Rational
Choice

**Murdock Learning Resource
Center
George Fox College**
Newberg, Oregon 97132

DEMCO

Rational Choice

The Contrast between Economics and Psychology

Edited by Robin M. Hogarth
and Melvin W. Reder

The University of Chicago Press
Chicago and London

The material in this volume first appeared in the supplement to the October 1986 issue of
THE JOURNAL OF BUSINESS (59:4,2).

The University of Chicago Press, Chicago 60637
The University of Chicago Press, Ltd., London
© 1986, 1987 by the University of Chicago
All rights reserved. Published 1987
Printed in the United States of America
95 94 93 92 91 90 89 88 87   5 4 3 2 1

Library of Congress Cataloging-in-Publication Data

Behavioral foundations of economic theory.
   Rational choice.

   Previously published as: The Behavioral foundations
of economic theory. 1986.
   Bibliography: p.
   Includes index.
   1. Economics—Psychological aspects—Congresses.
2. Choice (Psychology)—Congresses.   3. Rational
expectations (Economic theory)—Congresses.
4. Decision-making—Congresses.   I. Hogarth, Robin M.
II. Reder, Melvin Warren, 1919–   .   III. Title.
HB74.P8B44   1987   330'.01'9   86-27241
ISBN 0-226-34857-1 (alk. paper)
ISBN 0-226-34859-8 (pbk. : alk. paper)

The paper used in this publication meets the minimum requirements of American National Standard for Information Sciences—Permanence of Paper for Printed Library Materials, ANSI Z39.48-1984. ∞™

Contents

Preface

This volume contains the proceedings of a conference organized by Robin M. Hogarth and Melvin W. Reder and held at the University of Chicago on October 13–15, 1985. The stimulus for the conference was a growing body of evidence—mainly of an experimental nature—that has documented systematic departures from the dictates of rational economic behavior. Initially, these studies were conducted almost exclusively by psychologists, but recently also by an increasing number of economists, some of whom now routinely use experimental methods to address many substantive economic issues. The objectives of the conference were to bring together leading academics from both economics and psychology in order (1) to address the implications of the rationality assumptions underlying economics, (2) to assess the importance of evidence documenting violations of rational behavior for the development of both theoretical and applied economics, and (3) to provide a mechanism whereby both economists and psychologists could profit from being exposed to different perspectives.

In each of the four main sessions of the conference, two or three papers were presented and comments made by two or three discussants. In addition, there was a panel discussion at the end of the first full day of the conference, and, at the conference dinner that evening, George J. Stigler gave a delightful speech in which he discussed the relations between economics and psychology over approximately the last 150 years. The order in which the papers and comments are presented in this volume reflects the order in which they were presented at the conference.

The first two sessions of the conference presented many challenges to economic theory. First, Herbert A. Simon emphasized the need for economics to develop a sound empirical base. Second, a series of anomalous findings from both laboratory experiments and field surveys were reported in papers presented by Hillel J. Einhorn and Robin M. Hogarth and by Amos Tversky and Daniel Kahneman. Charles R. Plott, on the other hand, although presenting some data that were anomalous at the individual level, also showed that experimental data were often remarkably consistent with economic theory at the aggregate level. An important question raised by Tversky and Kahneman was whether psychologically descriptive models of choice could ever be reconciled with the axiomatic restrictions imposed by the kinds of positive models used in economics. In addition to the comments on the sessions that are included in this volume (by Richard H. Thaler, Howard Kunreuther, R. Duncan Luce, and Richard A. Shweder), Gary S. Becker (University of Chicago) was also a discussant in the first session and directed his remarks principally toward Simon's paper.

The panel discussion featured four speakers who brought quite different perspectives to the issues: Donald T. Campbell (with a viewpoint from psychology and evolutionary biology), James S. Coleman (sociology), John P. Gould (economics), and Laurence E. Lynn, Jr. (public policy). The four presentations were followed with useful interchange and debate among members of the audience and the speakers.

Speakers on the second day of the conference were all economists. In the morning session, Kenneth J. Arrow presented a thought-provoking discussion of the meaning of rationality in economics, and Robert E. Lucas, Jr., discussed several studies (empirical and experimental) from a viewpoint that saw rational behavior as the end product of an adaptive process. Comments on these papers included in this volume were made by Sidney G. Winter and Richard Zeckhauser. In addition, Zeckhauser extended his comments to a wider range of issues underlying the conference. Sanford J. Grossman (Princeton University) was also a discussant.

The final session was devoted to anomalies in financial markets. Merton H. Miller addressed the issue of whether the payment of dividends by firms is or is not anomalous vis-à-vis financial theory. Allan W. Kleidon provided a detailed discussion of the "excess volatility" of stock prices that had been documented in the earlier work of one of the discussants, Robert J. Shiller, who in turn replied to Kleidon's criticism. Of the other discussants at this session, Richard Roll (University of California, Los Angeles) considered the papers from his recent Wall Street perspective, and Stephen A. Ross (Yale University) presented a classification of different anomalies in finance. Neither Roll nor Ross provided written comments for this volume.

All the conference sessions were well attended, and despite what was thought would be adequate space in Swift Hall, even standing room was sometimes hard to find. The audience consisted of faculty and graduate students of the University of Chicago's Graduate School of Business as well as of the various departments of social sciences at the university. In addition, some sixty scholars from outside the University of Chicago attended the conference. The presentation of the papers and comments achieved a uniformly high standard, and a great level of intellectual excitement pervaded the entire proceedings. The difficult task of chairing the different sessions was admirably handled by William H. Kruskal, Edward O. Laumann, Paul J. H. Schoemaker,

Sherwin Rosen, and Eugene F. Fama (all of the University of Chicago).

On a historical note, it was learned early on October 15, the last day of the conference, that Professor Franco Modigliani of the Massachusetts Institute of Technology had been awarded the 1985 Nobel prize for economics, in part for his joint work with Merton H. Miller. A congratulatory telegram, proposed by Herbert A. Simon, was sent to Professor Modigliani on behalf of all attending the conference.

Many people deserve much thanks for facilitating both the organization and the holding of the conference. First, without a generous donation from the Irving B. Harris Foundation it would not have been possible to host the event at the University of Chicago. Second, the wholehearted support of the dean's office at the Graduate School of Business, and in particular of John P. Gould and Harry L. Davis, was instrumental to settling many key issues. Third, we were fortunate to have the able assistance of both Jean Howard and Charlesetta Wren, who most competently handled a mass of organizational details. Finally, we are grateful to the *Journal of Business* for providing an outlet for the publication of the conference proceedings.

Robin M. Hogarth
Melvin W. Reder

Introduction:
Perspectives from Economics
and Psychology*

The modern disciplines of economics and psychology are the direct descendants of a common body of philosophical ideas. As a result of their separate evolutions, however, the two disciplines interpret these ideas quite differently and generally pursue different research objectives using disparate methods of investigation and analysis. Nonetheless, since there are many areas of human activity where economists and psychologists study the same phenomena, it seems natural to ask whether the present separation is in the better interests of both disciplines. Moreover, even if one believes that economics and psychology should pursue separate paths, there may still be points at which they could and should make contact. In other words, can the modern disciplines of psychology and economics learn from each other, and, if so, what?[1]

The study of human choice behavior provides a focus for considering these issues in that it raises many thorny problems that underlie the behavioral assumptions or foundations of economic theory. One purpose of this paper is to sketch a response to the above questions that reflects the papers and discussions presented in

The paradigm of rational choice provides economics with a unity that is lacking in psychology. In the study of choice behavior, the two disciplines differ concerning (i) scope of phenomena: unlike economists, psychologists do not restrict research primarily to the market-level behavior of appropriately motivated experts; (ii) object of study: whereas psychologists deem process important, economists concentrate on outcomes; and (iii) data considered relevant: aggregate price-quantity relations are the focus of economic enquiry. Psychologists, on the other hand, are interested in different types of individual process data. Despite these differences, points of contact are indicated where each discipline could benefit from considering the alternative perspective.

* This work was supported, in part, by a contract from the Office of Naval Research.

1. As George Stigler commented in his speech at the conference dinner, there have been several attempts to find and develop links between economics and psychology within the last 150 years. However, these have had little effect.

this issue as well, of course, as our own prejudices. A second objective is to provide a context within which to view the contents of the issue.

Our discussion is organized as follows. We begin by considering different conceptualizations of "rationality" and "rational behavior" that are embedded in the various literatures dealing with these topics and especially those that surfaced in the conference papers and discussions. Second, we contrast the orientations taken by economists and psychologists to the study of choice behavior as well as noting the differential importance of this topic to the two disciplines. Third, we discuss how the rational choice paradigm adopted by economists delimits the scope of phenomena considered in empirical work. This, as we shall show, is critical since it lies at the source of disagreements between psychologists and economists as well as among economists. Fourth, we highlight differences in the methodological approaches used by the two disciplines in their empirical work and consider how these affect the types of substantive conclusions reached in the two disciplines. Finally, we speculate as to the extent to which economists and psychologists may make contact in their future work as well as indicating some promising areas for collaborative research.

Rationality and the Rational Choice Paradigm

A critical issue underlying many of the papers and discussions at the conference centered on what economists mean by the concept of rational choice behavior. We believe it is important to distinguish between two meanings, one quite broad and the other quite specific.

In the broad definition of rationality, economists are referring to a paradigm rather than to any particular theory. That is, decision makers are said to behave rationally when and only when behavior can be interpreted as conforming to the "rational choice" paradigm. This paradigm, expounded in many textbooks and treatises, supposes that the individual decision maker has a utility function whose arguments are defined as alternative uses of the resources with which he or she is endowed. The quantities of these resources are interpreted as constraints on the possible choices available to the decision maker, so that rational behavior consists of determining the set of resource quantities to be devoted to each of the possible uses as the solution to a constrained maximization problem.

Thus to provide an economic explanation of observed behavior is to show that the actions of the relevant decision makers conform to the rational choice paradigm and, where pertinent, that the behavior of multiperson aggregates is the result of individual choices made according to that paradigm. While no one at the conference argued that the rational choice paradigm was without valid applications, economists differed among themselves and a fortiori from other social scientists as to the paradigm's proper domain.

The rational choice paradigm can be considered a heuristic device for interpreting behavior, and, in this sense, it plays a role similar to that played by maximizing principles used in other sciences (e.g., physics) in generating hypotheses to explicate empirical phenomena. (For further discussion of this point, see Schoemaker [1984].) In essence the device is applied by interpreting phenomena as commodity quantities that can be varied—"supplied" in greater or less quantity—in response to changes in the resource constraints on the decision makers. For example, in addition to conventional commodities, recent applications of the paradigm have included descriptions of phenomena such as variations in the numbers of crimes committed, births, marriages, law suits, and so on as outcomes of changes in the costs (i.e., in the resource constraints) of such actions to the decision makers. The role of rationality is to provide a principle (or "rationale") to mediate the relations between changes in one or more resource constraints and changes in the quantities of the relevant phenomena. This takes the form of the maintained hypothesis that each of the individual decision makers behaves as if he or she were solving a constrained maximization problem.

As Simon (in this volume) points out, the maintained hypothesis of the rational choice paradigm is not by itself sufficient to generate the price-quantity relations that characterize economic models. Instead, specific auxiliary assumptions must be adduced for particular applications. However, the assumptions chosen are typically just those needed to bridge the gap(s) between actions implied by the rational choice paradigm at the level of the individual decision maker and price-quantity behavior at the level of the industry (or other aggregate), and, in this sense, the paradigm plays a central role.

It is important to note that the rational choice paradigm refers to individuals even though the price-quantity relations it is used to explain refer typically to the behavior of aggregates.[2] In most applied work, the paradigm is used as a "story" about the conjectured behavior of a hypothetical "representative" individual whose responses to changes in resource constraints (e.g., prices or wealth) parallel the changes of the relevant aggregate. To add credibility to the story, appeal is often made to everyday intuition concerning individual behavior. However, to apply the rational choice paradigm, few—if any—psychological assumptions are needed. The economic implications of the paradigm are compatible with virtually any account of the decision-making process

---

2. These statements should not be taken to imply that economists are not interested in individual behavior. Frequently, individual data are not available for the type of analysis economists wish to pursue. However, in cases in which the opportunity arises (e.g., when panel data on individuals coexist with intertemporal data on aggregates), economists have made serious attempts to provide coherent explanations of both individual and aggregate behavior.

so long as this generates appropriately sloped supply and demand curves.[3]

For many applications, however, this broad (rational choice paradigm) definition of rationality lacks specificity. It is therefore replaced by the narrower definition of maximizing expected utility (von Neumann and Morgenstern 1947), which does depend on strong assumptions of a psychological nature. Indeed, in recent decades the expected utility model has become the operational definition used in empirical work related to tests of rationality. Nonetheless, as pointed out at the conference (particularly by Arrow [in this volume]; and Gould [in this volume]), many important economic propositions can be derived without recourse to expected utility theory per se.[4]

It would be a mistake to believe that concepts of rational behavior are to be found only in economics. In fact, notions of rationality play important roles in other social sciences including psychology (for an enlightening discussion, see Simon [1978]). Freud's work, for example, depended heavily on conceptions of what was or was not rational behavior for people living in a particular society at a particular time, and all the social sciences seem to agree that most behavior is purposeful.

To contrast the application of rationality concepts in the different social sciences, it is useful to distinguish the rationality of means from the rationality of ends. The former refers to how given ends or goals are achieved and the latter to what ends or goals have been chosen in the first place. Whereas economic rationality refers only to means, the concept of rationality in other social sciences (as well as in everyday usage) typically involves some combination of the rationalities of means and ends (Einhorn and Hogarth 1981). Failure to appreciate these distinctions can and has led to considerable confusion when discussing issues of rationality in multidisciplinary settings.

Theories of Choice in Economics and Psychology

The rational choice paradigm provides economics with a disciplinary unity that is lacking in other social sciences. Psychology, in particular, is a fragmented discipline consisting of a number of separate research communities that do not share an easily identifiable paradigm. Moreover, the study of choice does not play a central role in this discipline.

3. That is, negatively sloped demand curves and (usually) non–negatively sloped supply curves. While it is certainly the case that in some situations the rational choice paradigm is compatible with negatively sloped supply curves, the paradigm loses much of its power when supply curves are of this nature.

4. By the expected utility model, we really refer to a broader class of models, including formulations such as that of Machina (1982), that permit a more generally characterized objective function.

Indeed, although decision making has become an increasingly important topic in psychology in recent years, this interest is fairly recent, dating from the 1950s, when psychologists first began systematic investigations of human choice behavior, investigations that, incidentally, were originally stimulated by economic models (Edwards 1954).

However, there are critical differences between explanations of choice behavior that are accepted by economists and by psychologists. As noted above, economic explanations involve showing that outcomes (i.e., what agents decide to do) are consistent with the maintained hypothesis of the rational choice paradigm. For psychologists, on the other hand, explanation requires specifying the process by which choices are made. Moreover, for an economist, the process explanation of a psychologist is, at most, of incidental interest unless it leads to outcomes at variance with the maintained hypothesis.

An illuminating example of these distinctions is provided by noting the differential reactions of economists and psychologists to a robust empirical finding known as the "preference reversal phenomenon" (for an overview, see Slovic and Lichtenstein [1983]). In these studies, subjects are asked to consider two gambles (of approximately equal expected value), one gamble having a high probability of winning a moderate stake and the other a low probability of winning a larger stake. The intriguing finding is that many of the subjects who prefer the former over the latter when required to choose between the gambles place a higher minimum selling price on the latter when asked to evaluate the same gambles.

For economists, these findings are disturbing and pose a challenge to the rational choice paradigm in that choice should be invariant as to how preference is elicited, that is, as a choice or a judgment of minimum selling price. (For further examples, see Tversky and Kahneman [in this volume].) Thus, when faced with such evidence, economists are forced into "rationalizing," discrediting, or arguing the irrelevance of the empirical findings.[5] Psychologists, on the other hand, are not threatened by the empirical result. The challenge to the psychologist is to construct a theory of the process that leads to preference reversals and to see whether this might generalize to domains other than choices between gambles (for one such theory, see Goldstein and Einhorn [in press]). In this volume, examples of this type of work include Einhorn and Hogarth's model of the effects of ambiguity about probabilities and Tversky and Kahneman's discussion of the implications of framing when people evaluate the outcomes of gambles using the psychological principles underlying prospect theory (Kahneman and Tversky 1979). In contrasting the alternative research orientations of the two disciplines, it has been suggested that, whereas psychologists delight in

5. For a specific example of this kind of behavior, see Grether and Plott (1979).

finding anomalous behavior that contradicts received wisdom, economists revel in showing how apparently anomalous behavior is in fact
consistent with the maintained hypothesis.

The Scope of Choice Theories in Economics and Psychology

In economics many investigators specifically delimit the type of phenomena to which the rational choice paradigm should be applied.
These limits refer both to characteristics of the environments in which
actions are taken and to characteristics of the agents; they are also the
subject of much controversy.

The Importance of Market Discipline

The economic paradigm focuses on actions taken in competitive circumstances.[6] The underlying assumption is that through competition
the actions of individual agents are subject to feedback that forces
them either to become effective or to withdraw from such actions. It is
further assumed that if people are ineffective at particular types of
activities they can still participate by appointing skilled agents to act in
their behalf. Either way, markets are assumed to reflect actions taken
by experienced decision makers seeking to maximize their own gains
and, simultaneously, keeping the market efficient by exploiting the
errors of others. Economists have little interest in modeling agents who
do not behave according to rational principles since they believe that
these agents will not survive in the market.

It is important to note that economists accept the fact that economic
agents, like ordinary people, are subject to errors and inconsistencies
in decision making. However, the fallibilities of economic agents are
assumed to be of a random rather than a systematic nature. That is,
since agents who make systematic errors would be exploited by other
agents and eventually forced to withdraw from the market, they would
no longer be the subject of economic enquiry.

Characteristics of Economic Agents

In many contexts, the rational choice paradigm is applied without condition on either information or skill of decision makers. But in others,
some economists—and this is a point of disagreement—feel the need
to make application of the paradigm conditional on the information
and/or skill of decision makers. For example, in discussing the per-

6. Of course economists are also concerned with monopoly, oligopoly, etc. as well as
competition. However, it is generally conceded that the heuristic power of the rational
choice paradigm is greatly reduced when the assumption of competition is abandoned. It
is worth noting that, among economists, those who stress the empirical importance of
competitive behavior tend to be strong adherents of the rational choice paradigm, and
conversely.

formance of pigeons as experimental subjects, Lucas (in this volume) points out that their behavior is consistent with the (rational choice) paradigm after they have had sufficient opportunity to adapt to the performance incentives operating in their environment, but not otherwise. Accordingly, he proposes (in effect) to restrict application of the paradigm to situations in which the environment can be considered as approximately stationary.

While this proposal may be a useful auxiliary assumption, it raises at least two important problems. (1) What criteria should be used to determine whether people (subjects, agents, or pigeons) have had sufficient time (for the purpose of the theory) to adapt to the performance incentives with which they are faced? For example, should consumers who shop regularly in supermarkets be considered sufficiently "expert" to meet the criteria? (2) As emphasized in Winter's (in this volume) comments, restricting the study of economics to situations that meet Lucas's specifications considerably limits the range of phenomena to which the discipline can be applied. In the arena of public policy, for example, it is important not only to know what equilibrium will eventually be reached when conditions change (e.g., following introduction of legislation such as deregulation in a particular industry) but also to understand the nature of the costs of moving from one state to another. At the individual level, consumers in many markets are often confronted by novel choices; thus it is important to understand how people make decisions under various conditions of ignorance.[7]

The Psychological Perspective

As became apparent at the conference, psychologists do not feel constrained to study decision making only in competitive market situations. They point out that many important decisions have to be taken in circumstances in which it is hard to imagine how market discipline would apply. It is thus artificial to limit the application and testing of behavioral choice models to only those circumstances that meet the approval of economists. Moreover, given their traditional interest in individual differences, psychologists consider the study of the decision-making capabilities of people with different levels of expertise to be a legitimate enterprise.

These issues were put in sharp focus in the paper by Tversky and Kahneman (in this volume). First, in discussing choice anomalies that could be attributed to "framing" effects, Tversky and Kahneman make a distinction between what they term "transparent" and "opaque" versions of choice problems. Briefly stated, when a problem

---

7. This point was particularly emphasized to the authors in conversation with Arnold Zellner. See also Einhorn and Hogarth (in this volume).

is presented in transparent form, choice behavior does not violate basic tenets of rationality. When choice problems are formulated in an opaque manner, however, people may well violate basic principles such as dominance or transitivity because of the effects of "framing" and so on. Whereas Tversky and Kahneman do not specify the conditions under which people perceive problems as transparent or opaque, it is reasonable to assume that these are related to structural aspects of problems and differences in individual levels of expertise. However, Tversky and Kahneman adduce evidence to the effect that professional expertise in a particular domain does not guarantee that people will see choice problems as transparent. Because this evidence is based on hypothetical questions, skeptical economists could still ask whether responses really affect what actions experts would take and/or if they would act differently as a result of considering their responses. On the other hand, if taken seriously, these findings are of great importance for economics in that they imply that descriptive models of choice need to include contextual variables that capture the effects of framing and other irrelevant factors. The basis on which this should be done, however, is unclear.

The second point relates to the assumption implicit in the argument concerning market discipline. This is that people learn from experience (see also Thaler, in this volume). Tversky and Kahneman admit that "there is no doubt that learning and selection do take place and tend to improve efficiency" but argue (in this volume, pp. 90–91) that

> effective learning takes place only under certain conditions: it requires accurate and immediate feedback about the relation between the situational conditions and the appropriate response. The necessary feedback is often lacking for the decisions faced by managers, entrepreneurs, and politicians because (i) outcomes are commonly delayed and not easily attributable to a particular action; (ii) variability in the environment degrades the reliability of the feedback, especially where outcomes of low probability are involved; (iii) there is often no information about what the outcome would have been if another decision had been taken; and (iv) most important decisions are unique and therefore provide little opportunity for learning (see Einhorn and Hogarth 1978). The conditions for organizational learning are hardly better. Learning surely occurs, for both individuals and organizations, but any claim that a particular error will be eliminated by experience must be supported by demonstrating that the conditions for effective learning are satisfied.

Tversky and Kahneman correctly anticipate that many economists would counter this argument with the contention that market forces, and particularly the actions of arbitrageurs, induce the appropriate corrective effects. However, they respond by stating (p. 91) that "there are situations in which this mechanism fails" and cite papers by

Hausch, Ziemba, and Rubenstein (1981), Haltiwanger and Waldman (1985), and Russell and Thaler (1985) as providing support for this assertion. More important, Tversky and Kahneman conclude (p. 91) by stating that "the normative and the descriptive analyses of choice should be viewed as separate enterprises. This conclusion suggests a research agenda. To retain the rational model in its customary descriptive role, the relevant bolstering assumptions must be validated. Where these assumptions fail, it is instructive to trace the implications of the descriptive analysis (e.g., the effects of loss aversion, pseudocertainty, or the money illusion) for public policy, strategic decision making, and macroeconomic phenomena (see Arrow 1982; Akerlof and Yellen 1985)."

Many of the disagreements between economists and psychologists can be framed as disputes about whether and how to pursue this research agenda. In particular, consider the contention that it is necessary to validate that the effects of errors of judgment and choice will be eliminated by some combination of learning through feedback and competition. While this will appear reasonable to most psychologists and also to some economists, its effects on the research practices of economics would be profound and—in the view of many economists—quite destructive. At the empirical level alone, there is likely to be such a wide diversity of decision processes among organizations that studying the process for any one entity would be more time consuming than studying the behavior of aggregates (e.g., industries, regions, or sectors). Moreover, having successfully modeled the behavior of individuals, it would then be necessary to model their interactions—or lack of them—that generate the aggregate regularities with which economics is primarily concerned.

This is not to say that economists have ignored the decision-making processes of individual entities. On the contrary, there is a literature of case studies—especially of business firms—that tries to describe such processes even though these descriptions are rarely integrated with formal economic models. Moreover, there have been several attempts to characterize the behavior of economic sectors as resulting from the behavior of typical individual decision-making units following particular rules of thumb (e.g., fixed markups, target pricing) rather than engaging in maximization of some objective function. However, many economists feel that such attempts, which often draw inspiration from case studies, have had—at best—indifferent success in predicting actual price-quantity behavior, and none has ever been taken to be more than a plausible conjecture whose applicability was limited in time and to a particular economic sector. On the other hand, critics of this position argue that frequently the data used in economists' explanations of decision making in naturally occurring situations are such that explanations incompatible with the rational choice paradigm cannot be even considered, let alone tested.

Methodological Differences

The manners in which economists and psychologists conduct their respective research programs differ on several dimensions. First, as noted above, whereas economists focus on outcomes, questions of process are central to psychologists. Thus, although both economists and psychologists stress the importance of predictive accuracy in assessing theories used in empirical work, psychologists are concerned with the manner in which decisions are made as well as with the characteristics of the participants and of their resource endowments.[8]

Second, the stimulus for much work in modern economics is deductive in nature. That is, given the general framework of the rational choice paradigm, economists are interested in testing and extending implications that have been deduced from the theory and are greatly concerned with reconciling observations with the maintained hypothesis. For many economists, the power of the paradigm lies in being able to make statements about areas of investigation where little data currently exist. However, as noted by Simon (in this volume) in his discussion of Becker's (1981) work on the family, to extend the theory into domains where there are no data on certain key variables may require empirically untested auxiliary assumptions the validity of which is essential to accurate prediction. Because psychologists do not work within the structure of a paradigm that is as general or as rigid as that of economists (see above), they are more ready to accommodate seemingly anomalous observations into their way of thinking. Since the focus in psychology is on how people do things, sets of "axioms" are not accorded the same esteem as their counterparts in economics.

For example, an important and active topic in psychology centers on how people decide that one particular variable is the cause of another. For an economist, however, this will not be a topic for research until such time as the resources, psychic or otherwise, used in formulating hypotheses of cause are specified along with their values in this and alternative uses. To discuss attributions of causality (or other "conceptual phenomena") the economist would have to tie judgments of cause into a larger framework involving costs of selecting different causal candidates as the particular agent involved in different circumstances. Indeed, it is instructive to note that economists who use experimental methods typically frame research questions as tests of the predictions of current economic theory (see, e.g., Plott, in this volume). Psychologists, in contrast, usually ask what hypothesis or theory could account for some phenomenon and/or experimental data without appealing to a more or less unified paradigm.

---

8. We note that few psychologists give much weight to many of the arguments outlined by Milton Friedman in his famous (1953) essay on the methodology of "positive science," apart from agreeing on the importance of prediction.

Third, the bulk of empirical evidence in psychology bearing on the rationality of decision makers is experimental in nature. On the other hand, despite a growing body of experimental work (see Plott, in this volume), empirical economics is overwhelmingly based on evidence from so-called natural experiments, that is, the historical record of observed "real world" behavior. Moreover, when laboratory results conflict with the implications of economic theory, economists typically question the relevance of the anomaly-producing laboratory experiments to real world phenomena.[9]

The questions raised by economists focus on three major issues: these relate to the expertise, motivation, and selection of subjects for experimental study. We now discuss each in turn.

Expertise of subjects. As noted above, economists often argue that rational behavior can be expected to occur only after individuals have had sufficient opportunity to learn the consequences of alternative choices. Hence experimental procedures must be carefully vetted to ensure that subjects have acquired sufficient opportunities for learning so that researchers can distinguish between inexperience and irrationality. However, establishing criteria for assessing whether sufficient learning has taken place is itself problematic.

Motivation of subjects. Both economists and psychologists agree that it is important to motivate subjects properly in experimental studies to ensure that responses are carefully made. There is some disagreement, however, as to what constitutes appropriate motivation. One advantage of the rational choice paradigm used by economists is that it suggests a criterion for judging this: specifically, motivation is appropriate only if rewards are an increasing function of the correctness of responses; also, if rewards are greater, subjects should be more likely to respond appropriately.

Psychologists, on the other hand, have greater difficulty in specifying the conditions under which subjects are appropriately motivated. In many psychological experiments, for example, it is not possible to construct appropriate incentive schemes since it is not clear what the correct responses are to particular questions. As an example, recall our previous discussion concerning causal judgments. Psychologists therefore tend to rely on judgment in deciding whether remuneration for participating in experiments is sufficient to ensure careful responses and on the beliefs that (*a*) subjects in experiments tend to "do as best

9. It is of interest to note that economists have been able to accept the results of experiments involving animal subjects as evidence favoring the rational choice paradigm (see Lucas, in this volume). Whereas the first experiments in this area were generally favorable to economic theory (e.g., Battalio et al. 1981), it is unclear how they will react to recent evidence showing that rats violate the substitution axiom (Battalio, Kagel, and MacDonald 1985) in the same manner as human subjects (Slovic and Tversky 1974).

they can" and (b) it would typically require far more effort on the part of subjects to falsify responses deliberately than to respond truthfully.

Parenthetically, when psychologists examine the procedures used in experimental economics (see Plott, in this volume) that do conform to the rational choice paradigm, they are often struck by two features. The first is that schemes introduced into the experiments to ensure incentive compatibility add considerable complexity to the problems of explaining the nature of the experimental task to the subjects. Moreover, it is not clear that subjects understand the full implications of such reward structures. (One of us, e.g., has experienced extreme difficulty in running experiments on probability assessment using proper scoring rules as incentives, even with fairly sophisticated M.B.A. subjects.) The second is that attempts to control the reward structure frequently require placing severe restrictions on the actions subjects are permitted to take in the experimental setting. For example, subjects are allowed to trade only within constraints placed on them by the supply or demand functions given to them by the experimenters (in accord with so-called induced value theory). These requirements, however, seem to place such severe restrictions on subjects' actions that psychologists may wonder whether the underlying economic theory is in fact being tested.

What evidence exists concerning the effects of different incentive schemes on the performance of experimental subjects? Einhorn and Hogarth (in this volume), Thaler (in this volume), and Tversky and Kahneman (in this volume) all cite studies in which, contrary to economic theory, greater incentives have been shown to lead to less rather than more "rational" behavior. However, in a 1961 study Siegel showed that, when incentives were introduced, irrational "probability-matching" behavior[10] disappeared and was replaced by economically appropriate maximizing behavior. Much still needs to be done to elucidate the relation between incentives and behavior (see also Arkes, Dawes, and Christensen 1986), and we believe that this is an important area in which joint cooperation by psychologists and economists could be most fruitful.

Selection of experimental subjects. As noted above, whereas psychologists are concerned with the behavior of individuals in many dif-

10. "Probability matching" has been investigated within the following type of paradigm. Subjects are asked to guess which of two lights (say, green and red) will appear on each of a sequence of trials. Unbeknownst to subjects, the appearance of the lights is governed by a stationary random process such that the probability of, say, green appearing on any given trial is p, with the complementary probability of $1 - p$ attaching to red. The empirical phenomenon known as probability matching refers to the finding that, over a series of trials, subjects' guesses tend to match the unknown probabilities in that the proportion of total guesses of, say, green tends toward p and that of red toward $1 - p$. To maximize the total number of correct guesses, however, the optimal strategy is simply to guess that the more frequently appearing color will appear on every trial.

ferent contexts, economists are not interested in behavior in contexts that lack the forces of a competitive market. That is, in the large number of cases in which decision making is ancillary to production of a good or service for sale on a competitive market or in which decision making can be delegated to an expert, economists are concerned only with the behavior of those who survive the selective process by which the market designates the decision makers who are to specialize in particular tasks. Thus departures from the axioms of rational behavior by large numbers of experimental subjects need not concern economists, although inability to find sufficiently large subsets who do not or cannot learn to avoid such departures must be of concern to them.

Although not inspired by beliefs in the corrective properties of market forces as such, many psychologists are aware of the need to validate experimental findings across both situations (e.g., experimental and field settings) and subjects (e.g., at varying levels of expertise). Moreover, in recent years several attempts have been made to replicate anomalous laboratory findings concerning choice behavior by using expert subjects in fieldlike settings. Results of these experiments have been equivocal in the sense that, whereas some experts make the same kinds of responses as novices, others do not.[11] One way of considering these results is to refer them to the "opaque-transparent" dimension discussed by Tversky and Kahneman (see above).

Relevant and Irrelevant Evidence

To point out procedural limitations in experiments that have found evidence of departures from rationality is to suggest an escape hatch for economists who wish to maintain the rational choice paradigm. But it does not imply that the observed departures from rationality are illusory or that they would vanish if experiments were always conducted using procedures acceptable to economists. There is a great need for empirical evidence generated across a wide range of environmental circumstances. Moreover, we believe that such research efforts could be greatly aided if one could devise a taxonomy of types of decision contexts and characteristics of decision makers that would allow meaningful classifications of empirical results.

A major difference between the predominant methodologies in psychology and economics centers on what data are considered "observable." Indeed, an important aspect of economists' seeming insensitivity to the details of decision-making processes is a tendency to treat these details as unobservable. That is, economists have a methodologi-

---

11. For example, in a study involving professional auditors, Joyce and Biddle (1981) failed to replicate studies that showed that college students had little understanding of the concept of regression toward the mean. On the other hand, Eddy (1982) found dramatic evidence that physicians made elementary errors in probabilistic reasoning when evaluating the outcomes of test results.

cal predilection for using models whose behavioral implications refer exclusively to interrelations of prices and quantities as reflected in market transactions and not to variables that reflect other aspects of the decision-making process.

Whereas these other aspects are not held to be irrelevant, economists put forth several arguments as to why they should be ignored. (i) The effects of the non-price-quantity variables are captured by variables reflecting prices and quantities observed in market transactions (i.e., transaction variables) and disturbance terms. (ii) Often non-price-quantity variables (i.e., "other" variables) are not observed or are not observable at all. (iii) Even when other variables are observable, they tend to be idiosyncratic to particular sectors or even to particular decision-making units, so that aggregation presents difficult problems. (iv) Translation of other variables into the categories of economic theory may be difficult and subject to disagreement. Thus, even when they are observable, it may be appropriate to ignore nontransaction variables, particularly if readings on them conflict with the implications of economic theory.

Point iv is especially likely to be contentious among psychologists and is also subject to dispute among economists. For example, Prescott (1977, p. 30) argues that, "like utility, expectations are not observed, and surveys cannot be used to test the rational expectations hypothesis. One can only test if some theory, whether it incorporates rational expectations or, for that matter, irrational expectations, is or is not consistent with observations." But Lovell (1986, p. 110) disagrees, arguing that "it may be a mistake to argue that we can divide variables into those that are observable and those that are not. . . . over the last several decades a number of economists . . . has found that survey observations on expectational variables can be of assistance in the empirical modeling of economic behavior and econometric forecasting." Lovell contends (inter alia) that reports of decision makers' forecasts (as reported in surveys) should be considered as evidence of the state of their expectations as of a given date and should not be dismissed as artifacts of the survey process when they appear to conflict with models involving observed price-quantity behavior exclusively. The contrary views of Prescott, Lucas, and a large number of other economists reflect a methodological preconception whose consequences are (i) to weight reports of prices and quantities in actual transactions more heavily than other types of empirical evidence such as forecasts, answers to hypothetical questions, statements of intention, and so on and (ii) to place greater credence on reports consistent with economic theory than those tending to contradict it. In a nutshell, if non-transaction-based measurements of expectations are consistent with transaction-based measurements, they are redundant; if inconsistent, they are probably erroneous. Therefore, treat expectations as though they were unobservable.

This attitude toward nontransaction measures of expectations is typical of the view taken of any variable—including those reflecting aspects of decision-making processes—that does not reflect the terms of the actual transactions. Implementation of the implied research strategy (i.e., attending only to phenomena recorded in transactions) is impeded in many areas by complexities in the measurement of prices and quantities that make tests of competing theories less decisive than they should be. It is for this reason that trades on organized exchanges, where the needs of commerce for unambiguous measurement of the terms of transactions coincide with the scientific imperatives of conceptual precision, are of special interest.

The Example of the Finance Paradigm

There are several reasons why evidence on the behavior of prices set on organized exchanges—especially those on which securities are traded—is of special importance. (1) The exigencies of organized exchanges require the establishment of uniform conditions of sale and the elimination of all characteristics of the assets traded that make for heterogeneity among units or traders. These conditions make for a nearly perfect realization of the theoretical construct of a one-price market that is continuously cleared. (2) Because securities are claims to cash flows, their own prices, together with interest rates on (almost) riskless bonds, form dual networks of actual prices and theoretical prices that would obtain if all opportunities for gain through arbitrage had been exploited. Any difference of relative prices between the two networks would imply the existence of an arbitrage opportunity, the exploitation of which is a sine qua non of rationality. Thus paucity of arbitrage opportunities and the speed with which they are eliminated become tests of the efficiency of the system of markets and the rationality of agents who participate in them. (3) The development of collateral markets in futures, options, and so on has increased the number of elements in the network of asset prices and the number of potential arbitrage opportunities. Still further, various characteristics of time series of security prices can be used to test the hypothesis that traders use all information contained in the history of these prices.

The combined effect of these distinguishing properties of organized exchanges is to make the behavior of their prices unusually accurate reflections of the behavior of wealth holders. As a result, economists generally agree that failure of observed prices to conform to theoretical predictions on these exchanges would be strong evidence of market inefficiency and associated irrationality of at least some agents.

Failure of asset prices on organized exchanges to reject the hypothesis of market efficiency would not, of course, imply anything as to the efficiency and rationality of behavior in other situations. But rejection of this hypothesis on organized exchanges would constitute a damaging blow to the whole of economic theory; failure to apply here, where circumstances are most favorable, would cast grave doubt on its applicability elsewhere. Moreover, the near continuous operation of an organized exchange generates a steady flow of publicly available data that makes hypothesis testing relatively easy.

Kleidon's paper (in this volume) provides an excellent example of how economists use information on security prices to make tests of market efficiency. This paper is in the nature of a reply to earlier work of Robert Shiller's purporting to show that security prices behave as though traders are affected by vagaries of fashion (mob psychology) that are incompatible with the hypothesis that they were utilizing all information contained in the relevant price histories. For our (methodological) purpose, the important point in the Kleidon-Shiller debate is that, despite Shiller's speculative remarks on investor psychology, the issues joined refer exclusively to the time-series properties of security prices. That is, although both Kleidon and Shiller, like other participants in this debate, consider that they are arguing about whether individual investors use information rationally, they do not adduce evidence from studies of individual behavior to support their respective positions.

In contrast, for psychologists who have been trained in conducting field studies as well as experimental methods, the empirical "ground rules" adopted in the Kleidon-Shiller debate seem curious at best. In psychology, collecting data from multiple sources is the way to illuminate conflict when trying to resolve issues in uncontrolled field studies (see, e.g., Cook and Campbell 1979).

Points of Contact

As our discussion has shown, the domains of choice behavior in psychology and economics differ in many important respects. Moreover, it is possible that the two disciplines will continue largely to ignore each other for many years to come. Indeed, given the different substantive interests that motivate enquiry in the two disciplines, we believe that the bulk of most work in both areas will continue to develop in their present separate ways. On the other hand, together the two disciplines offer communalities of interest and opportunity that we believe could become increasingly important. There are several reasons for this.

First, despite the usual quota of self-satisfaction that characterizes academic disciplines, there are sufficient numbers of both economists and psychologists who recognize lacunae in their approaches that could be addressed (at least partially) by considering other perspectives. Second, there are many applied areas of research that draw on both economics and psychology, thereby forcing some degree of confrontation between the two, for example, marketing, accounting, public policy, and so on. Third, as noted at this conference, representatives from both disciplines have made excursions across boundaries and attracted considerable attention. For example, economists have extended modes of economic analysis to behavior that has typically been conceptualized as noneconomic in nature (e.g., Becker 1981), and psychologists have systematically investigated the operational definitions of rationality proposed by economists.

In our view, the ultimate success of both the conference and this issue lies in the extent to which it will have facilitated productive interchanges between the two disciplines as opposed to reinforcing stereotypic prejudices (see also Zeckhauser, in this volume). We therefore address this issue.

We first note that choice behavior encompasses a wide range of phenomena for which neither economics nor psychology can currently provide a comprehensive account. Instead, each discipline can be thought of as providing only partial illumination. As already discussed, economics provides a strong, "rationalizing" metaphor in which the outcomes of choice processes are interpreted in a specific way. Moreover, in this metaphor, optimization principles play an important heuristic role in guiding how investigators approach certain problems. Psychology, on the other hand, lacks a unifying metaphor; nonetheless, psychologists typically have little difficulty in evaluating whether some explanation of a phenomenon is "psychological" in nature, thereby implicitly recognizing the existence of a psychological paradigm.

Our own prescription is to recognize that both economics and psychology provide different metaphors for studying complex phenomena. However, whereas each metaphor illuminates some aspects of decision making, it is necessarily limited. Thus more can be gained by viewing the world from the perspective of multiple metaphors. In addition, since the phenomena of concern are complex, we believe it would be foolish to abandon either approach. Indeed, in the division of labor that is necessary to make scientific progress, much can be gained by adhering to the "law of comparative advantage."

Nevertheless, several issues and topics raised at the conference suggested areas where collaboration between psychology and economics would be welcome. First, at the theoretical level Arrow, Lucas, and Gould all noted the nonuniqueness of the equilibria of certain rational expectations models. As these models embody the assumption that all decision makers take into account every implication of price-quantity history in optimizing (i.e., are—to use Winter's term—"super-optimizers"), it is frustrating to find that the models yield ambiguous implications. However, this frustration is considerably reduced when it is realized that, as Lucas (following Bray) shows, making explicit assumptions about the process by which economic agents form expectations is sufficient to establish the uniqueness of equilibrium.

From a psychological viewpoint, the interesting aspect of Lucas's observation is that the process suggested could be conceived of as an "anchoring-and-adjustment" model (Tversky and Kahneman 1974), a process that has been extensively studied and discussed in the literature on judgment and choice (see, e.g., Hogarth, 1981; Lopes, 1981; Einhorn and Hogarth 1985). In other words, Lucas's suggestion is highly plausible to psychologists and would provide a useful hypothesis for experimental testing. In another part of his paper, it will be noted that Lucas explicitly suggests an experiment to provide evidence on an issue for which economic intuition is lacking and where this could be aided by laboratory data.

Further specific connections between economics and psychology were suggested in other conference papers. Simon, for one, points out that there are many areas where the economic paradigm seems to force investigators into making bold assumptions as opposed to collecting data on the issues. Without disputing the influence of paradigmatic considerations, we believe that there are two reasons why economists may fail to collect such data. First, it is often difficult to do so (see above). Second, economists have not been trained to think of alternatives to collecting real world data.

However, as the conference papers by Plott and Lucas illustrate, when it is difficult to collect data in naturally occurring situations, it may be possible to generate experimental data that can, at least, shed partial light on the issues. The point here is that some experimental data may be better than none. Moreover, we believe that, following the pioneering work of both Smith and Plott, this point is now better understood by economists than it was, say, five years ago (see, in particular, Plott 1982; and Smith 1982). It also suggests that techniques and procedures for doing experiments should become an increasingly important part of the economist's tool kit and thus should be taught in graduate schools along with the more traditional methodological tools, such as econometrics.

A further way of fostering cooperative work between economists and psychologists would be to think of particular experiments or specific studies as forming parts of more comprehensive research programs as opposed to being ends in and of themselves. In particular, we urge both psychologists and economists to reflect on research findings from the perspective of paradigms other than the one in which the investigation was conceived and conducted. To use an analogy, one may have reason to be confident in the accuracy of a medical diagnosis if two physicians agree. However, confidence is liable to be far greater if one knows that the physicians have quite different backgrounds and training as opposed to having been schooled in the same tradition. It is both more important and more impressive when studies conducted within different paradigms converge on the same conclusions.

A good example of what we are recommending is provided by the work of Kunreuther et al. (1978) with respect to the purchase of disaster insurance (against floods and earthquakes). Kunreuther and his colleagues carried out two types of studies and confronted results on the same questions. One set of studies involved extensive field data, the second a series of laboratory experiments. Both studies provided rich sets of findings; however, the findings are that much more impressive when one sees that the outcomes of controlled laboratory experiments have parallels in data collected in the field, where control is problematic at best.

Applying these remarks to the papers presented at this conference suggests, for example, that the data presented by Einhorn and Hogarth in respect of reactions to ambiguity will have much more impact when they, or others, are able to indicate specific evidence of similar effects in more naturally occurring environments.

An important hindrance to this kind of work, however, is that economists and psychologists may not always share common interests and thus not wish to invest their time in common endeavors. This, in turn, suggests that funding agencies might wish to examine these issues and provide incentives that encourage cooperative efforts.

A further opportunity for fruitful interdisciplinary exchange arises from (occasional) parallels in intradisciplinary debates on methodological issues. Thus the ongoing debate within economics concerning what types of data are or are not to be considered in empirical work (see above) has a familiar ring to psychologists. In many ways, it parallels a debate (in psychology) as to whether certain kinds of data are "permissible" in inferring underlying mental processes. After misuse of introspective methods in the early development of the discipline, for a time the predominant methodology shifted under the strong influence of behavioral stimulus-response psychology to using only overt responses (i.e., actions) as data. This position has, however, changed in recent decades as psychologists have become more sophisticated in gathering different types of data bearing on subjects' mental processes (e.g., concurrent verbal protocols, physical records of eye movements, choice reaction times, and the like). The challenge today is to construct theories that are consistent with all data collected.

Still a further opportunity for fruitful interdisciplinary collaboration arises from the study of decision making by groups or teams as distinguished from individuals. In the context of this conference, an important problem that has received little attention to date centers on the extent to which choice anomalies would persist when, as often happens in naturally occurring situations, decisions are made in group or team settings. In one study using student subjects and simulated business decisions, Mowen and Gentry (1980) found greater propensity for groups as opposed to individuals to fall prey to the "preference reversal paradox." Other evidence on this issue, however, is sorely lacking, although one could easily generate alternative hypotheses (based on the extensive social psychological literature on groups) that the feedback that individuals receive by way of group processes could either exacerbate or correct possible deviations from rational behavior.

To this point, the discussion of this section has been directed mainly toward suggesting what economists can gain from psychologists. However, psychologists also have much to gain from economists in terms of both theory construction and methodological issues. First, even a casual perusal of the leading journals in economics and psychology indicates that the former have greater requirements in terms of modeling phenomena in precise quantifiable form. Whereas we do not advocate the use of mathematics in the social sciences simply for the sake of mathematics, we do believe that psychologists could benefit from more rigorous attempts to specify models in the style that is characteristic of work in economics. Thus, in the same manner that we would like to see experimental methodology enter more systematically into graduate programs in economics, we would like to see more quantitative modeling in the curricula of graduate programs in psychology. To a large extent, the contribution of psychology to the problems shared with economics has been negative in nature. Psychologists have been quick to point out deficiencies in economic reasoning and have amassed much experimental evidence on so-called anomalies. However, psychologists have been slow to propose alternative models that economists might use to overcome the noted descriptive deficiencies. As is well-known, you can "beat a model" only with a better model.

Second, we believe that psychologists should be less concerned with the importance of the internal validity of experiments and be more conscious of the economists' insistence on seeing whether the phenomena "matter in the real world" (for some concrete methodological advice on this issue, see Hammond, Hamm, & Grassia [in press]).

An interesting contrast in style between economists and psychologists is provided by comments in the conference papers by Miller, on the one hand, and Einhorn and Hogarth, on the other. Miller argues, in effect, that in looking at the complexity of economic behavior one must be careful not to be distracted by apparently interesting phenomena in that these could divert one's attention from understanding the major forces underlying what is observed. Einhorn and Hogarth, however, say that, given the richness of the phenomena that can be observed, one cannot afford to ignore them.

This difference "in style" suggests important research questions. How does one decide at what level a phenomenon should be studied and just how "realistic" do one's assumptions about behavior need to be? One strategy for considering this issue consists in determining the sensitivity of the conclusions of standard models of analysis to variations in basic assumptions. Indeed, some recent papers in the economics literature have started to examine precisely this issue by essentially endowing hypothetical actors in market situations with less than perfectly rational powers and then observing what effect this has on market behavior (see, e.g., Akerlof and Yellen [1985] and the references cited therein).

A further and critical problem was raised by Coleman (in this volume). He asks where the greatest research gains are to be had in the interface between psychology and economics. These are not, he believes, to be found so much in revising the descriptive accuracy of models of individual choice as in improving the "apparatus for moving from the level of the individual actor to the behavior of the system" (p. 184). Whether Coleman is correct or not in his assertion of which problem is the most critical, we believe that great and justified recognition awaits anyone who can meet the challenge implicit in his remark.

Finally, both the challenges and difficulties of fruitful coexistence of economics and psychology are encapsulated by the reductio ad absurdum cited by Arrow (in this volume): "There cannot be any money lying in the street, because someone else would have picked it up already" (p. 214). For the economist operating within the rational choice paradigm this statement can be taken to mean that, for all practical purposes, the world behaves as if there were no money lying in the street. The psychologist, however, has no reasons to accept this statement as a working hypothesis. Instead, he or she would accept the possibility that some money may be lying in the street and would consider it worth learning who finds it and how.

Robin M. Hogarth
Melvin W. Reder

References

Akerlof, G. A., and Yellen, J. L. 1985. Can small deviations from rationality make significant differences to economic equilibria? *American Economic Review* 75:708–20.

Arkes, H. R.; Dawes, R. M.; and Christensen, C. 1986. Factors influencing the use of a decision rule in a probabilistic task. *Organizational Behavior and Human Decision Processes* 37:93–110.

Arrow, K. J. 1982. Risk perception in psychology and economics. *Economic Inquiry* 20:1–9.

Arrow, K. J. In this volume. Rationality of self and others in an economic system.

Battalio, R. C.; Kagel, J. H.; Rachlin, H.; and Green, L. 1981. Commodity choice behavior with pigeons as subjects. *Journal of Political Economy* 89:67–91.

Battalio, R. C.; Kagel, J. H.; and MacDonald, D. N. 1985. Animals' choices over uncertain outcomes: Some initial experimental results. *American Economic Review* 75:597–613.

Becker, G. S. 1981. *A Treatise on the Family.* Cambridge, Mass.: Harvard University Press.

Coleman, J. S. In this volume. Psychological structure and social structure in economic models.

Cook, T. D., and Campbell, D. T. 1979. *Quasi-Experimentation: Design and Analysis Issues for Field Settings*. Boston: Houghton Mifflin.

Edwards, W. 1954. The theory of decision making. *Psychological Bulletin* 51:380–417.

Eddy, D. M. 1982. Probabilistic reasoning in clinical medicine: Problems and opportunities. In D. Kahneman, P. Slovic, and A. Tversky (eds.), *Judgment under Uncertainty: Heuristics and Biases*. New York: Cambridge University Press.

Einhorn, H. J., and Hogarth, R. M. 1978. Confidence in judgment: Persistence of the illusion of validity. *Psychological Review* 85:395–416.

Einhorn, H. J., and Hogarth, R. M. 1981. Behavioral decision theory: Processes of judgment and choice. *Annual Review of Psychology* 32:53–88.

Einhorn, H. J., and Hogarth, R. M. 1985. Ambiguity and uncertainty in probabilistic inference. *Psychological Review* 92:433–61.

Einhorn, H. J., and Hogarth, R. M. In this volume. Decision making under ambiguity.

Friedman, M. 1953. *Essays in Positive Economics*. Chicago: University of Chicago Press.

Goldstein, W. M., and Einhorn, H. J. In press. Expression theory and the preference reversal phenomena. *Psychological Review*.

Gould, J. P. In this volume. Is the rational expectations hypothesis enough?

Grether, D. M., and Plott, C. R. 1979. Economic theory of choice and the preference reversal phenomenon. *American Economic Review* 69:623–38.

Haltiwanger, J., and Waldman, M. 1985. Rational expectations and the limits of rationality: An analysis of heterogeneity. *American Economic Review* 75:326–40.

Hammond, K. R., Hamm, R. M.; and Grassia, J. In press. Generalizing over conditions by combining the multitrait multimethod matrix and the representative design of experiments. *Psychological Bulletin*.

Hausch, D. B.; Ziemba, W. T.; and Rubenstein, M. E. 1981. Efficiency of the market for racetrack betting. *Management Science* 27:1435–52.

Hogarth, R. M. 1981. Beyond discrete biases: Functional and dysfunctional aspects of judgmental heuristics. *Psychological Bulletin* 90:197–217.

Joyce, E. J., and Biddle, G. C. 1981. Are auditors' judgments sufficiently regressive? *Journal of Accounting Research* 19:323–49.

Kahneman, D., and Tversky, A. 1979. Prospect theory: An analysis of decision under risk. *Econometrica* 47:263–91.

Kleidon, A. W. In this volume. Anomalies in financial economics: Blueprint for change?

Kunreuther, H.; Ginsberg, R.; Miller, L; Sagi, P.; Slovic, P.; Borkan, B.; and Katz, N. 1978. *Disaster Insurance Protection: Public Policy Lessons*. New York: Wiley.

Lopes, L. L. 1981. Averaging rules and adjustment processes: The role of averaging in inference. Report 13. Madison: University of Wisconsin, Wisconsin Human Information Processing Program.

Lovell, M. C. 1986. Tests of the rational expectations hypothesis. *American Economic Review* 76:110–24.

Lucas, R. E., Jr. In this volume. Adaptive behavior and economic theory.

Machina, M. J. 1982. "Expected utility" analysis without the independence axiom. *Econometrica* 50:277–323.

Miller, M. H. In this volume. Behavioral rationality in finance: The case of dividends.

Mowen, J. C., and Gentry, J. W. 1980. Investigation of the preference-reversal phenomenon in a new product introduction task. *Journal of Applied Psychology* 65:715–22.

Plott, C. R. 1982. Industrial organization theory and experimental economics. *Journal of Economic Literature* 20:1485–1527.

Plott, C. R. In this volume. Rational choice in experimental markets.

Prescott, E. 1977. Should control theory be used for economic stabilization? In K. Brunner and A. Meltzer (eds.), *Optimal Policies, Control Theory, and Technological Exports*. Carnegie-Rochester Conferences on Public Policy, vol. 7. *Journal of Monetary Economics* 3, suppl.:13–38.

Russell, T., and Thaler, R. 1985. The relevance of quasi-rationality in competitive markets. *American Economic Review* 75:1071–82.

Schoemaker, P. J. H. 1984. Optimality principles in science: Some epistemological issues. In J. H. P. Paelinck and P. H. Vossen (eds.), *The Quest for Optimality*. Sussex: Gower.

Siegel, S. 1961. Decision making and learning under varying conditions of reinforcement. *Annals of New York Academy of Science* 89:766–83.

Simon, H. A. 1978. Rationality as process and as product of thought. *American Economic Review* 68:1–16.

Simon, H. A. In this volume. Rationality in psychology and economics.

Slovic, P., and Lichtenstein, S. 1983. Preference reversals: A broader perspective. *American Economic Review* 73:596–605.

Slovic, P., and Tversky, A. 1974. Who accepts Savage's axiom? *Behavioral Science* 19:368–73.

Smith, V. L. 1982. Microeconomic systems as an experimental science. *American Economic Review* 72:923–55.

Thaler, R. In this volume. The psychology and economics conference handbook: Comments on Simon, on Einhorn and Hogarth, and on Tversky and Kahneman.

Tversky, A., and Kahneman, D. 1974. Judgment under uncertainty: Heuristics and biases. *Science* 185:1124–31.

Tversky, A., and Kahneman, D. In this volume. Rational choice and the framing of decisions.

von Neumann, J., and Morgenstern, O. 1947. *Theory of Games and Economic Behavior.* 2d ed. Princeton, N.J.: Princeton University Press.

Winter, S. G. In this volume. Comments on Arrow and on Lucas.

Zeckhauser, R. In this volume. Comments: Behavioral versus rational economics: What you see is what you conquer.

Herbert A. Simon

Carnegie-Mellon University

Rationality in Psychology and Economics*

The task I shall undertake here is to compare and contrast the concepts of rationality that are prevalent in psychology and economics, respectively. Economics has almost uniformly treated human behavior as rational. Psychology, on the other hand, has always been concerned with both the irrational and the rational aspects of behavior. In this paper, irrationality will be mentioned only obliquely; my concern is with rationality. Economics sometimes uses the term "irrationality" rather broadly (e.g., Becker 1962) and the term "rationality" correspondingly narrowly, so as to exclude from the domain of the rational many phenomena that psychology would include in it. For my purposes of comparison, I will have to use the broader conception of psychology.

One point should be set immediately outside dispute. Everyone agrees that people have reasons for what they do. They have motivations, and they use reason (well or badly) to respond to these motivations and reach their goals. Even much, or most, of the behavior that is called abnormal involves the exercise of thought and reason. Freud was most insistent that there is method in madness, that neuroses and psychoses were patients' solutions—not very satisfactory solutions in the long run—for the problems that troubled them.

The assumption that actors maximize subjective expected utility (economic rationality) supplies only a small part of the premises in economic reasoning, and that often not the essential part. The remainder of the premises are auxiliary empirical assumptions about actors' utilities, beliefs, expectations, and the like. Making these assumptions correctly requires an empirically founded theory of choice that specifies what information decision makers use and how they actually process it. This behavioral empirical base is largely lacking in contemporary economic analysis, and supplying it is essential for enhancing the explanatory and predictive power of economics.

* In writing out my remarks for publication, I have had the benefit, of course, of hearing the observations of my discussants at the Chicago meeting. I shall take the liberty of commenting, from time to time, on their remarks, but I shall try to indicate when I do so, in order to avoid a confusing anachronism.

I emphasize this point of agreement at the outset—that people have reasons for what they do—because it appears that economics sometimes feels called on to defend the thesis that human beings are rational. Psychology has no quarrel at all with this thesis. If there are differences in viewpoint, they must lie in conceptions of what constitutes rationality, not in the fact of rationality itself.

The judgment that certain behavior is "rational" or "reasonable" can be reached only by viewing the behavior in the context of a set of premises or "givens." These givens include the situation in which the behavior takes place, the goals it is aimed at realizing, and the computational means available for determining how the goals can be attained. In the course of this conference, many participants referred to the context of behavior as its "frame," a label that I will also use from time to time. Notice that the frame must be comprehensive enough to encompass goals, the definition of the situation, and computational resources.

In its treatment of rationality, neoclassical economics differs from the other social sciences in three main respects: (*a*) in its silence about the content of goals and values; (*b*) in its postulating global consistency of behavior; and (*c*) in its postulating "one world"—that behavior is objectively rational in relation to its total environment, including both present and future environment as the actor moves through time.

In contrast, the other social sciences, in their treatment of rationality, (*a*) seek to determine empirically the nature and origins of values and their changes with time and experience; (*b*) seek to determine the processes, individual and social, whereby selected aspects of reality are noticed and postulated as the "givens" (factual bases) for reasoning about action; (*c*) seek to determine the computational strategies that are used in reasoning, so that very limited information-processing capabilities can cope with complex realities; and (*d*) seek to describe and explain the ways in which nonrational processes (e.g., motivations, emotions, and sensory stimuli) influence the focus of attention and the definition of the situation that set the factual givens for the rational processes.

These important differences in the conceptualization of rationality rest on an even more fundamental distinction: in economics, rationality is viewed in terms of the choices it produces; in the other social sciences, it is viewed in terms of the processes it employs (Simon 1976/ 1982). The rationality of economics is substantive rationality, while the rationality of psychology is procedural rationality.

Substantive and Procedural Rationality

If we accept values as given and consistent, if we postulate an objective description of the world as it really is, and if we assume that the decision maker's computational powers are unlimited, then two important consequences follow. First, we do not need to distinguish between the real world and the decision maker's perception of it: he or she perceives the world as it really is. Second, we can predict the choices that will be made by a rational decision maker entirely from our knowledge of the real world and without a knowledge of the decision maker's perceptions or modes of calculation. (We do, of course, have to know his or her utility function.)

If, on the other hand, we accept the proposition that both the knowledge and the computational power of the decision maker are severely limited, then we must distinguish between the real world and the actor's perception of it and reasoning about it. That is to say, we must construct a theory (and test it empirically) of the processes of decision. Our theory must include not only the reasoning processes but also the processes that generate the actor's subjective representation of the decision problem, his or her frame (Simon 1978/1982).

The rational person of neoclassical economics always reaches the decision that is objectively, or substantively, best in terms of the given utility function. The rational person of cognitive psychology goes about making his or her decisions in a way that is procedurally reasonable in the light of the available knowledge and means of computation.

Embracing a substantive theory of rationality has had significant consequences for neoclassical economics and especially for its methodology. Until very recently, neoclassical economics has developed no strong empirical methodology for investigating the processes whereby values are formed, for the content of the utility function lies outside its self-defined scope. It has developed no special methodology for investigating how particular aspects of reality, rather than other aspects, come to the decision maker's attention, or for investigating how a representation of the choice situation is formed, or for investigating how reasoning processes are applied to draw out the consequences of such representations.

All these investigations call for empirical inquiry at the micro level—detailed study of decision makers engaged in the task of choice (Simon 1979b/1982, 1982). They are not questions that are easily answered by even the most sophisticated econometric analysis of aggregate data. To understand the processes that the economic actor employs in making decisions calls for observing these processes directly while they are going on, either in real world situations or in the laboratory, and/or interrogating the decision maker about beliefs, expectations, and methods of calculation and reasoning.

Securing access in order to observe decision processes in business firms or government organizations is difficult but often quite feasible—there are already a substantial number of successful studies of this kind in the literature. To extrapolate and generalize the findings requires attention to problems of sampling and aggregation; but these problems are surely easier to solve than the problem of going from the micro level of hypothetical "representative firms" or "typical consumers" to the level of markets.

Laboratory experiments on decision processes raise questions of their generalizability to real world situations. Studies that depend on interrogation of one kind or another raise questions of the veridicality of responses. There is no dearth of methodological issues but no reason to suppose that these issues are any more intractable than those encountered in standard econometric practice. But since experimental economics is well represented at this conference, I will say no more about the methodological issues it faces. They are best discussed in the context of concrete examples, a number of which will be provided here.

To move from substantive to procedural rationality requires a major extension of the empirical foundations of economics. It is not enough to add theoretical postulates about the shape of the utility function, or about the way in which actors form expectations about the future, or about their attention or inattention to particular environmental variables. These are assumptions about matters of fact, and the whole ethos of science requires such assumptions to be supported by publicly repeatable observations that are obtained and analyzed objectively.

In the following sections of this paper, I should like to illustrate, with concrete examples, the difficulties that contemporary neoclassical economics faces on a number of fronts owing to the insufficiency of its empirical foundations. These examples will also suggest the directions in which empirical work needs to go. My topics will include the shape and dimensions of the utility function, the role of attentional processes, the formation of expectations, and the sources of the empirical parameters and models that characterize cost and supply functions.

In all these examples we will see that the conclusions that are reached by neoclassical reasoning depend very much on the "auxiliary" factual assumptions that have to be made to define the situation and very little on the assumptions of substantive rationality—in particular, the utility-maximization assumptions. Indeed, in many cases, provided that the factual assumptions are retained, the conclusions reached within the utility-maximization framework could be reached as readily from much weaker assumptions of "reasonableness" in behavior (Becker 1962). Almost all the action, all the ability to reach nontrivial conclusions, comes from the factual assumptions and very little from the assumptions of optimization. Hence it becomes critically important to submit the factual assumptions to careful empirical test.

Empirical Basis for the Utility Function

Contemporary neoclassical economics provides no theoretical basis for specifying the shape and content of the utility function, and this gap is very inadequately filled by empirical research using econometric techniques. The gap is important because many conclusions that have been drawn in the literature about the way in which the economy operates depend on assumptions about consumers' utility functions.

To illustrate this claim, I will take two examples from the work of one of my discussants, Gary Becker, at the risk, of course, of introducing circularity by discussing a discussant. Both examples are drawn from Becker's well-known *A Treatise on the Family* (1981).

The Opportunities of Children

My account of the first example is not original but follows an enlightening analysis that has been carried out recently by Arthur Goldberger (in press) of Becker's (1981, chs. 6, 7) theory of the opportunities of children and intergenerational mobility. On page 116 of his book, Becker follows a mathematical demonstration with the interpretation: "If parents correctly anticipate their children's luck and endowment, an increase in either would not add an equal amount to the income of children." This interpretation is later (pp. 125–26) used to question whether public compensatory education programs will achieve their goal since parents whose children participate in these programs simply reallocate elsewhere resources they would otherwise have invested in these children.

I will return in a moment to the empirical evidence for the conclusion and its application. First, however, I would like to report Goldberger's analysis of the underlying argument that leads up to it.

Goldberger shows that Becker's conclusion follows from specific assumptions that parents' utility grows positively with parent's consumption and child's income and that the child's income is an additive function of parents' investment and child's luck. If the latter function is multiplicative instead of additive, the conclusion does not follow. Moreover, the whole derivation employs a homothetic utility function. No empirical support is provided for these assumptions.

But Milton Friedman (1953) would tell us that we should concentrate our efforts on testing the conclusions, not the assumptions, and this is what Becker does. Three pieces of evidence are cited, one relating to compensatory education and two to other public "compensatory" programs. On education, Becker quotes Arthur Jensen's "famous and controversial essay" (the characterization is Becker's) to the effect that "compensatory education has been tried and it apparently has failed" (p. 125). The essay quoted is, indeed, controversial; others have subsequently reached quite different evaluations of Headstart and other compensatory education programs. Moreover, Jensen himself attributes their failure—if there was one—to causes very different from the utility functions of parents. To choose among Jensen's explanation, Becker's, and the thousand others that could be dreamed up, it would surely be important to find out directly whether families whose children participated in such programs diverted their money, nurturance, or attention away from those children. That would provide a relatively direct test of the nature of their preferences (although very far from a test either that they possessed consistent utility functions or that they were maximizing anything).

Becker's other two pieces of evidence are more to the point. It does appear that public health programs cause people to devote less of their private budgets to health matters (the programs are presumably intended to do this) and that food supplements to pregnant women are to some extent diverted by reallocation of private budgets. To that extent we can conclude that some substitutions of the sort that utility theory predicts do actually take place. But of course as Becker has pointed out elsewhere (Becker 1962), price elasticity of demand is not a very strong test of utility maximization.

What one sees in this example are matters of substantial practical as well as theoretical importance disposed of on the basis of unsupported theoretical assumptions and scanty evidence about the conclusions. Economics is too important, intellectually as well as practically, to be treated with this kind of casual empiricism.

What one also sees in this example is that the conclusions depend primarily not on the assumption of optimization but on the (untested) auxiliary assumption that the interaction of luck and endowment is additive rather than multiplicative. Utility maximization is neither a necessary nor a sufficient condition for compensatory behavior.

Finally, in this example one begins to understand the real decision making when one undertakes (as in the public health and food supplement research) to gather direct evidence about behavior through field studies or field experiments.

Labor Force Participation of Women

Let me now turn to a second example from Becker's (1981) book. On pages 245–56 he gives us his interpretation of the evolution of the American family since World War II. The salient fact around which the analysis revolves is that there has been a steady rise in the labor force participation of married women, including those with small children. At the outset (p. 245), Becker tells us that he believes "that the major cause of these changes is the growth in the earning power of women as the American economy developed." This credo is then buttressed by the empirical observation that the weekly earnings of employed women grew substantially during this period. This, he observes, implies an increase in the opportunity cost of staying in the home and also raises the relative cost of children, thereby reducing the demand for children.

However, the question is never raised as to (*a*) whether the increase in real earnings of women was more rapid than the increase in real earnings of men during this same period or (*b*) whether the increase in women's weekly earnings might not have been in some measure due to an increase in average hours worked—itself a form rather than a consequence of greater labor force participation.

Moreover, Becker places the whole weight of explanation on an unexplained shift in the demand curve for women's labor. No account is given of why this event should have taken place at this particular moment in American history or whether it was a sudden shock or a continuing development. Nor is any evidence provided (except the circular evidence that women moved into the labor force) that the event in fact took place. In particular, the possibility is not explored that a shift in the utility function of women caused a shift in the supply of women in the labor market in the face of a highly elastic demand curve and generally rising productivity in the economy.

So in this example as in the previous one, the action comes, not from the assumption of utility maximization, but from factual assumptions about the shifting or stability of particular supply and demand curves. The true explanation will be obtained not by raising the sophistication of the economic reasoning but only by painstaking examination of occupations in manufacturing and service industries and an even more difficult empirical examination of changes in women's attitudes about where they prefer to work. Utility maximization is neither a necessary nor a sufficient condition for the conclusion that was reached. The action comes from the empirical assumptions, including assumptions about how people view their world.

Attention and Representation

In a substantive theory of rationality there is no place for a variable like focus of attention. But in a procedural theory, it may be very important to know under what circumstances certain aspects of reality will be heeded and others ignored. I wish now to present two examples of situations in which focus of attention is a major determinant of behavior. The first rests on very strong empirical evidence; the second is more speculative, but I will try to make it plausible.

The Purchase of Flood Insurance

Kunreuther et al. (1978) have studied decisions of property owners whether to purchase insurance against flood damage. Neoclassical theory would predict that an owner would buy insurance if the expected reimbursable damage from floods was greater than the premium. The actual data are in egregious conflict with this claim. Instead it appears that insurance is purchased mainly by persons who have experienced damaging floods or who are acquainted with persons who have had such experiences, more or less independently of the cost/benefit ratio of the purchaser.

If we wish to understand the insurance-buying behavior, then we must determine, as Kunreuther and his colleagues did, the circumstances that attract the attention of a property owner to this decision alternative. Utility maximization is neither a necessary nor a sufficient condition for deducing who will buy insurance. The process of deciding—in this case, the process that puts the item on the decision agenda—is the important thing.

Voting Behavior

Voting behavior provides a more complex example of the role of attention in behavior. Both before and since Marx, it has been widely believed that voters respond, at least to an important extent, to their economic interests. Let us assume that is so. A substantial number of empirical studies have shown correlations between economic conditions and votes in American elections (Simon 1985). But such studies use a great variety of independent variables as measures of voters' perceptions of the economic consequences of their choices. (See, e.g., Hibbs 1982; and Weatherford 1983.) Some investigators have tried to measure the economic well-being of voters at the time of the election as compared with their well-being at some previous time. Others have measured the state of the economy—the level of the GNP, say, or of employment. Which of these (or what other measure) is the true measure of economic advantage? Quite different predictions can be made if different measures are chosen.

Consider the situation of a voter at the time of the 1984 presidential election who wished to maximize his or her economic well-being. Which of the following facts about the economy should influence the vote? (1) Real incomes of a majority have increased over the past 4 years but at less than the historical rate of a couple of decades earlier. (2) Dispersion of incomes has increased. (3) The rate of inflation has declined dramatically. (4) The rate of interest remains high compared with the historical past. (5) The national debt and deficit have increased dramatically. (6) The balance of trade has "worsened" dramatically. (7) Farm foreclosures have increased substantially. (8) Unemployment has decreased recently but is higher than it was 4 years previously. If we throw noneconomic considerations into the voter's utility function, we may add such facts as, The armament situation has changed in complex ways, et cetera, et cetera, moving into race tensions and equity to minorities, energy, the environment, creationism, abortion, and what not.

To predict how a voter, even a voter motivated solely by concern for his or her economic well-being, will vote requires much more than assuming utility maximization. A voter who attends to the rate of inflation may behave quite differently from a voter who attends to the federal deficit. Moreover, in order to predict where a voter's attention will focus, we may need to know his or her economic beliefs. A monetarist may consider different facts to be salient than the facts to which a Keynesian will attend. In any model of voting behavior that has any prospect of predicting behavior, almost all the action will lie in these auxiliary assumptions about attention and belief that define the decision maker's frame.

Expectations

Neoclassical theory, either with or without the assumption of rational expectations, cannot explain the phenomenon of the business cycle. In previous papers (e.g., Simon 1984) I have shown that auxiliary assumptions, which in this case amount to departures from objective rationality, must be annexed to the neoclassical model before a business cycle can be made to appear. I will repeat the argument here very briefly.

If we examine Keynes's reasoning in *The General Theory of Employment, Interest and Money* (1936), we see that, at most points, it fits perfectly the neoclassical mold of substantive rationality. Auxiliary assumptions (it does not matter whether we view them as "irrationalities" or simply as expectations) are introduced, however, at points that are critical to the explanation of the business cycle. One of these auxiliary assumptions is the postulate that labor suffers from the money illusion—that unions cannot distinguish between changes in real and money wages, respectively. The addition of this postulate is sufficient to produce underemployment stagnation in the Keynesian theory.

Remarkably enough, when we move from Keynes to the other end of the spectrum of economic theories—for example, to Lucas's (1981) rational expectations models—the same picture presents itself. The business cycle in these models derives, not from the assumptions of rationality, but from the appearance of money illusion in an erstwhile Eden. Only, in Lucas's theory, the illusion is suffered by businessmen, who cannot distinguish between general price movements and price changes in their industry, instead of by workers.

The action in business-cycle theories appears to reside not in the rationality assumptions but in auxiliary assumptions about the processes that people use to form expectations about future events. A theory of procedural rationality would have to employ empirical research to investigate these expectation-forming processes. Again, the assumption of utility or profit maximization provides neither a necessary nor a sufficient condition for the existence of business cycles.

We already have experience in using direct methods to learn how

people form expectations about the future. Direct inquiries into people's expectations about business conditions, pioneered by George
Katona (1951) at the University of Michigan, have for many years
supplied inputs to econometric models of the economy. Studies have
been made of planning methods and investment decision processes of
business firms (for examples, see Eliasson 1976; and Bromiley 1986)
that give us considerable information about what the forecasting firms
do and whether and how forecasting enters into the process of choosing investments. This kind of information, which could easily be multiplied, provides us with powerful means for testing the rational expectations theory or other theories about how expectations are formed.
There is no need to fall back on casual empiricism or on dubious
indirect inferences from econometric data.

Other Empirical Parameters

My two final examples of the role of facts in economic reasoning are a
little different from the previous ones. There are important cases in
which not only are assumptions of substantive rationality insufficient
to account for the observed phenomena but also parsimonious alternative explanations can be provided with only a minimal reference to
rationality. The two examples I will discuss are the distribution of
business firm sizes and the magnitudes of executive salaries.

Distribution of Business Firm Sizes

There is no unequivocal neoclassical theory of the distribution of business firm sizes. The traditional theory of the determinants of firm size
was expounded by Jacob Viner (1932) and, by some kind of intellectual
Gresham's Law, has survived to this day in elementary economics
textbooks and books on intermediate price theory. It postulates a family of U-shaped short-run cost curves; a U-shaped long-run cost curve
that is the envelope of the short-run curves; and a firm whose size
corresponds to the scale of minimum cost on the long-run curve.

There are innumerable difficulties with this account. The most serious is that empirical studies very often show cost curves to be J
shaped, without a recognizable minimum, rather than U shaped. With a
J-shaped curve, that is, decreasing costs at all sizes, there is no upper
bound on firm size. Nearly as serious is that the theory says nothing
about parameter values of the cost curves, hence nothing about what
sizes of firms will actually be observed. In particular, no conclusions
can be drawn about the distribution of firm sizes.

If the theory is interpreted to mean that all firms in an industry have
identical cost curves (which, in the absence of rents, should be the
case), then, in equilibrium, all firms will be the same size. But this
prediction is contradicted by the facts as squarely as any prediction

could be. The actual distributions are highly skewed, with many small firms and a few that are very large.

If, on the contrary, each firm has its own cost curve, bearing no relation to the curves of the others, then the theory predicts too little: any size distribution whatsoever can be accommodated. But the fact is that the actual distributions are quite regular and similar, approximating the Pareto distribution in the upper tail. The traditional theory is therefore a total failure in predicting actual firm size distributions and should be banished from the textbooks.

But here we face the difficulty that nature abhors a vacuum, that a bad theory is preferred to none. However, in this case, a wholly satisfactory alternative is available. It rests on plausible (although not well-tested) premises, and these premises are even consistent with possible behaviors of reasonable men and women. The key premise (Ijiri and Simon 1977) is that the expected rate of growth of a firm during any period is proportionate to the size it had attained at the beginning of that period—the so-called Gibrat assumption. With this assumption and a little attention to boundary conditions, the Pareto distribution can be deduced as the steady-state equilibrium of the system.

Such tests as have been made of the Gibrat assumption have had generally positive results. But even if we were satisfied that the assumption is empirically valid, we might wish to probe deeper. In a world in which people have reasons for their actions, why would such a relation hold? This is not the place for a full discussion of the matter, and I limit myself to two comments. First, if average rate of return on capital is independent of size of firm (as seems to be true to a first approximation), it is rather easy to think of reasons why access to internal or external capital for expansion should be, on average, roughly commensurate with present size. Second, we really do not need to do this kind of armchair guessing. We can undertake to study business firms to determine how growth comes about. What we should not do is to cling to a theory that predicts very little and that little incorrectly.

Distribution of Executive Salaries

My second example of a failure of classical theory that can be remedied within a framework of procedural rationality is the prediction of the distribution of the salaries of top executives.

Neoclassical theory would, of course, explain the salaries of executives in terms of individual abilities for managerial work. Moreover, a very able executive would presumably have greater productivity when engaged in large affairs, as in managing a large business firm. Hence the combined forces of supply and demand would produce a strong correlation of executive ability with firm size. Rees (1973, p. 201), in his textbook exposition of the theory, puts it this way: "The person who alone among hundreds of competing junior executives in a large corporation eventually rises to the presidency must surely have special qualities that account for this rise, although they differ from the qualities that make a successful scientist or a successful salesperson. In any event, a business that is not a monopoly would soon run at a loss if it selected executives without any regard to those kinds of ability relevant in managing a business well.''

The claim is moderate and plausible. It does not require any assumption of maximization, only the assumption that those who select executives will behave reasonably, by taking ability into account. It leaves open the question of the processes of selection: how ability is judged and how accurately it can be estimated. It also leaves open the question of whether the characteristics that allow a person to compete successfully for advancement are closely correlated with the characteristics that make for effective management. But we will ignore the Peter Principle and other postulates that have been put forward challenging the close relation between managerial ability and selectability.

Difficulty arises, however, when we try to move from these premises to an account of the observed salary distribution function. A number of studies (e.g., Roberts 1959) have shown that the average compensation of top executives increases with the cube root of the size of the firm. I have been told, though I have not seen the data, that this relation continues to hold when executive bonuses and fringe benefits are included in salary. How shall we explain this very regular and persistent distribution?

Neoclassical theory, without strong auxiliary assumptions, is helpless. As Lucas (1978) has pointed out, what are needed are an assumption about the marginal product of managerial work as a function of firm size and managerial ability and an assumption about the distribution of managerial ability measured in the same units as in the previously mentioned function. Since there are no empirical data either on the marginal productivity of managers (except the salary data themselves) or on the distribution of ability, it is easy to manufacture functions that will produce the desired distribution of salaries. However, it should be noted that certain "obvious" choices of function will not work—for example, the Gibrat assumption that the marginal productivity of a manager is proportional to the size of the firm. If a function is found that fits the data, it is, of course, not refutable and hence profoundly uninteresting as a theoretical premise.

As an alternative route to an explanation of the observed salary distribution (Simon 1979a/1982), we can introduce two factual assumptions that can be verified (and for one of which we already have sufficient empirical data). The first assumption is that business organizations have a pyramidal form and that the number of subordinates reporting directly to an executive does not vary much from one organization to another or from one organizational level to another—that the span of control is relatively constant. This is a well-known fact about business organizations. The second assumption is that, by some generally accepted norm of "fairness," the ratio of the salary of an executive to the salaries of his or her immediate subordinates is a constant over organizations and over levels.

With these two assumptions, it follows immediately that the log of the salary of the top executive will vary linearly with the log of company size; and with reasonable assumptions, fitting observed facts, about the sizes of the two parameters of the theory (the span of control and the "fair" ratio of salaries), the coefficient in this linear relation can be predicted to be in the neighborhood of .3—very close to the observed value.

Of course, we will be more confident that this is the correct explanation when we have more direct evidence that the postulated norm of fairness really exists in peoples' minds. My only claim at the moment is that here we have an explanation that takes process into account, that does not rely on any assumption of utility or profit maximization, and that does describe a realizable decision process that is not dependent on quantities that are unobservable by the actors and by economists studying the phenomena. Of course this explanation does make the correct prediction—quantitatively as well as qualitatively.

Neoclassical economists have raised several objections to the explanation I have just outlined. Rees (1973, p. 201) argues that the theory "is too special, since it applies only to hierarchical organizations." He points out that the salary distributions of such professionals as architects and attorneys, who typically work in small organizations, also are highly skewed. Of course, there is no reason to suppose that salaries in all occupations are fixed in the same way. A procedural theory of rationality would predict that the method of salary determination would depend on what kinds of information were available for assessing worth.

Position in hierarchy provides such information in large organizations. In the case of architectural and legal firms, direct measures are generally available of the magnitude of the revenues associated with an associate's work and the magnitude of the contracts he or she is able to attract. Moreover, the sizes of jobs have a highly skewed distribution for a variety of reasons that we could explore empirically. Hence the fact that the salaries of professionals other than executives of business firms are skewed hardly seems a reason for rejecting the theory of executive compensation I have proposed.

Recently, new information has been gained about bonuses and other nonsalary awards that make up an increasing part of executive compensation. This information shows that bonuses vary strongly with profits and other statistics that might be taken as measures of the effectiveness of executive performance. But such evidence merely shows that companies try to motivate their executives to make profits (often, alas, with excessive attention to short-run profits, as has been pointed out in the literature). It does not show that the incentives bear any close relation to the marginal worth of the executives or even that the fluctuations in profits are the result of the incentive compensation.

The evidence that incentives are offered to executives to increase profits is just what a procedural theory would predict. It would predict also that the rewards would be related to available statistics of company performance, even in the absence of reliable information about the exact relation between performance and managerial behavior. It would make no assumption that profits are maximized since the observable evidence provides no basis for that assumption. It would assume only that executives (and corporate boards) believe that executives can influence profits through their behavior and that a bonus plan would thereby motivate them to try harder.

A procedural theory would assume that people have reasons for what they do when they set executive salaries and that these reasons take account of the highly imperfect and incomplete information available to them. However, it would be essential, in order to predict behavior more precisely, to have good empirical information both about the kinds of information to which the decision makers have ready access and about their beliefs and opinions on the mechanisms of the world on which their decisions operate. The most likely sources of such information are direct studies of the behaviors, values, beliefs, and opinions of the actors.

Summing Up

Between supporters of substantive and procedural theories of rationality there are fundamental differences about what constitutes a principled, parsimonious, scientific theory. We may put the matter in Bayesian terms. Neoclassical economists attach a very large prior probability (.9944?) to the proposition that people have consistent utility functions and in fact maximize utilities in an objective sense. As my examples show, they are prepared to make whatever auxiliary empirical assumptions are necessary in order to preserve the utility-maximization postulate, even when the empirical assumptions are unverified. When verification is demanded, they tend to look for evidence that the theory makes correct predictions and resist advice that they should look instead directly at the decision mechanisms and processes.

Given the magnitude of the Bayesian prior that expresses confidence in the theory and the weakness of the kinds of indirect evidence that are allowed for testing it, neoclassical economics becomes, as has been observed more than once, essentially tautological and irrefutable. Because of its preoccupation with utility maximization, it fails to observe that most of its "action"—the force of its predictions—derives from the, usually untested, auxiliary assumptions that describe the environment in which decisions are made. The examples show that the important conclusions it draws can usually also be drawn, with the aid of the auxiliary assumptions, from the postulate that people are procedurally rational and without assuming that they maximize utility.

It is too easy, within the neoclassical methodological framework, to save the theory from unpleasant evidence by modifying the auxiliary assumptions and providing a new framework within which the actor "must have been operating." Hence neoclassical theory, as usually applied, is an exceedingly weak theory, as shown by the difficulty of finding sets of facts, actual or hypothetical, that cannot be rationalized and made consistent with it.

Behavioral theories of rationality attach a high prior probability (.9944?) to the assumption that economic actors use the same basic processes in making their decisions as have been observed in other human cognitive activities and that these processes are indeed observable. In situations that are complex and in which information is very incomplete (i.e., virtually all real world situations), the behavioral theories deny that there is any magic for producing behavior even approximating an objective maximization of profits or utilities. They therefore seek to determine what the actual frame of the decision is, how that frame arises from the decision situation, and how, within that frame, reason operates.

In this kind of complexity, there is no single sovereign principle for deductive prediction. The emerging laws of procedural rationality have much more the complexity of molecular biology than the simplicity of classical mechanics. As a consequence, they call for a very high ratio of empirical investigation to theory building. They require painstaking factual study of the decision-making process itself.

What is to be done? What prescription for economic research derives from my analysis?

First, I would recommend that we stop debating whether a theory of substantive rationality and the assumptions of utility maximization provide a sufficient base for explaining and predicting economic behavior. The evidence is overwhelming that they do not.

We already have in psychology a substantial body of empirically tested theory about the processes people actually use to make boundedly rational, or "reasonable," decisions. This body of theory asserts that the processes are sensitive to the complexity of decision-making contexts and to learning processes as well.

The application of this procedural theory of rationality to economics requires extensive empirical research, much of it at micro-micro levels, to determine specifically how process is molded to context in actual economic environments and the consequences of this interaction for the economic outcomes of these processes. Economics without psychological and sociological research to determine the givens of the decision-making situation, the focus of attention, the problem representation, and the processes used to identify alternatives, estimate consequences, and choose among possibilities—such economics is a one-bladed scissors. Let us replace it with an instrument capable of cutting through our ignorance about rational human behavior.

References

Becker, G. S. 1962. Irrational behavior and economic theory. *Journal of Political Economy* 70:1–13.
Becker, G. S. 1981. *A Treatise on the Family*. Cambridge, Mass.: Harvard University Press.
Bromiley, P. 1986. Corporate planning and capital investment. *Journal of Economic Behavior and Organization* 7:147–70.
Eliasson, G. 1976. *Business Economic Planning*. New York: Wiley.
Friedman, M. 1953. *Essays in Positive Economics*. Chicago: University of Chicago Press.
Goldberger, A. S. In press. *Modeling the Economic Family*. Ann Arbor: University of Michigan Press.
Hibbs, D. A., Jr. 1982. Economic outcomes and political support for British governments among occupational classes. *American Political Science Review* 76:259–79.
Ijiri, Y., and Simon, H. A. 1977. *Skew Distributions and the Sizes of Business Firms*. Amsterdam: North-Holland.
Katona, G. 1951. *Psychological Analysis of Economic Behavior*. New York: McGraw-Hill.
Keynes, J. M. 1936. *The General Theory of Employment, Interest and Money*. London: Macmillan.
Kunreuther, H., with Ginsberg, R.; Miller, L.; Sagi, P.; Slovic, P.; Borkan, B.; and Katz, N. 1978. *Disaster Insurance Protection: Public Policy Lessons*. New York: Wiley.
Lucas, R. E., Jr. 1978. On the size distribution of business firms. *Bell Journal of Economics* 9:508–23.
Lucas, R. E., Jr. 1981. *Studies in Business Cycle Theory*. Cambridge, Mass.: MIT Press.
Rees, A. 1973. *The Economics of Work and Pay*. New York: Harper & Row.
Roberts, D. R. 1959. *Executive Compensation*. Glencoe, Ill.: Free Press.
Simon, H. A. 1976. From substantive to procedural rationality. In S. J. Latsis (ed.), *Method and Appraisal in Economics*. Cambridge: Cambridge University Press. Reprinted in *Models of Bounded Rationality*. 2 vols. Cambridge, Mass.: MIT Press, 1982.
Simon, H. A. 1978. Rationality as process and product of thought. *American Economic Review: Proceedings* 68:1–16. Reprinted in *Models of Bounded Rationality*. 2 vols. Cambridge, Mass.: MIT Press, 1982.
Simon, H. A. 1979a. On parsimonious explanations of production relations. *Scandinavian Journal of Economics* 81:459–74. Reprinted in *Models of Bounded Rationality*. 2 vols. Cambridge, Mass.: MIT Press, 1982.
Simon, H. A. 1979b. Rational decision making in business organizations. *American Economic Review* 69:493–513. Reprinted in *Models of Bounded Rationality*. 2 vols. Cambridge, Mass.: MIT Press, 1982.
Simon, H. A. 1982. *Models of Bounded Rationality*. 2 vols. Cambridge, Mass.: MIT Press.
Simon, H. A. 1984. On the behavioral and rational foundations of economic dynamics. *Journal of Economic Behavior and Organization* 5:35–55.
Simon, H. A. 1985. Human nature in politics: The dialogue of psychology with political science. *American Political Science Review* 79:293–304.
Viner, J. 1932. Cost curves and supply curves. *Zeitschrift für Nationalökonomie* 3:23–
Weatherford, M. S. 1983. Economic voting and the "symbolic politics" argument. *American Political Science Review* 77:158–74.

Hillel J. Einhorn
Robin M. Hogarth
University of Chicago

Decision Making under Ambiguity*

The study of decision making under uncertainty has been dominated by a single approach—the closely related theories of expected utility and subjective expected utility. As formulated and axiomatized by von Neumann and Morgenstern (1944) and Savage (1954), these theories rank among the most important in twentieth-century social science. They have had a profound influence on the manner in which social scientists (in particular, economists, psychologists, statisticians, sociologists, and political scientists) describe choice under uncertainty. Moreover, they have provided the foundation for prescriptive approaches to decision making (e.g., decision analysis; see Raiffa [1968]; Keeney and Raiffa [1976]). In one area, however, expected utility and subjective expected utility (hereafter called "utility theory") have met with mixed success. This is represented by a host of experiments on choice behavior, conducted principally by psychologists but also by an increasing number of economists (for a comprehensive review, see Schoemaker [1982]). On the one hand, utility theory has been enormously fruitful in providing a framework within which choice can be studied. On the other, it has failed to predict certain phenomena, resulting in so-called choice paradoxes

* This research was supported by a contract from the Office of Naval Research. We thank Mel Reder for his comments on an earlier version.

Ellsberg's paradox shows that ambiguous probabilities derived from choices between gambles are not coherent. A descriptive model of judgment under ambiguity is developed in which an initial estimate serves as an anchor and adjustments are made for ambiguity via a mental simulation process. The model specifies conditions for ambiguity seeking and avoidance and sub- and superadditivity of complementary probabilities. Three experiments involving Ellsberg's paradox and the setting of buying and selling prices for insurance and a warranty test the model. A choice rule under ambiguity is proposed that implies the nonindependence of ambiguous probabilities and the sign of payoff utilities. Extensions of the model to choices with explicit probabilities and the handling of context effects are discussed.

or anomalies. Furthermore, these failings have been noted for several decades (cf. Edwards 1954, 1961).

Utility theory has nonetheless proven to be remarkably resilient to the experimental evidence that has accumulated against it. Indeed, we make this remark despite the fact that recent alternative theories succeed in explaining several choice paradoxes (e.g., Chew and MacCrimmon 1979; Kahneman and Tversky 1979; Bell 1982; Machina 1982; Quiggin 1982). We believe that three factors have contributed to the longevity of utility theory. (1) The criterion of maximizing expected (or subjectively expected) utility follows logically from a parsimonious set of axioms. In addition, each axiom specifies a reasonable principle (e.g., transitivity) such that it provides a description of how a "rational" actor might behave. (2) The theory has provided a useful framework for deriving empirically testable propositions in many areas of applied economics, for example, finance, marketing, political economy, and so on. (3) The theory is difficult to falsify with naturally occurring data since exogenous variables can be called on to explain violations of predictions. Moreover, tests of utility theory are not as rigorous as they seem in that specific alternatives to the theory are rarely considered (for exceptions, see Kunreuther [1976]; Thaler [1980]). In practice, tests of the theory have not followed a "strong inference" approach (Platt 1964).

In our view, both utility theory and its alternatives fail to capture three important elements that characterize risky decision making.

1. *The nature of uncertainty in choice.* The dominant metaphor used to conceptualize risky decision making involves choices between explicit gambles. Moreover, in both experimental and theoretical work, this notion is made operational by using explicit gambling devices such as dice, urns, bingo cages, and the like. However, we argue that the nature of the uncertainty people experience in real world decisions is often quite different from that inherent in gambling devices.

2. *Effects of context.* The gamble metaphor allows one to study the structure of decisions within a particular context (i.e., the gambling context). However, people are highly sensitive to contextual variables, and changes in context can strongly affect the evaluation of risk.

3. *Dependence between probabilities and payoffs.* All models proposed to date maintain the assumption that utilities and probabilities combine independently in determining the overall worth of risky options. We believe that payoffs can systematically affect the weight given to uncertainty, especially in the presence of ambiguity.

Purpose and Plan of the Paper

Our focus in this paper concerns the first issue raised above—the nature of uncertainty and its representation in theories of choice. The other two issues are briefly considered, particularly in light of the model developed for dealing with judgments under ambiguity. The paper is organized as follows. We first discuss the difference between exact probabilities and the more realistic ambiguous probabilities that characterize most decision-making situations. In this regard, we consider the paradox presented by Daniel Ellsberg (1961), in which choices under ambiguity violate Savage's (1954) subjective expected utility model. A quantitative, psychological model of how people assess uncertain probabilities is then developed, and various implications are derived. Three experimental studies that test the model are presented. These deal with variations of Ellsberg's paradox and the setting of buying and selling prices for an insurance policy and a warranty. Finally, our results and model are discussed with respect to a choice rule for decision making under ambiguity and extensions of this rule to situations in which probabilities are precisely known.

The Nature of Uncertainty and Ambiguity

There are important psychological differences in the way people experience the uncertainty inherent in gambling devices as compared with those faced in everyday life. In gambling devices, the nature of uncertainty is explicit since there is a well-defined sampling space and sampling procedure. In contrast, when assessing uncertainty in real world tasks, the precision of the gambling analogy can be misleading. Specifically, beliefs about uncertain events are typically loosely held and ill defined. Moreover, feelings of uncertainty are not limited to random influences that affect outcomes from a well-defined process (e.g., the proportions of different colored balls in an urn) but can extend to uncertainty about the underlying data generating process itself. In short, ambiguity or "uncertainty about uncertainties" is a pervasive element of much real world decision making. We now turn to an important demonstration of this fact by discussing Ellsberg's paradox (Ellsberg 1961).

Ellsberg used the following example to demonstrate that uncertainty in choice is not totally captured by the concept of a "probability." Imagine two urns each containing red and black balls. In urn 1 there are 100 balls with unknown proportions of red and black. Urn 2 contains 50 red and 50 black balls. Now consider a gamble such that, if you bet on red and it is drawn from the urn, you get a $100 payoff; similarly for black. If, on the other hand, you bet on the wrong color, the payoff is $0. First, consider urn 1 and ask yourself whether you prefer, or are indifferent to, betting on a red or a black ball (designated R_1 and B_1, respectively). Most people are indifferent between red and black, thereby implying that the subjective probabilities of the two events are equal; that is, $p(R_1) = p(B_1) = .5$. Next consider the choice of balls in urn 2, in which the proportion of red and black is known to be .5. Again, most people are indifferent between R_2 and B_2, implying that $p(R_2) = p(B_2) = .5$.

Imagine that you are now asked to indicate whether you would prefer to draw a red from urn 1 (unknown proportion of red) or from urn 2 (proportion of red = .5). When faced with this question, many people prefer urn 2 (rather than express indifference). Note that the choice of urn 2 over urn 1 implies that $p(R_2) > p(R_1)$. However, from the previous choices, $p(R_1) = .5$ and $p(R_2) = .5$. Hence there is a contradiction between the probabilities derived from choices within the urns and those derived from choices between the urns. Finally, consider being asked to choose betwen urn 1 and urn 2 if a black ball is to be drawn. Again, most people prefer to draw from urn 2, which implies that $p(B_2) > p(B_1)$. The overall pattern of choices within and between urns leads to the following:

$$p(R_2) > p(R_1) = .5, \quad p(B_2) > p(B_1) = .5;$$

or

$$p(R_2) = .5 > p(R_1), \quad p(B_2) = .5 > p(B_1).$$

In the first case, the sum of $p(R_2)$ and $p(B_2)$ is greater than one (hereafter called "superadditivity"); in the second case, the sum of $p(R_1)$ and $p(B_1)$ is less than one (hereafter called "subadditivity"). Thus either urn 2 has complementary probabilities that sum to more than one, or urn 1 has complementary probabilities that sum to less than one. As we will show, the nonadditivity of complementary probabilities is central to judgments under ambiguity.

Ellsberg's paradox demonstrates that, although it may seem strange and awkward to speak of uncertainty as being more or less certain itself, such a concept is crucial for understanding how people make judgments and decisions in their natural environment. In fact, the notion of uncertainty about uncertainty has been discussed under a variety of rubrics, for example, ambiguous probabilities, second-order uncertainty, and probabilities for probabilities (e.g., Marschak 1975). Moreover, current work on fuzzy sets (Zadeh 1978), Shafer's (1976) theory of evidence, Cohen's (1977) attempt to formalize uncertainty in legal settings, and the elicitation of probability ranges (Wallsten, Forsyth, and Budescu 1983) all contain ideas regarding the vagueness that can underlie probabilities. However, it should be noted that the concept of ambiguous probabilities has not received universal acceptance (e.g., de Finetti [1977]; see also the various responses to Ellsberg's original article—Raiffa [1961]; Ellsberg [1963]; Roberts [1963]). Be that as it may, empirical evidence (e.g., Becker and Brownson 1964; Yates and Zukowski 1976; Gärdenfors and Sahlin 1982; Curley and Yates 1985) has shown that ambiguity affects judgments and choices and should not, therefore, be ignored. However, it is one thing to acknowledge the importance of ambiguity (cf. Keynes 1921, p. 71; Knight 1921) and another to develop a theory that incorporates it in the assessment of probabilities and the determination of choices. Before turning to that task, we need to define the concept of ambiguity more precisely.

Reconsider urn 1 (unknown proportion) in Ellsberg's problem, and note that all probability distributions over the proportions of red and black are equally likely. Now imagine that one samples four balls (without replacement) and gets three reds and one black. The proportion of red is now restricted to $.03 + x$ (where $0 \leq x \leq .96$) and the proportion of black to $.97 - x$. This result rules out certain probability distributions, thereby making others more likely. Indeed, as sample size increases, further distributions are ruled out until only one is left. We can now distinguish between ignorance, ambiguity, and risk, according to the degree to which one can rule out alternative distributions; that is, ambiguity is an intermediate state between ignorance (no distributions are ruled out) and risk (all distributions but one are ruled out). Thus, ambiguity results from the uncertainty associated with specifying which of a set of distributions is appropriate in a given situation. Moreover, the amount of ambiguity is an increasing function of the number of distributions that are not ruled out by one's knowledge of the situation.

As pointed out by Ellsberg (1961), various factors can affect ambiguity in addition to the amount of information (such as sample size). For example, ambiguity will generally be high when evidence is unreliable and conflicting or when the causal process generating outcomes is poorly understood. On the other hand, well-known random processes (such as flipping coins or dice) are uncertain but not ambiguous since the probabilities are well specified. The following example, given by Gärdenfors and Sahlin (1982, pp. 361–62), is useful in distinguishing between uncertainty, ignorance, and ambiguity.

> Consider Miss Julie who is invited to bet on the outcome of three different tennis matches. As regards match A, she is very well-informed about the two players. . . . Miss Julie predicts that it will be a very even match and a mere chance will determine the winner. In match B she knows nothing whatsoever about the relative strength of the contestants. . . . Match C is similar to match B except that Miss Julie has happened to hear that one of the contestants is an excellent tennis player although she does not know anything about which player it is, and that the second player is indeed an amateur so that everyone considers the outcome of the match a foregone conclusion.

We argue that match A is uncertain but not ambiguous (analogous to urn 2 in Ellsberg's paradox), that match B reflects ignorance (analogous to Ellsberg's urn 1 since all distributions over the probability of winning are equally likely), and that match C is ambiguous since the probability of each player winning is either zero or one.

Ellsberg's paradox demonstrates ambiguity avoidance since people prefer to draw from the unambiguous urn. Indeed, Ellsberg (1961, p. 666) stated that ambiguity avoidance helps to explain why new technologies are resisted more than one would expect on the basis of their first-order probabilities of accidents, failures, and so on. However, are there conditions under which ambiguity will be sought rather than avoided? Another Ellsberg example (quoted in Becker and Brownson 1964, pp. 63–64, n. 4) illustrates ambiguity preference. Consider two urns with 1,000 balls each. In urn 1, each ball is numbered from 1 to 1,000, and the probability of drawing any number is .001. In urn 2, there are an unknown number of balls bearing any single number. For example, the proportion of balls bearing the number 687 could vary from zero to one. If there is a prize for drawing number 687 from the urn, would you prefer to draw from urn 1 or urn 2? Urn 1 contains no ambiguity since the probability of winning is exactly .001; urn 2 involves ignorance since all probabilities of winning are equally likely. For many people, urn 2 seems a more attractive bet than urn 1. Hence there are situations in which ambiguity is preferred rather than avoided. We consider this in more detail in the next section but note that accounting for such shifts in "attitudes toward ambiguity" is an important criterion for judging the adequacy of any theory of ambiguity.

The Ambiguity Model

We now develop a model of how people assess uncertainty in ambiguous situations. To judge the adequacy of our model, we establish the following criteria. (1) The model must be able to explain the pattern of choices in Ellsberg's paradox. This means that the model should allow for sub- *and* superadditivity of complementary probabilities. (2) The model should specify the conditions under which people will avoid or seek ambiguity. (3) Individual differences should be captured by different parameter values within the same general model. (4) The model should be empirically testable and falsifiable.

Anchoring-and-Adjustment Strategy

The basic idea underlying the ambiguity model is that people use an anchoring-and-adjustment strategy in which an initial probability is used as the anchor (or starting point) and adjustments are made for ambiguity. The anchor probability can come from a variety of sources; it may be a probability that is salient in memory, the best guess of experts, or a probability that is otherwise available. Denote the anchor probability as p and the judged probability that results from the anchoring-and-adjustment process as $S(p)$. Thus

$$S(p) = p + k, \tag{1}$$

where k is defined as the net effect of the adjustment process. The adjustment process is assumed to involve a mental simulation in which higher and lower values of p are imagined. The rationale for this is that, since p can come from any one of a number of distributions, the imagining of different values allows one to evaluate which of these distributions is more or less plausible. For example, in assessing the probability of a defect in a new type of computer chip, one may have an estimate from the engineering department that is based on meager data. One could then "try out" other values of p to see if they are "in the ballpark." Once values of p are imagined and evaluated, they are incorporated into the adjustment term, thereby allowing one to maintain sensitivity to both uncertainty and ambiguity.

To model the net effect of the mental simulation process, k is assumed to be a function of three factors.

1. *Level of the anchor,* p. Since $0 \leq S(p) \leq 1$, k must lie in the interval $-p \leq k \leq 1 - p$. This means that the sign of the adjustment must be partly due to the size of the anchor. Indeed, if $p = 1$, k must be negative (or zero) and the adjustment will be downward; similarly, if $p = 0$, k will be positive (or zero) and the adjustment will be upward. When $0 < p < 1$, adjustments can be either upward or downward.

2. *Amount of ambiguity.* The greater the amount of ambiguity, the larger the size of the simulation (the bigger the ballpark). In the limiting case of no ambiguity, a mental simulation process is unnecessary since the value of p is exactly known. In the case of ignorance, ambiguity is at its maximum, and all values of p are equally plausible. We denote the parameter θ as the amount of ambiguity in the situation ($0 \leq \theta \leq 1$).

3. *Attitude toward ambiguity.* This refers to the relative weighting of (imagined) probabilities that are higher and lower than the anchor. We denote β as a parameter reflecting this relative weighting ($\beta \geq 0$). Note that one's attitude toward ambiguity is crucial in determining whether one adjusts upward or downward. For example, if one gives more weight to higher probabilities than lower ones, this generally results in upward adjustments to the anchor. On the other hand, if one gives more weight to lower probabilities, downward adjustments are more likely. The sign of k is thus determined by β and p.

To model the adjustment process, let

$$k = k_g - k_s, \tag{2}$$

where k_g denotes the effect of imagining values of p *greater* than the anchor and k_s the effect of imagining *smaller* values. Note that the maximum values of k_g and k_s are $1 - p$ and p, respectively (since

$-p \leqslant k \leqslant 1 - p$). However, the size of the simulation depends on the amount of ambiguity, θ. We assume that k_g and k_s can be represented as proportions of the maximum adjustments, where θ is the constant of proportionality; that is,

$$k_g = \theta(1 - p),$$
$$k_s = \theta p.$$ (3)

Note that, under no ambiguity, $\theta = 0$, $k = 0$, and $S(p) = p$ for all p. Thus adjustments to the anchor occur only under ambiguity.

Now consider one's attitude toward ambiguity, β. Since β represents the relative weighting of higher versus lower probabilities, we need only weight either k_g or k_s to affect k. For convenience, we weight k_s by β as follows:

$$k_s = \theta p^\beta.$$ (4)

By substituting (3) and (4) into (2), the net effect of the adjustment for ambiguity (k) is given by

$$k = \theta(1 - p - p^\beta).$$ (5)

When equation (5) is substituted into equation (1), the full model becomes

$$S(p) = p + \theta(1 - p - p^\beta).$$ (6)

Note that the full model can also be expressed as

$$S(p) = (1 - \theta)p + \theta(1 - p^\beta).$$ (7)

Equation (7) implies that the judged ambiguous probability is a weighted average of p and $1 - p^\beta$, where the weights reflect the amount of ambiguity, θ.

Implications of the Model

Although the ambiguity model is derived from a small number of psychological assumptions, it is nevertheless rich in implications. We now consider these in some detail.

1. The ambiguity model implies that $S(p)$ is regressive with respect to p. This can best be seen in figure 1, which shows $S(p)$ as a function of p for different values of β, holding θ constant ($\theta > 0$). In figure 1a, $0 < \beta < 1$, which implies that probabilities lower than the anchor are weighted more heavily than those above the anchor. This leads to downward adjustments (i.e., $k < 0$) over most of the range of p; hence $S(p) < p$. However, it is important to note that β defines a "crossover" point (denoted p_c) at which $S(p) = p$. When $p < p_c$, $S(p) > p$ even though lower probabilities in the mental simulation receive more weight than higher ones. Why does this occur? Recall that the sign of

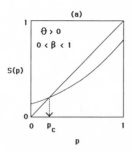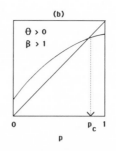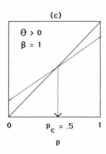

F<small>IG</small>. 1.—$S(p)$ as a function of p for values of θ and β. (© 1985 by the American Psychological Association. Reprinted by permission of the publisher from H. J. Einhorn and R. M. Hogarth, "Ambiguity and Uncertainty in Probabilistic Inference," *Psychological Review* 92, no. 4 [October 1985]: 433–61.)

the adjustment is determined by β *and* the level of p. For example, when p is small, there are fewer lower probabilities to imagine, and thus the net effect of the adjustment process is positive.

In figure 1*b*, $\beta > 1$, which implies that probabilities higher than the anchor are weighted more than lower ones. This results in upward adjustments over much of the range of p; hence $S(p) > p$ when $p < p_c$. On the other hand, when $p > p_c$, the greater weight for imagined higher probabilities does not compensate for their reduced number, and $S(p) < p$. Now consider figure 1*c*, in which $\beta = 1$. This implies that higher and lower probabilities are equally weighted in the simulation process; hence $S(p) = p$ at .5.

2. Equation (6) specifies the conditions under which judgments of complementary probabilities are additive (sum to one). Specifically,

$$S(p) + S(1 - p) = 1 + \theta[1 - p^\beta - (1 - p)^\beta]. \qquad (8)$$

There are three sufficient conditions for additivity: (*a*) no ambiguity ($\theta = 0$); (*b*) equal weighting of imagined probabilities ($\beta = 1$); and (*c*) the anchor probability expresses either certainty or impossibility ($p = 0, 1$). Otherwise, $\beta < 1$ implies subadditivity (shown in fig. 1*a*), and $\beta > 1$ implies superadditivity (shown in fig. 1*b*).

3. We now discuss how the ambiguity model explains the various patterns of responses to Ellsberg's paradox. First, consider someone with parameter values as shown in figure 1*a*; that is, $\theta > 0$ and $0 < \beta < 1$. In decisions under ambiguity, such a person will effectively underweight $p > p_c$ and overweight $p < p_c$, thereby generating the typical pattern of responses in Ellsberg's original problem. According to our model, most people choose the nonambiguous urn when $p = .5$ because $S(p = .5) < .5$. Such a choice seems to reflect "ambiguity avoidance." However, the same person who chooses the unambiguous urn when $p = .5$ often chooses the ambiguous urn when $p = .001$. From our perspective, if $p = .001$ is less than the crossover point (p_c),

$S(p = .001) > .001$ and "ambiguity seeking" at low probabilities is perfectly consistent with ambiguity avoidance at moderate to high probabilities (for positive payoffs). This also explains some otherwise puzzling results in which lotteries with low but unreliable probabilities are chosen over those with equally low and reliable probabilities (Gärdenfors and Sahlin 1982).

The ambiguity function shown in figure 1a does not explain why some people in the Ellsberg task prefer to choose the ambiguous urn when $p = .5$ (see the next section for empirical evidence). However, consider a person with parameter values as shown in figure 1b; that is, $\theta > 0$ and $\beta > 1$. In this case, $S(p = .5) > .5$, which is consistent with ambiguity seeking in Ellsberg's original problem. Because individual differences are rarely considered in decision making under uncertainty, our model has the distinct advantage of positing a general process yet allows for individual variations via different parameter values. This is illustrated by considering people who are indifferent between ambiguous and nonambiguous urns at $p = .5$. Our model distinguishes between two types; those for whom $\theta = 0$ and those with parameters values as shown in figure 1c (i.e., $\theta > 0$, $\beta = 1$). This latter group does not adjust at $p = .5$ but does adjust at all other values of p. Hence these people will be indifferent between lotteries only at $p = .5$.

4. The ambiguity model presented here is static; it gives an account of judgment under ambiguity at a given point in time. However, what happens as more information is obtained? In the simple case in which new information reduces ambiguity without changing the anchor probability (i.e., new data increases the absolute amount of information without changing the relative balance of positive and negative evidence), our model can be extended as follows. Let v denote the amount of new information acquired in time period t. Furthermore, let the judged ambiguous probability after time period t, $S(p)_t$, be written as

$$S(p)_t = p + \frac{\theta}{v}(1 - p - p^\beta). \tag{9}$$

Therefore, as v increases, the effect of ambiguity on the adjustment process decreases. Indeed, as v gets very large, $S(p)_t$ approaches p. This also means that complementary probabilities will approach additivity as v increases since

$$S(p)_t + S(1 - p)_t = 1 + \frac{\theta}{v}[1 - p^\beta - (1 - p)^\beta]. \tag{10}$$

5. The version of the ambiguity model shown in figure 1a bears a striking resemblance to the decision weight function of prospect theory (Kahneman and Tversky 1979). In that theory, the effects of uncertainty on choice are modeled via a decision weight function, $\pi(p)$, that is subadditive, has undefined end points, and displays "subproportion-

ality.'' This latter characteristic implies that the slope of the decision weight function is less than one and decreases as p gets smaller. These characteristics, together with a value function defined on gains and losses, account for many choice paradoxes. Since prospect theory concerns gambles with well-defined probabilities, its domain is different from ours. Nevertheless, we believe that the similarity in representing how uncertainty affects choice is not coincidental (see Discussion section below).

6. We have implicitly assumed that the parameters θ and β are such that $S(p)$ is monotone increasing with p. However, the function shown in equation (6) is sufficiently flexible so that nonmonotone as well as decreasing monotone functions are possible. In fact, we have found some evidence for nonmonotonicity in studies fitting the θ and β parameters to probability judgments under ambiguity (Einhorn and Hogarth 1985). Moreover, a situation in which $S(p)$ is likely to be a decreasing function of p arises when the surface meaning of data suggests the opposite conclusion; for example, imagine someone who ''protesteth too much'' or a suspect who is ''framed'' for a crime. If we denote θ^* as reflecting the credibility of the data (where higher values of θ^* mean lower credibility), then lack of credibility ($\theta^* = 1$) implies that

$$S(p) = 1 - p^\beta. \tag{11}$$

Thus, as p increases, $S(p)$ decreases. More generally, as θ^* increases, it reaches a point, conditional on p and β, at which the data for a hypothesis start to count against it.

Empirical Evidence

The ambiguity model can be tested in a variety of ways. Three studies are presented that investigate (*a*) variations of the Ellsberg paradox and (*b*) implications of the model for buyers and sellers of insurance and a warranty (Einhorn and Hogarth 1985; Hogarth and Kunreuther 1985*a*, 1985*b*).

Ellsberg Revisited

The ambiguity model predicts both ambiguity seeking and avoidance, depending on p, the size of the anchor probability, and β, one's attitude toward ambiguity. To examine this, first consider choices involving positive payoffs. Recall that, in the original version of the paradox, people are offered a $100 payoff if they choose a specified colored ball drawn from one of the urns. The basic result is that most people prefer to draw from the unambiguous urn, indicating ambiguity avoidance. However, if the probability of winning is small, Ellsberg conjectured that people would prefer to draw from the ambiguous urn, thereby displaying ambiguity seeking. To our knowledge, this latter hypothesis has not been put to an empirical test. Since the ambiguity model can predict both ambiguity avoidance for $p = .5$ and ambiguity seeking for low probabilities (see fig. 1*a*), a simple choice experiment that varies the probability of winning should provide evidence on Ellsberg's conjecture as well as the adequacy of the model.

In addition to varying the probabilities in Ellsberg's paradox, we investigated whether attitudes toward ambiguity change when negative, rather than positive, payoffs are involved. This is important since loss gambles with ambiguous probabilities are quite common, especially in insurance (see the next section for empirical evidence). Moreover, the simulation process underlying our model can be taken to imply that the assessment of ambiguous probabilities will result in a differently shaped function for losses as opposed to wins. To see this, assume that people are generally cautious in assessing uncertain probabilities. When assessing loss probabilities, they should therefore give more weight to higher values of the (simulated) loss probabilities than to lower values. This will result in an overestimation of loss probabilities, especially in the low to moderate range. Note that both the overestimation of ambiguous loss probabilities *and* the underestimation of ambiguous win probabilities are consistent with a general conservative attitude toward ambiguity. We now turn to a test of these ideas.

Experimental design and results.   There were two tasks in which subjects were asked to choose (or express indifference) between drawing a specified type of ball from either an ambiguous or a nonambiguous urn. In the first task, subjects were asked to imagine two urns each containing 100 balls. They were further told that half the balls in one urn were red and half black (the unambiguous case), but they were not informed as to the proportions of red and black balls in the second urn (the ambiguous case). The payoff was contingent on drawing a ball of a specified color (red or black). In the second task, subjects were asked to imagine two urns each containing 1,000 balls. In the nonambiguous urn, the balls were numbered consecutively from 1 to 1,000, and subjects were told that the payoff was contingent on drawing ball number 687 ($p = .001$). In the ambiguous case, subjects were told that any proportion of the 1,000 balls could be number 687.

Thus the first task involved choosing (or expressing indifference) between an ambiguous or a nonambiguous urn where the probability of the payoff was known to be .5 for the latter urn. The second task was similar in structure except that the probability of the payoff in the nonambiguous case was .001. The study investigated the effects of positive and negative payoffs by asking subjects to imagine prizes or penalties of $100. All subjects responded to both tasks but were randomly allocated to two groups. In one group, subjects were given the first task ($p = .5$) with a positive payoff and the second ($p = .001$) with a negative payoff. In the second group, this manipulation was reversed (i.e., negative payoff at .5 and positive payoff at .001).

The subjects were 274 M.B.A. students at the University of Chicago who responded to questionnaires distributed at the beginning of a course on decision making. The main results are shown in table 1. First, consider the results for positive payoffs when the choice is between an urn with known $p = .5$ and an ambiguous urn. The modal response (47%) favors the nonambiguous urn, thereby supporting Ellsberg's hypothesis of ambiguity avoidance. However, a considerable proportion exhibits indifference (34%) (perhaps reflecting business school training), and a surprising 19% of subjects are ambiguity seeking. Now consider the choice pattern when the known probability is small ($p = .001$). Although the modal response still favors the nonambiguous urn (43%), the choice of the ambiguous urn increases from 19% to 35%. Next, consider the results for negative payoffs when $p = .5$. The modal response is now indifference (56%), and ambiguity seeking is sharply reduced to 14%. Furthermore, when $p = .001$, ambiguity seeking is further reduced (to 5%), and the modal response shifts to strong ambiguity avoidance (75%). Hence there are large differences in responses to ambiguity between gambles with positive and negative payoffs.

In terms of the ambiguity model, the overall pattern of results can be summarized by referring back to figure 1a and c. Note that figure 1a shows an ambiguity function that is consistent with the experimental results for positive payoffs. Thus there is ambiguity avoidance for $p = .5$ but ambiguity preference for $p = .001$. The shape of the ambiguity function for negative payoffs is consistent with figure 1c. In this case, loss probabilities are overestimated until $p = .5$—at which point $S(p) = p$—but underestimated when $p > .5$. This latter prediction was not explicitly tested in this study but is investigated below.

TABLE 1   **Ellsberg's Paradox with Gains and Losses at Two Probability Levels**

Conditions	Ambiguous Urn (%)	Nonambiguous Urn (%)	Indifference (%)	Total (%)
Win $100:				
$p = .5$	19	47	34	100
	(25)	(63)	(45)	(133)
$p = .001$	35	43	22	100
	(48)	(60)	(30)	(138)
Lose $100:				
$p = .5$	14	30	56	100
	(18)	(40)	(75)	(133)
$p = .001$	5	75	20	100
	(7)	(106)	(20)	(141)

NOTE.—Numbers of responses are shown in parentheses.

Insurance

The buying and selling of insurance provides an important context to test the ambiguity model for two reasons. (1) Buyers and sellers often have different amounts of information concerning the probability of the event to be insured. Thus they may not experience the same amount of ambiguity in assessing the occurrence of a potential loss. (2) Buyers of insurance are trying to transfer their risk and are willing to pay a premium (thus suffering a sure loss) to do so. On the other hand, sellers of insurance are taking on a risk in the belief that the probability of losing the bet with the buyer is in their favor. In terms of the simulation process underlying our model, we hypothesize that sellers will give *more* weight than will buyers to the higher simulated loss probabilities. The rationale for this is based on the greater cost to the seller of underestimating loss probabilities. Note that the buyer may also overestimate the probability of loss by weighting higher loss probabilities more than lower ones, but our hypothesis concerns the comparison between buyers and sellers. In fact, there is some empirical evidence consistent with the notion that the person who assumes a risk gives more attention to higher values of the loss probability than someone who transfers the risk (Thaler 1980; Hershey, Kunreuther, and Schoemaker 1982). In terms of our model, the above hypothesis implies that $\beta_{seller} > \beta_{buyer}$.

In order to explicate how these differences can be captured by our model, consider figure 2, which shows a simplified 2×2 classification of buyers and sellers in either an ambiguous or a nonambiguous state. In cell 1, buyers and sellers are well acquainted with the probabilities of the potential loss and are thus in a nonambiguous state. In this case, $\theta = 0$ and $S(p) = p$ for both buyers and sellers. If it is assumed that selling and buying prices for insurance are the same monotonic function of $S(p)$, then we predict that buyers and sellers should have the same buying and selling prices for insurance over the full range of loss probabilities. Thus we expect that the sellers' premiums will be equal to the prices buyers are willing to pay. Now consider the more typical case shown in cell 2, in which the seller is not ambiguous (due to actuarial data, e.g.) but the buyer is. In this situation, $\theta = 0$ and $S(p) = p$ for the seller; however, the ambiguous buyer will overestimate most of the loss probabilities, $S(p) > p$, until the ambiguity function crosses the diagonal, after which $S(p) < p$. We therefore predict that the buyer will be willing to pay more for insurance than the seller asks at small and even moderate values of p. However, above some value of p, the buyer will not be willing to pay the premium asked by the seller.

The situation shown in cell 3 is less likely, although one example may be the case of new technologies in which inside information is

BUYERS

	Nonambiguous	Ambiguous
Nonambig.	Well known processes (1)	Typical situation (2)
Ambiguous	New technologies-inside information for buyers (3)	New technologies-processes poorly understood (4)

SELLERS appears to the left, spanning the two seller rows.

FIG. 2.—Classification of insurance situations

available to buyers (e.g., owners of the new companies) but not to the sellers. In any event, we predict that sellers will overestimate the loss probabilities over most of the range of p—that is, $S(p) > p$—while $S(p) > p$ for the buyers. This implies that, for most probabilities, sellers will set premiums that are higher than buying prices. Finally, consider cell 4, which shows the situation in which buyers and sellers are both ambiguous, and assume that $\theta_{seller} = \theta_{buyer}$. According to our argument, if $\beta_{seller} > \beta_{buyer}$, then $S(p)_{seller} > S(p)_{buyer}$ over the full range of p. Hence we predict that the sellers' premiums will be higher than buying prices for all loss probabilities.

The four predictions that follow from the ambiguity model are summarized in figure 3, which shows the implied ambiguity functions for buyers and sellers under both ambiguous and nonambiguous conditions. Prediction 1 states that buyers and sellers will have equal prices when they are both nonambiguous; that is, $S(p) = p$ for both buyers and sellers. Prediction 2 concerns nonambiguous sellers and ambiguous buyers. Note that the buyers should be willing to pay more for insurance than the sellers ask, up to the point at which $S(p) = p$; after this point, buyers should be unwilling to pay what sellers ask. Prediction 3 concerns ambiguous sellers and nonambiguous buyers. In this case, sellers' premiums should be larger than buying prices over most of the range of p. Finally, prediction 4 concerns the case in which buyers and sellers are both ambiguous. This situation results in premiums that are higher than buying prices over the whole range of loss probabilities.

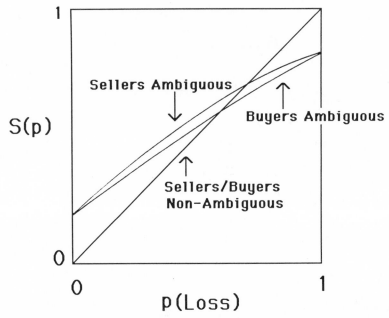

Fig. 3.—Approximate ambiguity functions for buyers and sellers of insurance. (© 1985 by the American Psychological Association. Reprinted by permission of the publisher from H. J. Einhorn and R. M. Hogarth, "Ambiguity and Uncertainty in Probabilistic Inference," *Psychological Review* 92, no. 4 [October 1985]: 433–61.)

Experimental design and results.   Prices for insurance were investigated for ambiguous and nonambiguous loss probabilities of .01, .35, .65, and .90. Subjects were given a scenario in which the owner of a small business with assets of $110,000 was seeking to insure against a possible $100,000 loss. The probability of the loss (due to a defective product) was given at one of the four levels in both the ambiguous and the nonambiguous conditions. However, a comment was added as to whether one could "feel confident" (nonambiguous case) or "experience considerable uncertainty" (ambiguous case) concerning the estimate. In addition, half the subjects were told that they were sellers of insurance, and the other half were assigned the role of buyers. The sellers were asked to imagine they headed a department in an insurance company and were authorized to set premiums. The buyers were told to imagine that they were the owner of the company. As far as possible, the same wording was used in both the buyer and the seller versions of the scenario. After reading the scenario, subjects were asked to state maximum buying prices (for buyers) or minimum selling prices (for sellers).

The experimental design involved having different subjects as buyers or sellers at each of the four probability levels. Thus there were eight different groups of subjects (2 × 4). Each subject was given both the ambiguous and the nonambiguous version of the scenario. Therefore, the design involved a within-subjects factor (ambiguity/ nonambiguity) and two between-subjects factors (probability levels and buyer versus seller). The subjects were 112 M.B.A. students at the University of Chicago. These subjects had prior training in business, economics, and statistics, and the insurance context was familiar to them. The basic results are shown in table 2, which shows the median prices for all experimental conditions (medians are reported since several distributions within conditions are quite skewed).

Our first prediction concerns columns 1 and 3, buyers and sellers nonambiguous. We predicted that the prices would be equal for buyers and sellers, and the results support the prediction. The second prediction concerns columns 2 and 3, buyers ambiguous and sellers nonambiguous. Note that the buyers are willing to pay more for insurance than the sellers ask at $p = .01$ ($1,500 vs. $1,000), but the prices are (approximately) equal at $p = .35$; thereafter, the buying price is less than the sellers' asking price. This pattern is exactly predicted by our model. The third prediction concerns columns 1 and 4, nonambiguous buyer and ambiguous seller. Here the seller's price is higher than the buyer's over the range of p, in accord with our prediction. However, our model also implies that, at very high p, the seller's price should be lower than the buyers, and this is not observed in these data. On the other hand, the ratio of premiums to buying prices decreases as p increases, which does accord with our model. Finally, consider our fourth prediction, which involves columns 2 and 4, buyer and seller both ambiguous. As predicted, the seller's price is higher than the buyer's for all values of p. In Hogarth and Kunreuther (1985a, 1985b), the results of several related experiments are reported using different scenarios, research designs, subjects, and response modes. The results of those experiments are consistent with the findings reported here.

Warranty Pricing

A warranty is a particular type of insurance contract in which the seller agrees to fix, replace, or otherwise make good the product sold to the buyer. The buyer, in turn, agrees to pay a premium for the warranty (we assume that products sold with warranties have the premium incorporated into the price of the product). The purpose of the present study was to test the ambiguity model in the context of buying and selling a warranty. In addition, the subjects in the experiment were executives in life insurance companies rather than business students. This gave us a chance to see whether our previous results would replicate in a different context and with a more sophisticated and knowledgeable subject population.

TABLE 2   Median Buying and Selling Prices for Insurance

	Buyers		Sellers	
Probability	Nonambiguous (1)	Ambiguous (2)	Nonambiguous (3)	Ambiguous (4)
.01	1,000	1,500	1,000	2,500
.35	35,000	35,000	37,500	52,500
.65	65,000	45,000	65,000	70,000
.90	82,500	60,000	90,000	90,000

Experimental design and results.   The subjects were 136 executives in life insurance companies attending a management seminar. They completed a questionnaire given to them the evening before the seminar began. The question of interest for this study involved a scenario describing a new personal computer that was about to be distributed by the owner of a computer store. The probability of a defect in the computer requiring repair was given as .05, .25, .75. In the ambiguous probability condition, it was stated that there was little experience with the actual use of the computer and that there was considerable disagreement among experts concerning the probability of a defect. In the nonambiguous condition, it was stated that there was considerable testing of the computer and one could be confident in the estimated defect probabilities on which all experts agreed. Half the subjects were assigned to the ambiguous condition and the other half to the nonambiguous condition. In addition, for each of these groups, subjects were further divided into buyers (i.e., consumers) or sellers (computer store owners). The sellers were asked to set a minimum price for the warranty on the computer; the buyers were asked to state the maximum price they would pay for a warranty. The cost of fixing the defect was stated to be $400. To summarize, the design of the study involved four separate groups, depending on whether subjects were buyers or sellers and whether the probabilities were ambiguous. Furthermore, each subject was asked to state either a buying or a selling price for each of the three probability levels. Thus probability levels were varied as a within-subjects factor. The median prices for all experimental conditions are shown in table 3.

We discuss these results in terms of the four predictions made in the insurance study. First, when buyers and sellers are nonambiguous (cols. 1 and 3), premiums and buying prices should be equal. This holds for $p = .05$ and approximately so for $p = .25$ but not for $p = .75$. Second, when buyers are ambiguous and sellers are unambiguous (cols. 2 and 3), our model predicts that buyers are willing to pay more

TABLE 3   Median Buying and Selling Prices for Warranty

	Buyers		Sellers	
Probability	Nonambiguous (1)	Ambiguous (2)	Nonambiguous (3)	Ambiguous (4)
.05	20	25	20	40
.25	90	50	100	120
.75	200	100	300	300

than sellers ask at low probabilities but less than sellers ask for moderate to high probabilities. This pattern is supported by the data. Third, when buyers are nonambiguous and sellers are ambiguous (cols. 1 and 4), the model predicts that premiums will be higher than buying prices over most of the range of p. Note that this is indeed the case. However, as was the case in the insurance study, we do not find that the buyer's price is above the seller's at very high probabilities. Fourth, when buyers and sellers are both ambiguous (cols. 2 and 4), we predict that the seller's price will be higher than the buying price over the whole range of p. As can be seen, this is the case. Taken together, these findings essentially replicate the results from the insurance study.

Although we have presented three experiments testing the implications of the ambiguity model, the interested reader is referred to further experiments in Einhorn and Hogarth (1985). These concern the fitting of θ and β parameters to individual subjects' probability judgments, the prediction of sub- and superadditivity of complementary probabilities, and the prediction of choices on the basis of the fit of the model to probability judgments. In general, the results of these studies are consistent with the implications from the model.

Discussion

We first consider our theoretical and empirical results with regard to choice under ambiguity. Thereafter we discuss possible extensions of the model to the case in which probabilities are not ambiguous.

Our model for assessing ambiguous probabilities can be extended in a straightforward way to include an explicit decision rule for choice under ambiguity. We first assume, in accord with prospect theory (Kahneman and Tversky 1979), that the subjective worths of outcomes are defined over gains and losses rather than final asset positions. Denote w_G and w_L as the subjective worths of the amounts to be gained and lost in a two-outcome gamble, respectively. We then define the concept of expected worth under ambiguity (EWA) as

$$\text{EWA} = w_G S(p_G) + w_L S(p_L). \tag{12}$$

where $S(p_G)$ and $S(p_L)$ are the ambiguous probabilities of gaining and losing. Moreover, we assume that people choose among ambiguous gambles in accord with expected worth under ambiguity; that is, one chooses to maximize EWA. We make several points with respect to the rule embodied in (12). (a) Under no ambiguity, $S(p_G) = p_G$, $S(p_L) = p_L$, and expected worth under ambiguity is equivalent to the expected utility model (except that subjective worths are defined over gains and losses). (b) Although our model implies that $S(p)$ can be both nonmonotonic and negatively related to p (depending on the values of θ and β), we restrict these parameters in choice under ambiguity (and uncertainty—see below) so that $S(p)$ is always an increasing function of p. To do otherwise would permit violations of dominance. However, we do permit violations of dominance to occur in judgments. Indeed, some evidence for this has been found by Goldstein and Einhorn (in press), using attractiveness ratings of gambles. Since judgment and choice may not be psychologically equivalent (Einhorn and Hogarth 1981; Slovic, Fischhoff, and Lichtenstein 1982), the distinction between the ambiguity model for judgment and the model of expected worth under ambiguity for choice is not unreasonable. (c) We are aware of only two other rules for dealing with ambiguous choice; one propounded by Ellsberg (1961, pp. 664–69) and the other by Gärdenfors and Sahlin (1982). However, neither of these rules allows for ambiguity seeking *and* avoidance. Moreover, these rules do not imply different ambiguity functions for gains and losses. On the other hand, equation (12) does account for ambiguity seeking and avoidance for both gains and losses. Recall that, in experiment 1, the results for the $100 payoff showed ambiguity avoidance at $p_G = .5$ but considerable ambiguity preference at $p_G = .001$. If the ambiguity function for gains is as shown in figure 1a, it follows from (12) that

$$w(\$100)S(p_G = .5) < w(\$100)(.5),$$

$$w(\$100)S(p_G = .001) > w(\$100)(.001).$$

Hence there is ambiguity avoidance at moderate- to high-gain probabilities and ambiguity preference at low-gain probabilities. It is possible, with appropriate values of θ and β, to account for other patterns of choice. In particular, since many people in experiment 1 chose to avoid the ambiguous urn at $p_G = .001$, β could be made smaller so that it crosses the diagonal at a p_G value less than .001. We believe that $S(p_G)$ will eventually cross the diagonal at some point; otherwise a person would prefer a sure probability of no gain (i.e., $p_G = 0$) to an ambiguous probability of no gain, $S(p_G = 0)$. Because the latter offers some nonzero chance of a gain as opposed to no chance, we would expect ambiguity seeking to occur below some value of p_G.

Now consider the choices under ambiguity for the loss payoff in experiment 1. Recall that, in this case, when $p_L = .5$, indifference between the urns was the largest response; when $p_L = .001$, ambiguity avoidance was the overwhelming response. This pattern implies that

$$w(-\$100)S(p_L = .5) = w(-\$100)(.5),$$

$$w(-\$100)S(p_L = .001) < w(-\$100)(.001).$$

This pattern is consistent with an ambiguity function for losses such as that shown in figure 1c. Note that this function also implies ambiguity seeking for losses when $p_L > .5$; that is, $S(p_L) < p_L$ for $p_L > .5$. Reasoning in a manner analogous to the case for gains, we believe that ambiguity seeking will occur for some (high) loss probabilities; otherwise a sure loss ($p_L = 1$) would be preferred to an ambiguous loss, $S(p_L = 1)$. It is an empirical question as to what the crossover point will be in any particular situation.

An interesting aspect of our model is that it implies a lack of independence between ambiguous probabilities and the sign of utilities; that is, different ambiguity functions depend on whether one is dealing with gains or with losses. Furthermore, since we have assumed that $\beta_{gain} < \beta_{loss}$, choices under ambiguity that deal with pure gain gambles are likely to imply subadditivity of complementary probabilities ($\beta_G < 1$), while those dealing with pure loss gambles should lead to less subadditivity, including additivity ($\beta_L = 1$) and even superadditivity ($\beta_L > 1$). While more data are needed to test this hypothesis, it suggests the need for a "dual probability function" in choices under ambiguity (cf. Marks 1951; Irwin 1953; Luce and Narens 1985; Nygren and Isen 1985). In fact, Edwards (1962) commented on the nonindependence of the sign of utilities and probabilities some 25 years ago: "All of these findings strongly indicate that there is at least an interaction between the *sign* of the utility of a bet and the subjective probability associated with the event. . . . Furthermore, the direction of the effects is in general the direction predicted by the Irwin subjective probability theory. None of the evidence, however, indicates an interaction between value and subjective probability provided that the signs of the utilities involved do not change" (pp. 45–46).

Our results regarding buying and selling prices for insurance and a warranty (experiments 2 and 3) raise the important question as to how one's "perspective" influences the assessment of ambiguous uncertainties. For example, consider the difference between those who live near the site of a planned nuclear power plant and the nuclear engineers who are designing it. The former may experience a great deal of ambiguity about the probability of an accident and greatly overestimate this relative to the engineers' "best guess." The importance of perspective can also be seen in situations in which the participants to a dispute code the outcomes in terms of gains versus losses. For example, consider a defendant and a plaintiff in a lawsuit in which the lawyers for both sides estimate the probability of winning as .5 but neither side is confident in the estimate. From the plaintiff's point of view, one needs to assess the ambiguous probability of a gain, $S(p_G)$; from the defendant's point of view, one needs to assess the ambiguous probability of a loss, $S(p_L)$. If these two functions are not the same (as we have argued), the relative sizes of β_L and β_G will determine whether both sides are overconfident or underconfident (and thus settle out of court) or whether one side wishes to settle but the other refuses. According to our analysis, we expect that, in general, $\beta_G < \beta_L$, reflecting cautious attitudes and thus underconfidence by both parties. This implies that most lawsuits will be settled out of court, as indeed occurs in 95% of cases (see Gould [1973], in which an expected utility analysis assuming known probabilities is also consistent with this evidence). While the decision to go to trial or settle out of court is more complicated than indicated by our present discussion, our purpose is to emphasize that one's perspective can affect the assessment of ambiguous probabilities and the decisions on which they are based.

Extension to Known Probabilities

The simulation process underlying the assessment of ambiguous probabilities provides a plausible psychological mechanism to account for probability "weights" that differ from stated probabilities in descriptive theories of risk. To see how such weights can result from a simulation process when probabilities are explicitly given, an auxiliary process must be hypothesized that accounts for imagining and differentially weighting higher and lower values of the stated probabilities. Imagine that the size of a payoff, like the size of the planet, exerts a gravitational force on those objects or factors (such as uncertainties) that are associated with it. The effect of this "force" could be modeled via the simulation process (including optimistic or pessimistic attitudes captured by different values of β) such that decision weights would differ from stated probabilities. If this were the case, utilities and probabilities would be not only sign dependent (as discussed before) but size dependent as well. In fact, evidence for size dependence has been found by Wothke (1985) and Hogarth and Einhorn (in preparation). For example, choices in many well-known utility-theory paradoxes (e.g., Allais 1953) are not paradoxical vis-à-vis utility theory when payoffs are small as opposed to large.

If one equates choices that are consistent with utility theory as reflecting "rationality" (cf. Einhorn and Hogarth 1981), there is considerable irony in the fact that in these cases large incentives produce less rational choices than small incentives. On the other hand, such results are consistent with evidence showing that the relation between

TABLE 4   Effect of Insurance versus Gambling Context for a
           Possible $10,000 Loss

Probability	Sure Loss	% Preferring Sure Loss— Insurance	% Preferring Sure Loss— Gambling
.001	10	81	54
.01	100	66	46
.10	1,000	59	29
.50	5,000	39	32
.90	9,000	34	24
.99	9,900	27	22
.999	9,990	17	17

performance and motivation (which we equate with incentive size) is single peaked (e.g., Yerkes and Dodson 1908). Hence there is often an optimal amount of motivation beyond which performance declines. Performance, however, depends on both cognition and motivation. Thus, if incentive size can be thought of as analogous to the speed with which one travels in a given direction, cognition determines the direction. Therefore, if incentives are high but cognition is faulty, one gets to the wrong place faster. Clearly, much remains to be done in explicating the relations between incentive size, the assessment of uncertainty, and the effects of both on choice.

In addition to the effects of size and sign of payoff on probabilities, the simulation process suggests that changes in the β parameter can be used to model context effects in the choice process. For example, consider the work of Hershey and Schoemaker (1980) on choices between a sure loss and a gamble, as compared to deciding whether to buy insurance (which also involves a sure loss vs. a gamble). Table 4 shows the different responses when structurally equivalent gambles are framed in terms of both an insurance and a gambling context. The results show a higher percentage of risk-averse choices for the former. Why? We argue that, relative to gambling, the insurance context induces a greater attitude toward caution (i.e., more weight is given to imagining values of the probability greater than the anchor), and this is reflected in different β parameters in the two contexts; specifically, $\beta_{\text{insurance}} > \beta_{\text{gambling}}$. This implies that $S(p_L)_{\text{insurance}} > S(p_L)_{\text{gambling}}$, such that greater risk aversion is observed in the insurance as compared to the gambling context.

Conclusion

The study of risk has been dominated by a single metaphor—the explicit lottery with stated probabilities and payoffs. However, as noted by Lopes (1983), "The simple, static lottery or gamble is as indispensible to research on risk as is the fruitfly to genetics. The reason is obvious; lotteries, like fruitflies, provide a simplified laboratory model of the real world, one that displays its essential characteristics while allowing for the manipulation and control of important experimental variables" (p. 137). We believe that it is time to move beyond the tidy experiments and axiomatizations built on the explicit lottery. The real world of risk involves ambiguous probabilities, dependencies between probabilities and utilities, context and framing effects (Tversky and Kahneman 1981; Thaler 1985), regret (Bell 1982), "illusions of control" (Langer 1975), and superstitions (Skinner 1966). Given the richness of the phenomena before us, our biggest risk would be to ignore them.

References

Allais, M. 1953. Le comportement de l'homme rationnel devant le risque: Critique des postulats et axiomes de l'Ecole Américaine. *Econometrica* 21:503–46.

Becker, S. W., and Brownson, F. O. 1964. What price ambiguity? Or the role of ambiguity in decision making. *Journal of Political Economy* 72:62–73.

Bell, D. 1982. Regret in decision making under uncertainty. *Operations Research* 30:961–81.

Chew, S. H., and MacCrimmon, K. R. 1979. *Apha-Nu Choice Theory: A Generalization of Expected Utility Theory.* Working Paper no. 669. Vancouver: University of British Columbia, Faculty of Commerce and Business Administration.

Cohen, L. J. 1977. *The Probable and the Provable.* Oxford: Clarendon.

Curley, S. P., and Yates, J. F. 1985. The center and range of the probability interval as factors affecting ambiguity preferences. *Organizational Behavior and Human Decision Processes* 36:273–87.

de Finetti, B. 1977. Probabilities of probabilities: A real problem or a misunderstanding? In A. Aykaç and C. Brumat (eds.), *New Directions in the Application of Bayesian Methods.* Amsterdam: North-Holland.

Edwards, W. 1954. The theory of decision making. *Psychological Bulletin* 51:380–417.

Edwards, W. 1961. Behavioral decision theory. *Annual Review of Psychology* 12:473–98.

Edwards, W. 1962. Utility, subjective probability, their interaction, and variance preferences. *Journal of Conflict Resolution* 6:42–51.

Einhorn, H. J., and Hogarth, R. M. 1981. Behavioral decision theory: Processes of judgment and choice. *Annual Review of Psychology* 32:53–88.

Einhorn, H. J., and Hogarth, R. M. 1985. Ambiguity and uncertainty in probabilistic inference. *Psychological Review* 92:433–61.

Ellsberg, D. 1961. Risk, ambiguity, and the Savage axioms. *Quarterly Journal of Economics* 75:643–69.

Ellsberg, D. 1963. Reply. *Quarterly Journal of Economics* 77:336–42.

Gärdenfors, P., and Sahlin, N. E. 1982. Unreliable probabilities, risk taking, and decision making. *Synthese* 53:361–86.

Goldstein, W. M., and Einhorn, H. J. In press. Expression theory and the preference reversal phenomena. *Psychological Review.*

Gould, J. P. 1973. The economics of legal conflicts. *Journal of Legal Studies* 11:279–300.

Hershey, J. C.; Kunreuther, H. C.; and Schoemaker, P. J. H. 1982. Sources of bias in assessment procedures for utility functions. *Management Science* 28:936–54.

Hershey, J. C., and Schoemaker, P. J. H. 1980. Risk taking and problem context in the domain of losses: An expected utility analysis. *Journal of Risk and Insurance* 47:111–32.

Hogarth, R. M., and Einhorn, H. J. In preparation. Venture theory: A model of risky decision making. Chicago: University of Chicago, Graduate School of Business, Center for Decision Research.

Hogarth, R. M., and Kunreuther, H. C. 1985*a*. Ambiguity and insurance decisions. *American Economic Association Papers and Proceedings* 75:386–90.

Hogarth, R. M., and Kunreuther, H. C. 1985*b*. Risk, ambiguity, and insurance. Unpublished manuscript. Chicago: University of Chicago, Graduate School of Business, Center for Decision Research.

Irwin, F. W. 1953. Stated expectations as functions of probability and desirability of outcomes. *Journal of Personality* 21:329–35.

Kahneman, D., and Tversky, A. 1979. Prospect theory: An analysis of decision under risk. *Econometrica* 47:263–91.

Keeney, R. L., and Raiffa, H. A. 1976. *Decisions with Multiple Objectives: Preferences and Value Tradeoffs.* New York: Wiley.

Keynes, J. M. 1921. *A Treatise on Probability.* London: Macmillan.

Knight, F. H. 1921. *Risk, Uncertainty, and Profit.* Boston: Houghton Mifflin.

Kunreuther, H. C. 1976. Limited knowledge and insurance protection. *Public Policy* 24:227–61.

Langer, E. J. 1975. The illusion of control. *Journal of Personality and Social Psychology* 32:311–28.

Lopes, L. L. 1983. Some thoughts on the psychological concept of risk. *Journal of Experimental Psychology: Human Perception and Performance* 9:137–44.

Luce, R. D., and Narens, L. 1985. Classification of concatenation measurement structures according to scale type. *Journal of Mathematical Psychology* 29:1–72.

Machina, M. J. 1982. "Expected utility" analysis without the independence axiom. *Econometrica* 50:277–323.

Marks, R. W. 1951. The effect of probability, desirability, and "privilege" on the stated expectations of children. *Journal of Personality* 19:332–51.

Marschak, J. 1975. Personal probabilities of probabilities. *Theory and Decision* 6:121–53.

Nygren, T. E., and Isen, A. M. 1985. Examining probability estimation: Evidence for dual subjective probability functions. Paper presented at the meeting of the Psychonomics Society, Boston.

Platt, J. R. 1964. Strong inference. *Science* 146:347–53.

Quiggin, J. 1982. A theory of anticipated utility. *Journal of Economic Behavior and Organization* 3:323–43.

Raiffa, H. A. 1961. Risk, ambiguity, and the Savage axioms: Comment. *Quarterly Journal of Economics* 75:690–94.

Raiffa, H. A. 1968. *Decision Analysis.* Reading, Mass.: Addison-Wesley.

Roberts, H. V. 1963. Risk, ambiguity, and the Savage axioms: Comment. *Quarterly Journal of Economics* 77:327–36.

Savage, L. J. 1954. *The Foundations of Statistics.* New York: Wiley.

Schoemaker, P. J. H. 1982. The expected utility model: Its variants, purposes, evidence and limitations. *Journal of Economic Literature* 20:529–63.

Shafer, G. A. 1976. *A Mathematical Theory of Evidence.* Princeton, N.J.: Princeton University Press.

Skinner, B. F. 1966. The phylogeny and ontogeny of behavior. *Science* 153:1205–13.

Slovic, P.; Fischhoff, B.; and Lichtenstein, S. 1982. Response mode, framing, and information-processing effects in risk assessment. In R. M. Hogarth (ed.), *Question Framing and Response Consistency.* San Francisco: Jossey-Bass.

Thaler, R. 1980. Toward a positive theory of consumer choice. *Journal of Economic Behavior and Organizations* 1:39–60.

Thaler, R. 1985. Mental accounting and consumer choice. *Marketing Science* 4:199–214.

Tversky, A., and Kahneman, D. 1981. The framing of decisions and the psychology of choice. *Science* 211:453–58.

von Neumann, J., and Morgenstern, O. 1944. *The Theory of Games and Economic Behavior.* Princeton, N.J.: Princeton University Press.

Wallsten, T. S.; Forsyth, B. H.; and Budescu, D. 1983. Stability and coherence of health experts' upper and lower subjective probabilities about dose-response functions. *Organizational Behavior and Human Performance* 31:277–302.

Wothke, W. 1985. Allais' paradox revisited: The implications of the ambiguity adjustment model. Unpublished manuscript. Evanston, Ill.: Northwestern University, Department of Psychology, September.

Yates, J. F., and Zukowski, L. G. 1976. Characterization of ambiguity in decision making. *Behavioral Science* 21:19–25.

Yerkes, R. M., and Dodson, J. D. 1908. The relation of strength of stimulus to rapidity of habit-formation. *Journal of Comparative and Neurological Psychology* 18:459–82.

Zadeh, L. A. 1978. Fuzzy sets as a basis for a theory of possibility. *Fuzzy Sets and Systems* 1:3–28.

Amos Tversky
Stanford University

Daniel Kahneman
University of British Columbia

Rational Choice and the Framing of Decisions*

The modern theory of decision making under risk emerged from a logical analysis of games of chance rather than from a psychological analysis of risk and value. The theory was conceived as a normative model of an idealized decision maker, not as a description of the behavior of real people. In Schumpeter's words, it "has a much better claim to being called a logic of choice than a psychology of value" (1954, p. 1058).

The use of a normative analysis to predict and explain actual behavior is defended by several arguments. First, people are generally thought to be effective in pursuing their goals, particularly when they have incentives and opportunities to learn from experience. It seems reasonable, then, to describe choice as a maximization process. Second, competition favors rational individuals and organizations. Optimal decisions increase the chances of survival in a competitive environment, and a minority of rational individuals can sometimes impose rationality on the

Alternative descriptions of a decision problem often give rise to different preferences, contrary to the principle of invariance that underlies the rational theory of choice. Violations of this theory are traced to the rules that govern the framing of decision and to the psychophysical principles of evaluation embodied in prospect theory. Invariance and dominance are obeyed when their application is transparent and often violated in other situations. Because these rules are normatively essential but descriptively invalid, no theory of choice can be both normatively adequate and descriptively accurate.

* This work was supported by contract N00014-84-K-0615 from the Office of Naval Research to Stanford University. The present article reviews our work on decision making under risk from a new perspective, discussed primarily in the first and last sections. Most of the empirical demonstrations have been reported in earlier publications. Problems 3, 4, 7, 8, and 12 are published here for the first time. Requests for reprints should be addressed to Amos Tversky, Department of Psychology, Stanford University, Stanford, California 94705, or to Daniel Kahneman, Department of Psychology, University of California, Berkeley, California 94720.

whole market. Third, the intuitive appeal of the axioms of rational choice makes it plausible that the theory derived from these axioms should provide an acceptable account of choice behavior.

The thesis of the present article is that, in spite of these a priori arguments, the logic of choice does not provide an adequate foundation for a descriptive theory of decision making. We argue that the deviations of actual behavior from the normative model are too widespread to be ignored, too systematic to be dismissed as random error, and too fundamental to be accommodated by relaxing the normative system. We first sketch an analysis of the foundations of the theory of rational choice and then show that the most basic rules of the theory are commonly violated by decision makers. We conclude from these findings that the normative and the descriptive analyses cannot be reconciled. A descriptive model of choice is presented, which accounts for preferences that are anomalous in the normative theory.

I. A Hierarchy of Normative Rules

The major achievement of the modern theory of decision under risk is the derivation of the expected utility rule from simple principles of rational choice that make no reference to long-run considerations (von Neumann and Morgenstern 1944). The axiomatic analysis of the foundations of expected utility theory reveals four substantive assumptions—cancellation, transitivity, dominance, and invariance—besides the more technical assumptions of comparability and continuity. The substantive assumptions can be ordered by their normative appeal, from the cancellation condition, which has been challenged by many theorists, to invariance, which has been accepted by all. We briefly discuss these assumptions.

Cancellation. The key qualitative property that gives rise to expected utility theory is the "cancellation" or elimination of any state of the world that yields the same outcome regardless of one's choice. This notion has been captured by different formal properties, such as the substitution axiom of von Neumann and Morgenstern (1944), the extended sure-thing principle of Savage (1954), and the independence condition of Luce and Krantz (1971). Thus, if A is preferred to B, then the prospect of winning A if it rains tomorrow (and nothing otherwise) should be preferred to the prospect of winning B if it rains tomorrow because the two prospects yield the same outcome (nothing) if there is no rain tomorrow. Cancellation is necessary to represent preference between prospects as the maximization of expected utility. The main argument for cancellation is that only one state will actually be realized, which makes it reasonable to evaluate the outcomes of options separately for each state. The choice between options should therefore depend only on states in which they yield different outcomes.

Transitivity. A basic assumption in models of both risky and risk-less choice is the transitivity of preference. This assumption is necessary and essentially sufficient for the representation of preference by an ordinal utility scale u such that A is preferred to B whenever $u(A) > u(B)$. Thus transitivity is satisfied if it is possible to assign to each option a value that does not depend on the other available options. Transitivity is likely to hold when the options are evaluated separately but not when the consequences of an option depend on the alternative to which it is compared, as implied, for example, by considerations of regret. A common argument for transitivity is that cyclic preferences can support a "money pump," in which the intransitive person is induced to pay for a series of exchanges that returns to the initial option.

Dominance. This is perhaps the most obvious principle of rational choice: if one option is better than another in one state and at least as good in all other states, the dominant option should be chosen. A slightly stronger condition—called stochastic dominance—asserts that, for unidimensional risky prospects, A is preferred to B if the cumulative distribution of A is to the right of the cumulative distribution of B. Dominance is both simpler and more compelling than cancellation and transitivity, and it serves as the cornerstone of the normative theory of choice.

Invariance. An essential condition for a theory of choice that claims normative status is the principle of invariance: different representations of the same choice problem should yield the same preference. That is, the preference between options should be independent of their description. Two characterizations that the decision maker, on reflection, would view as alternative descriptions of the same problem should lead to the same choice—even without the benefit of such reflection. This principle of invariance (or extensionality [Arrow 1982]), is so basic that it is tacitly assumed in the characterization of options rather than explicitly stated as a testable axiom. For example, decision models that describe the objects of choice as random variables all assume that alternative representations of the same random variables should be treated alike. Invariance captures the normative intuition that variations of form that do not affect the actual outcomes should not affect the choice. A related concept, called consequentialism, has been discussed by Hammond (1985).

The four principles underlying expected utility theory can be ordered by their normative appeal. Invariance and dominance seem essential, transitivity could be questioned, and cancellation has been rejected by many authors. Indeed, the ingenious counterexamples of Allais (1953) and Ellsberg (1961) led several theorists to abandon cancellation and the expectation principle in favor of more general representations. Most of these models assume transitivity, dominance, and invariance (e.g., Hansson 1975; Allais 1979; Hagen 1979; Machina 1982; Quiggin 1982; Weber 1982; Chew 1983; Fishburn 1983; Schmeidler 1984; Segal 1984; Yaari 1984; Luce and Narens 1985). Other developments abandon transitivity but maintain invariance and dominance (e.g., Bell 1982; Fishburn 1982, 1984; Loomes and Sugden 1982). These theorists responded to observed violations of cancellation and transitivity by weakening the normative theory in order to retain its status as a descriptive model. However, this strategy cannot be extended to the failures of dominance and invariance that we shall document. Because invariance and dominance are normatively essential and descriptively invalid, a theory of rational decision cannot provide an adequate description of choice behavior.

We next illustrate failures of invariance and dominance and then review a descriptive analysis that traces these failures to the joint effects of the rules that govern the framing of prospects, the evaluation of outcomes, and the weighting of probabilities. Several phenomena of choice that support the present account are described.

II. Failures of Invariance

In this section we consider two illustrative examples in which the condition of invariance is violated and discuss some of the factors that produce these violations.

The first example comes from a study of preferences between medical treatments (McNeil et al. 1982). Respondents were given statistical information about the outcomes of two treatments of lung cancer. The same statistics were presented to some respondents in terms of mortality rates and to others in terms of survival rates. The respondents then indicated their preferred treatment. The information was presented as follows.[1]

Problem 1 (Survival frame)

Surgery: Of 100 people having surgery 90 live through the post-operative period, 68 are alive at the end of the first year and 34 are alive at the end of five years.

Radiation Therapy: Of 100 people having radiation therapy all live through the treatment, 77 are alive at the end of one year and 22 are alive at the end of five years.

Problem 1 (Mortality frame)

Surgery: Of 100 people having surgery 10 die during surgery or the post-operative period, 32 die by the end of the first year and 66 die by the end of five years.

1. All problems are presented in the text exactly as they were presented to the participants in the experiments.

Radiation Therapy: Of 100 people having radiation therapy, none die during treatment, 23 die by the end of one year and 78 die by the end of five years.

The inconsequential difference in formulation produced a marked effect. The overall percentage of respondents who favored radiation therapy rose from 18% in the survival frame ($N = 247$) to 44% in the mortality frame ($N = 336$). The advantage of radiation therapy over surgery evidently looms larger when stated as a reduction of the risk of immediate death from 10% to 0% rather than as an increase from 90% to 100% in the rate of survival. The framing effect was not smaller for experienced physicians or for statistically sophisticated business students than for a group of clinic patients.

Our next example concerns decisions between conjunctions of risky prospects with monetary outcomes. Each respondent made two choices, one between favorable prospects and one between unfavorable prospects (Tversky and Kahneman 1981, p. 454). It was assumed that the two selected prospects would be played independently.

Problem 2 ($N = 150$). Imagine that you face the following pair of concurrent decisions. First examine both decisions, then indicate the options you prefer.

Decision (i) Choose between:
A. a sure gain of $240 [84%]
B. 25% chance to gain $1000 and 75% chance to gain nothing [16%]

Decision (ii) Choose between:
C. a sure loss of $750 [13%]
D. 75% chance to lose $1000 and 25% chance to lose nothing [87%]

The total number of respondents is denoted by N, and the percentage who chose each option is indicated in brackets. (Unless otherwise specified, the data were obtained from undergraduate students at Stanford University and at the University of British Columbia.) The majority choice in decision i is risk averse, while the majority choice in decision ii is risk seeking. This is a common pattern: choices involving gains are usually risk averse, and choices involving losses are often risk seeking—except when the probability of winning or losing is small (Fishburn and Kochenberger 1979; Kahneman and Tversky 1979; Hershey and Schoemaker 1980).

Because the subjects considered the two decisions simultaneously, they expressed, in effect, a preference for the portfolio A and D over the portfolio B and C. However, the preferred portfolio is actually dominated by the rejected one! The combined options are as follows.

A & D: 25% chance to win $240 and 75% chance to lose $760.
B & C: 25% chance to win $250 and 75% chance to lose $750.

When the options are presented in this aggregated form, the dominant option is invariably chosen. In the format of problem 2, however, 73% of respondents chose the dominated combination A and D, and only 3% chose B and C. The contrast between the two formats illustrates a violation of invariance. The findings also support the general point that failures of invariance are likely to produce violations of stochastic dominance and vice versa.

The respondents evidently evaluated decisions i and ii separately in problem 2, where they exhibited the standard pattern of risk aversion in gains and risk seeking in losses. People who are given these problems are very surprised to learn that the combination of two preferences that they considered quite reasonable led them to select a dominated option. The same pattern of results was also observed in a scaled-down version of problem 2, with real monetary payoff (see Tversky and Kahneman 1981, p. 458).

As illustrated by the preceding examples, variations in the framing of decision problems produce systematic violations of invariance and dominance that cannot be defended on normative grounds. It is instructive to examine two mechanisms that could ensure the invariance of preferences: canonical representations and the use of expected actuarial value.

Invariance would hold if all formulations of the same prospect were transformed to a standard canonical representation (e.g., a cumulative probability distribution of the same random variable) because the various versions would then all be evaluated in the same manner. In problem 2, for example, invariance and dominance would both be preserved if the outcomes of the two decisions were aggregated prior to evaluation. Similarly, the same choice would be made in both versions of the medical problem if the outcomes were coded in terms of one dominant frame (e.g., rate of survival). The observed failures of invariance indicate that people do not spontaneously aggregate concurrent prospects or transform all outcomes into a common frame.

The failure to construct a canonical representation in decision problems contrasts with other cognitive tasks in which such representations are generated automatically and effortlessly. In particular, our visual experience consists largely of canonical representations: objects do not appear to change in size, shape, brightness, or color when we move around them or when illumination varies. A white circle seen from a sharp angle in dim light appears circular and white, not ellipsoid and grey. Canonical representations are also generated in the process of language comprehension, where listeners quickly recode much of what they hear into an abstract propositional form that no longer discriminates, for example, between the active and the passive voice and often does not distinguish what was actually said from what was implied or presupposed (Clark and Clark 1977). Unfortunately, the mental machinery that transforms percepts and sentences into standard forms does not automatically apply to the process of choice.

Invariance could be satisfied even in the absence of a canonical representation if the evaluation of prospects were separately linear, or nearly linear, in probability and monetary value. If people ordered risky prospects by their actuarial values, invariance and dominance would always hold. In particular, there would be no difference between the mortality and the survival versions of the medical problem. Because the evaluation of outcomes and probabilities is generally non-linear, and because people do not spontaneously construct canonical representations of decisions, invariance commonly fails. Normative models of choice, which assume invariance, therefore cannot provide an adequate descriptive account of choice behavior. In the next section we present a descriptive account of risky choice, called prospect theory, and explore its consequences. Failures of invariance are explained by framing effects that control the representation of options, in conjunction with the nonlinearities of value and belief.

III.   Framing and Evaluation of Outcomes

Prospect theory distinguishes two phases in the choice process: a phase of framing and editing, followed by a phase of evaluation (Kahneman and Tversky 1979). The first phase consists of a preliminary analysis of the decision problem, which frames the effective acts, contingencies, and outcomes. Framing is controlled by the manner in which the choice problem is presented as well as by norms, habits, and expectancies of the decision maker. Additional operations that are performed prior to evaluation include cancellation of common components and the elimination of options that are seen to be dominated by others. In the second phase, the framed prospects are evaluated, and the prospect of highest value is selected. The theory distinguishes two ways of choosing between prospects: by detecting that one dominates another or by comparing their values.

For simplicity, we confine the discussion to simple gambles with numerical probabilities and monetary outcomes. Let $(x, p; y, q)$ denote a prospect that yields x with probability p and y with probability q and that preserves the status quo with probability $(1 - p - q)$. According to prospect theory, there are values $v(\cdot)$, defined on gains and losses, and decision weights $\pi(\cdot)$, defined on stated probabilities, such that the overall value of the prospect equals $\pi(p)v(x) + \pi(q)v(y)$. A slight modification is required if all outcomes of a prospect have the same sign.[2]

---

2. If $p + q = 1$ and either $x > y > 0$ or $x < y < 0$, the value of a prospect is given by $v(y) + \pi(p)[v(x) - v(y)]$, so that decision weights are not applied to sure outcomes.

The Value Function

Following Markowitz (1952), outcomes are expressed in prospect theory as positive or negative deviations (gains or losses) from a neutral reference outcome, which is assigned a value of zero. Unlike Markowitz, however, we propose that the value function is commonly S shaped, concave above the reference point, and convex below it, as illustrated in figure 1. Thus the difference in subjective value between a gain of $100 and a gain of $200 is greater than the subjective difference between a gain of $1,100 and a gain of $1,200. The same relation between value differences holds for the corresponding losses. The proposed function expresses the property that the effect of a marginal change decreases with the distance from the reference point in either direction. These hypotheses regarding the typical shape of the value function may not apply to ruinous losses or to circumstances in which particular amounts assume special significance.

A significant property of the value function, called *loss aversion*, is that the response to losses is more extreme than the response to gains. The common reluctance to accept a fair bet on the toss of a coin suggests that the displeasure of losing a sum of money exceeds the pleasure of winning the same amount. Thus the proposed value function is (i) defined on gains and losses, (ii) generally concave for gains and convex for losses, and (iii) steeper for losses than for gains. These properties of the value function have been supported in many studies of risky choice involving monetary outcomes (Fishburn and Kochenberger 1979; Kahneman and Tversky 1979; Hershey and Schoemaker 1980; Payne, Laughhunn, and Crum 1980) and human lives (Tversky 1977; Eraker and Sox 1981; Tversky and Kahneman 1981; Fischhoff 1983). Loss aversion may also contribute to the observed discrepancies between the amount of money people are willing to pay for a good and the compensation they demand to give it up (Bishop and Heberlein 1979; Knetsch and Sinden 1984). This effect is implied by the value function if the good is valued as a gain in the former context and as a loss in the latter.

Framing Outcomes

The framing of outcomes and the contrast between traditional theory and the present analysis are illustrated in the following problems.

Problem 3 (*N* = 126): Assume yourself richer by $300 than you are today. You have to choose between
a sure gain of $100 [72%]
50% chance to gain $200 and 50% chance to gain nothing [28%]

Problem 4 (*N* = 128): Assume yourself richer by $500 than you are today. You have to choose between
a sure loss of $100 [36%]
50% chance to lose nothing and 50% chance to lose $200 [64%]

VALUE

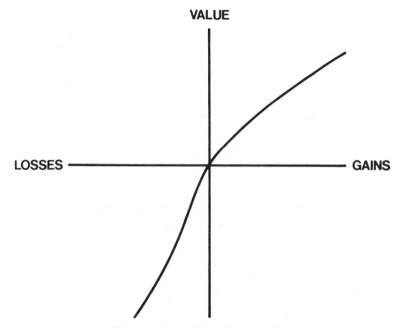

LOSSES ———————————————— **GAINS**

FIG. 1.—A typical value function

As implied by the value function, the majority choice is risk averse in problem 3 and risk seeking in problem 4, although the two problems are essentially identical. In both cases one faces a choice between $400 for sure and an even chance of $500 or $300. Problem 4 is obtained from problem 3 by increasing the initial endowment by $200 and subtracting this amount from both options. This variation has a substantial effect on preferences. Additional questions showed that variations of $200 in initial wealth have little or no effect on choices. Evidently, preferences are quite insensitive to small changes of wealth but highly sensitive to corresponding changes in reference point. These observations show that the effective carriers of values are gains and losses, or changes in wealth, rather than states of wealth as implied by the rational model.

The common pattern of preferences observed in problems 3 and 4 is of special interest because it violates not only expected utility theory but practically all other normatively based models of choice. In particular, these data are inconsistent with the model of regret advanced by Bell (1982) and by Loomes and Sugden (1982) and axiomatized by Fishburn (1982). This follows from the fact that problems 3 and 4 yield identical outcomes and an identical regret structure. Furthermore, regret theory cannot accommodate the combination of risk aversion in problem 3 and risk seeking in problem 4—even without the corresponding changes in endowment that make the problems extensionally equivalent.

Shifts of reference can be induced by different decompositions of outcomes into risky and riskless components, as in the above problems. The reference point can also be shifted by a mere labeling of outcomes, as illustrated in the following problems (Tversky and Kahneman 1981, p. 453).

Problem 5 (N = 152): Imagine that the U.S. is preparing for the outbreak of an unusual Asian disease, which is expected to kill 600 people. Two alternative programs to combat the disease have been proposed. Assume that the exact scientific estimates of the consequences of the programs are as follows:

If Program A is adopted, 200 people will be saved. [72%]

If Program B is adopted, there is 1/3 probability that 600 people will be saved, and 2/3 probability that no people will be saved. [28%]

In problem 5 the outcomes are stated in positive terms (lives saved), and the majority choice is accordingly risk averse. The prospect of certainly saving 200 lives is more attractive than a risky prospect of equal expected value. A second group of respondents was given the same cover story with the following descriptions of the alternative programs.

Problem 6 (N = 155):
If Program C is adopted 400 people will die. [22%]

If Program D is adopted there is 1/3 probability that nobody will die, and 2/3 probability that 600 people will die. [78%]

In problem 6 the outcomes are stated in negative terms (lives lost), and the majority choice is accordingly risk seeking. The certain death of 400 people is less acceptable than a two-thirds chance that 600 people will die. Problems 5 and 6, however, are essentially identical. They differ only in that the former is framed in terms of the number of lives saved (relative to an expected loss of 600 lives if no action is taken), whereas the latter is framed in terms of the number of lives lost.

On several occasions we presented both versions to the same respondents and discussed with them the inconsistent preferences evoked by the two frames. Many respondents expressed a wish to remain risk averse in the "lives saved" version and risk seeking in the "lives lost" version, although they also expressed a wish for their answers to be consistent. In the persistence of their appeal, framing effects resemble visual illusions more than computational errors.

Discounts and Surcharges

Perhaps the most distinctive intellectual contribution of economic analysis is the systematic consideration of alternative opportunities. A basic principle of economic thinking is that opportunity costs and out-of-pocket costs should be treated alike. Preferences should depend only on relevant differences between options, not on how these differences are labeled. This principle runs counter to the psychological tendencies that make preferences susceptible to superficial variations in form. In particular, a difference that favors outcome A over outcome B can sometimes be framed either as an advantage of A or as a disadvantage of B by suggesting either B or A as the neutral reference point. Because of loss aversion, the difference will loom larger when A is neutral and B-A is evaluated as a loss than when B is neutral and A-B is evaluated as a gain. The significance of such variations of framing has been noted in several contexts.

Thaler (1980) drew attention to the effect of labeling a difference between two prices as a surcharge or a discount. It is easier to forgo a discount than to accept a surcharge because the same price difference is valued as a gain in the former case and as a loss in the latter. Indeed, the credit card lobby is said to insist that any price difference between cash and card purchases should be labeled a cash discount rather than a credit surcharge. A similar idea could be invoked to explain why the price response to slack demand often takes the form of discounts or special concessions (Stigler and Kindahl 1970). Customers may be expected to show less resistance to the eventual cancellation of such temporary arrangements than to outright price increases. Judgments of fairness exhibit the same pattern (Kahneman, Knetsch, and Thaler, in this volume).

Schelling (1981) has described a striking framing effect in a context of tax policy. He points out that the tax table can be constructed by using as a default case either the childless family (as is in fact done) or, say, the modal two-child family. The tax difference between a childless family and a two-child family is naturally framed as an exemption (for the two-child family) in the first frame and as a tax premium (on the childless family) in the second frame. This seemingly innocuous difference has a large effect on judgments of the desired relation between income, family size, and tax. Schelling reported that his students rejected the idea of granting the rich a larger exemption than the poor in the first frame but favored a larger tax premium on the childless rich than on the childless poor in the second frame. Because the exemption and the premium are alternative labels for the same tax differences in the two cases, the judgments violate invariance. Framing the consequences of a public policy in positive or in negative terms can greatly alter its appeal.

The notion of a money illusion is sometimes applied to workers' willingness to accept, in periods of high inflation, increases in nominal wages that do not protect their real income—although they would strenuously resist equivalent wage cuts in the absence of inflation. The essence of the illusion is that, whereas a cut in the nominal wage is always recognized as a loss, a nominal increase that does not preserve real income may be treated as a gain. Another manifestation of the money illusion was observed in a study of the perceived fairness of economic actions (Kahneman, Knetsch, and Thaler, in press). Respondents in a telephone interview evaluated the fairness of the action described in the following vignette, which was presented in two versions that differed only in the bracketed clauses.

> A company is making a small profit. It is located in a community experiencing a recession with substantial unemployment [but no inflation/and inflation of 12%]. The company decides to [decrease wages and salaries 7%/increase salaries only 5%] this year.

Although the loss of real income is very similar in the two versions, the proportion of respondents who judged the action of the company "unfair" or "very unfair" was 62% for a nominal reduction but only 22% for a nominal increase.

Bazerman (1983) has documented framing effects in experimental studies of bargaining. He compared the performance of experimental subjects when the outcomes of bargaining were formulated as gains or as losses. Subjects who bargained over the allocation of losses more often failed to reach agreement and more often failed to discover a Pareto-optimal solution. Bazerman attributed these observations to the general propensity toward risk seeking in the domain of losses, which may increase the willingness of both participants to risk the negative consequences of a deadlock.

Loss aversion presents an obstacle to bargaining whenever the participants evaluate their own concessions as losses and the concessions obtained from the other party as gains. In negotiating over missiles, for example, the subjective loss of security associated with dismantling a missile may loom larger than the increment of security produced by a similar action on the adversary's part. If the two parties both assign a two-to-one ratio to the values of the concessions they make and of those they obtain, the resulting four-to-one gap may be difficult to bridge. Agreement will be much easier to achieve by negotiators who trade in "bargaining chips" that are valued equally, regardless of whose hand they are in. In this mode of trading, which may be common in routine purchases, loss aversion tends to disappear (Kahneman and Tversky 1984).

IV. The Framing and Weighting of Chance Events

In expected-utility theory, the utility of each possible outcome is weighted by its probability. In prospect theory, the value of an uncertain outcome is multiplied by a decision weight $\pi(p)$, which is a monotonic function of p but is not a probability. The weighting function π

has the following properties. First, impossible events are discarded, that is, $\pi(0) = 0$, and the scale is normalized so that $\pi(1) = 1$, but the function is not well behaved near the end points (Kahneman and Tversky 1979). Second, for low probabilities, $\pi(p) > p$, but $\pi(p) + \pi(1 - p) \leq 1$ (subcertainty). Thus low probabilities are overweighted, moderate and high probabilities are underweighted, and the latter effect is more pronounced than the former. Third, $\pi(pr)/\pi(p) < \pi(pqr)/\pi(pq)$ for all $0 < p, q, r \leq 1$ (subproportionality). That is, for any fixed probability ratio r, the ratio of decision weights is closer to unity when the probabilities are low than when they are high, for example, $\pi(.1)/\pi(.2) > \pi(.4)/\pi(.8)$. A hypothetical weighting function that satisfies these properties is shown in figure 2. Its consequences are discussed in the next section.[3]

Nontransparent Dominance

The major characteristic of the weighting function is the overweighting of probability differences involving certainty and impossibility, for example, $\pi(1.0) - \pi(.9)$ or $\pi(.1) - \pi(0)$, relative to comparable differences in the middle of the scale, for example, $\pi(.3) - \pi(.2)$. In particular, for small p, π is generally subadditive, for example, $\pi(.01) + \pi(.06) > \pi(.07)$. This property can lead to violations of dominance, as illustrated in the following pair of problems.

Problem 7 ($N = 88$). Consider the following two lotteries, described by the percentage of marbles of different colors in each box and the amount of money you win or lose depending on the color of a randomly drawn marble. Which lottery do you prefer?

Option A

90% white	6% red	1% green	1% blue	2% yellow
$0	win $45	win $30	lose $15	lose $15

Option B

90% white	6% red	1% green	1% blue	2% yellow
$0	win $45	win $45	lose $10	lose $15

It is easy to see that option B dominates option A: for every color the outcome of B is at least as desirable as the outcome of A. Indeed, all

---

3. The extension of the present analysis to prospects with many (nonzero) outcomes involves two additional steps. First, we assume that continuous (or multivalued) distributions are approximated, in the framing phase, by discrete distributions with a relatively small number of outcomes. For example, a uniform distribution on the interval (0, 90) may be represented by the discrete prospect (0, .1; 10, .1; . . . ; 90, .1). Second, in the multiple-outcome case the weighting function, $\pi_p(p_i)$, must depend on the probability vector p, not only on the component p_i, $i = 1, \ldots, n$. For example, Karmarkar (1978) used the function $\pi_p(p_i) = \pi(p_i)/[\pi(p_1) + \ldots + \pi(p_n)]$. A more elaborate extension that ensures stochastic dominance was proposed by Quiggin (1982). As in the two-outcome case, the weighting function is assumed to satisfy subcertainty, $\pi_p(p_1) + \ldots + \pi_p(p_n) \leq 1$, and subproportionality.

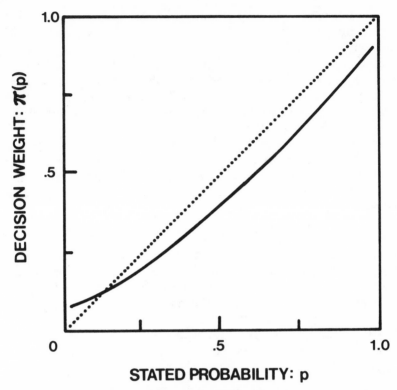

FIG. 2.—A typical weighting function

respondents chose B over A. This observation is hardly surprising
because the relation of dominance is highly transparent, so the dominated prospect is rejected without further processing. The next problem is effectively identical to problem 7, except that colors yielding
identical outcomes (red and green in B and yellow and blue in A) are
combined. We have proposed that this operation is commonly performed by the decision maker if no dominated prospect is detected.

Problem 8 (N = 124). Which lottery do you prefer?

Option C

90% white	6% red	1% green	3% yellow
$0	win $45	win $30	lose $15

Option D

90% white	7% red	1% green	2% yellow
$0	win $45	lose $10	lose $15

The formulation of problem 8 simplifies the options but masks the
relation of dominance. Furthermore, it enhances the attractiveness of

C, which has two positive outcomes and one negative, relative to D, which has two negative outcomes and one positive. As an inducement to consider the options carefully, participants were informed that one-tenth of them, selected at random, would actually play the gambles they chose. Although this announcement aroused much excitement, 58% of the participants chose the dominated alternative C. In answer to another question the majority of respondents also assigned a higher cash equivalent to C than to D. These results support the following propositions. (i) Two formulations of the same problem elicit different preferences, in violation of invariance. (ii) The dominance rule is obeyed when its application is transparent. (iii) Dominance is masked by a frame in which the inferior option yields a more favorable outcome in an identified state of the world (e.g., drawing a green marble). (iv) The discrepant preferences are consistent with the subadditivity of decision weights. The role of transparency may be illuminated by a perceptual example. Figure 3 presents the well-known Müller-Lyer illusion: the top line appears longer than the bottom line, although it is in fact shorter. In figure 4, the same patterns are embedded in a rectangular frame, which makes it apparent that the protruding bottom line is longer than the top one. This judgment has the nature of an inference, in contrast to the perceptual impression that mediates judgment in figure 3. Similarly, the finer partition introduced in problem 7 makes it possible to conclude that option D is superior to C, without assessing their values. Whether the relation of dominance is detected depends on framing as well as on the sophistication and experience of the decision maker. The dominance relation in problems 8 and 1 could be transparent to a sophisticated decision maker, although it was not transparent to most of our respondents.

Certainty and Pseudocertainty

The overweighting of outcomes that are obtained with certainty relative to outcomes that are merely probable gives rise to violations of the expectation rule, as first noted by Allais (1953). The next series of problems (Tversky and Kahneman 1981, p. 455) illustrates the phenomenon discovered by Allais and its relation to the weighting of probabilities and to the framing of chance events. Chance events were realized by drawing a single marble from a bag containing a specified number of favorable and unfavorable marbles. To encourage thoughtful answers, one-tenth of the participants, selected at random, were given an opportunity to play the gambles they chose. The same respondents answered problems 9–11, in that order.

Problem 9 ($N = 77$). Which of the following options do you prefer?
A. a sure gain of $30 [78%]
B. 80% chance to win $45 and 20% chance to win nothing [22%]

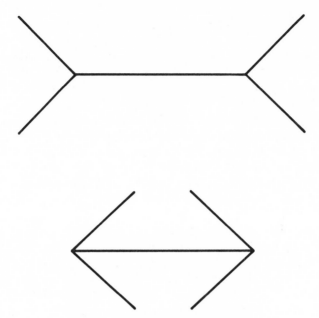

FIG. 3.—The Müller-Lyer illusion

Problem 10 (N = 81). Which of the following options do you prefer?
C. 25% chance to win $30 and 75% chance to win nothing [42%]
D. 20% chance to win $45 and 80% chance to win nothing [58%]

Note that problem 10 is obtained from problem 9 by reducing the probabilities of winning by a factor of four. In expected utility theory a preference for A over B in problem 9 implies a preference for C over D in problem 10. Contrary to this prediction, the majority preference switched from the lower prize ($30) to the higher one ($45) when the probabilities of winning were substantially reduced. We called this phenomenon the *certainty effect* because the reduction of the probability of winning from certainty to .25 has a greater effect than the corresponding reduction from .8 to .2. In prospect theory, the modal choice in problem 9 implies $v(45)\pi(.80) < v(30)\pi(1.0)$, whereas the modal choice in problem 10 implies $v(45)\pi(.20) > v(30)\pi(.25)$. The observed violation of expected utility theory, then, is implied by the curvature of π (see fig. 2) if

$$\frac{\pi(.20)}{\pi(.25)} > \frac{v(30)}{v(45)} > \frac{\pi(.80)}{\pi(1.0)}.$$

Allais's problem has attracted the attention of numerous theorists, who attempted to provide a normative rationale for the certainty effect by relaxing the cancellation rule (see, e.g., Allais 1979; Fishburn 1982, 1983; Machina 1982; Quiggin 1982; Chew 1983). The following problem

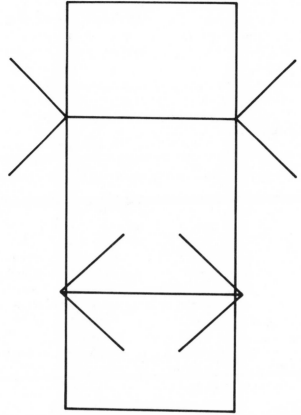

Fig. 4.—A transparent version of the Müller-Lyer illusion

illustrates a related phenomenon, called the *pseudocertainty effect*, that cannot be accommodated by relaxing cancellation because it also involves a violation of invariance.

Problem 11 ($N = 85$): Consider the following two stage game. In the first stage, there is a 75% chance to end the game without winning anything, and a 25% chance to move into the second stage. If you reach the second stage you have a choice between:

    E. a sure win of $30 [74%]
    F. 80% chance to win $45 and 20% chance to win nothing [26%]

Your choice must be made before the outcome of the first stage is known.

Because there is one chance in four to move into the second stage, prospect E offers a .25 probability of winning $30, and prospect F offers a .25 × .80 = .20 probability of winning $45. Problem 11 is therefore identical to problem 10 in terms of probabilities and outcomes. However, the preferences in the two problems differ: most subjects made a risk-averse choice in problem 11 but not in problem 10. We call this phenomenon the pseudocertainty effect because an outcome that is actually uncertain is weighted as if it were certain. The framing of problem 11 as a two-stage game encourages respondents to apply cancellation: the event of failing to reach the second stage is discarded prior to evaluation because it yields the same outcomes in both options. In this framing problems 11 and 9 are evaluated alike.

Although problems 10 and 11 are identical in terms of final outcomes and their probabilities, problem 11 has a greater potential for inducing regret. Consider a decision maker who chooses F in problem 11, reaches the second stage, but fails to win the prize. This individual knows that the choice of E would have yielded a gain of $30. In problem 10, on the other hand, an individual who chooses D and fails to win cannot know with certainty what the outcome of the other choice would have been. This difference could suggest an alternative interpretation of the pseudocertainty effect in terms of regret (e.g., Loomes and Sugden 1982). However, the certainty and the pseudocertainty effects were found to be equally strong in a modified version of problems 9–11 in which opportunities for regret were equated across problems. This finding does not imply that considerations of regret play no role in decisions. (For examples, see Kahneman and Tversky [1982, p. 710].) It merely indicates that Allais's example and the pseudocertainty effect are primarily controlled by the nonlinearity of decision weights and the framing of contingencies rather than by the anticipation of regret.[4]

The certainty and pseudocertainty effects are not restricted to monetary outcomes. The following problem illustrates these phenomena in a medical context. The respondents were 72 physicians attending a meeting of the California Medical Association. Essentially the same pattern of responses was obtained from a larger group ($N = 180$) of college students.

Problem 12 ($N = 72$). In the treatment of tumors there is sometimes a choice between two types of therapies: (i) a radical treatment such as extensive surgery, which involves some risk of imminent death,

4. In the modified version—problems 9'–11'—the probabilities of winning were generated by drawing a number from a bag containing 100 sequentially numbered tickets. In problem 10', the event associated with winning $45 (drawing a number between one and 20) was included in the event associated with winning $30 (drawing a number between one and 25). The sequential setup of problem 11 was replaced by the simultaneous play of two chance devices: the roll of a die (whose outcome determines whether the game is on) and the drawing of a numbered ticket from a bag. The possibility of regret now exists in all three problems, and problem 10' and 11' no longer differ in this respect because a decision maker would always know the outcomes of alternative choices. Consequently, regret theory cannot explain either the certainty effect (9' vs. 10') or the pseudocertainty effect (10' vs. 11') observed in the modified problems.

(ii) a moderate treatment, such as limited surgery or radiation therapy. Each of the following problems describes the possible outcome of two alternative treatments, for three different cases. In considering each case, suppose the patient is a 40-year-old male. Assume that without treatment death is imminent (within a month) and that only one of the treatments can be applied. Please indicate the treatment you would prefer in each case.

Case 1

Treatment A: 20% chance of imminent death and 80% chance of normal life, with an expected longevity of 30 years. [35%]

Treatment B: certainty of a normal life, with an expected longevity of 18 years. [65%]

Case 2

Treatment C: 80% chance of imminent death and 20% chance of normal life, with an expected longevity of 30 years. [68%]

Treatment D: 75% chance of imminent death and 25% chance of normal life, with an expected longevity of 18 years. [32%]

Case 3

Consider a new case where there is a 25% chance that the tumor is treatable and a 75% chance that it is not. If the tumor is not treatable, death is imminent. If the tumor is treatable, the outcomes of the treatment are as follows:

Treatment E: 20% chance of imminent death and 80% chance of normal life, with an expected longevity of 30 years. [32%]

Treatment F: certainty of normal life, with an expected longevity of 18 years. [68%]

The three cases of this problem correspond, respectively, to problems 9–11, and the same pattern of preferences is observed. In case 1, most respondents make a risk-averse choice in favor of certain survival with reduced longevity. In case 2, the moderate treatment no longer ensures survival, and most respondents choose the treatment that offers the higher expected longevity. In particular, 64% of the physicians who chose B in case 1 selected C in case 2. This is another example of Allais's certainty effect.

The comparison of cases 2 and 3 provides another illustration of pseudocertainty. The cases are identical in terms of the relevant outcomes and their probabilities, but the preferences differ. In particular, 56% of the physicians who chose C in case 2 selected F in case 3. The conditional framing induces people to disregard the event of the tumor not being treatable because the two treatments are equally ineffective in this case. In this frame, treatment F enjoys the advantage of pseudocertainty. It appears to ensure survival, but the assurance is conditional on the treatability of the tumor. In fact, there is only a .25 chance of surviving a month if this option is chosen.

The conjunction of certainty and pseudocertainty effects has significant implications for the relation between normative and descriptive theories of choice. Our results indicate that cancellation is actually obeyed in choices—in those problems that make its application transparent. Specifically, we find that people make the same choices in problems 11 and 9 and in cases 3 and 1 of problem 12. Evidently, people "cancel" an event that yields the same outcomes for all options, in two-stage or nested structures. Note that in these examples cancellation is satisfied in problems that are formally equivalent to those in which it is violated. The empirical validity of cancellation therefore depends on the framing of the problems.

The present concept of framing originated from the analysis of Allais's problems by Savage (1954, pp. 101–4) and Raiffa (1968, pp. 80–86), who reframed these examples in an attempt to make the application of cancellation more compelling. Savage and Raiffa were right: naive respondents indeed obey the cancellation axiom when its application is sufficiently transparent.[5] However, the contrasting preferences in different versions of the same choice (problems 10 and 11 and cases 2 and 3 of problem 12) indicate that people do not follow the same axiom when its application is not transparent. Instead, they apply (nonlinear) decision weights to the probabilities as stated. The status of cancellation is therefore similar to that of dominance: both rules are intuitively compelling as abstract principles of choice, consistently obeyed in transparent problems and frequently violated in nontransparent ones. Attempts to rationalize the preferences in Allais's example by discarding the cancellation axiom face a major difficulty: they do not distinguish transparent formulations in which cancellation is obeyed from nontransparent ones in which it is violated.

V. Discussion

In the preceding sections we challenged the descriptive validity of the major tenets of expected utility theory and outlined an alternative account of risky choice. In this section we discuss alternative theories

---

5. It is noteworthy that the conditional framing used in problems 11 and 12 (case 3) is much more effective in eliminating the common responses to Allais's paradox than the partition framing introduced by Savage (see, e.g., Slovic and Tversky 1974). This is probably due to the fact that the conditional framing makes it clear that the critical options are identical—after eliminating the state whose outcome does not depend on one's choice (i.e., reaching the second stage in problem 11, an untreatable tumor in problem 12, case 3).

and argue against the reconciliation of normative and descriptive analyses. Some objections of economists to our analysis and conclusions are addressed.

Descriptive and Normative Considerations

Many alternative models of risky choice, designed to explain the observed violations of expected utility theory, have been developed in the last decade. These models divide into the following four classes. (i) Nonlinear functionals (e.g., Allais 1953, 1979; Machina 1982) are obtained by eliminating the cancellation condition altogether. These models do not have axiomatizations leading to a (cardinal) measurement of utility, but they impose various restrictions (i.e., differentiability) on the utility functional. (ii) The expectations quotient model (axiomatized by Chew and MacCrimmon 1979; Weber 1982; Chew 1983; Fishburn 1983) replaces cancellation by a weaker substitution axiom and represents the value of a prospect by the ratio of two linear functionals. (iii) Bilinear models with nonadditive probabilities (e.g., Kahneman and Tversky 1979; Quiggin 1982; Schmeidler 1984; Segal 1984; Yaari 1984; Luce and Narens 1985) assume various restricted versions of cancellation (or substitution) and construct a bilinear representation in which the utilities of outcomes are weighted by a nonadditive probability measure or by some nonlinear transform of the probability scale. (iv) Nontransitive models represent preferences by a bivariate utility function. Fishburn (1982, 1984) axiomatized such models, while Bell (1982) and Loomes and Sugden (1982) interpreted them in terms of expected regret. For further theoretical developments, see Fishburn (1985).

The relation between models and data is summarized in table 1. The stub column lists the four major tenets of expected utility theory. Column 1 lists the major empirical violations of these tenets and cites a few representative references. Column 2 lists the subset of models discussed above that are consistent with the observed violations.

TABLE 1   **Summary of Empirical Violations and Explanatory Models**

Tenet	Empirical Violation	Explanatory Model
Cancellation	Certainty effect (Allais 1953, 1979; Kahneman and Tversky 1979) (problems 9–10, and 12 [cases 1 and 2])	All models
Transitivity	Lexicographic semiorder (Tversky 1969) Preference reversals (Slovic and Lichtenstein 1983)	Bivariate models
Dominance	Contrasting risk attitudes (problem 2) Subadditive decision weights (problem 8)	Prospect theory
Invariance	Framing effects (Problems 1, 3–4, 5–6, 7–8, 10–11, and 12)	Prospect theory

The conclusions of table 1 may be summarized as follows. First, all the above models (as well as some others) are consistent with the violations of cancellation produced by the certainty effect.[6] Therefore, Allais's "paradox" cannot be used to compare or evaluate competing nonexpectation models. Second, bivariate (nontransitive) models are needed to explain observed intransitivities. Third, only prospect theory can accommodate the observed violations of (stochastic) dominance and invariance. Although some models (e.g., Loomes and Sugden 1982; Luce and Narens 1985) permit some limited failures of invariance, they do not account for the range of framing effects described in this article.

Because framing effects and the associated failures of invariance are ubiquitous, no adequate descriptive theory can ignore these phenomena. On the other hand, because invariance (or extensionality) is normatively indispensable, no adequate prescriptive theory should permit its violation. Consequently, the dream of constructing a theory that is acceptable both descriptively and normatively appears unrealizable (see also Tversky and Kahneman 1983).

Prospect theory differs from the other models mentioned above in being unabashedly descriptive and in making no normative claims. It is designed to explain preferences, whether or not they can be rationalized. Machina (1982, p. 292) claimed that prospect theory is "unacceptable as a descriptive model of behavior toward risk" because it implies violations of stochastic dominance. But since the violations of dominance predicted by the theory have actually been observed (see problems 2 and 8), Machina's objection appears invalid.

Perhaps the major finding of the present article is that the axioms of rational choice are generally satisfied in transparent situations and often violated in nontransparent ones. For example, when the relation of stochastic dominance is transparent (as in the aggregated version of problem 2 and in problem 7), practically everyone selects the dominant prospect. However, when these problems are framed so that the relation of dominance is no longer transparent (as in the segregated version of problem 2 and in problem 8), most respondents violate dominance, as predicted. These results contradict all theories that imply stochastic dominance as well as others (e.g., Machina 1982) that predict the same choices in transparent and nontransparent contexts. The same conclusion applies to cancellation, as shown in the discussion of pseudocertainty. It appears that both cancellation and dominance have normative appeal, although neither one is descriptively valid.

The present results and analysis—particularly the role of transparency and the significance of framing—are consistent with the concep-

---

6. Because the present article focuses on prospects with known probabilities, we do not discuss the important violations of cancellation due to ambiguity (Ellsberg 1961).

tion of bounded rationality originally presented by Herbert Simon (see, e.g., Simon 1955, 1978; March 1978; Nelson and Winter 1982). Indeed, prospect theory is an attempt to articulate some of the principles of perception and judgment that limit the rationality of choice.

The introduction of psychological considerations (e.g., framing) both enriches and complicates the analysis of choice. Because the framing of decisions depends on the language of presentation, on the context of choice, and on the nature of the display, our treatment of the process is necessarily informal and incomplete. We have identified several common rules of framing, and we have demonstrated their effects on choice, but we have not provided a formal theory of framing. Furthermore, the present analysis does not account for all the observed failures of transitivity and invariance. Although some intransitivities (e.g., Tversky 1969) can be explained by discarding small differences in the framing phase, and others (e.g., Raiffa 1968, p. 75) arise from the combination of transparent and nontransparent comparisons, there are examples of cyclic preferences and context effects (see, e.g., Slovic, Fischhoff, and Lichtenstein 1982; Slovic and Lichtenstein 1983) that require additional explanatory mechanisms (e.g., multiple reference points and variable weights). An adequate account of choice cannot ignore these effects of framing and context, even if they are normatively distasteful and mathematically intractable.

Bolstering Assumptions

The assumption of rationality has a favored position in economics. It is accorded all the methodological privileges of a self-evident truth, a reasonable idealization, a tautology, and a null hypothesis. Each of these interpretations either puts the hypothesis of rational action beyond question or places the burden of proof squarely on any alternative analysis of belief and choice. The advantage of the rational model is compounded because no other theory of judgment and decision can ever match it in scope, power, and simplicity.

Furthermore, the assumption of rationality is protected by a formidable set of defenses in the form of bolstering assumptions that restrict the significance of any observed violation of the model. In particular, it is commonly assumed that substantial violations of the standard model are (i) restricted to insignificant choice problems, (ii) quickly eliminated by learning, or (iii) irrelevant to economics because of the corrective function of market forces. Indeed, incentives sometimes improve the quality of decisions, experienced decision makers often do better than novices, and the forces of arbitrage and competition can nullify some effects of error and illusion. Whether these factors ensure rational choices in any particular situation is an empirical issue, to be settled by observation, not by supposition.

It has frequently been claimed (see, e.g., Smith 1985) that the observed failures of rational models are attributable to the cost of thinking and will thus be eliminated by proper incentives. Experimental findings provide little support for this view. Studies reported in the economic and psychological literature have shown that errors that are prevalent in responses to hypothetical questions persist even in the presence of significant monetary payoffs. In particular, elementary blunders of probabilistic reasoning (Grether 1980; Tversky and Kahneman 1983), major inconsistencies of choice (Grether and Plott 1979; Slovic and Lichtenstein 1983), and violations of stochastic dominance in nontransparent problems (see problem 2 above) are hardly reduced by incentives. The evidence that high stakes do not always improve decisions is not restricted to laboratory studies. Significant errors of judgment and choice can be documented in real world decisions that involve high stakes and serious deliberation. The high rate of failures of small businesses, for example, is not easily reconcilied with the assumptions of rational expectations and risk aversion.

Incentives do not operate by magic: they work by focusing attention and by prolonging deliberation. Consequently, they are more likely to prevent errors that arise from insufficient attention and effort than errors that arise from misperception or faulty intuition. The example of visual illusion is instructive. There is no obvious mechanism by which the mere introduction of incentives (without the added opportunity to make measurements) would reduce the illusion observed in figure 3, and the illusion vanishes—even in the absence of incentives—when the display is altered in figure 4. The corrective power of incentives depends on the nature of the particular error and cannot be taken for granted.

The assumption of the rationality of decision making is often defended by the argument that people will learn to make correct decisions and sometimes by the evolutionary argument that irrational decision makers will be driven out by rational ones. There is no doubt that learning and selection do take place and tend to improve efficiency. As in the case of incentives, however, no magic is involved. Effective learning takes place only under certain conditions: it requires accurate and immediate feedback about the relation between the situational conditions and the appropriate response. The necessary feedback is often lacking for the decisions made by managers, entrepreneurs, and politicians because (i) outcomes are commonly delayed and not easily attributable to a particular action; (ii) variability in the environment degrades the reliability of the feedback, especially where outcomes of low probability are involved; (iii) there is often no information about what the outcome would have been if another decision had been taken; and (iv) most important decisions are unique and therefore provide little opportunity for learning (see Einhorn and Hogarth 1978). The conditions for organizational learning are hardly better. Learning surely occurs, for both individuals and organizations, but any claim that a particular error will be eliminated by experience must be supported by demonstrating that the conditions for effective learning are satisfied.

Finally, it is sometimes argued that failures of rationality in individual decision making are inconsequential because of the corrective effects of the market (Knez, Smith, and Williams 1985). Economic agents are often protected from their own irrational predilections by the forces of competition and by the action of arbitrageurs, but there are situations in which this mechanism fails. Hausch, Ziemba, and Rubenstein (1981) have documented an instructive example: the market for win bets at the racetrack is efficient, but the market for bets on place and show is not. Bettors commonly underestimate the probability that the favorite will end up in second or third place, and this effect is sufficiently large to sustain a contrarian betting strategy with a positive expected value. This inefficiency is found in spite of the high incentives, of the unquestioned level of dedication and expertise among participants in racetrack markets, and of obvious opportunities for learning and for arbitrage.

Situations in which errors that are common to many individuals are unlikely to be corrected by the market have been analyzed by Haltiwanger and Waldman (1985) and by Russell and Thaler (1985). Furthermore, Akerlof and Yellen (1985) have presented their near-rationality theory, in which some prevalent errors in responding to economic changes (e.g., inertia or money illusion) will (i) have little effect on the individual (thereby eliminating the possibility of learning), (ii) provide no opportunity for arbitrage, and yet (iii) have large economic effects. The claim that the market can be trusted to correct the effect of individual irrationalities cannot be made without supporting evidence, and the burden of specifying a plausible corrective mechanism should rest on those who make this claim.

The main theme of this article has been that the normative and the descriptive analyses of choice should be viewed as separate enterprises. This conclusion suggests a research agenda. To retain the rational model in its customary descriptive role, the relevant bolstering assumptions must be validated. Where these assumptions fail, it is instructive to trace the implications of the descriptive analysis (e.g., the effects of loss aversion, pseudocertainty, or the money illusion) for public policy, strategic decision making, and macroeconomic phenomena (see Arrow 1982; Akerlof and Yellen 1985).

References

Akerlof, G. A., and Yellen, J. 1985. Can small deviations from rationality make significant differences to economic equilibria? *American Economic Review* 75:708–20.
Allais, M. 1953. Le comportement de l'homme rationnel devant le risque: Critique des postulats et axiomes de l'Ecole Américaine. *Econometrica* 21:503–46.

Allais, M. 1979. The foundations of a positive theory of choice involving risk and a criticism of the postulates and axioms of the American School. In M. Allais and O. Hagen (eds.), *Expected Utility Hypotheses and the Allais Paradox.* Dordrecht: Reidel.

Arrow, K. J. 1982. Risk perception in psychology and economics. *Economic Inquiry* 20:1–9.

Bazerman, M. H. 1983. Negotiator judgment. *American Behavioral Scientist* 27:211–28.

Bell, D. E. 1982. Regret in decision making under uncertainty. *Operations Research* 30:961–81.

Bishop, R. C., and Heberlein, T. A. 1979. Measuring values of extra-market goods: Are indirect measures biased? *American Journal of Agricultural Economics* 61:926–30.

Chew, S. H. 1983. A generalization of the quasilinear mean with applications to the measurement of income inequality and decision theory resolving the Allais paradox. *Econometrica* 51:1065–92.

Chew, S. H., and MacCrimmon, K. 1979. Alpha utility theory, lottery composition, and the Allais paradox. Working Paper no. 686. Vancouver: University of British Columbia.

Clark, H. H., and Clark, E. V. 1977. *Psychology and Language.* New York: Harcourt Brace Jovanovich.

Einhorn, H. J., and Hogarth, R. M. 1978. Confidence in judgment: Persistence of the illusion of validity. *Psychological Review* 85:395–416.

Ellsberg, D. 1961. Risk, ambiguity, and the Savage axioms. *Quarterly Journal of Economics* 75:643–69.

Eraker, S. E., and Sox, H. C. 1981. Assessment of patients' preferences for therapeutic outcomes. *Medical Decision Making* 1:29–39.

Fischhoff, B. 1983. Predicting frames. *Journal of Experimental Psychology: Learning, Memory and Cognition* 9:103–16.

Fishburn, P. C. 1982. Nontransitive measurable utility. *Journal of Mathematical Psychology* 26:31–67.

Fishburn, P. C. 1983. Transitive measurable utility. *Journal of Economic Theory* 31:293–317.

Fishburn, P. C. 1984. SSB utility theory and decision making under uncertainty. *Mathematical Social Sciences* 8:253–85.

Fishburn, P. C. 1985. Uncertainty aversion and separated effects in decision making under uncertainty. Working paper. Murray Hill, N.J.: AT & T Bell Labs.

Fishburn, P. C., and Kochenberger, G. A. 1979. Two-piece von Neumann–Morgenstern utility functions. *Decision Sciences* 10:503–18.

Grether, D. M. 1980. Bayes rule as a descriptive model: The representativeness heuristic. *Quarterly Journal of Economics* 95:537–57.

Grether, D. M., and Plott, C. R. 1979. Economic theory of choice and the preference reversal phenomenon. *American Economic Review* 69:623–38.

Hagen, O. 1979. Towards a positive theory of preferences under risk. In M. Allais and O. Hagen (eds.), *Expected Utility Hypotheses and the Allais Paradox.* Dordrecht: Reidel.

Haltiwanger, J., and Waldman, M. 1985. Rational expectations and the limits of rationality: An analysis of heterogeneity. *American Economic Review* 75:326–40.

Hammond, P. 1985. Consequential behavior in decision trees and expected utility. Institute for Mathematical Studies in the Social Sciences Working Paper no. 112. Stanford, Calif.: Stanford University.

Hansson, B. 1975. The appropriateness of the expected utility model. *Erkenntnis* 9:175–93.

Hausch, D. B.; Ziemba, W. T.; and Rubenstein, M. E. 1981. Efficiency of the market for racetrack betting. *Management Science* 27:1435–52.

Hershey, J. C., and Schoemaker, P. J. H. 1980. Risk taking and problem context in the domain of losses: An expected utility analysis. *Journal of Risk and Insurance* 47:111–32.

Kahneman, D.; Knetsch, J. L.; and Thaler, R. H. In this volume. Fairness and the assumptions of economics.

Kahneman, D.; Knetsch, J. L.; and Thaler, R. In press. Perceptions of fairness: Entitlements in the market. *American Economic Review.*

Kahneman, D., and Tversky, A. 1979. Prospect theory: An analysis of decision under risk. *Econometrica* 47:263–91.

Kahneman, D., and Tversky, A. 1982. The psychology of preferences. *Scientific American* 246:160–73.

Kahneman, D., and Tversky, A. 1984. Choices, values, and frames. *American Psychologist* 39:341–50.

Karmarkar, V. S. 1978. Subjectively weighted utility: A descriptive extension of the expected utility model. *Organizational Behavior and Human Performance* 21:61–72.

Knetsch, J. L., and Sinden, J. A. 1984. Willingness to pay and compensation demanded: Experimental evidence of an unexpected disparity in measures of value. *Quarterly Journal of Economics* 99:507–21.

Knez, P.; Smith, V. L.; and Williams, A. W. 1985. Individual rationality, market rationality and value estimation. *American Economic Review: Papers and Proceedings* 75:397–402.

Loomes, G., and Sugden, R. 1982. Regret theory: An alternative theory of rational choice under uncertainty. *Economic Journal* 92:805–24.

Luce, R. D., and Krantz, D. H. 1971. Conditional expected utility. *Econometrica* 39:253–71.

Luce, R. D., and Narens, L. 1985. Classification of concatenation measurement structures according to scale type. *Journal of Mathematical Psychology* 29:1–72.

Machina, M. J. 1982. "Expected utility" analysis without the independence axiom. *Econometrica* 50:277–323.

McNeil, B. J.; Pauker, S. G.; Sox, H. C., Jr.; and Tversky, A. 1982. On the elicitation of preferences for alternative therapies. *New England Journal of Medicine* 306:1259–62.

March, J. G. 1978. Bounded rationality, ambiguity, and the engineering of choice. *Bell Journal of Economics* 9:587–608.

Markowitz, H. 1952. The utility of wealth. *Journal of Political Economy* 60:151–58.

Nelson, R. R., and Winter, S. G. 1982. *An Evolutionary Theory of Economic Change*. Cambridge, Mass.: Harvard University Press.

Payne, J. W.; Laughhunn, D. J.; and Crum, R. 1980. Translation of gambles and aspiration level effects in risky choice behavior. *Management Science* 26:1039–60.

Quiggin, J. 1982. A theory of anticipated utility. *Journal of Economic Behavior and Organization* 3:323–43.

Raiffa, H. 1968. *Decision Analysis: Introductory Lectures on Choices under Uncertainty*. Reading, Mass.: Addison-Wesley.

Russell, T., and Thaler, R. 1985. The relevance of quasi-rationality in competitive markets. *American Economic Review* 75:1071–82.

Savage, L. J. 1954. *The Foundations of Statistics*. New York: Wiley.

Schelling, T. C. 1981. Economic reasoning and the ethics of policy. *Public Interest* 63:37–61.

Schmeidler, D. 1984. Subjective probability and expected utility without additivity. Preprint Series no. 84. Minneapolis: University of Minnesota, Institute for Mathematics and Its Applications.

Schumpeter, J. A. 1954. *History of Economic Analysis*. New York: Oxford University Press.

Segal, U. 1984. Nonlinear decision weights with the independence axiom. Working Paper in Economics no. 353. Los Angeles: University of California, Los Angeles.

Simon, H. A. 1955. A behavioral model of rational choice. *Quarterly Journal of Economics* 69:99–118.

Simon, H. A. 1978. Rationality as process and as product of thought. *American Economic Review: Papers and Proceedings* 68:1–16.

Slovic, P.; Fischhoff, B.; and Lichtenstein, S. 1982. Response mode, framing, and information processing effects in risk assessment. In R. M. Hogarth (ed.), *New Directions for Methodology of Social and Behavioral Science: Question Framing and Response Consistency*. San Francisco: Jossey-Bass.

Slovic, P., and Lichtenstein, S. 1983. Preference reversals: A broader perspective. *American Economic Review* 73:596–605.

Slovic, P., and Tversky, A. 1974. Who accepts Savage's axiom? *Behavioral Science* 19:368–73.

Smith, V. L. 1985. Experimental economics: Reply. *American Economic Review* 75:265–72.

Stigler, G. J., and Kindahl, J. K. 1970. *The Behavior of Industrial Prices*. New York: National Bureau of Economic Research.

Thaler, R. H. 1980. Towards a positive theory of consumer choice. *Journal of Economic Behavior and Organization* 1:39–60.

Tversky, A. 1969. Intransitivity of preferences. *Psychological Review* 76:105–10.

Tversky, A. 1977. On the elicitation of preferences: Descriptive and prescriptive considerations. In D. E. Bell, R. L. Keeney, and H. Raiffa (eds.), *Conflicting Objectives in Decisions*. New York: Wiley.

Tversky, A., and Kahneman, D. 1981. The framing of decisions and the psychology of choice. *Science* 211:453–58.

Tversky, A., and Kahneman, D. 1983. Extensional versus intuitive reasoning: The conjunction fallacy in probability judgment. *Psychological Review* 90:293–315.

von Neumann, J., and Morgenstern, O. 1944. *Theory of Games and Economic Behavior*. Princeton, N.J.: Princeton University Press.

Weber, R. J. 1982. The Allais paradox, Dutch auctions, and alpha-utility theory. Working paper. Evanston, Ill.: Northwestern University.

Yaari, M. E. 1984. Risk aversion without decreasing marginal utility. Report Series in Theoretical Economics. London: London School of Economics.

Richard H. Thaler

Cornell University

The Psychology and Economics Conference Handbook: Comments on Simon, on Einhorn and Hogarth, and on Tversky and Kahneman

I. Guide to Discussants

While most of George Stigler's articles have received the attention they deserve, there is one piece that I think has been neglected, though its potential contribution to the knowledge transmitted at a conference like this one is enormous. The article I refer to is titled "The Conference Handbook" (Stigler 1977). In this incisive piece Stigler argues that conferences could be run much more efficiently if discussants could utilize a standard list of comments that could be called out by number, much as in the old story about the prisoners who told their jokes by number. Stigler offers several introductory remarks and 32 specific comments. For example, introductory remark F could be used nicely at an interdisciplinary conference like this one: "It is good to have a nonspecialist looking at our problem. There is always a chance of a fresh viewpoint, although usually, as in this case, the advantages of the division of labor are reaffirmed." The specific comments begin with the classic 1: "Adam Smith said that." Two others that might come in handy at this conference are 23: "The motivation of the agents in this theory is so narrowly egotistic that it cannot possibly explain the behavior of real people"; and 24: "The flabby economic actor in this impressionistic model should be replaced by the utility-maximizing individual" (pp. 442, 443).

While Stigler's comments are insightful and quite versatile, I have found that conferences that combine psychologists and economists present a special set of problems to discussant and attendee alike, and so I am taking this opportunity to provide a customized list of comments that can be used in these situations. The comments I will mention are those that are most frequently offered by economists when discussing the work of psychologists. For the sake of fairness, a subject in which I have recently become interested, I will also offer brief responses.

1. *If the stakes are large enough, people will get it right.* This comment is usually offered to rebut a demonstration of embarrassing inconsistency on the part of a group of undergraduate students participating in an experiment at one of our leading universities. Many such demonstrations have offered the subjects little or no incentive to think hard or to get the "right" answer, so it is reasonable to ask whether financial incentives might not eliminate less than fully rational answers. This, of course, is an empirical question. Do people tend to make better decisions when the stakes are high? There is little evidence that they do.

Some investigators have tested to see whether the introduction of moderate-sized financial incentives will eliminate irrational behavior. For example, Grether and Plott (1979) replicated Lichtenstein and Slovic's (1971) demonstration of the preference reversal phenomenon with and without financial incentives. They discovered to their surprise that the preference reversals were somewhat stronger when financial incentives were used. Of course, no one has received enough financial support to replicate preference reversal phenomena at very large stakes, but the assertion that systematic mistakes will always disappear if the stakes are large enough should be recognized for what it is— an assertion unsupported by any data.

2. *In the real world people will learn to get it right.*   This comment, as is the first one, is derived from a reasonable concern that many experiments have not offered the subjects much if any opportunity to learn. The validity of the assertion again comes down to an empirical question. Do real world environments facilitate learning? Unfortunately, there is little reason to be optimistic. Accurate learning takes place only when the individual receives timely and organized feedback. As Einhorn and Hogarth (1978) have shown, many repetitive decision-making tasks do not provide this type of learning opportunity. For example, a common, well-documented decision-making failing is overconfidence. Subjects in many contexts have been shown to display this trait. Einhorn and Hogarth have shown that in decision-making tasks in which the decision maker usually succeeds, such as selecting students for admission into a highly selective college with a very attractive applicant pool, experience will tend to increase confidence regardless of the ability of the decision maker to discriminate good from bad applicants. Thus experience does not necessarily lead to learning.

3. *In the aggregate, errors will cancel.*   This remark should be used with caution since the errors that have been discovered by the psychologists studying decision making are systematic. Similarly, the statement, If it is not rational, it is random and thus unpredictable, is incorrect. Behavior can be (and is often shown in the laboratory to be) purposeful, regular, and yet systematically different from the axioms of economic theory. I like the term "quasi rational" to describe such

behavior. Someone who systematically overreacts to new information in violation of Bayes's rule is predictable yet only quasi rational.

4. *In markets, arbitrage and competition will eliminate the effects of irrational agents.* Markets can provide a unique context for agents to choose in an environment with both monetary incentives and learning opportunities. Moreover, the existence of other agents, ready to exploit the slightest slip, could create a situation in which mistakes are quickly eliminated. Under what circumstances will arbitrage and competition render the choices of quasi-rational agents irrelevant? This question is addressed in my recent paper with Tom Russell (Russell and Thaler 1985). We investigate the operation of competitive markets in which some agents are fully rational and others are quasi rational. We then find the conditions that are sufficient to guarantee that such markets will yield rational equilibria, that is, the equilibria that would obtain if all the agents were rational. We find that these conditions are quite restrictive and are unlikely to occur in any but the most efficient of financial markets. In goods markets, a mistake by one individual will generally not create an arbitrage or profit opportunity for someone else. In these circumstances, mistakes can persist. While it is wrong to assume that behavior discovered in the psychologist's lab will necessarily survive in real world markets, it is also wrong to assume that markets will always eliminate such behavior.

5. *Where is the theory?* The original contributions to what is now referred to as behavioral decision theory were simply empirical anomalies, such as those discovered by Allais and by Ellsberg. Even without theories, however, these results were very useful in showing where the existing theory (expected utility theory) made predictions about behavior that were systematically wrong. The papers presented in this session by Tversky and Kahneman (in this volume) and by Einhorn and Hogarth (in this volume) have taken these original anomalies and tried to develop descriptive theories that can account for the observed behavior. These explicitly descriptive theories cannot be derived from normative axioms. Nevertheless, they are theories, and they seem to do a good job of predicting behavior.

6. *Economic theory has done very well so far, and if it is not broken . . .* How successful is economic theory? The answer to this question depends on what constitutes a test. I propose the following ground rules. A test can be used as supporting evidence by the proponents of a theory if and only if the same test would have been accepted as a refutation had it come out the other way. Let me illustrate by example. If you look through a typical microeconomics textbook you will find few if any "tests" of the theory. However, there is one frequently reported test by Ray Battalio, John Kagel, and their colleagues, who perform experimental studies using animal subjects. (See, e.g., Kagel et al. 1975.) These studies have demonstrated that

rats and pigeons have downard-sloping demand curves and upward-sloping labor supply curves. Such results are cited as supporting the theory. However, if rats were found to violate the substitution axiom, would that count as a refutation of expected utility theory? If rat markets failed to clear, would we abandon the efficient market hypothesis in finance?

More productive than the selective citing of supporting evidence by both sides would be the adoption of the research procedure recommended by the Dutch psychologist Willem Hofstee. Hofstee (1984) recommends that scientists engage in reputational bets. Suppose that X thinks that rational models predict well and that Y thinks otherwise. Then X and Y must stipulate an experiment or other empirical investigation on which they agree in advance to disagree about their predictions of the outcome of the experiment. Hofstee has developed an incentive compatible method for eliciting probabilistic forecasts from each scientist about the outcomes of the experiment. Once the bets are made, a third scientist is brought in to run the experiment, and the three publish the results. A new bureau would be necessary to keep track of each scientist's rating, as is done in chess. Perhaps a rule could be adopted that in order to maintain "grand master" status a bet has to be made every so often.

Economists and psychologists who genuinely made an effort to find some propositions to bet on might discover that there is less disagreement than was suspected. Perhaps economists do not really believe their models are descriptively accurate or psychologists do not believe their laboratory experiments would generalize to the market. Let us find out! My betting parlor in Ithaca is now open for business.

II. Positive Steps

Many of the results that have created the stimulation for this conference have been negative—counterexamples to the received theory. What positive steps can be taken? In many cases economic theory imposes restrictions on models by specifying variables that should not enter the analysis. For example, marginal analysis, the heart of microeconomic theory, specifies that only marginal costs and benefits should alter decisions. Historical or sunk costs should be irrelevant. Yet anyone who has tried to teach this concept knows that ignoring sunk costs does not come naturally to the uninitiated. Therefore it should not be surprising to discover that sunk costs often influence choices (Thaler 1980; Arkes and Blumer 1985). Positive theories of choice, then, will relax the restriction that sunk costs are irrelevant and will investigate the role they may play in actual decision making. The size of the first part of a two-part pricing scheme, for example, might affect utilization at the margin. (If I paid for it, I am going to use it!) The three papers presented in this session (Einhorn and Hogarth, in this volume; Simon, in this volume; and Tversky and Kahneman, in this volume) provide other examples of opportunities for improving the descriptive validity of economic theories by relaxing the restrictions.

Herb Simon has stressed for years the importance of cognitive limitations on human decision making. One example of the way his twin concepts of bounded rationality and "satisficing" can be used to enrich economic theory is to incorporate task complexity into descriptive models. Research has demonstrated that, as tasks become more complex, individuals adopt simplifying decision-making strategies (Payne 1976; Russo and Dosher 1983). Economic theorists usually leave task complexity out of their models by assuming that any decision-making problem, no matter how complex, will be solved optimally. Descriptive validity would be increased by assuming that the use of simplifying rules and heuristics (with their accompanying biases) will be used more often in complex situations (even when the stakes are high).

Einhorn and Hogarth (in this volume) suggest relaxing the assumption that perceived ambiguity is irrelevant to choice. Since ambiguity is aversive in many (though not all) situations, the inclusion of ambiguity in a model of individual decision making under uncertainty may help enrich models of insurance purchases (see, e.g., Hogarth and Kunreuther 1985).

Kahneman and Tversky's research has demonstrated repeatedly that even the most innocuous of assumptions, such as the invariance of choice to problem formulation, may need to be relaxed. Here the possibilities for enriching the economic model are endless. What are the comparative effects on consumption of a "temporary tax increase" compared to an equally large "temporary tax surcharge"? Can we be sure, without any empirical evidence, that the two are identical?

III. Two False Statements

I will end my remarks with the following two false statements.

1. Rational models are useless.
2. All behavior is rational.

I have offered these false statements because both sides in the debate that will be taking place at this conference and at similar conferences in the future have a tendency to misstate the other side's views. If everyone would agree that these statements are false, then no one would have to waste any time repudiating them.

References

Allais, Maurice. 1953. Le comportement de l'homme rationnel devant le risque: Critique des postulats et axiomes de l'Ecole Américane. *Econometrica* 21 (October): 503–46.

Arkes, H. R., and Blumer, C. 1985. The psychology of sunk cost. *Organizational Behavior and Human Decision Process* 35:124–40.

Einhorn, H., and Hogarth, R. 1978. Confidence in judgment: Persistence in the illusion of validity. *Psychological Review* 85, no. 5:395–416.

Einhorn, Hillel J., and Hogarth, Robin M. In this volume. Decision making under ambiguity.

Ellsberg, D. 1961. Risk, ambiguity, and the Savage axioms. *Quarterly Journal of Economics* 75 (November): 643–69.

Grether, D., and Plott, C. 1979. Economic theory and the preference reversal phenomenon. *American Economic Review* 69:623–38.

Hofstee, W. K. B. 1984. Methodological decision rules as research policies: A betting reconstruction of empirical research. *Acta Pscyologica* 56:93–109.

Hogarth, R., and Kunreuther, H. 1985. Risk, ambiguity and insurance. Working paper. Chicago: University of Chicago, Graduate School of Business, Center for Decision Research.

Kagel, J.; Rachlin, H.; Green, L.; Battalio, R. C.; Basmann, R. L.; and Klemm, W. R. 1975. Experimental studies of consumer demand using laboratory animals. *Economic Inquiry* 13 (March): 22–38.

Lichtenstein, S., and Slovic, P. 1971. Reversal of preferences between bids and choices in gambling decision. *Journal of Experimental Psychology* 89:46–55.

Payne, J. 1976. Task complexity and contingent processing in decision making: An informational search and protocol analysis. *Organizational Behavior and Human Performance* 26:366–87.

Russell, T., and Thaler, R. 1985. The relevance of quasi rationality and competitive markets. *American Economic Review* 75, no. 5 (December): 1071–82.

Russo, J. E., and Dosher, B. 1983. Strategies for multiattribute choice. *Journal of Experimental Psychology: Memory, Learning and Cognition* 9:676–696.

Simon, Herbert A. In this volume. Rationality in psychology and economics.

Stigler, G. J. 1977. The conference handbook. *Journal of Political Economy* 85, no. 2:441–43.

Thaler, R. 1980. Toward a positive theory of consumer choice. *Journal of Economic Behavior and Organziation* 1 (March): 39–60.

Tversky, Amos, and Kahneman, Daniel. In this volume. Rational choice and the framing of decisions.

Daniel Kahneman
University of California, Berkeley

Jack L. Knetsch
Simon Fraser University

Richard H. Thaler
Cornell University

Fairness and the Assumptions of Economics*

The advantages and disadvantages of expanding the standard economic model by more realistic behavioral assumptions have received much attention. The issue raised in this article is whether it is useful to complicate—or perhaps to enrich—the model of the profit-seeking firm by considering the preferences that people have for being treated fairly and for treating others fairly.

The absence of considerations of fairness and loyalty from standard economic theory is one of the most striking contrasts between this body of theory and other social sciences—and also between economic theory and lay intuitions about human behavior. Actions in many domains commonly conform to standards of decency that are more restrictive than the legal ones: the institutions of tipping and lost-and-found offices rest on expectations of such actions. Nevertheless, the standard microeconomic model of the profit-maximizing firm assigns essentially no role to

The traditional assumption that fairness is irrelevant to economic analysis is questioned. Even profit-maximizing firms will have an incentive to act in a manner that is perceived as fair if the individuals with whom they deal are willing to resist unfair transactions and punish unfair firms at some cost to themselves. Three experiments demonstrated that willingness to enforce fairness is common. Community standards for actions affecting customers, tenants, and employees were studied in telephone surveys. The rules of fairness, some of which are not obvious, help explain some anomalous market phenomena.

* The research for this paper was supported by the Department of Fisheries and Oceans Canada. Kahneman and Thaler were also supported, respectively, by the U.S. Office of Naval Research and by the Alfred P. Sloan Foundation. Conversations with J. Brander, R. Frank, and A. Tversky were very helpful. We also thank Leslie McPherson and Daniel Treisman for their assistance. The paper presented at the conference and commented on by the discussants included a detailed report of study 3, which is only summarized here. It did not contain study 1, which was incomplete at the time. Daniel Kahneman is now in the Department of Psychology, University of California, Berkeley 94720.

generosity and social conscience or even to good will or indignation. The economic agent is assumed to be law-abiding but not "fair"—if fairness implies that some legal opportunities for gain are not exploited. This nonfairness assumption expresses a resistance to explanations of economic actions in moral terms that has deep roots in the history of the discipline. The central insight that gave rise to modern economics is that the common good is well served by the free actions of self-interested agents in a market.

Like the assumption of rationality, the assumption of nonfairness could take several forms, which may be ordered from "pure as-if" to "true believer." The as-if position is methodological rather than substantive. It assigns the entire burden of proof to anyone who would complicate the basic model and accepts as grounds for its revision only improved predictions of economic variables, not direct tests of its assumptions. A moderate true-believer position would be that the economic arena, like a boxing ring or a poker game, is an environment in which many of the rules that govern other human interactions are suspended. In the extreme true-believer position any appearance of concern for values of fairness or for the welfare of strangers is interpreted in terms of self-interest and strategic behavior.

Although not logically required for the pursuit of standard economic analyses, true belief in nonfairness appears to be common among economists. It is often viewed as an embarrassment to the basic theory that people vote, do not always free ride, and commonly allocate resources equitably to others and to themselves when they are free to do otherwise. There is a clear preference for treating apparent indications of fairness (or of irrationality) as isolated phenomena of little economic significance.

In opposition to the dominant trend several economists have invoked a notion of fairness in their interpretations of regulation (Zajac 1978, in press) and of the market phenomena of price and wage stickiness (Hirschman 1970; Arrow 1973; Akerlof 1979, 1982; Solow 1980). Arthur Okun (1981) offered a notably detailed account of the demands of customers and employees for fair treatment and of the role of perceived unfairness in triggering a search for alternative suppliers. Okun made a strong case that many customer markets resemble labor markets more than they do pure auction models. Like labor markets, customer markets sometimes fail to clear, an observation that Okun explained by the hostility of customers to price increases that are not justified by increased costs.

The opposition to price rationing as a response to a shortage is easily documented. An example is provided by the following question, which was put to 191 adult residents of the Vancouver metropolitan region as part of a telephone survey.

A football team normally sells some tickets on the day of their games. Recently, interest in the next game has increased greatly, and tickets are in great demand. The team owners can distribute the tickets in one of three ways. (1) By auction: the tickets are sold to the highest bidders. (2) By lottery: the tickets are sold to the people whose names are drawn. (3) By queue: the tickets are sold on a first-come first-served basis. Rank these three in terms of which you feel is the most fair and which is the least fair—the auction, the lottery, and the queue.

The results for this question are given in table 1.

In terms of economic efficiency, the three procedures are ranked from the auction, which would allocate the good to the customers willing to pay the most for it, down to the wasteful method of queueing. The inverse ordering obtains when the allocation procedures are ranked by their fairness.

In what ways could community standards of fairness deter firms from exploiting excess demand? A radical possibility, which corresponds to lay beliefs (Kahneman, Knetsch, and Thaler, in press), is that there is a significant incidence of cases in which firms, like individuals, are motivated by concerns of fairness. The characteristic of these cases is that the firm behaves "fairly" in the absence of inducements such as the promise of future custom or the threat of regulation. An important example that appears to satisfy this criterion was documented by Olmstead and Rhode (1985) in their analysis of the behavior of a dominant supplier during the West Coast oil famine of 1920.

A less radical position is that actions that the public will perceive as unfair are deterred by the resistance of potential transactors. This resistance will be most effective if it is backed up by a willingness on the part of customers and employees to pay some cost to avoid unfair transactions and unfair firms. There are indications that such a willingness may exist.

The following pair of questions, reported in Thaler (1985), was administered to two groups of participants in an executive education program. One group received the version including the passages in brackets, while the other received the passages in parentheses.

You are lying on the beach on a hot day. All you have to drink is ice water. For the past hour you have been thinking about how much you would enjoy a nice cold bottle of your favorite brand of beer. A companion gets up to go make a phone call and offers to bring back a beer from the only nearby place where beer is sold, [a fancy resort hotel] (a run-down grocery store). He says that the beer might be expensive and so asks how much you would be willing to pay for the beer. He says he will buy the beer if it costs as much or less than the price you state, but if it costs more than the price you state he will

TABLE 1   Ranking of Allocation Methods

Allocation Method	Most Fair (%)	Least Fair (%)
Auction	4	75
Lottery	28	18
Queue	68	7

not buy it. You trust your friend, and there is no chance of bargaining with the [bartender] (store owner). What price do you state?

The median response for the fancy-hotel version was $2.65, while the median response for the grocery-store version was $1.50. Evidently, people are willing to pay different amounts for a beer to be consumed on the beach, depending on where it was purchased. Put another way, people would refuse to buy a beer from the grocery store at a price less than their reservation price rather than pay what they consider to be an excessive amount. Note that, because different prices are considered appropriate for the grocery and for the hotel, the two establishments face different demands for a physically identical good to be consumed under identical circumstances.

These introductory considerations lead to several questions. How prevalent is "fair" behavior in the absence of enforcement? Does resistance to unfair treatment occur in real as well as in hypothetical problems? Do people only resist unfair transactions in which they are directly involved, or are they willing to incur costs to punish unfair actors? What are the specific rules of fairness that apply to firms in their transactions? Could the inclusion of considerations of fairness improve the understanding of significant economic facts? We will now review three studies that dealt with these questions.

The first study includes three experiments that are concerned with the enforcement of fairness. The second study uses a survey of public opinion to investigate whether the public considers cost-plus markup the rule of fair pricing. The third study, which is only summarized here (Kahneman et al., in press), consists of an extensive survey of rules of fairness that the public would apply to retailers, employers, and landlords.

Study 1: Resisting Unfairness

The behavior that we label resistance to unfairness was recently observed in experiments by Guth, Schmittberger, and Schwarz (1982) and by Binmore, Shaked, and Sutton (1985). The first of these experiments introduced the following ultimatum game. One player, A (allocator), is asked to propose a division of a sum of money, X, between himself or herself and an anonymous player, R (recipient). Player R may either accept A's proposal or reject it, in which case both players receive nothing. The game-theoretic solution to this problem is that A should offer R a token payment and that R should accept any positive offer. The results were not consistent with this presumption. Most allocators offered more than a token payment, and many offered an equal split. Also, some positive offers were declined by recipients, indicating a resistance to unfair allocations and a willingness to pay to avoid them. Guth et al. were not able to report much about this behavior because most offers in their experiment were obviously fair and occasions for resistance correspondingly rare. Experiment 1 was designed to elicit a response to unfair proposals from all participants.

The experiment was conducted in a psychology class and in a commerce (business administration) class at the University of British Columbia. Each participant was given a sheet that included instructions and a response form. An example of the instructions for the first part of the experiment is given below.

> In this experiment you are matched at random with a student in the class—call him or her X. You will not get to know who X is. A sum of $10 has been provisionally allocated to the two of you. Because our budget does not permit us to pay everybody, 20 pairs of students will be chosen in a random draw and will be paid according to their responses. In responding to this questionnaire you should assume that you will be among those who are paid. X will propose a division of the $10 between the two of you, by selecting one of the options listed below. You must decide now which options are acceptable to you and which, if any, are unacceptable. If the option actually proposed by X is one that you marked acceptable, the $10 will be paid out accordingly. If the option that X proposes is unacceptable to you, neither of you gets anything. To make sure you understand the rules, please answer the following two questions before continuing. (1) If X allocates you $3.00 and you marked that value acceptable, you get $_____, and X gets $_____. (2) If X allocates you $3.00 and you marked that value unacceptable, you get $_____, and X gets $_____.

The possible allocations ranged from $9.50 to X and $0.50 to the recipient to an even split of $5.00 each, in steps of $0.50. The participants were instructed to designate each offer as acceptable or unacceptable. Half the students in the psychology class were informed that they would be paired with an unknown undergraduate student in a commerce class. All the participants in the commerce class were informed that they would be paired with a psychology student.

After completing the first task the participants turned to the next page, which instructed them to allocate $10.00 to themselves or to "a student, Z (*not* the one whom we called X)." The rules were the same as they were for the first part. The answers to the second question were used to determine the payoffs as indicated. The verbal instructions to the subjects promised that all payoffs would be in sealed envelopes to protect their privacy. The main results are shown in table 2.

Contrary to the game-theoretic prediction but in accordance with other experimental observations the actual allocations were quite generous (Selten 1978; Guth et al. 1982; Hoffman and Spitzer 1982; but see also Binmore et al. 1985; Hoffman and Spitzer 1985).

Of greater interest here is the observation that a substantial proportion of participants were willing to reject positive offers. The results do not indicate whether these individuals were motivated by a reluctance to participate in an unfair transaction, or by a wish to punish an unfair allocator, or perhaps by both. In either case the resistance to unfairness exhibited in this experiment is of the type that might deter a profit-maximizing agent or firm from seeking to exploit some profit opportunities. A widespread readiness to resist unfair transactions or to punish unfair actors even at some cost could present a significant threat to firms in competitive environments.

Experiment 2 was designed to obtain an indication of the prevalence of unenforced fairness in anonymous transactions and to establish whether people are willing to incur a cost to reward fairness and to punish unfairness when the fair or unfair actions were directed at someone else. Subjects in this experiment were students in an undergraduate psychology class at Cornell University. In the first part of the experiment subjects were instructed to divide $20 with an anonymous student in the same class, with no possibility of rejection by the recipient. The allocation was made by choosing between two possibilities: $18 to self and $2.00 to the other, or $10 to each. The participants were informed that eight pairs (selected at random from 161 students) would actually be paid according to their responses. Precautions were taken to ensure the privacy of payoffs.

The second part of the experiment, introduced after the first was completed, is explained in the following instructions.

This part of the experiment will be limited to those members of the class who were not selected to be paid in the first part. You will be matched at random with two other students, and you will get to share some money with one or both of them. If the two people made different decisions in the first stage (e.g., one of them took $10 and one took $18), then you must make a decision about how to allocate the money. Call the person who took $10 and gave the other one $10 student E (for even). Call the person who took $18 and gave the other one $2.00 student U (for uneven). Your choices are as follows: you may allocate $5.00 to yourself, $5.00 to student E, and nothing to student U; or you may allocate $6.00 to yourself, nothing to student E, and $6.00 to student U. If both the students with whom you are grouped made the same decision, then you will receive

TABLE 2   Experiment 1 Results

	Class		
	Psychology/ Psychology	Psychology/ Commerce	Commerce/ Psychology
Mean amount offered ($)	4.76	4.47	4.21
Equal split offers (%)	81	78	63
Mean of minimum acceptable ($)	2.59	2.24	2.00
Demands > $1.50 (%)	58	59	51
Participants (N)	43	37	35

NOTE.—Data presented are by subsample; the results do not include 22 subjects whose answers to the test questions indicated a misunderstanding of the instructions.

$6.00, and each of them will receive $3.00. For this stage 15 groups of students will actually be paid.

The results of the first part of the experiment show that fair allocations are observed even under conditions of complete anonymity and with no possibility of retaliation. Of the 161 students, 122 (76%) divided the $20 evenly. This is stronger evidence for the prevalence of fairness to strangers than was obtained in experiment 1. A fair allocation in an ultimatum game could be explained by the allocator's fear, often justified, that the recipient might reject a small positive offer.

The second stage of the experiment was designed to see whether the subjects would pay $1.00 to punish an unfair allocator and simultaneously reward a fair one. A clear majority (74%) made that choice, indicating a preference to divide $10 evenly with a fair allocator rather than divide $12 with an unfair allocator. Not surprisingly, there was a substantial correlation between the choices made in the two stages. Of 122 subjects who took $10 in the first stage, 107 (88%) preferred to share with student E in the second stage. In contrast, of the 39 subjects who took $18, only 12 (31%) shared with student E.

A class in the Cornell School of Industrial and Labor Relations was used for experiment 3, in which only the second part of experiment 2 was administered. The subjects were told (truthfully) that they would be matched with members of another class that had participated in part 1 of the experiment but had not been selected to be paid. Unlike the previous experiments, all the participants in experiment 3 were paid in accordance with their expressed preferences. These procedural differences did not affect the willingness to pay for justice: 26 of the 32 subjects (81%) preferred to share $10 with a fair allocator rather than share $12 with an unfair one.

Two hypotheses that were mentioned in the introduction could explain why firms might sometimes fail to exploit legal but "unfair" profit opportunities. The radical hypothesis is that the owners and managers of firms have a preference for acting fairly. The alternative hypothesis is that transactors may be willing to punish an offending firm by with-holding their current and future business. The results of these experiments provide clear evidence for the willingness to punish invoked in the second hypothesis. The prevalence of unenforced fairness in experiment 2 and in others reported in the literature lends some credence to the more radical possibility as well.

Study 2: Cost Plus Is Not the Rule of Fair Pricing

The second study was motivated by a hypothesis that turned out to be wrong: that the community standard for fair pricing is that the prices of goods should be determined by adding a markup to unit costs. The hypothesis had some initial support in the observation of cost-plus pricing as a routine procedure in firms (Cyert and March 1963). Okun (1981, p. 153) noted that "many supplying firms present themselves to their customers as procurement agencies operating under a brokerage arrangement" in which "the broker receives a specified fraction of the total value of the transaction."

The critical test for the fairness hypothesis of cost-plus pricing arises when the supplier's costs decrease. Consider the simple example of a monopolist who sells a fixed supply of a particular kind of table for $150 each and now realizes a $20 reduction in costs for each table. By a cost-plus rule with constant profit per unit the supplier should lower the price of each table by $20. By brokerage rules with proportional markup the price should be reduced by more than $20. To test whether cost plus is the rule of fair pricing this basic scenario of a supplier facing decreased costs was presented to respondents in a telephone survey.

Additional hypotheses considered possible qualifications to a general cost-plus rule of pricing, which would link the notion of fair profit to the nature of the value added by the firm or to the source of the opportunity for increased profit. Specifically, the predictions were (1) that the cost-plus rule might apply strictly only to middlemen, not to producers, and (2) that the cost-plus rule might apply only to savings due to reduced input costs but not to savings achieved by increasing efficiency. The instructive result of the study was that all these hypotheses were either completely or partially contradicted by the data.

The surveys were included in telephone interviews with adult residents in the Toronto metropolitan area. One of eight different versions of the basic questionnaire was presented to each respondent. One of these versions is presented below in full.

My first questions are about the behavior of people in business. Suppose a factory produces a particular table, which it sells to wholesalers. The factory has been selling all the tables it can produce for $150 each. Suppose that the factory has now found a supplier who charges $20 less for the materials needed to make each table. Does fairness require the factory to change its price from $150? [Respondents who answered "yes" were now asked, "What is a fair price that it could charge the wholesalers?"] [All respondents were then asked the following question.] Imagine instead that the factory saved $20 on each table not by getting less expensive supplies but by inventing a more efficient way of making the tables. Does fairness require the factory to change its price from $150 in this case? [Continued as above.]

Different groups of respondents were asked these questions about four kinds of firms: a factory, as in the example above; "a carpenter works alone in his workshop to make tables, which he sells directly to individual customers"; "a wholesaler is the only one that distributes a particular kind of table"; and "a furniture store is the only one that sells a particular kind of table." Four other versions were generated by asking the same two questions in the opposite order. A total of 975 responses were obtained, divided about equally among the eight versions. Table 3 shows the main results for the first question asked in each version.

The main hypothesis of this study is unequivocally rejected. Even in the cases that are the most favorable to a cost-plus pricing rule (a wholesaler or retailer facing reduced input costs) only about one-third of the respondents applied that rule in designating a fair price. Half the respondents stated that fairness does not require the firm to pass on any part of its savings. The standards of fairness that respondents applied were far more favorable to firms than was suggested by the cost-plus rule.

The other two hypotheses concerning the determinants of fair pricing fared no better. Although the carpenter working alone was favored significantly more than other firms, this effect appears due to the size of the firm rather than to its role as producer. The results for the furniture factory lend no support to the general hypothesis that a producer can fairly retain a larger share of an incremental profit than can a middleman.

Finally, the prediction concerning the source of the profit increment also finds no support in table 3. The notion of a brokerage agreement suggested that it might be fair for a supplier to retain a profit increment that it obtains by increasing efficiency, although a similar increment due to decreased input costs should be passed on to customers. Contrary to this hypothesis, the proportion allowing the firm to maintain its price appeared to be slightly higher in the case of cheaper supplies than in the case of increased efficiency.

The results reported so far were all derived from comparisons between the responses to the first of the two questions that each respon-

TABLE 3   Results of Cost-plus Questions

| | Seller | | | |
Source of Savings	Store	Wholesaler	Carpenter	Factory
Cheaper supply:				
Cost-plus responses				
($130 or less) (%)	34	31	19	20
No-price-change-required				
responses (%)	47	51	63	48
Means of fair prices ($)	141.11	142.32	144.12	142.97
Increased efficiency:				
Cost-plus responses				
($130 or less) (%)	31	23	13	40
No-price-change-required				
responses (%)	39	46	60	35
Means of fair prices ($)	141.73	142.19	145.54	140.15

dent answered. The effect of the source of the profit increment could also be tested in a second way because each respondent was asked to evaluate the two possibilities in immediate succession. The conclusion of this within-individual analysis is rather different from the conclusion reached by comparing the responses of different samples. Most respondents (67%) stated the same fair price for an efficiency gain and for a reduction of input costs. Among those who distinguished between the two cases, however, a majority (62% overall) stated a lower fair price in the case of a cost reduction than in the case of an efficiency gain. This result confirms the original hypothesis and is highly reliable ($p <$ .001 by chi square test for correlated proportions).

The difference between these results and those of table 3 could reflect the higher statistical power of within-individual comparisons. It may also reflect a more interesting distinction between levels of strength for factors or rules of fairness. We define a weak factor (or rule) as one that affects evaluations of contrasting cases only when these cases are judged in relation to each other, as is likely to happen with successive questions. The effects of stronger factors can be demonstrated without the benefit of such implicit comparisons. No comparison is required, for example, to evoke different evaluations of a hardware store that raises the price of snow shovels in a blizzard and of one that does not.

A determinant or rule of fairness can be both weak and clear. For an example from another domain consider two prizes: (1) a week in Paris and (2) a week in Paris and $1.00 in cash. Separate evaluations of the attractiveness of these prizes would surely be indistinguishable, although everyone will prefer the second to the first in a direct choice.

In these terms, the distinction between cost reduction and efficiency gains was shown by the within-respondent comparisons to have some validity as a rule of fairness. The rule was not clear, however, as the agreement between respondents was far from perfect. The between-respondent design showed it to have little or no strength. The proposed cost-plus rule failed a test of strength because respondents did not generally apply it to set a fair price in a particular case considered in isolation. It remains possible that respondents might follow a cost-plus rule if asked to consider together the appropriate price response to increases and to reductions of costs. The rule is at best weak, then, but it could still be valid and even clear. A rule that is weak by the present definition can be of much theoretical interest. When the task is to predict which actions of firms will be generally rejected as unfair, however, it is reasonable to start with the strongest rather than with the clearest rules.

The present analysis suggests a caution to theorists not to rely on the clarity of their own intuitions to estimate the strength of fairness rules. Any systematic speculation about rules of fairness inevitably involves explicit comparisons of contrasting cases. Intuitions derived from such comparisons may prove a poor guide to the relative importance of different factors in a between-respondent design. The methodological conclusions of this discussion are (1) that theoretical speculation about rules of fairness is not a substitute for observation of community standards and (2) that between-respondent comparisons are necessary to measure the strength of rules rather than their clarity. These considerations led us to adopt a between-respondent design in subsequent surveys of rules of fairness.

Study 3: Rules of Fairness

The failure of the cost-plus hypothesis in study 2 prompted a more extensive study of community standards of fairness for firms, which is described in detail elsewhere (Kahneman et al., in press). Telephone surveys were conducted in the Vancouver and Toronto metropolitan areas, using a broader range of examples and a different question format than those used in study 2. Most questions required the respondents to evaluate the fairness of an action in which a firm sets a price, rent, or wage that affects the outcomes of a transactor (customer, tenant, or employee) and deviates from a relevant precedent (the reference transaction). The following examples illustrate the method.

A landlord owns and rents out a single small house to a tenant who is living on a fixed income. A higher rent would mean the tenant would have to move. Other small rental houses are available. The landlord's costs have increased substantially over the past year, and the landlord raises the rent to cover the cost increases when the tenant's lease is due for renewal.

A small photocopying shop has one employee who has worked in the shop for 6 months and earns $9.00 per hour. Business continues to be satisfactory, but a factory in the area has closed, and unemployment has increased. Other small shops have now hired reliable workers at $7.00 per hour to perform jobs similar to those done by the photocopy-shop employee. The owner of the photocopying shop reduces the employee's wage to $7.00.

The results of these examples are shown in table 4.

The examples illustrate two of the general rules that were found to govern fairness judgments in the surveys. (1) It is unfair for a firm to exploit an increase in its market power to alter the terms of the reference transaction at the direct expense of a customer, tenant, or employee. (2) It is acceptable for a firm to maintain its profit at the reference level by raising prices or rents or by cutting wages as necessary.

The rule against adjusting prices to changed market conditions implies that it is unfair for a firm to exploit excess supply of labor to cut the wages of its employees. In the context of consumer markets and rental housing the same rule implies that an increase in demand unaccompanied by an increase in costs is not an acceptable reason to raise prices or rents. The opposition to exploitation of market power also entails strong rejection of excessive monopoly gains (see also Zajac in press) and of price discrimination. The introduction of auctions as an instrument of rationing is also opposed: most respondents think, for example, that if a single Cabbage Patch doll is discovered in a storeroom, it would be quite unfair for the store to auction it to the highest bidder. The spirit of this rule is well expressed in Okun's sardonic remark (1981, p. 153): "No price announcement has ever explained to customers that the supplier has moved to a new position to capture a larger share of the surplus in the relation as a result of a stronger market."

An interpretation of the hostility of respondents to exploitations of excess demand is that transactors (customers, tenants, and employees) are considered to have an entitlement to the terms of the reference transaction, which cannot be violated arbitrarily by firms to increase their profits (Bazerman 1985; Zajac, in press). The other side of the coin is that the public considers the firm entitled to its reference profit. In a conflict between the transactor's claim to the reference price (or wage) and the firm's claim to its reference profit, it is acceptable for the firm to impose its claim rather than compromise. As illustrated by the tenant example, respondents agreed that a firm may protect its profit by passing on a cost increase in its entirety, even when doing so causes considerable loss or inconvenience.

There is a notable asymmetry between the rules of fairness that apply when circumstances increase or decrease the profits of a firm. The rules of fairness evidently permit firms to pass on the entire

TABLE 4   Responses to Illustrative Survey Questions

Landlord Example	%	Photocopying Shop Example	%
Completely fair	39	Completely fair	4
Acceptable	36	Acceptable	13
Somewhat unfair	18	Somewhat unfair	34
Very unfair	7	Very unfair	49

amount of a cost increase, but, as was shown in study 2 and further confirmed in study 3, firms are allowed to retain most of the benefits of a cost reduction.

Fairness and Framing

The concepts that economists use in their analyses of transactions are not always apt for a descriptive treatment of individual choice or of fairness judgments. A descriptive treatment must sometimes ignore distinctions that are normatively essential or introduce distinctions that are normatively irrelevant. In particular, a descriptive analysis requires that the outcomes of participants in a transaction should be defined as changes relative to a reference state rather than in absolute and objective terms (Kahneman and Tversky 1979). The determination of the reference level in a choice is subject to framing effects, which can yield inconsistent preferences for the same objective consequences (Tversky and Kahneman, in this volume). Similarly, judgments of fairness cannot be understood without considering the factors that determine the selection of a reference transaction.

Reference transactions are often tied to a particular good. For example, most respondents believe that it is unfair for a store to mark up the jars of peanut butter in its stock when wholesale prices rise, apparently because they associate the cost to the individual jar. The reference transaction may also reflect the history of relations between the firm and a particular individual: different rules apply to a current employee or tenant and to their potential replacements.

The notion of a reference state defines the gains and losses of participants in a way that violates the logic of economic analysis. Consider, for example, the contrasting rules that govern what a firm may fairly do when its reference profit is threatened or when its market power increases. In an economic analysis a firm that does not exploit its market power incurs an opportunity cost, which is considered equivalent to a decreased profit. This is the case, for example, when an employer pays an employee more than the replacement wage. Community standards of fairness—at least as indicated by the Canadian respondents surveyed—require employers and landlords to absorb such opportunity costs, just as they require hardware stores to maintain their price for snow shovels after a spring blizzard. On the other hand, fairness rules allow firms complete recovery of actual cost increases without any requirement to share the pain. A theory that assumes the equivalence of opportunity costs and out-of-pocket losses cannot do justice to these strong intuitions.

A number of economic phenomena can be predicted on the assumption that the rules of fairness have some influence on the behavior of firms (Kahneman et al., in press). The rules of fairness tend to induce stickiness in wages and asymmetric price rigidities. They also favor a much greater use of temporary discounts than of temporary surcharges in price adjustments. Where costs for a category of goods are similar, opposition to price rationing may lead to sellouts for the most desirable items (e.g., the main game on the football calendar or the Christmas week in a ski resort). There is some evidence for all these predictions, which represent anomalies in the standard model.

Discussion

The most striking aspect of the basic microeconomic model, and the one that distinguishes it most sharply from other social sciences, is its conceptual parsimony. The behavior of economic agents is attributed to a well-defined objective—for firms it is the maximization of profits—that is pursued with complete rationality within legal and budgetary constraints. The idea that maximizing agents, all endowed with complete information, interact in a Walrasian auction is used to obtain predictions of market outcomes from a minimal set of assumptions about individual participants. The model of the agents is so simple that their decisions become predictable from an objective description of the environment.

There is a similarity in the programs of economics and classical stimulus-response behaviorism: both approaches seek to predict behavior from a specification of its circumstances. The environment considered in elementary microeconomics is quite simple. It can be completely described in terms of specific opportunities to maximize the objective function, and it is assumed that all such opportunities are exploited.

There are two ways of enriching this basic model. They differ in their cost and in the resistance that they may arouse among many economists. An uncontroversial move is to adopt a more complex view of the environment and of the interactions among transacting agents. Many subtleties become evident when the assumption of perfect information is dropped, allowing ignorance and risk, and when the costs of searching and transacting are considered. Much current research in economics is in this vein.

A more controversial move is to complicate the model of the agent. This can be done by allowing market behavior to be affected by added motives besides buying cheap and selling dear or by abandoning the standard assumption of rational expectations. There are at least two good reasons to resist such moves. First, adding complexity to the model of the agent generally makes it more difficult to derive unequivocal predictions of behavior from a specification of the environment. Second, there is a threat of a slippery slope. It appears all too easy to lengthen the lists of noneconomic motives or cognitive errors that might affect economic behavior.

In spite of these cautions it is sometimes useful to enrich the model of economic agents by explicitly introducing a behavioral factor that is ignored in the standard theory. Such an effort is ultimately tested by whether it helps to resolve recognized anomalies and to identify new ones. Parsimony requires that a new behavioral assumption should be introduced only if it specifies conditions under which observations deviate significantly from the basic model and only if it predicts the direction of these deviations.

Norms of fairness may satisfy this test of usefulness if, as some evidence suggests, they have a significant effect on market phenomena. A conservative revision of the standard theory will retain the model of the profit-maximizing firm and alter only the model of the transactors with which the firm must deal by endowing them with explicit rules for the judgment of fairness and with a willingness to reject unfair transactions and to discriminate against unfair firms. These characteristics of transactors affect the environment in which profit-maximizing firms operate and alter the behavior of these firms in predictable ways. A more radical revision of the standard model would incorporate a preference for fairness in the objective function of at least some firms.

The contribution of the present study has been to identify some of the criteria that people use in their fairness judgments and to demonstrate the willingness of people to enforce fairness at some cost to themselves. A realistic description of transactors should include the following traits. (1) They care about being treated fairly and treating others fairly. (2) They are willing to resist unfair firms even at a positive cost. (3) They have systematic implicit rules that specify which actions of firms are considered unfair. Further, fairness rules are not describable by the standard economic model or by a simple cost-plus rule of thumb. Instead, judgments of fairness are influenced by framing and other factors considered irrelevant in most economic treatments. By incorporating these traits into an enriched model of customers, tenants, and employees, better predictions about the behavior of the firms with which they deal may be obtained.

Perhaps the most important lesson learned from these studies is that the rules of fairness cannot be inferred either from conventional economic principles or from intuition and introspection. In the words of

Sherlock Holmes in "The Adventure of the Copper Beeches": "Data! Data! Data! I cannot make bricks without clay."

References

Akerlof, G. 1979. The case against conservative macroeconomics: An inaugural lecture. *Economica* 46 (August): 219–37.

Akerlof, G. 1982. Labor contracts as partial gift exchange. *Quarterly Journal of Economics* 97 (November): 543–69.

Arrow, K. 1973. Social responsibility and economic efficiency. *Public Policy* 21 (Summer): 303–17.

Bazerman, M. H. 1985. Norms of distributive justice in interest arbitration. *Industrial and Labor Relations* 38 (July): 558–70.

Binmore, K.; Shaked, A.; and Sutton, J. 1985. Testing noncooperative bargaining theory: A preliminary study. *American Economic Review* 75 (December): 1178–80.

Cyert, R. M., and March, J. G. 1963. *A Behavioral Theory of the Firm*. Englewood Cliffs, N.J.: Prentice-Hall.

Guth, W.; Schmittberger, R.; and Schwarz, B. 1982. An experimental analysis of ultimatum bargaining. *Journal of Economic Behavior and Organization* 3:367–88.

Hirschman, A. L. 1970. *Exit, Voice and Loyalty*. Cambridge, Mass.: Harvard University Press.

Hoffman, E., and Spitzer, M. L. 1982. The Coase theorem: Some experimental tests. *Journal of Law and Economics* 25:73–98.

Hoffman, E., and Spitzer, M. L. 1985. Entitlements, rights, and fairness: An experimental examination of subjects' concepts of distributive justice. *Journal of Legal Studies* 14, no. 2:259–97.

Kahneman, D.; Knetsch, J. L.; and Thaler, R. H. In press. Fairness as a constraint on profit seeking: Entitlements in the market. *American Economic Review*.

Kahneman, D., and Tversky, A. 1979. Prospect theory: An analysis of choice under risk. *Econometrica* 47 (March): 263–91.

Okun, A. 1981. *Prices and Quantities: A Macroeconomic Analysis*. Washington, D.C.: Brookings Institution.

Olmstead, A. L., and Rhode, P. 1985. Rationing without government: The West Coast gas famine of 1920. *American Economic Review* 15 (December): 1044–55.

Selten, R. 1978. The equity principle in economic behavior. In Hans W. Gottinger and Werner Leinfellner (eds.), *Decision Theory and Social Ethics: Issues in Social Choice*. Dordrecht: Reidel.

Solow, R. M. 1980. On theories of unemployment. *American Economic Review* 70:1–11.

Thaler, R. H. 1985. Mental accounting and consumer choice. *Marketing Science* 4:199–214.

Tversky, A., and Kahneman, D. In this volume. Rational choice and the framing of decisions.

Zajac, E. E. 1978. *Fairness or Efficiency: An Introduction to Public Utility Pricing*. Cambridge, Mass.: Ballinger.

Zajac, E. E. In press. Perceived economic justice: The example of public utility regulation. In H. Peyton Young (ed.), *Cost Allocation: Methods, Principles and Applications*. Amsterdam: North-Holland.

Charles R. Plott
California Institute of Technology

Rational Choice in Experimental Markets*

The theory of rational individual choice has many different uses in experimental economics. The uses must be considered in any realistic evaluation of the theory. This paper is organized around that perspective.

If the only question posed is, Rational choice, true or false? then the answer is clearly false. Many critics of economics have claimed that the discipline is built on untestable foundations. Economists are indebted to psychologists for debunking such critics and demonstrating that the theory can indeed be tested. However, the gratitude can go only so far. During the process of demonstrating testability, the psychologists disconfirmed the theory. Preference transitivity experiments (Tversky 1969) and preference reversal experiments (Grether and Plott 1979) both demonstrate that the weakest forms of the classical preference hypothesis[1] are systematically at odds with facts.

The theory of rational behavior has several different uses. First, it is used at the most fundamental level of experimental methodology to induce preferences used as parameters in models. Second, it appears repeatedly in experimentally successful mathematical models of complex phenomena such as speculation, bidding, and signaling. Third, it is used as a tool to generate ex post models of results that are otherwise inexplicable. Finally, it has been used as a tool successfully to design new institutions to solve specific problems. When tested directly, the theory can be rejected. It is retained because neither an alternative theory nor an alternative general principle accomplishes so much.

* Financial support from the National Science Foundation and from the Caltech Program of Enterprise and Public Policy is gratefully acknowledged. I wish to thank Kemal Guler for his help in processing the data used in Sec. III. I also wish to thank Barry Weingast and Harvey Reed for their collaboration on the ideas and background data processing that form that section.

1. The classical hypothesis is taken to be that attitudes of preference can be represented by total, reflexive, negatively acyclic binary relations. For generalizations and alternatives to this hypothesis, see Aizerman (1985).

It follows that theories of markets for which rational individual choice is a necessary component are either discomfirmed by the same evidence or cannot be applied because the preconditions for application are not present. The logic is compelling, and an awareness of its existence has colored how experimental economists pose questions, how they do experiments, and what they conclude. If one wants only to "test" a theory in the sense of rejection, then one should examine its most suspect predictions. If, as part of its formulation of market behavior, a theory predicts acyclic individual choice behavior—as is the case with almost all economics models—then one seeking a disconfirmation of the theory knows exactly where to look and how to proceed. Existing experiments on individual choice behavior provide ample machinery.

The rejection of a theory of markets on the terms described above is not an especially challenging research objective. Those who study experimental markets tend to pose the questions in different ways. Rather than inquire whether a theory is true or false, they ask if the magnitude of error in the predictions of market phenomena is acceptable; or, if no concept of degree of acceptability is readily available, the question becomes which of several competing models is the most accurate, fully realizing that the best model might still be "poor." When confronted with data that suggest the existence of erratic or irrational individual behavior, the implications are immediately evaluated in terms of the possible implications for a market level of analysis. Of course, when unusual market behavior is observed, one might then turn to models of irrational individual behavior to see if they contain the seeds of an explanation.

In brief it is almost impossible to assess the importance of any problem with rationality postulates as found in experimental market studies without assessing the performance of the market models based on such postulates. In Section I, I will discuss hypotheses about rational behavior that are built directly into the foundations of laboratory market procedures. In Section II, three examples of laboratory experiments will be discussed. The accuracy of the models and the rationality postulates that form the structure of the models will be covered. Section III will demonstrate how ideas of rationality can be used to explain otherwise very confusing market behavior. Section IV will examine unusual phenomena that models of rational behavior suggest might exist, and Section V will discuss some pending problems for concepts of rationality as they are currently used.

I. Laboratory Market Procedures and Rationality

For the most part, laboratory markets are created as a challenge to theory. One research objective is to construct simple markets that are special cases of the complicated phenomena to which the models are ordinarily applied. The relative accuracies of models are assessed. The models are changed in light of the data from the special case. It is hoped, as a result, that the revised models will be more useful when applied to the complex. While other research strategies can be identified (Plott 1982, esp. pp. 1519–23), this particular strategy is frequently used.

The above objective demands that laboratory economics procedures permit some reasonably direct correspondence between parameters of models and what is controlled in an experiment. The important variables of almost all economic models are preferences (as opposed to sources of motivation), beliefs, resources, market organization (institutions), technology, commodities, prices, allocations, and incomes. If a model is to be evaluated, all these variables need to be observed and sometimes controlled. If a variable cannot be observed directly, then it is always suspected of having gone awry when the model itself does not fit the data. Of course, in this context, the preferences and beliefs are key because (*a*) they can be used to explain almost any pattern of the other variables (Ledyard, in press) and (*b*) they cannot be observed directly.

Laboratory techniques control preferences or, in a sense, allow them to be observed indirectly. The basic insight is that preferences are parameters to economic models, but the source of preferences is not a parameter. The key idea is to use monetary incentives to induce preferences for abstract commodities that exist only for the purpose of the experiment. Consider the following axioms, which are a combination of the precepts used by Smith (1976) and the axioms used by Plott (1979). If the following axioms are accepted, then preferences can be induced and controlled for purposes of experimentation.

1. More reward medium (money) is preferred to less, other things being equal (salience and nonsatiation).

2. Individuals place no independent value on experimental outcomes other than that provided by the reward medium (neutrality).

3. Individuals optimize.

Suppose, for example, that a commodity is the set of nonnegative integers, which are called units of the commodity X. Another commodity, Y, is simply U.S. currency. An individual, i, is assigned a function, $R^i(x)$, indicating the reward (dollar amount) he will receive from the experimenter should he acquire x units of the commodity. If postulates 1–3 are satisfied, then we can take as a parameter in a model, defined over $X \cdot Y$ where the operation $\cdot$ is a Cartesian product, the binary relation P_i, defined by $(x, y)P^i(x', y') \Leftrightarrow R^i(x) + y > R^i(x') + y'$. The relation P_i is the preference relation of i. If the axioms are satisfied, then P_i is in fact the individual's preference relation in the same sense that it will reflect actual individual choices from the pairs in $X \cdot Y$. Since the experimenter controls the functional form of $R^i(\cdot)$, the preference relation of each individual can be controlled as desired.

Carrying the example further, we could view $R^i(x) - R^i(x - 1)$ as the willingness to pay for additional units of X. In some circumstances the difference would be interpreted as an (inverse) demand function. That is, supose p is a constant price that a subject must pay for units of X. An optimizing subject would want to maximize $R^i(x) - px$. The optimum occurs (ignoring the problem caused by the discrete formulation) at the point $\hat{x}$ such that $R^i(\hat{x}) - R^i(\hat{x} - 1) = p$. Solving the equation for $\hat{x}$, we obtain a function, $\hat{x} = D_i(p)$, which can be interpreted as an individual demand function for X.

Notice that, if any of the conditions, 1, 2, or 3, is not satisfied, then a key parameter is misspecified. When asked to choose over $X \cdot Y$, the subject's choices would not be those predicted by P_i. If this occurs, and if the experimenter is not aware of the problem, a model might be discarded as inaccurate when in fact the experiment was not properly controlled. The point to be emphasized is that a theory of rationality is basic to experimental procedures and to the interpretation of the results. If rationality is not reliable behaviorally, then one would expect economic models to be poor predictors of experimental market behavior because the basic parameters of the economic models would not be controllable.

The nature of the argument just outlined suggests a first line of defense that can be used by anyone whose pet theory has been abused by experimental data. Were the payoffs of a sort that assures that postulate 1 is satisfied? For the most part economists have used money in amounts that will accumulate to amounts comparable to wage rates (for equivalent time) of employed members of the subject pools. Typically, this amount is between $8.00 and $20 per hour. A failure to provide adequate incentives is known to affect results at a group level of performance in ways that do not disappear with large samples.[2] Results regarding the importance of incentives when studying individual choices have been mixed. For example, Grether and Plott (1979) found no incentive effects. The most recent study is by Grether (1981), who demonstrated that the instances of seemingly confused behavior go up when incentives go down.

The second postulate substantially differentiates those who study markets from those who study individuals. Psychologists frequently

2. Only two examples exist. Once problems were detected along this line, subsequent experiments used more incentives. The committee experiments studied by Fiorina and Plott (1978) used incentives as a control. Means and variances were affected substantially. Plott and Smith (1978) demonstrate that traders tend not to trade units for which positive profits will be made. Just breaking even is not enough.

use rich descriptions of situations to elicit responses. From an economist's point of view, this practice is one that is to be viewed with suspicion.[3] Data that lead to a model's rejection can always be explained away by hypotheses that take advantage of any ambiguity that might exist over what preferences "really" existed in the experiment.

The final condition, 3, depends not only on human nature but also on whether the subject understands the relation $R^i(\cdot)$. This function is seldom simply verbally communicated to the subject. If the function involves random elements, they are made operational with real random devices (the word "probability" is not used). Subjects are given experience with the properties of $R^i(\cdot)$ and tested on their understanding of it. Sometimes the instructions of a complicated market experiment involve exercises in which subjects choose over $X \cdot Y$ or its equivalent as a check on conditions 1–3. While these precautions are taken as a defense against disgruntled theorists who might dismiss results on the (self-serving) claim that the preferences were not controlled, they also comment on implicit assumptions about the nature of rationality: intelligence is important; verbal communication is suspect; analytical and cognitive abilities are not dependable over experience. So the experiment proceeds, allowing for the possibility that individuals might be satisficers in the Simon (1979) sense and fail to explore the nature of $R^i(x)$ if left to their own devices.

Acknowledged problems with the concept of rational choice have shaped experimental market procedures in still a third way that was mentioned in the opening paragraphs. Almost all economic models postulate the existence (on an "as if" basis) of a transitive preference over lotteries. Thus transitive choice over lotteries can be viewed as a prediction made by the models. We know from Tversky's (1969) work on transitivity and from preference reversal experiments (Grether and Plott 1979) that those particular predictions of the models will be disconfirmed; that is, we know that models of this type make predictions that are wrong. Logic thus compels us to realize that the "truth" of the models is not necessarily the only goal of the research effort because we already have the answer to that question. Instead the research question becomes the degree to which one model is better than another at capturing market behavior. Experiments should be designed to make comparisons among models whenever such comparisons are

---

3. I am aware of one documented example of a problem caused by the descriptions of the alternatives. In Cohen, Levine, and Plott (1978) subjects were involved in a voting experiment. The objects of choice (letters of the alphabet) were labeled in humorous ways. Traditional financial incentives were also operative. The group-choice model, which had worked well in other experiments, was not working well, so subjects were asked to explain the reasons for their votes. The recorded votes and the reasons given by subjects indicated that subjects neglected the financial incentives and chose in ways they imagined reasonable in light of the humorous description of the options.

possible. Which model throws light on market behavior? Which model is true is a different question.

II. Performance of Market Models

If rationality assumptions are totally unreliable, then one would expect market models based on them to be similarly unreliable. Preferences for outcomes might be induced by the procedures outlined above, but it does not follow that the market supply and demand functions can be constructed from those preferences. An uncontrolled aspect of rationality is required to go from preferences to market demand; or demands and supplies might have been controlled, but laboratory markets are complicated and involve expectations formation, strategy, and so forth. The demand and supply model itself might not work as a predictor of price; or events in the market could override the incentives used. People simply might not be able to cope or might become irritated or frustrated so easily that no market model would work. If people are erratic and/or irrational, the induced preferences will not guarantee the accuracy of economic models.

Three different examples of market experiments are now summarized. Each relies on different features of human capacities. All are "success stories" in the sense that a mathematical model based on principles of rational choice seems to capture much of what is observed. The replications of these experiments have occurred in enough similar situations that the inferences drawn from the examples probably reliably reflect the facts as opposed to outlying or fortuitous observations.

A. *Middlemen*

The first example comes from a paper by Plott and Uhl (1981). The concern was with middlemen. Each of a group of suppliers was given a marginal cost function by application of induced preferences theory. If price was constant and each followed the competitive optimizing response, the market supply curve would be as shown in figure 1. Similarly, final buyers each had a derived demand. Should final buyers have responded in an optimizing fashion to a fixed price, the market demand would have been as shown in the figure. Each agent was assigned a different number to use as a name during the experiment. The numbers on the market demand and supply functions refer to the agent who had the limit value at the indicated level.

Final buyers and suppliers were in different rooms and could neither trade nor communicate. A group of four middlemen (speculators) were allowed first to visit the suppliers' room, at which time a market, A, was opened. Having acquired inventories, the middlemen were then taken to the final buyers' room, where they were able to sell in market

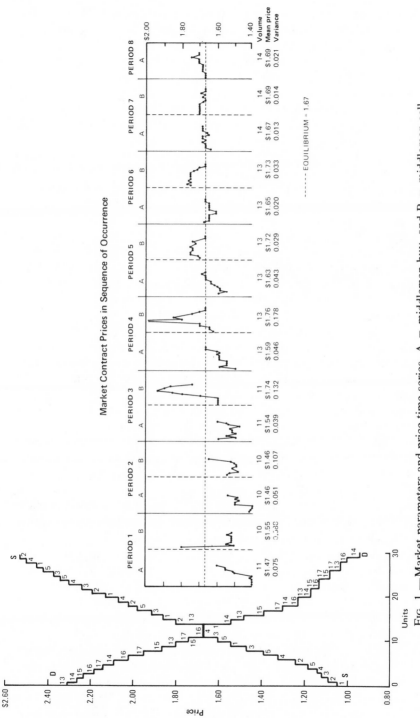

FIG. 1.—Market parameters and price time series. A = middlemen buy, and B = middlemen sell

B what they had previously purchased in market A. After market B was closed, the middlemen returned to market A to start a new period (of two markets). Inventories could not be carried forward to succeeding periods. Everything acquired in A had to be sold in B or forgotten. Both markets were organized in a manner similar to oral double auctions.

If the individuals serving the middleman function were optimizers and correctly assessed the probability of sales in market B, then the prices in markets A and B should have approached equality. The level of price should have been at the demand and supply intersection. Profits of middlemen should have approached zero. The volume in both markets should have been 14 units. It would be as if demanders and suppliers were in the same market and middlemen did not exist.

As shown in figure 1, the predictions of the model are approximately correct, and there is a time series of all contract prices in the order in which they occurred. With time and replication of periods the prices in both markets converged to the predicted equilibrium price of $1.67. The predicted carryforward of 14 units was close to the actual volume. Profits of middlemen dissipated to near zero as predicted.

From a practical perspective the competitive model works rather well when applied to the middleman markets. No model of which I am aware, based on principles other than some form of rationality, does as well as does the competitive model. Indeed, in this simple example there are many chances for things to go wrong. First, notice that the theory of derived demand is working twice removed. Derived demand theory was used to postulate the market demand of final consumers as induced by the experimenter. Derived demand for a factor of production was used by middlemen when they purchased a "resource" from the sellers in room A and transformed it into a product for sale in room B. Notice that this transformation took place under conditions of extreme uncertainty. The middlemen did not know the demand function, prices, or any other aspect of the market (or market theory). Somehow they assessed the consequences of their actions with reasonable accuracy. Once having acquired inventories, the middlemen showed no evidence of falling prey to the sunk-cost fallacy. When mistakes appeared to have been made, that is, when middlemen seem to have carried too much forward, the middlemen readily sold at a loss and recovered as much as possible. (In the first period, 1 unit was carried forward and not sold, but in subsequent periods this problem never occurred.) Notice also that we have some confirmation of the "free riding" or "prisoner's dilemma" model as applied to public goods. Middlemen had a common interest in keeping prices low in market A and high in market B. Outbidding a fellow middleman and gaining the associated personal profits is the market analogue of free riding. These participants were not characterized by such a concern for fellow middlemen that they would forgo advantages of individual gain in order that the profits of all might be higher. Not only is there support here for a "rational" perspective, but there is support for the additional proposition that these people in this setting were not naturally concerned about others; or, if they were so concerned, it was not apparent in their collective actions.

While the middleman type of market experiment suggests that elements of the rational agent model can capture much of the actual human behavior, we cannot assume that this is the end of the story. Even this simple market exhibits behavior that at best is not predicted by the model and at worst is wholly inconsistent with the model. Notice first that the model becomes accurate only after a process of convergence. The model says nothing about that. Notice that the adjustment process contains events that are hard to reconcile with rationality. In the A market, prices existed that were substantially below those observed in the previous A market, and prices tended to move up during a period. Why did sellers simply not wait and capture the higher prices? Why in period 7 did the buyer pay \$2.31 when such high prices had never been necessary before? Notice that in market B of periods 1–2 an excess demand existed but that prices were below equilibrium. The model predicts equilibrium, and in periods 1–2 this did not occur.

B. Auctions

Some of the most extensive use of the precision afforded by rationality postulates is found in the auction literature. This example is of special importance because it is the only example of which I am aware that the full implications of rationality axioms have been deduced in operational terms in a form that can be examined by an experimenter. Put another way, this is the only example in all of economics where a reasonably complete theory about rational behavior in markets exists.

Compare two types of sealed-bid auctions in which a single item is to be sold. Each bidder tenders a single bid in private that is collected and examined (privately) by the market (auctioneer). The object will be awarded to the highest bidder. If the auction is a first-price auction, the winning bidder will pay the amount of his own bid. If the auction is a second-price auction, the winner will pay the amount of the second-highest bid.

The scientific challenge is to compare the bids tendered in each type of market and, more ambitiously, to predict the bids tendered. Suppose that N agents are participating and that all participants know that v_i, the value of the object to each bidder i, is drawn from a probability distribution with support on the interval $[\underline{V}, \overline{V}]$. Notice three aspects of the challenge. First, the institution can be viewed as a treatment variable, so, even if the theory fails to predict individual agent behavior, it still might add insight about market behavior. When dealing with economics, the role of the market as an aspect of inquiry should always be kept in focus. Second, it is the actions taken by agents and not their thoughts, thought processes, feelings, or attitudes that are to be studied. Finally, the concepts of value and probability that are frequently a cause for concern by critics of economics are built into the theory at the outset.

An experimental approach to the problem was first developed by Coppinger, Smith, and Titus (1980) and has since expanded dramatically. To appreciate the role of rationality in this investigation we will consider only a simple case. The values v_i are independently drawn from a constant density on [0, 1], so, by expressing bids as a fraction of the largest possible value, any interval can be considered. Each agent knows his own value before bidding but not the value of others. The above facts are public knowledge and can be controlled for experimental purposes; that is, auctions can actually be created that objectively have the requisite properties.

How might one go about developing a model of the situation? The auction theory literature suggests that the system will behave as if the following are true. (a) Agents choose in accord with the expected utility hypothesis. To obtain a model that can be solved we will assume each player has a utility function of wealth, $U_i(y) = y^r$, where r is distributed across the population by a publicly known probability distribution, ϕ, on [0, 1]. The constant r is a risk-aversion factor. This assumption will be treated as a maintained hypothesis for purposes of analyzing the data and testing the theory. (b) At the time of choice each agent, i, knows (v_i, r_i), his own value and risk parameter, but knows only the probability distribution from which those of others were drawn. (c) Each individual follows Bayes's law in forming expectations. (d) Each individual will choose a Nash equilibrium bidding function. (e) There are N agents.

Under all the above assumptions the symmetric Nash equilibrium bidding functions are

$$
b_i = \begin{cases} v_i, & \text{for all } i \text{ if the second-price auction is used;} \\ \dfrac{(N-1)v_i}{N-1+r_i}, & \text{for all } i \text{ if the first-price auction is used.} \end{cases}
$$

The comparative institutional prediction is that the expected price under the first-price auction is greater than the expected price under the second-price auction. Table 1 reproduces the results of some of Smith's experiments. The range of the support function [0, $\overline{V}$] was varied with N to keep expected profits, as calculated by the model, the same as N increased. First, notice that the model is very accurate when applied to the second-price auction for $N > 3$. For example, if $N = 6$, the model predicts a mean price of 12.1, and the actual price averaged

TABLE 1   Theoretical Predictions and Means and Variances
           Pooled over N Markets

Number and Statistics	First-Price Auction		Second-Price Auction	
	Observed Price	Risk Neutral Theoretical ($r \equiv 1$)	Observed Price	Theoretical
3:*				
Mean	2.44	2.5	1.97	2.5
Variance	.589	.384	.759	.96
4:†				
Mean	5.64	4.9	...	...
Variance	1.80	.96	...	...
5:†				
Mean	9.14	8.1	...	...
Variance	1.37	1.83	...	...
6:†				
Mean	13.22	12.1	11.21	12.1
Variance	4.31	3.0	8.20	6.4
9:‡				
Mean	31.02	28.9	27.02	28.9
Variance	4.91	8.38	18.66	18.85

Source.—Cox, Roberson, and Smith (1982).
* $N = 70$.
† $N = 60$.
‡ $N = 30$.

11.21. The predicted variances are also close to those observed. As predicted by the model, people tend to bid their value when they participate in the second-price auction. Second, notice that the prediction about the market treatment variable is also correct. The average price for the second-price auctions is below the average price of the first-price auctions for every value of N. The first-price auction generates more revenue as predicted.

The risk-neutral model ($r = 1$) tends to develop inaccuracies when applied to the magnitude of first-price auction bids. Of course the risk-neutrality parameter was not controlled in these experiments. In any case, prices in the first-price auction are higher than those predicted by the model if we assume that $r = 1$. If the data are tested for every value of N against the risk-averse model, which predicts that observed prices will be above the risk-neutral prediction, the model cannot be rejected for $N > 3$.

The support for the Nash-equilibrium-based models has continued as research has expanded to a study of the multiple units case, although the model has encountered difficulties for some values of N. For the single-unit case, however, the full Nash equilibrium model with all its implicit and explicit rationality assumptions is the most accurate model that exists. To the extent that the model places restrictions on data it is consistent with the facts in an absolute sense.

C. Signaling

The third example is a demonstration that the equilibrium notions motivated by concepts of optimizing behavior can capture the essence of very complicated and interdependent phenomena. The model itself was originally motivated by a cynical view of education (Spence 1974). Imagine a world in which education has no intrinsic value but is very costly in terms of time and effort to all but the smartest people. By paying an appropriate premium for educated employees, employers can make education a profitable investment for smart people but not for others. Thus the employers can hire just the people they wish (smart) by paying a premium for an attribute they do not value (education). Theoretically, the employers can do this even though the intelligence level of the prospective employee prior to employment can be observed by no one other than the employee himself; and, when asked, a prospective employee has an incentive to lie.

The point of the exercise is not to explore the appropriateness of the reasoning when applied to investments in education. The purpose is to explore the nature of equilibrium when such asymmetric information exists in markets. We inquire about the appropriateness of equilibrating principles that are asserted to be operative and the ability of mathematical statements to capture them.

The example was intended only to help one understand the laboratory market that was created. In the laboratory market several sellers have 2 units each of a commodity that can be sold. The units have two characteristics: grade, which can be either Regular (R) or Super (S), and quality, which initially is zero but can be added by the seller. Grade is like a {dumb, smart} variable, and quality is like education that can be added at cost. A seller's 2 units are either both R or both S. Half the sellers have R's, and the other half have S's, as determined randomly and secretly before any trading begins. Before purchase, N buyers can observe quality added, but the underlying grade is discovered only after purchase and after the market period is closed.

Buyers like Supers better than Regulars, and buyers place some value on any additional quality added by sellers (i.e., education has some value). In particular, for each unit purchased buyers have the following value (determined by the experimenter by using the techniques of induced preference described in the introduction):

$$V(g, q) = G(g) + Q(q),$$

where

$g \in \{R, S\} \equiv \{\text{Regular, Super}\}$;
$q \in [0, \infty) = \text{quality added by seller}$;
$$G(g) = \begin{cases} \$2.50 & \text{if } g = S, \\ \$.50 & \text{if } g = R; \end{cases}$$

$$Q(q) = \begin{cases} \$.205q - \$.005q^2 & \text{if } q \le 20, \\ \$[(.205)(20) - (.005)(20^2)] + \$.01q & \text{if } q > 20. \end{cases}$$

Sellers face costs of adding quality of $\$.15q$ and $\$.02q$ if the units are Regulars or Supers, respectively. It costs less to add q (get educated) if the unit is a Super (smart).

The most efficient signaling equilibrium is a fascinating concept when considered from a rationality perspective. The equilibrium is defined by the following equations:

> all Regulars will be produced at the same quality, q_R,
> and will sell at the same price, P_R;
> all Supers will be produced at the same quality, q_S,
> and will sell at the same price, P_S.

(1)

The two conditions in (1) follow from an underlying axiom requiring that no arbitrage exists. If different prices and qualities existed within grades, then profit opportunities would exist, and rational agents would take advantage of them:

$$V(R, q_R) = P_R;$$
$$V(S, q_S) = P_S.$$

(2)

The equations in (2) pick up two aspects of behavior. First, having observed the quality level, q_R or q_S, the buyer can infer the grade, R or S, with certainty. Quality and grade are perfectly correlated. Second, once this is known the demand and supply model under certainty becomes applicable. For any unit with characteristics (g, q) a horizontal demand exists. Recall that the values of consumers were defined per unit, so, without budget constraints and with prices below value and no uncertainty, the buyer would want an infinite quantity of all possible commodities. The limited supply (vertical supply curve) and horizontal demand curve drive prices to the maximum, that is, the demand price:

$$P_R - .15q_R \ge P_S - .15q_S;$$
$$P_S - .02q_S \ge P_R - .02q_R.$$

(3)

The two conditions in (3) require that truthful revelation is incentive compatible. Regular sellers maximize profits by selling units at the quality level recognized by buyers as Regulars. Super sellers maximize profits by selling units at quality levels recognized by buyers as Supers:

$$\max\{[V(R, q_R) - .15q_R] + [V(S, q_S) - .02q_S]\}.$$

(4)

Condition (4) captures a type of "market rationality." It says that profits of the system will be maximized subject to the behavioral constraints defined in (1)–(3).

In less opaque terms, the final condition (4) can be interpreted as another type of demand and supply condition. The q_S and q_R will be adjusted to reflect gains from exchange. The maximization formulation captures the idea that this adjustment in the quality levels of the commodity will continue until further adjustments would negate the signaling value implicit in (1). The idea is explained geometrically in figure 2. The value functions for a single buyer are drawn from Regulars and Supers. The increases in value with additional quality are as shown. Equation (2) says that the price of an S will be along the top curve and that the price of an R will be along the bottom curve. The qualities, q_R and q_S, must be such that they are not equal and thereby signal to the buyer the underlying grade. The qualities should also be located such that sellers of R's have no interest in marketing their units at (P_S, q_S), and so forth, as demanded by (2). Finally, q_R should be located to maximize system profits, and q_S should be the minimum possible level consistent with (2). A check of the equations will demonstrate that $(q_R, q_S) = (6, 27)$, as shown in the figure, have the requisite properties.

Twelve markets with the above (and related) parameters were reported in Miller and Plott (1985). The results were mixed in the sense that other variations of the model outlined above were more accurate than was that particular model. However, the interesting thing from the perspective of this paper is that the model captured any of the market data at all; yet in two of the 11 markets this complicated model that is filled with rationality postulates is very accurate. The data points are shown in figure 2 near the predicted equilibrium. The quality of Regulars, q_R, is correct, and the quality of supers, q_S, is a little too high. Variances in qualities and prices are very low. Prices are slightly below the predicted level, reflecting a frequently observed property of markets that agents will not trade for zero reward. Behavior of the type described in this model is certainly not beyond human or market capabilities.

III. Ex Post Rationalization (Reparameterization)

When markets perform in unusual or unexpected ways, the rationality postulates suggest hypotheses to explain why. The econometrics and field studies literature are filled with ex post rationalization techniques, but very little has been said about them in laboratory economics papers.

The idea of reparameterization is important in a second way. Rationality at a market level of analysis can be separated from rationality at the individual level. Suppose that the market model works well given the individual agent's personal decision rules. So, from observed market behavior we can make some reasonable inferences about what actual individual decision rules must have been. Suppose further that from induced preference theory we obtain an independent theoretical idea about what a rational individual's decision rule would have been in

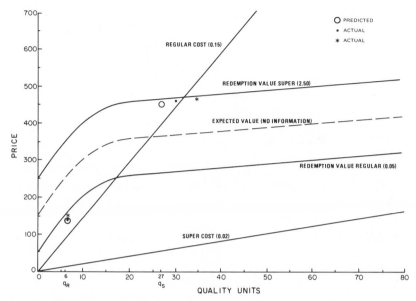

Fɪɢ. 2.—Model parameters and predictions displayed with actual experimental outcomes.

the experiment. By comparing the inferred actual with the theoretical rational we can perhaps develop a methodology for testing the latter as they are relevant for economics.

To demonstrate how rationality principles can be used in this capacity, the data from four experiments are analyzed. These are experiments that would have been discarded because of (allegedly) poor experimental control. These experiments were done in the mid-1960s and early 1970s before some of the experimental techniques currently used had been developed. They are all oral auction markets that differed in various ways from the oral double auction now in use. Each trader had 2 units and could tender an all-or-none offer. Offers remain open until canceled or taken. The instructions were not administered carefully. No tests on procedures or practice rounds were allowed. The accounting was not checked for confused or cheating participants, and so on. In essence the current operational procedures for making certain that subjects understand the reward medium and the market technology were not followed—or so we would like to believe.

The nature of the markets was to induce simple demand and supply functions different from those that had previously been examined. Also present were multiple units, which, at the time of the experiments, had not been studied. The question posed was whether the observed prices and volume would converge to the equilibrium predictions of the model.

The answer was a rather resounding "no." The initial parameters are shown as the solid-line demand and supply functions in figures 3–4. For the most part the data are well removed from the predictions of the model.

Whenever data are trashed, a danger exists that the problem is the principles that guided the models, not the lack of parametric control. However, when examining subjects' decisions, many seemed to violate the intuitive notions of rationality stemming from confusion or a willingness to violate the rules of the market.

An exercise was undertaken to "reparameterize" the experiments. We wished to provide a method of adjusting individual preference parameters in light of their choices and determine the extent to which the revised market model fits the data. The rules used were as follows. (a) If a buyer (seller) buys (sells) a unit for more (less) than the redemption value (cost) of the unit, then the limit price is adjusted to the transaction price. (b) If an agent never bid or traded during the entire experiment and passed up profitable opportunities (suitably defined), then the parameters are adjusted as if the agent were not present. (c) If an agent failed to trade for 2 consecutive periods and passed up profitable opportunities (suitably defined), then the limit prices are revised to equal the highest (lowest) bid to buy (offer to sell) that the agent tendered or accepted for that unit in any period throughout the experiment. (d) If an agent transacts for more units than the maximum permitted, then the units are adjusted to the maximum number of such extra units traded in any period, and the limit prices are the highest (lowest) price paid (received) for those units during the entire experiment.

The revised demand and supplies are the dotted curves in figures 3–4. The price predictions of the revised model fit much better than they do in the original in three of the four cases, and in the fourth case the price predictions are identical. The volume figures are worse after reparameterization because in all cases the actual volume was low relative to the original model and because the revised parameters predicted even lower volume.

The exercise demonstrates two properties of rationality-based theories. First, the adjustment of parameters need not induce circularity in the reasoning. Ex post theories based on rationality can certainly be rejected. For example, the observed volume can be used to reject the revised model. Second, in view of subsequent experimentation, the decision to discard the data was probably correct. If these subjects are "equivalent" to those used in subsequent experiments, and if the market organization had no special effects, then the actual preferences used by the subjects were not those the experimenter attempted to induce. If preferences are stable, we know now that under the double oral auction prices converge to the competitive equilibrium. Thus sub-

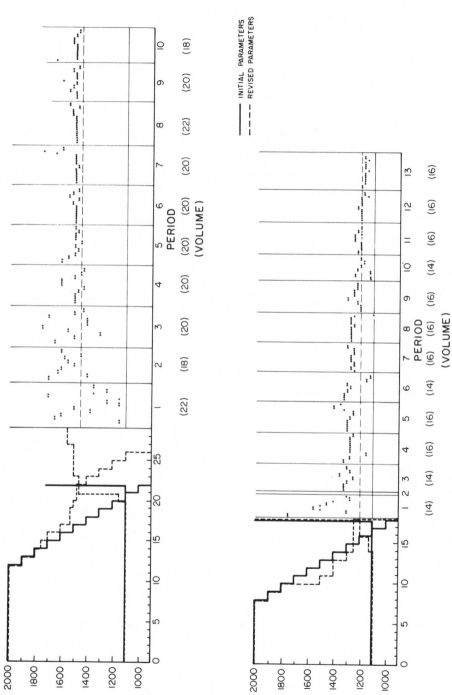

Fig. 3.—Parameters of initial and revised models, predictions, and price time series of two experimental markets

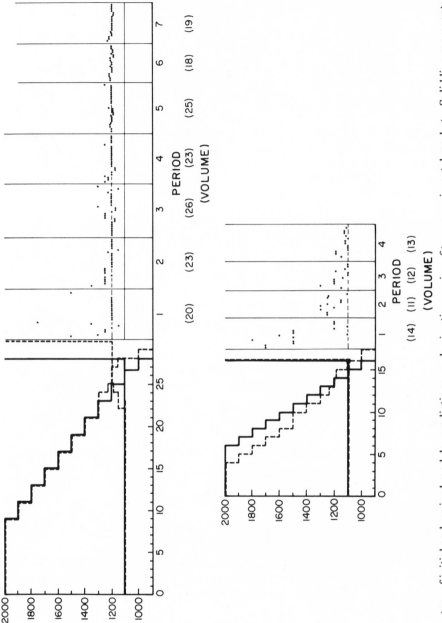

FIG. 4.—Parameters of initial and revised models, predictions, and price time series of two experimental markets. Solid line represents initial parameters and broken line revised parameters.

sequent experiments tell us that the markets in the figures above had adjusted to the actual preferences. Even if participants are confused and "irrational" from certain perspectives, the market model can still be applied.

The only other attempt to revise parameters of a market model based on decisions made during the experiment is the ongoing work by Knez, Smith, and Williams (1985). They have attempted to measure individual attitudes during a market, and to use those parameters for prediction they tested a market model based on measured parameters against the model with parameters as specified a priori by the experimenter. The markets themselves are for lotteries in which subjects stated their limit prices—maximum (minimum) willingness to pay (sell)—prior to the opening of each market period. Their conclusions are (*a*) that the act of measurement does not appear to affect the market; (*b*) that the market model drawn from the measured parameters is more accurate than is the model constructed from induced preferences; and (*c*) that many subjects (in the 40% range) exhibited a willingness to violate their own stated limit prices. Knez et al. suggest that the elicited parameters are analogous to guesses about how subjects will trade or, perhaps, are similar to wishes as opposed to true limit prices. Nevertheless, the measured parameters improve predictions about market prices.

IV. New Institutions

The rationality postulates have been useful in suggesting new institutional arrangements that have never before existed. The research on public goods provision mechanisms is a good example. Other examples include the work by Grether, Isaac, and Plott (1981) on the allocation of landing rights by auction or the work by Rassanti, Smith, and Bulfin (1982) on a combinatorial auction to solve the same problem. Experimental methods have been the only source of data about how these new institutions might perform.

An interesting example, with possibly limited social usefulness, is the unstable dollar auction.[4] The idea is to create processes that applications of rationality theory suggest will have bizarre properties. In this case the objective is to attempt to sell a dollar to perfectly informed people for much more than a dollar. Intuitively, it seems that rational consumers would never do such a thing, but intuition is not always a reliable scientific tool.

Subjects, after having attended an economics experiment, are fre-

---

4. This auction process first appears in print in Shubik (1971). In conversation Shubik tells me that he hesitates to take full credit for having invented the process because many unusual processes were proposed in conversation among game theorists at Princeton in the early 1950s. The theorists were using game theory to invent processes in which rational behavior by individuals would lead to surprising behavior.

quently in a room calculating their earnings. Having calculated their earnings and having not yet been paid, a dollar auction is announced. Subjects are carefully told that an English auction will be used. The market will stop if 45 seconds elapse after a bid with no intervening bid. The dollar will be given to the highest bidder, but the second-highest bidder must pay the amount of his own bid; that is, high bidder gets the dollar, but the second-highest bidder pays for it. Bids cannot exceed the amount earned in the previous experiment, and no talking is allowed.

The game is not well understood from a game-theoretic perspective. The version with unlimited budgets and unlimited time has no solution except infinite bids. With limitations on endowments, under no circumstances can nonparticipation by everyone be a Nash equilibrium. Models of the situation exist in which a solution involves participation from everyone and in which everyone should be prepared to bid their endowment.[5] The point is that models based on concepts of rationality suggest that rational people might produce intuitively impossible, or perhaps irrational, results (i.e., selling a dollar for much more than a dollar).

The data from five such auctions are in figure 5. The dots are the actual bids in dollars as they occurred in sequence. As can be seen, the dollar always sold for much more than a dollar. In auction 1, for example, the dollar went to a bid of $27, and the price actually paid by the second-highest bidder was $20. Some of the relevant data are in table 2. Participants are indexed according to the size of their budget, with the person with the largest budget called person number 1. In auction 1 the

---

5. A complete game-theoretic treatment of the auction is not available. Kim Border and Joel Sobel (private correspondence) have produced the following model. The insight of the model is to treat the auction like a sealed-bid auction. The sealed bid is interpreted as a reservation price above which the subject will not go during the actual English auction bidding process. Consider only the two-person case for exposition purposes with the following rules: (i) high bidder receives $1.00 and pays nothing; (ii) second-highest bidder receives zero and pays his bid; (iii) bids must be nonnegative and no more than wealth; and (iv) common knowledge is that wealth is independently and identically distributed from cumulative density function $F(\cdot)$, is supported on $[0, A]$, and has continuous density $f(\cdot)$. Let $V(x) = (1 + x)F(x) - x$; $M(W) = \max\{x \leq W: x$ max's V on $[0, W]\}$; and $b(W) = W - \{V[M(W)] - V(W)\}/[1 - F(W)]$, using the convention that, if $F(W) = 1$, then $\{V[M(W)] - V(W)\}/[1 - F(W)] = 0$. The bidding function, $b(W)$, is the equilibrium strategy of a symmetric Bayesian Nash equilibrium with risk-neutral players. Generalization to N bidders is straightforward. As an example consider the two-person case in which $F(\cdot)$ is uniform over $[0, A]$. The optimum bidding function is

$$b(W) = \begin{cases} W, & \text{if } W \geq A - 1; \\ \dfrac{W}{A - W}, & \text{if } W < A - 1. \end{cases}$$

In this case the equilibrium strategy is to be prepared to bid all your wealth if your wealth is one less than the maximum possible wealth. Border has also produced an example in which the optimal strategy is for all bidders to always bid all their wealth.

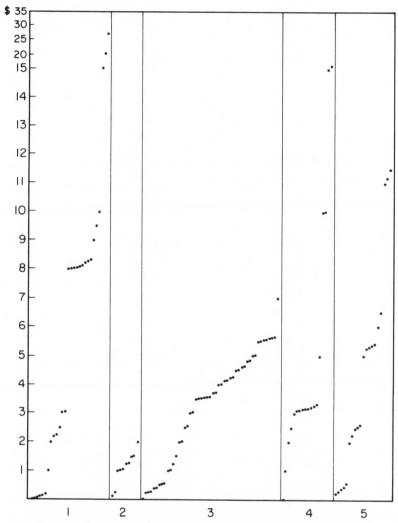

FIG. 5.—Bid time series from five dollar auctions (see table 2)

person with the largest endowment had $40. The auction winner had the sixth-largest endowment at $27.54. The person who paid $20 had an endowment of $20.70. These were the only two bidders after the fourteenth bid of $8.00. Frequently, the auction stopped only after a bidder hit a constraint. The individual who acquired the dollar tended to have an above-average endowment. On the average, people lost a great deal of money.

The phenomenon suggested by the models actually exists. The data contain three interesting lessons. First, models of rational choice help us look beyond the market organizations that have evolved through

TABLE 2   Parameters for Five Dollar Auctions, Bids That Initiate Two-Person Sequences, and the Number of People Bidding

Auction 1: PCC	Auction 2: PCC	Auction 3: PCC	Auction 4: CIT	Auction 5: CGS
Fourteen Participants	Fourteen Participants	Five Participants	Fourteen Participants	Eleven Participants
$L_1 = \$40.00$	$L_1 = \$30.87$	$L_1 = \$31.68$	$L_1 = \$41.70$	$L_1 = \$14.70$
$L_W = L_6 = \$27.56$	$L_W = L_{13} = \$23.07$	$L_W = L_1 = \$31.68$	$L_W = L_5 = \$21.30$	$L_W = L_3 = \$11.90$
$L_L = L_{16} = \$20.70$	$L_L = L_6 = \$25.44$	$L_L = L_5 = \$11.28$	$L_L = L_{11} = \$15.05$	$L_L = L_6 = \$11.20$
$B_W = \$27.00$	$B_W = \$2.00$	$B_W = \$7.00$	$B_W = \$16.00$	$B_W = \$11.50$
$B_L = \$20.00$	$B_L = \$1.51$	$B_L = \$5.63$	$B_L = \$15.00$	$B_L = \$11.20$
Only traders 6 and 16, beginning with $B = \$8.00$ (fourteenth bid)	Only traders 6 and 13, beginning with $B = \$1.02$ (fifth bid)	Only traders 1 and 5, beginning with $B = \$.52$ (ninth bid)	Only traders 5 and 11, beginning with $B = \$2.00$ (third bid)	Only traders 3 and 6, beginning with $B = \$11.20$ (nineteenth bid)
Eight people bid at least once	Five people bid at least once	Three people bid at least once	Four people bid at least once	Five people bid at least once

NOTE.—PCC = Pasadena City College, CIT = California Institute of Technology, and CGS = Claremont Graduate School. L_i = limit price of the person with the ith highest limit price, L_W = limit price of the auction winner, B_W = bid of auction winner, and B_L = bid of auction loser—the person who paid.

history to find institutions that might be capable of performing some specific task. One might imagine nobler tasks than to sell a dollar for more than a dollar, but that is not the issue. Second, the existence of intuitively "irrational" market behavior is not conclusive evidence that models based on concepts of individual rationality are inappropriate or ill-equipped to be useful in applications. Finally, the example demonstrates that models based on optimization principles are filled with subtleties often unappreciated by critics of rationality. As far as I am aware, the game described above has never been solved with any degree of generality. We do not know some of the major properties of the Nash equilibrium strategies should they exist. Given the current development of theory, the data cannot be used either to confirm or to reject a theory.

V. Pending Problems

The review above contains no examples of the failure of an economic model to confront the data successfully. I do not want to leave the reader with the impression that such examples do not exist. This section is intended to disabuse anyone of the notion that our models are in perfect shape and that the rationality foundation needs neither examination nor modification. Many problems and paradoxes exist. This paper was not organized around the failure of the models because the reasons for the failures are not clear. Arguments like those in Section III that show differences of procedures and incentives as explanations for unexpected market behavior are very much in contention with arguments that would change entirely the way we think about economics.

The potential problems with rational choice models that have been identified by psychologists and that might be manifest in market behavior have not been systematically explored. This lack of study reflects a resource constraint and not a lack of interest or enthusiasm. Two exceptions to the general rule exist currently, and I understand that more attempts to study markets for evidence of "heuristics" are under way.

In an experimental study by Plott and Wilde (1982) the "representativeness" heuristic (Tversky and Kahneman 1974) was given an opportunity to work. Subjects had valuations for commodity units that were contingent on an underlying state of nature. Prior probabilities were generated by a bingo cage. Once a state of nature was chosen (one for each buyer), a clue to the state was generated by a draw from a second bingo cage. The distribution governing the draws from the second cage was contingent on the state determined by the first draw. After receiving their personal clue, buyers would participate in a market in which the units were being sold. After this process was repeated for several periods (during which the market equilibrated in the usual fashion), the

market supply was shifted. The representativeness heuristic predicted
no change in volume due to the lowered price. In reality, slight increases occurred as would be anticipated from risk-averse expected
utility behavior with Bayesian agents.

A more direct examination of the base-rate fallacy has been conducted by Duh and Sunder (1985). The experiment was similar to the
Plott and Wilde experiment, but the supply was completed inelastic,
thereby letting price serve as a measure of valuation, and the markets
were organized differently. The experiments also varied the base rate
to see if the markets responded appropriately. A model based on the
principle that base rates would be ignored was rejected in favor of a
model based on the principle that people would follow Bayes's law.

The present lack of support in experimental markets for the psychol-
ogy-based ideas is not going to be the end of the story. Many properties
of markets have been observed that are not explicable in terms of
current models. Posted prices have an independent effect on market
prices (Plott and Smith 1978); nonbinding price ceilings affect market
convergence (Isaac and Plott 1981; Smith and Williams 1981); and
bubbles can be observed in asset markets (Plott and Sunder 1983;
Camerer 1984; Smith, Suchanek, and Williams 1986). The dynamics of
the convergence process in equilibrating markets is not theoretically
understood at all (Davis and Williams, in press). In fact we have only
begun to develop a theory based on individual strategic decisions about
why equilibrium is attained in any experimental markets where equilibrium has been observed (Wilson 1982; Friedman 1984; Easley and
Ledyard 1986). The Dutch auction behaves differently from the first-
price auction even though they are supposed to be behaviorally
isomorphic (Coppinger et al. 1980). The signaling experiments discussed above contain events that suggest that some of the markets
studied failed to incorporate information that was clearly present in a
statistical sense. The markets appeared to adjust appropriately only
after a change in experimental procedure drew attention to the statistical regularity. The questions that now exist about the need for economists to consider the decision process used by individuals in addition
to observed choices are likely to occur with increasing frequency.

The role of morality, altruism, and ethical predispositions in forming
choice is another area of potential discoveries. Needless to say, there
has been no way of separating theories of altruistically based behavior
and moralistic behavior from preference theory or rational choice theories. Furthermore, since preference theory requires no theory about
the source of preferences, no overriding need for a separate theory of
moral behavior has been solidly demonstrated. The fact that preferences might include or reflect moral considerations does not, on the
surface, contradict a theory of rational choice or maximizing behavior.
Moral considerations might influence the shape and form of prefer-

ences, but that does not contradict the existence of preferences or choices based on them. One can argue that the existence of morally based behavior provides evidence of rational choice. Experimental markets with externalities, public goods decision processes, and related commons dilemma experiments have not shown the domination of moral considerations over financial motivation (Dawes 1980). Thus no review of procedures and theories has been forced on experimentalists. Nevertheless, evidence of morally based decisions does exist (Palfrey and Rosenthal 1985). In committee experiments the evidence is pronounced especially when as few as three participants are involved (Isaac and Plott 1978; Eavey and Miller 1984). Furthermore, a methodology for investigating experimentally the phenomena and related theories of moral choices is being explored. Hoffman and Spitzer (1985) formulate a strong case that it is possible to formulate in operational terms competing theories about moral attitudes and that it is possible to use experimental techniques to assess their relative accuracy. How our models of rational choice become modified to include the technical features of moral attitudes (consistent? myopic? stable? sensitivity and responsiveness of choice to evidence?), if such exist, remains an open question.

VI. Closing Remarks

The tone of this paper is defensive. Claims about the irrelevance of models of rational choice and the consequent irrelevance of economics are not uncommon topics of conversation. Even economists sometimes engage in disparaging remarks about the discipline because of doubts about either the testability or the validity of the optimization hypothesis. If one looks at experimental markets for evidence, the pessimism is not justified. Market models based on rational choice principles (including the subspecies of satisficing) do a pretty good job of capturing the essence of very complicated phenomena.

On the other hand, the evidence presented here should provide no one with a feeling of overconfidence. Referees who summarize experimental papers by saying, The results are obvious because they follow immediately from rational choice, have not looked very closely at the theory and the data. While the theory of rational choice provides a very useful set of general principles, it is a mistake to elevate the theory to the status of irrefutable law that always reliably operates and need not be challenged.

References

Aizerman, M. A. 1985. New problems in the general choice theory: Review of a research trend. *Social Choice and Welfare* 2 (December): 235–82.

Camerer, Colin. 1984. Speculative price bubbles in asset markets: A theoretical survey and experimental design. Unpublished manuscript. Philadelphia: University of Pennsylvania, Wharton School.

Cohen, Linda; Levine, Michael E.; and Plott, Charles R. 1978. Communication and agenda influence: The chocolate pizza design. In H. Sauermann (ed.), *Coalition Forming Behavior: Contributions to Experimental Economics*. Vol. 8. Tübingen: Mohr (Siebeck).

Coppinger, Vicki M.; Smith, Vernon L.; and Titus, Jon A. 1980. Incentives and behavior in English, Dutch and sealed-bid auctions. *Economic Inquiry* 18 (January): 1–22.

Cox, James C.; Roberson, Bruce; and Smith, Vernon L. 1982. Theory and behavior of single object auctions. In V. L. Smith (ed.), *Research in Experimental Economics*. Vol. 2. Greenwich, Conn.: JAI.

Davis, Douglas D., and Williams, Arlington W. In press. The effects of rent asymmetries in posted offer markets. *Journal of Economic Behavior and Organization*.

Dawes, Robyn M. 1980. Social dilemmas. *Annual Review of Psychology* 31:169–93.

Duh, Rong Ruey, and Sunder, Shyam. 1985. Incentives, learning and processing of information in a market environment: An examination of the base rate fallacy. Department of Accounting Working Paper 1985–5. Minneapolis: University of Minnesota at Minneapolis St. Paul.

Easley, David, and Ledyard, John. 1986. Theories of price formation and exchange in double oral auctions. Social Science Working Paper no. 611. Pasadena: California Institute of Technology.

Eavey, Cheryl, and Miller, Gary J. 1984. Fairness in majority rule games with a core. *American Journal of Political Science* 28 (August): 570–86.

Fiorina, Morris P., and Plott, Charles R. 1978. Committee decisions under majority rule. *American Political Science Review* 72 (June): 575–98.

Friedman, Dan. 1984. On the efficiency of experimental double auction markets. *American Economic Review* 74 (March): 60–72.

Grether, David M. 1981. Financial incentive effects and individual decision making. Social Science Working Paper no. 401. Pasadena: California Institute of Technology.

Grether, David M.; Isaac, R. Mark; and Plott, Charles R. 1981. The allocation of landing rights by unanimity among competitors. *American Economic Review* 71 (May): 166–71.

Grether, David M., and Plott, Charles R. 1979. Economic theory of choice and the preference reversal phenomenon. *American Economic Review* 69 (September): 623–38.

Hoffman, Elizabeth, and Spitzer, Matthew L. 1985. Entitlements, rights, and fairness: Some experimental results. *Journal of Legal Studies* 14 (June): 259–98.

Isaac, R. Mark, and Plott, Charles R. 1978. Cooperative game models of the influence of the closed rule in three person, majority rule committees: Theory and experiments. In P. C. Ordeshook (ed.), *Game Theory and Political Science*. New York: New York University Press.

Isaac, R. Mark, and Plott, Charles R. 1981. Price controls and the behavior of auction markets: An experimental examination. *American Economic Review* 71 (June): 448–59.

Knez, P.; Smith, Vernon L.; and Williams, A. 1985. Individual rationality, market rationality and value estimation. *American Economic Review* 75 (May): 397–402.

Ledyard, John O. In press. The scope of the hypothesis of Bayesian equilibrium. *Journal of Economic Theory*.

Miller, Ross M.; and Plott, Charles R. 1985. Product quality signaling in experimental markets. *Econometrica* 53 (July): 837–71.

Palfrey, Thomas R., and Rosenthal, Howard. 1985. Altruism and participation in social dilemmas. Graduate School of Industrial Administration Working Paper no. 35-84-85. Pittsburgh: Carnegie-Mellon University.

Plott, Charles R. 1979. The application of laboratory experimental methods to public choice. In C. S. Russell (ed.), *Collective Decision Making: Applications from Public Choice Theory*. Baltimore: Johns Hopkins University Press.

Plott, Charles R. 1982. Industrial organization theory and experimental economics. *Journal of Economic Literature* 20 (December): 1485–1527.

Plott, Charles R., and Smith, Vernon L. 1978. An experimental examination of two exchange institutions. *Review of Economic Studies* 45 (February): 133–53.

Plott, Charles R., and Sunder, Shyam. 1983. Rational expectations and the aggregation of diverse information in laboratory security markets. Social Science Working Paper no. 363. Pasadena: California Institute of Technology.

Plott, Charles R., and Uhl, Jonathan T. 1981. Competitive equilibrium with middlemen: An empirical study. *Southern Economic Journal* 47 (April): 1063–71.

Plott, Charles R., and Wilde, Louis L. 1982. Professional diagnosis versus self diagnosis: An experimental examination of some special features of markets with uncertainty. In V. L. Smith (ed.), *Research in Experimental Economics*. Vol. 2. Greenwich, Conn.: JAI.

Rassenti, S.; Smith, Vernon; and Bulfin, R. 1982. A combinatorial auction for airport time slot allocation. *Bell Journal of Economics* 13 (Autumn): 402–17.

Shubik, Martin. 1971. The dollar auction game. *Journal of Conflict Resolution* 15 (Fall): 109–11.

Simon, H. A. 1979. Rational decision making in business organizations. *American Economic Review* 69 (September): 493–514.

Smith, Vernon L. 1976. Experimental economics: Induced value theory. *American Economic Review* 66 (May): 274–79.

Smith, Vernon L.; Suchanek, Gerry L.; and Williams, Arlington W. 1986. Bubbles, crashes and endogenous expectations in experimental asset markets. Working Paper no. 86-2. Tucson: University of Arizona, Department of Economics.

Smith, Vernon L., and Williams, Arlington W. 1981. On nonbinding price controls in a competitive market. *American Economic Review* 71 (June): 467–74.

Spence, M. A. 1974. *Market Signaling: Informational Transfer in Hiring and Related Screening Processes*. Cambridge, Mass.: Harvard University Press.

Tversky, Amos. 1969. Intransitivity of preferences. *Psychological Review* 76 (January): 31–48.

Tversky, A., and Kahneman, D. 1974. Judgment under uncertainty: Heuristics and biases. *Science* 185:1124–31.

Wilson, Robert. 1982. Double auctions. Technical Report 391. Stanford, Calif.: Stanford University, Institute for Mathematical Studies in the Social Sciences, October. Reprinted in T. Groves, R. Radner, and S. Reiter (eds.), *Information Incentives and Economic Mechanisms: Essays in Honor of Leonid Hurwicz*. Minneapolis: University of Minnesota Press (in press).

Howard Kunreuther

University of Pennsylvania

Comments on Plott and on Kahneman, Knetsch, and Thaler*

Both of these papers raise a number of interesting questions as to the factors that are important in determining market outcomes. The Kahneman, Knetsch, and Thaler (in this volume) paper explores whether the introduction of fairness can help explain behavior by firms that could not be easily explained by standard economic analyses. Charles Plott's (in this volume) summary of experimental economic evidence suggests that market models based on rational choice principles do rather well for a certain class of problems but that there are a number of areas where the jury is still out.

Let me first turn to the Kahneman et al. paper. In my opinion the importance of this paper is that it lays out a set of testable propositions that are based on the deviations between a new transaction from a reference transaction. On the basis of these propositions the authors offer testable hypotheses such as the following.

Firms will not raise prices if there is an increase in demand unaccompanied by an increase in cost.

Firms will not introduce an auction as a method of allocating scarce consumer goods.

Firms will not cut wages of existing employees if there is excess supply of labor.

According to Kahneman et al., firms will not follow these and other practices because customers or employees consider them to be unfair, and hence firms may be hurt sufficiently in the future to offset any short-run gains they may achieve.

The key empirical test for these and other hypotheses is what actually happens in a market setting. There are a set of considerations that

* These comments reflect helpful discussions with Colin Camerer and Paul Klein-dorfer.

will influence firm behavior that make the answers to the above questions somewhat open.

1. Referring to the length of the time horizon associated with a particular problem, is it fair to raise prices when there is a shortage of goods (the response is likely to be conditional on whether the relevant horizon is short, medium, or long)?

As an illustration of a short-run problem consider the New York City power failure of 1965. There is anecdotal evidence that the prices of flashlights and candles went way up. People may have considered this unfair, but they were willing to pay. An open question is, Would the same have happened in a small town?

The medium-run situation is illustrated by the 1964 Alaska earthquake, in which there were food and housing shortages. Here the behavior is in the direction that Kahneman et al. would predict. Safeway lowered the price of orange juice even though demand was very high and rationed two cans to each customer. Rents for homes during the immediate postdisaster period slightly decreased or stayed the same even though there was severe damage in the area. The Safeway store wanted to preserve its reputation for being a good neighbor and not hitting people when they were down (Dacy and Kunreuther 1968).

The recent example of Michael Jackson's promotional tour illustrates how he violated this intrinsic notion of fairness by charging prices that his promoters felt would just clear the market. His goodwill and future reputation were affected by this action—both my son and daughter have a more negative view of him today, as do their friends who went to the concert. Part of this may be due to fad, but I believe fairness also played a role with respect to his decrease in popularity.

A long-run shortage is illustrated by famine. Prices are likely to rise even though people consider it unfair. This may lead to regulation or attempts at regulation on the basis of a just price. There is a precedent for this behavior going back to the Roman Empire when Emperor Diocletian issued two price edicts in A.D. 285 and A.D. 301, fixing maximum prices for 700–800 different articles on the basis of production cost. The reason for this action was fear of revolution by the poorer classes (Glaeser 1927, pp. 157–58).

2. Fairness may influence behavior by enabling businesses to frame the situation so that it is viewed as acceptable by consumers without affecting the profitability of the firm. An example given by Kahneman et al. is a restaurant charging a $5.00 reservation fee on Saturday night. This was considered unfair by many people. However, restaurants face another alternative. Rather than charging a fee for reservations, they can achieve the same effect by having music during the week as well as on Saturday night but levying a cover charge only on Saturday. If asked whether such a practice were fair, my guess is that the general public would find this acceptable. In fact one observes this in places today.

3. What effect does problem context and culture have on what is considered fair? Airlines consider it fair to have a schedule of rates depending on how far in advance you book. People seem to consider it unfair in hotels. Here is one counterexample. There is one small hotel in New York City that does follow this policy by charging $130 for advance reservations and $150 if they are 80% filled 1 week before the arrival date. Those who have previously spent a night at the hotel at $150 per night are frequently surprised to learn when making an advance reservation that the price is now only $130. They refuse to believe that there is not a quality difference between this room and the one they previously had. At an extreme level, if a resort offered me a room at marginal cost, I might think twice about accepting it because I would suspect that the low price was the result of inferior quality.

4. If concepts of fairness differ between specific groups of individuals, what effect, if any, will this have on market behavior? My colleague, Colin Camerer, administered parts of the Kahneman et al. questionnaire to 48 first-year M.B.A. students. Here is a brief summary of the results.

Price data. One question in Kahneman et al. was whether people felt it was appropriate to raise prices if there was a shortage. An example given was auctioning off the lone Cabbage Patch doll in a store. In Kahneman et al.'s survey 24% found this to be acceptable in contrast with 64% of the M.B.A. students.

Another question asked whether people felt it was acceptable to raise the price of current stock of peanut butter when the owner learns that the wholesale price has risen? In Kahneman et al.'s survey 21% found this practice acceptable, while 73% of the M.B.A. students did so.

If individuals who will be running businesses in future years generally feel it is fair to raise prices even though the public does not, what would we expect would happen in the "market"? The answer depends partly on the competitive environment as well as on whether firms have private information that buyers cannot obtain directly (e.g., their costs of peanut butter); that is, firms having more monopoly power and more private information on costs will be more likely than others to raise the price of peanut butter on existing stock when wholesale prices rise.

Wage data. The M.B.A. survey yielded results similar to Kahneman et al.'s; namely, it is unfair to lower wages if there is excess supply. For these questions, students possibly saw themselves as future employees on getting an M.B.A.

5. Finally, are there explanations based on arguments regarding asymmetry of information between buyers and sellers that may explain firm behavior without having to rely on fairness? To illustrate, Kahneman et al. implied that, because of considerations of fairness, differences in income will be insufficient to eliminate excess demand for individuals considered to be most valuable and excess supply of those considered most dispensable.

An alternative explanation is that firms obtain private information on the quality of their own workers that they do not share with others. Workers are unable to convey this information to others because it will be hard to convince them of their internal value to the firm. In the context of a university, this asymmetry of information partially explains why teaching is not rewarded as much as is research and leads us to allocate considerable time to visible activities such as attending and presenting papers at conferences. In a broader labor market context, current employers may offer a wage lower than that which appears to be market clearing because other firms have imperfect information on special skills that are not measurable in direct output by the employee and because the worker has no way to signal them (Kunreuther and Pauly 1985).[1]

Let us turn now to market-based experiments, in which Charles Plott has undertaken pioneering studies. His paper suggests that the market models based on rational choice principles work well, but the data suggest the importance of different institutional arrangements as well as the decision process in characterizing final outcomes.

On the institutional side, Plott (1982) reports on an experiment by Vernon Smith and his colleagues on the effect of different institutions on equilibrium prices. In a double oral auction there was a tendency for equilibrium to erode from the monopoly price to competitive equilibrium. On the other hand, in a posted-price auction, where monopolists post both the price and an available quantity at the beginning of a period, the monopoly price and quantity survived as an equilibrium.

On the decision process side, a recent experimental study by Hoffman and Spitzer (1985) also suggests that differences emerge if an individuals feel they have gained special advantages through a fortuitous event rather than by special skills or hard work. In Hoffman and Spitzer's experiment two individuals had an opportunity to work out a sharing arrangement for a total prize of $14; however, one of the two participants would specify a noncooperative outcome unilaterally.

In one version of their experiment a coin was flipped, and the winner could choose any outcome he or she wished. The other player was free to accept it or to receive nothing. The coin flip "winner" was guaranteed $12 if the other player did not accept the proposed split. The final offer made by the winner of the coin flip frequently was $7.00. In another version of the experiment a game of some skill was played to determine who had "earned" the entitlement to propose the split.

---

1. At the other end of the spectrum there may be cost-based explanations with respect to why firms pay some workers more than they appear to be worth. Carl Shapiro and Joseph Stiglitz (1984) suggest that firms may pay more than a "going wage" to induce workers not to shirk. Employees know that if they are fired they will pay a penalty for their behavior. Hence involuntary unemployment may occur.

Then the participant who won the game was very likely to request $13, with the other player receiving $1.00 if he or she accepted the proposal.

A principal thrust of Plott's paper is that experimental markets offer a way of determining whether individual behavior that appears to violate rational choice principles will be corrected by market activity. He points to a recent study by Knez, Smith, and Williams (1985), where trading assets in a double oral auction corrected for violations of expected utility theory when there is a probabilistic outcome on dividends. Other experimental studies such as those by Plott and Sunder (1982), where some traders have inside information on dividends while others do not, also reveal that the market is consistent with predictions from expected utility theory even though specific individuals may not be rational.

There is a general recognition that the key to a stable equilibrium is learning and the ability to learn. Experimental market research is one of the most promising areas for understanding how different institutions, contexts, and assumptions on available information may affect behavior. Several areas seem to be fruitful avenues for exploring these questions.

1. How well does the market correct for biases with respect to low-probability events? We know that individuals appear to violate expected utility theory when the probabilities of certain outcomes are very low. The failure to buy flood insurance at subsidized rates, to wear seat belts, or to utilize safety equipment on the job characterizes this behavior. Are there ways in which learning can take place in a market setting?

For example, one could undertake insurance market experiments where there is a very small probability of suffering a large loss to see how this event affects market outcomes. On the basis of empirical data, one would predict that individuals would not be interested in insurance even at subsidized premia because they assume that the disaster "will not happen to me." If people have a difficult time learning optimal long-run strategy from small samples, then we would not expect the market to correct for this behavior.

From a prescriptive vantage point it would be helpful to understand why such behavior occurs. If the cost of processing information on low-probability events is difficult, it may be desirable to present information in different forms to "correct" certain biases. For example, consider an insurance market experiment in which an individual knew he or she would be in the market for 25 periods and that the chance of receiving a large loss in any given period was .01. If subjects were told that the chance that a loss would occur at least once in the 25-period stretch was greater than .2, then they may consider this low-probability event to be relatively high. The resulting equilibrium market premia might be higher than in the situation in which subjects were given the probability for only a single period.

2. When individuals do not exhibit probabilistic biases in making choices, will the market correct for this behavior? For example, Grether (1980) has shown that individuals exhibit the Kahneman and Tversky representativeness bias rather than using a Bayesian updating rule. Camerer (1985) investigated this bias in a market setting and found that it still persisted.

A key question in moving from the individual to the market is whether people can learn from those who behave according to optimal statistical decision rules. As Arrow (1982) has pointed out, if everyone else is irrational, it by no means follows that one can make money by being rational, at least in the short run.

3. What effect does ambiguity on probabilities have on market behavior? Hogarth and Kunreuther (1985) have studied individual behavior in the context of insurance markets to determine what happens to premiums charged by buyers and sellers when people are given uncertain information on probabilities in contrast to certain information. Behavior appears to be inconsistent with that predicted by utility theory. It is not clear what happens in a market setting when there can be trading between buyers and sellers.

Tversky and Kahneman (1981) have presented examples designed to show that framing questions that contain identical statistical information in different ways affects preferences. One could determine whether this type of inconsistency also holds in a market setting. For example, one could endow all participants with a certain amount of cash and expose them to a lottery where there is a potential loss. Equilibrium prices for this lottery could be contrasted with the situation in which no initial endowment is given and the lottery is in terms of gains. With the appropriate adjustments in initial endowments one can construct lotteries where the market equilibrium prices should be the same in both situations. Will market behavior correct for framing effects induced by presenting information in terms of losses instead of gains? We do not know.

In summary, both of these papers offer a large menu for future research on individual and market equilibria. We need to understand how other attributes such as "fairness" effect behavior and how the learning process effects equilibrium. The work of Kahneman, Knetsch, and Thaler on fairness and the experimental market paradigms of Plott and his colleagues offer a springboard for determining how markets affect individual choice.

References

Arrow, K. 1982. Risk perception in psychology and economics. *Economic Inquiry* 20:1–9.

Camerer, C. 1985. Do biases in probability judgment affect market outcomes? Some experimental evidence. Wharton Risk and Decision Processes Center Working Paper no. 83-12-05. Philadelphia: University of Pennsylvania, Wharton School.

Dacy, D., and Kunreuther, H. 1968. *The Economics of Natural Disasters.* New York: Free Press.

Glaeser, M. 1927. *Outlines of Public Utility Economics.* New York: Macmillan.

Grether, D. 1980. Bayes rule as a descriptive model: The representativeness heuristic. *Quarterly Journal of Economics* 95:537–57.

Hoffman, B., and Spitzer, M. 1985. Entitlements, rights and fairness: An experimental examination of subjects' concepts of distributive justice. *Journal of Legal Studies* 14:259.

Hogarth, R. M., and Kunreuther, H. 1985. Ambiguity and insurance decisions. *American Economic Association Papers and Proceedings* 75:386–90.

Kahneman, D.; Knetsch, J.; and Thaler, R. In this volume. Fairness and the assumptions of economics.

Knez, P.; Smith, V.; and Williams, A. 1985. Individual rationality, market rationality and value estimation. *American Economic Association Papers and Proceedings* 75:397–402.

Kunreuther, H., and Pauly, M. 1985. Market equilibrium with private knowledge: An insurance example. *Journal of Public Economics* 26:269–88.

Plott, C. 1982. Industrial organization theory and experimental economics. *Journal of Economic Literature* 10 (December): 1485–1527.

Plott, C. In this volume. Rational choice in experimental markets.

Plott, C., and Sunder, S. 1982. Efficiency of experimental markets with inside information: An application of rational expectations models. *Journal of Political Economy* 90:663–98.

Shapiro, C., and Stiglitz, J. 1984. Equilibrium unemployment as a worker discipline device. *American Economic Review* 74:433–44.

Tversky, A., and Kahneman, D. 1981. The framing of decisions and the psychology of choice. *Science* 211:453–58.

R. Duncan Luce

Harvard University

Comments on Plott and on Kahneman, Knetsch, and Thaler

Commenting on papers by top researchers (Kahneman, Knetsch, and Thaler, in this volume; and Plott, in this volume) can be, and in this case has been, difficult because of the paucity of valid objections around which to organize one's comments. Of course, this may just reflect the fact that neither paper is close to my major areas of interest. In any event, when facing such a problem—because when asked to be a discussant some time ago I failed to anticipate what should have been obvious—three courses of action come to mind.

The most obvious, although cowardly, possibility was to call in "sick." On reflection, I realized that this task really would not resolve my problem because a conference publication typically lurks in the background, and the organizers would surely demand that I write out my undelivered comments anyhow. It is awkward to argue continued illness when one is up and about, attending other public meetings.

A second plausible tack is to think up a few questions that the authors of the paper may or may not be able to answer. Of course, if one expects to have anything left for the publication, it is wise to make sure that at least one of the questions is unanswerable using the present data or theory.

A third tack is either to extract a phrase or paragraph—the "lesson of the day," as the minister used to say when I was a boy—or to select another paper from the conference as a point of departure to discuss what one would have said at somewhat greater length had the organizers of the conference invited one to be a speaker rather than a discussant.

Having failed to adopt the first approach, I shall illustrate each of the others, first, by asking a few, hopefully sage questions of Kahneman et al. and, second, by using a phrase from Plott's paper and the entire nonassigned Tversky and Kahneman (in this volume) paper as two points of departure for what I really want to say.

For Kahneman et al., three questions occurred to me. As I said when I raised them at the conference, I was sure they could deal readily with the first two, but I doubted the third was answerable from the data. And indeed, they have rewritten their paper eliminating the classification scheme about which the first two questions were centered. So I am left with the last question I raised.

Although the results presented are very striking indeed, the fact remains that in many cases something between a quarter and a third of the respondents disagreed with the majority. This certainly suggests that we do not all have the same moral judgments in specific cases; but does it mean more than that? Is it pretty much a matter of chance whether an individual will be in a minority on a question, or is holding the minority view likely to be a behavioral pattern for all judgments of fairness? One can well imagine that there may be two or (probably) more patterns of morality in society and that, if one knew a person's answers to a few of the questions, their answers to the others would become quite predictable. If I understand how these data were collected, one can only use them indirectly to approach that question. Each respondent answered questions about only a small subset of the questions, whereas to verify strongly patterned behavior it would be necessary to have responses to all, or most, of the questions. It might be useful to find out if there is such patterning.

When I turn to Plott's summary of market experiments I am rather more at a loss to come up with a question, in part because I know little from first-hand experience about experimental markets. In this one, I have therefore decided to adopt a ministerial stance and seek out a theme on which to reflect—it is "rational choice." Plott remarks that the market models are based on individual rationality, and, despite the fact there is substantial evidence that rationality is not descriptively adequate, the market models are reasonably descriptive. In addition, he writes (p. 119): "If the following axioms are accepted, then preferences can be induced and controlled for purposes of experimentation.

1. More reward medium (money) is preferred to less, other things being equal (salience and nonsatiation).

2. Individuals place no independent value on experimental outcomes other than that provided by the reward medium (neutrality).

3. Individuals optimize."

From this he "derives" that the preference order over pairs (x, y), where x is the amount of a single commodity and y is money, is necessarily an additive conjoint structure with the representation $R^i(y) + x$, where R^i is an experimenter-determined conversion from the commodity to money. Since the experimenter controls R^i, a wide range of preference orders can be induced on the subject.

Plott argues that assumption 2 is where economists and psychologists part company. That is certainly the case if the nonmonetary commodity has any intrinsic worth to the subject. But if the experiment is so contrived that it is simply a recoding for money, then the assumption is true, but the procedure seems artificial, if not trivial. Let me not get stuck on this point, for it is assumption 3, I believe, that really separates the economists from the psychologists. It is here that something having to do with rationality appears. Just what does that mean, and just what have the experiments shown us? That is, of course, the main topic of the paper by Tversky and Kahneman (in this volume).

I think we will all agree that a major keystone of rationality is transitivity. We must have that if we are to have any kind of numerical theory that associates numbers to individual alternatives and permits us to describe behavior as equivalent to maximizing value. But we all know (thanks in large part to the careful experimental work of Tversky [1969], Lichtenstein and Slovic [1971], Grether and Plott [1979], and Slovic and Lichtenstein [1983]) of circumstances in which transitivity fails. This continues to strike me as one of the most surprising results in the area and one that I believe needs continued investigation.

Recall too that when it is brought to a person's attention that he or she has made strictly intransitive choices, considerable discomfort is exhibited. People seem to feel it to be an inconsistency they do not like, and with good reason since it can be made to bankrupt them. What is not at all clear to me is whether these sorts of intransitivities are in fact relevant to the market situations discussed by Plott. If they are, I would expect that considerable advantage could be taken of the person exhibiting them. Let me leave, albeit uneasily, transitivity and turn to what else is involved in rationality.

Here we enter a great morass of examples and experiments that are, in my opinion, less than perfectly clear in their significance. Tversky and Kahneman (in this issue) conclude that these findings imply that the development of rational and descriptive theories are separate enterprises. I am not yet convinced, in part because there is a theory (Luce and Narens 1985, sec. 7, p. 56) that seems potentially able to encompass both.

Let us take as the domain of discussion an algebra, $\mathscr{E}$, of events and a set, X, of gambles that is closed under binary operations of forming gambles from the events. This is often called a mixture space. More specifically, if A is an event in $\mathscr{E}$ and x, y are gambles in X, then the following gamble is also in X: if the experiment underlying event A is carried out, then x is received when A occurs, and y is received when $\bar{A}$ occurs. I use an operator notation to denote this gamble, namely, $xo_A y$. The more complex gamble $(xo_A y)o_B z$ is interpreted to be a two-stage gamble in which the experiment underlying B is first run, and, if B occurs, then independent of that experiment the one underlying A is run to select between x and y. In particular B may equal A, in which case two independent realizations of the same experiment are involved, as in generating a random sample. Now, assuming a transitive preference ordering $\gtrsim$ on X, I formulate for this structure three additional principles, each of which is true in subjective expected utility (SEU). These are all discussed by Tversky and Kahneman.

PRINCIPLE 1—*Monotonicity of composition* (which is an example of what Tversky and Kahneman call "dominance"). For all x, y, z in X and A in $\mathscr{E}$,

$$x \gtrsim y$$

if and only if

$$xo_A z \gtrsim yo_A z$$

if and only if

$$zo_A x \gtrsim zo_A y.$$

(In a more careful presentation, I would have to restrict A to be nonnull in some suitable sense.) As we are all aware, this property is really very compelling, and it underlies numerous social dilemmas, such as versions of the prisoner's dilemma. Let me not comment on it until I lay out the other two principles.

PRINCIPLE 2—*Irrelevance of framing* (which is an example of what Tversky and Kahneman call "invariance"). Given any two gambles that are equivalent in the sense that the several outcomes occur under exactly the same conditions, except possibly for the order in which independent experiments are carried out, the gambles should be judged indifferent in preference.

Thus, for example, this principle implies, as is easily verified, that each of the following indifferences should hold:

$$(xo_A y)o_B y \sim (xo_B y)o_A y, \tag{1}$$

which is called "commutativity in the mixture space";

$$xo_A y \sim yo_{\sim A} x, \tag{2}$$

which is called "complementation in the mixture space";

$$(xo_A y)o_A z \sim (xo_A z)o_A(yo_A z), \tag{3}$$

which is called "right autodistributivity" in the mixture space.

I shall refer to such equations where the only real difference is one of framing as "accounting equations." Again, let me hold off on comments.

PRINCIPLE 3—*Event monotonocity* (which Tversky and Kahneman call "cancellation" and the "sure-thing principle"). Suppose $x > y$ and A, B, C in $\mathscr{C}$ are such that $A \cap C = B \cap C = \emptyset$. Then

$$xo_A y \gtrsim xo_B y$$

if and only if

$$xo_{A \cup C} y \gtrsim xo_{B \cup C} y.$$

Violations of this property are often called the Ellsberg paradox.

Note well the difference between principles 1 and 3. The former concerns monotonicity under formation of new gambles from old ones, whereas the latter concerns monotonicity when the outcomes associated with the events are systematically altered by changing the outcome on both sides over an event, C, that is disjoint from both A and B. These two principles are not to be confused since, as will soon be clear, they play very different roles in utility theory. The fact that the term "sure-thing principle" has been applied to both suggests that they may not always be clearly distinguished, although they certainly are distinguished by Tversky and Kahneman.

As was emphasized by Tversky and Kahneman, SEU satisfies all three properties, and it is descriptively wrong. Are all three principles wrong, or are only some of them? According to my reading of the literature we know that the Ellsberg paradox is exhibited by many people, and thus event monotonicity, principle 3, is not descriptively valid in general. We also know, as is well summarized in Tversky and Kahneman, that versions of principle 2, invariance, and versions of principles 1 and 2 combined, dominance and invariance, are not descriptively correct. They assert that when dominance is made transparent, as it is in the statement of principle 1, people abide by it. I think, however, I am correct in saying that we do not have any true experimental test of that claim. But let me assume that it will be confirmed. Then it is interesting to ask what sort of theory can be based on just transitivity and monotonicity of composition (dominance). Ignoring possible failures of transitivity such a theory might be descriptively adequate and, with additional postulates such as principles 2 and 3, reduce to SEU.

Such a theory, called "dual bilinear utility," can be found in Luce and Narens (1985). I will not attempt to recount the argument, which is intricate and depends in part on deducing the form of the most general concatenation structure that has an interval scale representation onto the real numbers. Suffice it here to give the representation that results from these considerations: there is a utility function, U over X, and two weighting functions, S^+ and S^-, on $\mathscr{C}$ such that U is order preserving and

$$U(xo_A y) = \begin{cases} S^+(A)U(x) + [1 - S^+(A)]U(y), & \text{if } x > y, \\ U(x), & \text{if } x \sim y, \\ S^-(A)U(x) + [1 - S^-(A)]U(y), & \text{if } x < y. \end{cases}$$

The utility function is an interval scale, as is easily verified. Note that this form degenerates into SEU provided that $S^+ = S^- = $ a probability measure; otherwise, it has some differences of importance. Let me point out five.

First, given the way the representation was derived, it necessarily satisfies monotonicity of composition (principle 1), a fact that is easily verified directly.

Second, this representation satisfies the framing principle of commutativity in the mixture space that is embodied in equation (1). This corresponds to the idea that the order in which experiments are conducted does not have any special significance. Personally, I am a bit more suspicious of this than I am of monotonicity of composition, and it certainly needs to be studied in isolation.

Third, this representation satisfies complementation in the mixture space (eq. [2]) if and only if, for each A in $\mathscr{E}$,

$$S^+(A) + S^-(\bar{A}) = 1.$$

This is not yet the same as saying that S^+ and S^- are identical.

Fourth, it satisfies right autodistributivity (eq. [3]) if and only if $S^+ = S^-$, in which case there is a single bilinear weighting rather than different ones that depend on the relative value of the components. I should point out that many other similar accounting equations, such as bisymmetry, lead to the same conclusion. Indeed it appears that any accounting equation that involves either more than two outcomes or more than two events forces this much of SEU. This means that, if we are to have the real flexibility of the dual bilinear model, the principle of irrelevance of framing must be invoked in a most limited way.

Fifth, the dual bilinear utility model satisfies principle 3 (monotonicity of events or cancellation) if and only if for each A, B, C in $\mathscr{E}$ with $A \cap C = B \cap C = \emptyset$ and for each $i = +, -,$

$$S^i(A) \geq S^i(B)$$

if and only if

$$S^i(A \cup C) \geq S^i(B \cup C).$$

This property holds, of course, when the S^i are probability measures.

I will not go into the calculations (they may be found in Luce and Narens [1985]), but the general dual bilinear model is closely similar to, and more general than, the prospect theory of Kahneman and Tversky (1979), which means that it can encompass many of the empirical results that are inconsistent with SEU. One of the major differences between the two theories, and one that no doubt can be exploited to distinguish between them empirically, is that the dual bilinear model exhibits a form of relativity internal to the gamble, placing different weights on the more preferred outcome than on the less preferred, whereas the prospect model has a form of relativity that is embodied in the form of the utility function, vis-à-vis present wealth.

In terms of empirical work, the dual bilinear model suggests that we should study monotonicity of composition in isolation from the framing questions, and such a study is currently under way. In addition, I think it would be interesting to examine carefully several of the accounting equations, in particular, equations (1) and (2). And, of course, it would be interesting to see what sorts of economic models would arise on the assumption of this somewhat more limited notion of rationality, one that does not invoke the strong analytic abilities implicit in the irrelevance-of-framing principle. In its present form the dual bilinear model is unsatisfactory in at least two important respects. First, it does not explicitly talk about gambles having more than two outcomes except to the extent that they can be decomposed into compositions of binary gambles. Second, no axiomatization of it has been developed in terms of preference as a primitive. I have shown how to axiomatize general interval scale concatenation structures (Luce 1986), but it is not immediately obvious how to use that to obtain an effective axiomatization of dual bilinear utilities. Considerable work remains to be done, but I think this model demonstrates the real possibility of evolving descriptive theories based on limited (bounded) forms of rationality, which, when sufficient properties are added, becomes SEU.

References

Grether, D. M., and Plott, C. R. 1979. Economic theory of choice and the preference reversal phenomenon. *American Economic Review* 69 (September): 623–38.

Kahneman, D.; Knetsch, J. L.; and Thaler, R. H. In this volume. Fairness and the assumptions of economics.

Kahneman, D., and Tversky, A. 1979. Prospect theory: An analysis of decision under risk. *Econometrics* 47 (March): 263–91.

Lichtenstein, S., and Slovic, P. 1971. Reversal of preferences between bids and choices in gambling decisions. *Journal of Experimental Psychology* 89, no. 1:46–55.

Luce, R. D. In press. Uniqueness and homogeneity of ordered relational structures. *Journal of Mathematical Psychology*.

Luce, R. D., and Narens, L. 1985. Classification of concatenation measurement structures according to scale type. *Journal of Mathematical Psychology* 29 (March): 1–72.

Plott, C. R. In this volume. Rational choice in experimental markets.

Slovic, P., and Lichtenstein, S. 1983. Preference reversals: A broader perspective. *American Economic Review* 73 (September): 596–605.

Tversky, A. 1969. Intransitivity of preference. *Psychological Review* 76 (January): 31–48.

Tversky, A., and Kahneman, D. In this volume. Rational choice and the framing of decisions.

Richard A. Shweder

University of Chicago

Comments on Plott and on Kahneman, Knetsch, and Thaler*

Being an anthropologist, and feeling a bit more like a participant observer than a native in these marvelously theological proceedings,[1] I think I will start my comments with a joke about the market for brains in Papua New Guinea. That is where they practice cannabalism, and in Papua New Guinea every encounter with another person can be represented as a choice situation in which each decides whether or not to take the other's head.

So this fellow walks into a supermarket in Papua New Guinea. He goes to the meat section where he sees several bins. The first bin says "psychologists' brains—$2.32 a pound." The second bin says "economists' brains—$2.49 a pound." The third bin says "anthropologists' brains—$15 a pound." He goes to the guy behind the meat counter and says, "What's this! I mean brains are brains. I can understand a slight difference in price for psychologists' brains and economists' brains, but $15 a pound for anthropologists' brains. That's ridiculous. It's downright unfair!" The guy behind the counter replies, "Do you know how many anthropologists we had to kill before we could get a pound of brains!"

I confess that I feel a little bit that way today (i.e., lacking in unbounded rationality) when I hear speakers like Simon, Einhorn,

* This commentary was written while I was a John Simon Guggenheim Fellow and a fellow at the Center for Advanced Study in the Behavioral Sciences. I am also grateful for the financial support provided by the Spencer Foundation.

1. With regard to the theological dimension of the conference, I confess to the suspicion that it is not so much, as Herbert Simon suggested in his opening remarks, that in the modern era business has displaced religion but, rather, that in the modern era a new religion has come along. It is the religion associated with individualism and the famous "spirit" of capitalism (Weber 1958) in which individual choice becomes a fetish. And it becomes everyone's mission to encourage everyone else to expand as far as possible the realm of things over which one makes rational decisions. Suspicions aside, the physical setting of the conference—the Swift Lecture Hall on the third floor of the Divinity School at the University of Chicago—seemed like a perfectly arranged scene for deep and passionate reconsiderations of the foundations of rational choice theory.

Tversky, Kahneman, Plott, and others talk so lucidly about an issue—the so-called problem of rationality and its relation to the apparently irrational—that has concerned, mystified, and divided anthropologists for at least a century.

In fact what I feel like doing is sitting down and saying nothing. Given the likelihood of exciting exchanges—real and symbolic—it would be quite pleasurable just to sit back, observe, and learn. Unfortunately, I have to balance that likelihood against an absolute certainty that Robin Hogarth and Mel Reder would not like it if I just sat things out. And, since I have recently learned that "there is a nonlinear weighting function for subjective worth such that it hurts more to lose status than it pleases to gain and that greater value is attached to absolutely certain outcomes," I think I will say a few things and risk getting myself into deep trouble, which is a risk I would normally like to avert at almost any cost, except Robin's and Mel's displeasure.

Kahneman, Knetsch, and Thaler (in this volume) document an ethical side (what years ago might have been called a sentimental or artificial side) to economic transactions. While their main goal is to discover generalizations that describe whether an economic action is considered fair, they go on to argue that fairness judgments are not coincidental with judgments of market efficiency or self-interest, that fairness judgments do not form part of a coherent normative system, that fairness judgments are themselves motivating and have real world effects on economic behavior, and that fairness judgments cannot be deduced from the normative axioms of rational choice theory.

One implication of their work is that anyone who actually lived by rational choice theory as a matter of literal and general policy (e.g., someone who represented every encounter as a choice and always raised prices to meet increased demand) would be morally defective. It is noteworthy that our everyday language of moral abuse is rich in adjectives, verbs, and nouns encoding in folk wisdom exactly that perception of the unbound, unembedded, unsocialized rational actor. Thus we condemn someone as "self-interested," "calculating," "manipulative," "opportunistic"—as a "profiteer." We speak of "being scalped," and so on. Unbounded, self-interested behavior seems to be held in deep distrust by common sense. Perhaps that is for good reasons—good rational reasons—although to comprehend the rationality of our everyday attitude of moral disapproval toward opportunistic self-interest one may have to move away from a perspective of individual self-interest to a perspective of detached, impartial rationality. I shall have more to say about that in a moment.

Charles Plott (in this volume) starts his paper by thanking psychologists for showing that the axioms of rational choice are testable and by suggesting that as a general account of individual decision-making processes the deep maxims of choice theory do not hold—the theory is false. He then goes on to document cases in which the rational agent model, the optimization assumptions, and risk-averse expected utility theory work well to model complicated behavior in experimental markets. Plott describes choice situations in which potential "irrationalities" of individual decision making and judgment (the sunk-cost fallacy and representativeness heuristic) do not play a part in, or interfere with, rational choice. (How rational outcomes are produced without an appeal to the rational processes of individuals still remains to be explained.) Plott notes in passing that the need for a separate theory of moral behavior (separate from rational choice theories) has not been documented, a possible point of tension with the position of Kahneman et al.

A common issue motivating or presupposed by both papers is the relation between the normative and descriptive functions of rational choice theories. Given space constraints I will try to raise one or two questions about each paper and then conclude by trying to bridge the gap between "is" and "ought," between descriptive accounts of why people do the things they do and normative accounts of what people should and would do if they acted rationally. I want to point to a way in which normative and descriptive studies need each other.

In its own very elegant way, the paper by Kahneman et al. connects with classic issues in social theory. It has long been argued in certain sociological traditions that, from the point of view of utilitarian models of optimizing individuals pursuing their self-interest, there is in any society an extra- or nonrational force associated with communal or solidarity interests. The work of Durkheim (1964, 1965) comes to mind on morality, retributive justice, and the idea of the sacred as opposed to the profane. Durkheim focused on the deeply felt need for revenge in systems of punishment. For example, it somehow feels deeply wrong simply to let people who kill their spouses go free, even if it could be demonstrated that crimes of passion were "one time" events, that it is costly to maintain prisons, that spouse murderers do not need to be rehabilitated, and that there is no deterrent effect traceable to their incarceration. Some extra- or nonrational force, a deeply felt sense of justice, requires punishment. Classic work in anthropology on taboos and rituals (see Shweder [1984] for an overview) develops the idea of a nonrational component to human behavior, although there is always someone eager to try their hand at rationalizing such things as the Hindus' prohibition against eating beef (the sacred cow) or the failure of most Americans to categorize cats, dogs, horses, or rats as something to eat.

The research also has parallels in work on contract law (Kennedy 1982), especially the issue of why there are innumerable limits on the freedom to enter into contract, limits on the freedom to set any terms one wants in a contract, and impositions of mandatory terms that parties to a contract cannot waive, whatever their perception of their interests. On the surface of it, it would seem that fairness and other ethical considerations place limits on freedom of contract. For example, large classes of actors (children, the insane, and the incompetent) are protected from exploitation by not allowing them to enter into contracts; certain agreements are simply morally repugnant (e.g., agreeing to be a slave in return for free housing or agreeing to waive one's right to get married in exchange for $50,000). And many terms imposed on contracting parties regardless of their wishes (e.g., a legal requirement that a deal is not binding until after a waiting period) would seem to involve paternalistic or ethical considerations. So even though the paper by Kahneman et al. may seem "narrowly" focused on fairness in economic transactions, the issues run deep.

I find myself a bit reluctant to accept, as yet, the expressed view that the fairness judgments described do not form a coherent system and cannot be derived from any philosophical or economic theory of morality. I would concede that at the level where the paper tries to locate generalizations about fairness judgments they do not seem to form a coherent package and that, at that level, such generalizations as "an increase in demand unaccompanied by an increase in cost is not an acceptable reason to raise prices" seem to require a lot of qualification. For example, what about the market for summer rentals on Nantucket or in Southampton? What if every year during the past 30 when there had been a blizzard the hardware store had raised the price of snow shovels from $15 to $20, and everyone is aware of it? In such cases raising the price without reference to cost might not be considered unfair. Why not?

I suspect there are ways to see more unity, generality, and coherence in these judgments of fairness. As a start one might focus research on the ideal and idealized conditions presupposed by the notion of a rational choice by a voluntary agent. The presupposed idealized agent of unbounded rationality made choices free of duress or emotional impulse, with foresight and advice, armed with accurate information and an intelligence able to calculate consequences accurately, and so on. Thus implicit contracts, whether economic contracts or contracts of other kinds, are unfair and disallowable by courts and are offensive to the collective conscience to the extent that either of the agents involved deviated from a condition of voluntariness at the time of giving consent. When parties to contracts are sufficiently vulnerable (i.e., in a state of involuntariness) courts often disallow the contract. Thus, for example, a woman in a postpartum depression who consents to give her child to an adoption agency for a fee and then later wants the child back might well succeed at getting society to disqualify the contract.

One basic goal of our social attitudes, sentiments, and institutions seems to be to protect the vulnerable from exploitation and defend the communal or solidarity interests of the "tribe." If the blizzard and consequent price increase could have been anticipated, that is, if foresight were possible, the price hike may not have seemed unfair. But if foresight was not possible, then the purchaser was not a voluntary agent but rather a vulnerable individual being taken advantage of, the perception of which activates ethical feelings, which in this case may reflect communal interests. A theory of voluntary agency, a theory expanding the concepts of duress and fraud, might give unity and generality to the account of everyday judgments about fairness. I suspect that judgments about fairness are generated not from a list of generalizations about supply and demand and opportunity costs but rather by assessing the degree to which conditions of voluntariness failed to hold in any particular transaction.

One area for future development in the examplary paper by Kahneman et al. would be systematically to face the anticipated counterargument that fairness judgments are rational as matters of social policy or as cultural values or as institutions or even as matters of long-term, as distinguished from short-term, self-interest. In principle the existence of a code of good conduct enforced by social pressure, or guilt, and possibly supported by received doctrines about evil is not incompatible with rational choice models, although it may prove impossible to make sense of things only from the level of analysis of individual or egoistic calculators.

When an attempt is made in moral philosophy or religious ethics to give a rational account of fairness values or ethical principles, what typically happens is that the argument gets displaced to another level of analysis. For example, we invoke the idea of an impartial agent or a rational actor who is indifferent to his particular position or advantage in society and who has the wisdom and power to create sensible ethics and institutions. That is what is done by Rawls (1971), who tries, perhaps unsuccessfully, to derive a just society from a social contract among self-interested actors, each of whom is imagined to be ignorant of the ways he differs from others in wealth, power, intelligence, beauty, and so on. That is, the hypothetical actor does not know where he is going to end up in the society that is formed. Just social institutions (including a market) are meant to work to the advantage of everyone wherever he or she might happen to end up in society. It is a controversial and debatable issue whether one can theoretically derive an ethical motive as the product of rational self-interested calculation. Nonetheless, it would be nice to know where Kahneman et al. stand on attempts to model ethics after rational choice models, as in social contract theories.

Plott demonstrates that rational choice models can predict complex behavior in experimental markets. He describes his paper as a defense against claims about the descriptive irrelevance of such models. Reading Plott's paper side by side with the paper by Tversky and Kahneman (in this volume), I understand why some economists may feel defensive. Tversky and Kahneman argue that it is not possible to construct a theory of choice that is both normatively acceptable and descriptively adequate and that, therefore, the normative and descriptive analyses of choice should be viewed as separate enterprises.

I can see how those are fighting words to economists, yet when it comes down to particulars it is fascinating that there are really very few substantive differences between Plott and Tversky and Kahneman. There are differences in emphasis and especially in what is put in the foreground and what is left in the background; yet a list of substantial claims would not reveal much disagreement. Despite some rhetorical flourishes, none of them is making radical claims.

Thus Tversky and Kahneman acknowledge that the dominance rule and other axioms of rational choice are obeyed when their application is sufficiently transparent, and they seem to restrict their claim that the normative theory is descriptively invalid to those choice situations where the axioms are embedded in nontransparent frames. Moreover, Tversky and Kahneman acknowledge that what they call, with a rhetorical flourish, the "bolstering" assumptions of rational choice theory are often valid. Thus feedback and markets can correct individual deviations from rationality, and so on. On the other hand, Plott grants that markets may behave in unusual ways that might have to be explained by models of irrational or normatively unacceptable individual behavior.

No one seems to be advocating any of the following possible radical positions: (a) that the normative model is normatively inadequate; (b) that rational choice models never model real world choices; (c) that the axioms of rational choice models are tautologically true or that they are incapable of justification; or (d) that significant error in judgment and choice never occurs in real world situations. It is less clear whether Tversky and Kahneman and Plott believe that all individual behavior ought to be represented as a choice or whether they believe that the rationality of values, practices, or institutions can be explained by reference to egoistic real world calculations, whether long or short term.

Some remarks by Churchman (1961, p. 234) have helped me in thinking about the relation between the normative and the descriptive sides of our deepest normative maxims. Churchman seeks a middle ground between the two extreme views (a) that the axioms are always descriptively valid and (b) that the axioms are irrelevant for describing behavior. I like his middle-of-the-road position. I hope it is not the golden mean between right and wrong!

Churchman starts out with an analogy from logic—the maxim that nothing can be both A and not A. The analogy is of special interest to me because several generations of anthropologists, starting with Lucien Lévy-Bruhl in 1910, have spent their time debating whether the rules of logic had any part to play in the thinking of primitive peoples. Some of the arguments turned on one's interpretation of such assertions as, "We are red parrots," and, "Sorcerers are bush cats." Lévy-Bruhl argued that when the natives said, "We are red parrots," they were not committing logical errors that the native could be led to recognize and correct but rather were engaging in a mode of thought governed by alternative, nonlogical rules. In the 1930s Lévy-Bruhl recanted (perhaps prematurely), and today most anthropologists believe that the laws of identity and noncontradiction are relevant and important for understanding primitive thought.

Examples of apparent violations of the idea that nothing can be both A and not A ("We are red parrots") are treated as either metaphors, parallel descriptive systems of the table-salt-is-sodium-chloride variety, or else bad translations. Some scholars believe there are special contexts (e.g., ritual occasions or dream states) in which normative logical principles such as identity, noncontradiction, and the excluded middle are irrelevant or inapplicable or in which their violation is the point of the ritual experience.

Churchman (1961, p. 234) has the following to say about the maxim that nothing can be both A and not A. To paraphrase, the table before me is both green (on top) and black (underneath). I guess nothing can be both A and not A in the same place and at the same time. The top is green to me but gray to you (who is color blind). I guess nothing can be both A and not A in the same place and at the same time and to the same person. It is green to my eye but hard to my hand. Well, I guess it cannot be both A and not A in the same place and time and to the same person and in the same aspect of his experience.

Reflecting on the maxim (nothing can be both A and not A) Churchman argues that it is intuitively available in our mental equipment yet has a dynamic, almost dialectical, relation to experience. On the one hand, the maxim makes it possible for us to order and record our experiences; experiences get structured as we apply the maxim. On the other hand, the maxim gets reinterpreted as we order these experiences—we reinterpret what A and not A and can "be" mean. The maxim itself is empty; it comes uninterpreted in our mental equipment, and how we end up ordering experience is underdetermined by the maxim alone. Yet it is indispensable for ordering objects and events into contrast sets and for deciding which things we will treat as the relevant set of things that an A cannot be (e.g., "dimes" are not "birds," but it is more relevant on most occasions to contrast them with "pennies" or "nickels," etc.). One implication of this dialectical approach is that a "reconciliation" of what is (actual decision making) and what ought to be (the normative model) is something that is sometimes sought after, even if not accomplished, by each individual actor. A descriptive account of decision making must pay attention to the individual's own normative self-regulation.

By extension, Churchman argues that the rationality maxims are ways of ordering events. He points out that, in a sense, they can never be shown to be false because we can always maintain them by reinterpreting the concept of preference or choice or the terms that denote the objects of preference. Still we may end up rejecting the relevance of one or more of the maxims if we are driven to very awkward interpretations of preference or to awkward interpretations of the domain of objects over which choice or preference relations are said to apply. I find it awkward, for example, to represent routine, ritualized, or habitual behavior, which is done without conscious deliberation or calculation, as an unconscious choice on the part of the individual between continuing the habit and not continuing the habit.

From that point of view behavior is underdetermined by the rationality maxims in several senses. For one thing there is much negotiation and conflict in any society about which areas of experience are properly represented as choices, for example, whether to sell one's body parts, to feed your children, or to convince your wife to make her womb available to others for hire to produce children. It would be illuminating to know whether marriage rates go down as divorce rates and lawyers fees go up or whether, instead, the routine practice of marrying goes on at the same rate regardless of the consequences or risks involved. For many people in our culture it is deeply troubling to think about marriage in terms of self-interested calculation—of costs and benefits. Many cultural factors enter in here—guilt, repression, ethical codes, and the concept of evil rule out rational calculation in many domains. It is the realm of the sacred or the ethical—which is pretty much the same thing.

In those domains where we are permitted to represent things as choices we may well strive to get the choice situation and our preferences into equilibrium with the maxims of choice theory (invariance, transitivity, etc.), and in some cases we succeed, perhaps assisted by market forces, feedback, and transparent framing. But we do not always succeed. Many psychological factors enter in here, for example, the biases associated with certain heuristics, indifference to evidence, tastes influencing beliefs about the likelihood of outcomes, snap decisions, logical lapses, lack of clarity about goals, lack of foresight, and so on. As has been powerfully demonstrated, problems of the same logical form but of different content differ substantially in difficulty or transparency—and for many reasons. The problem with the idea of abstract or formal axioms is not that the axioms are false but rather the implication that one can focus on them alone (ignoring content and framing) and still comprehend or predict actual functioning. If you succeed at predicting functioning, it is because you know more than you realized about the content and the proper way to frame things.

In conclusion, it seems to me that any metalanguage for talking about real world behavior is going to have to be rich enough to acknowledge the existence of differences between rational, irrational, and nonrational behavior, at least at the level of individual functioning.

Of course the discussion can be shifted from individual rationality and calculation to the rationality of practices, ethical codes, or institutions. Perhaps social rules and customary practices are a rational solution to the problem that many people are vulnerable to irrationalities much of the time and fall short of ideal voluntary control. Perhaps institutions (e.g., the family and social and professional hierarchies) evolve or are created so that, in effect, the weak give deference, loyalty, and admiration to the strong in exchange for care, nurturance, guidance, and protection. Perhaps in a well-organized society no individual need calculate for himself the advantages or disadvantages of his institutions and ethics or be aware of the bargain implicit in them.

The importance of rationality models is clearly revealed in various attempts to account for institutions and social practices and ethics. Yet, ironically, no one can identify the real human actor who would make the choice to set up sensible institutions and fair practices. And, to end with a theological dimension for the conference, many have thought and continue to think that the only entity with enough power and intelligence and foresight and impartiality to make such choices is some hypothetical rational actor called God. "God," as sociologists since Durkheim have been prone to remark, is a representation of the community, of solidarity interests. The "conscience collective" is not only conscience but consciousness of the collective. It is a global or collective rationality bigger than ego and his "self"-interest. And there are many who haunt this Swift Hall of the Divines of the University of Chicago who still think that something like God—an impartial observer who sees things from all perspectives at once and takes regard of what it sees—is a necessary inference from a rationalistic perspective on society. Perhaps he has an invisible hand. But he or she or it is a very long way from those individual mortal decision makers, you and me, whose vulnerabilities—in our unbounded and admirable desire to be gods—we sometimes overlook.

References

Churchman, C. W. 1961. *Prediction and Optimal Decision.* Englewood Cliffs, N.J.: Prentice-Hall.

Durkheim, E. 1964. *The Division of Labor in Society.* New York: Free Press.

Durkheim, E. 1965. *The Elementary Forms of the Religious Life.* New York: Free Press.

Kahneman, D.; Knetsch, J. L.; and Thaler, R. H. In this volume. Fairness and the assumptions of economics.

Kennedy, D. 1982. Distributive and paternalistic motives in contract and tort law, with special reference to compulsory terms and unequal bargaining power. *Maryland Law Review* 41:563–658.

Plott, C. In this volume. Rational choice in experimental markets.

Rawls, J. 1971. *A Theory of Justice*. Cambridge, Mass.: Harvard University Press.

Shweder, R. A. 1984. Anthropology's romantic rebellion against the enlightenment. In R. A. Shweder and R. A. LeVine (eds.), *Culture Theory: Essays on Mind, Self and Emotion*. New York: Cambridge University Press.

Tversky, A., and Kahneman, D. In this volume. Rational choice and the framing of decisions.

Weber, M. 1958. *The Protestant Ethic and the Spirit of Capitalism*. New York: Scribner's.

Donald T. Campbell

Lehigh University

Rationality and Utility from the Standpoint of Evolutionary Biology

A major motive of these comments is to offer a perspective in which the important paper on perceptions of fairness by Kahneman, Knetsch, and Thaler (in this volume) is moved from being a description of an exogenous factor "distorting" market rationality and becomes instead an integral part of a theory of collective rationality. In anticipatory summary, perceptions of fairness (like moral norms in general) are our individually rational preferences as to how others behave. If the collective-goods payoffs are sufficient so that the cooperative system is worth maintaining and if that social system is intact, then it may be individually rational to abide by those norms oneself as a rationally paid cost in a strategy of getting others to live up to them.

This will be argued on grounds drawn from evolutionary biology and, in particular, from the issues surrounding "altruism" that are so focal to sociobiology. A growing number of economists are participating in a potential integration of economics and evolutionary theory. From participants in this conference this includes, at least, Simon (1973, 1983), Becker (1976), Nelson and Winter (1982), and Lucas (in this volume). Among our nonpresent colleagues participating are Hirshleifer (1977, 1978) and Samuelson (1983). Because I believe this is a trend that should be further developed, I am going to preface my analysis of the issues raised by Kahneman et al.'s paper by an overview of other aspects of the sociobiological perspective relevant to the total agenda of this conference.

Shared in common by biology's "population genetics" (the mathematical theory of the evolutionary process) and econometrics are models in which populations of individual decision makers that are optimizing utilities produce macro effects. The concepts of "decision making," "utilities," "self-interest," and self-sacrificial "altruism" are, of course, used in biology as a convenient metaphorical shorthand rather than as a literal description of cognitive decision processes and subjective utilities. I, for one, condone and participate in this usage and regard it as rarely misleading. I do not have space to argue this here, other than to assert (1) that the selective processes operate in such ways as to select for animals that act "as though" they had such decision processes and utilities and (2) that—conceived of as a linguistic shorthand—such invoking of "teleonomy" does not imply "teleological causation," being consistent with a thoroughgoing physicalism (i.e., ontological priority of the inorganic). (For an able and highly readable defense of such usage, see Dawkins [1976].)

My disagreement with Dawkins is not in the use of "selfish" but rather that he confounds the unit of retention, the gene, with the unit of selection, the whole organism (see Sober 1984). It is the unit of selection that, in this biological shorthand, will be "selfish" and that will manifest "teleonomy" or "goals" or "purposiveness."

One could regard macroeconomic theory as using "rationality" and "interests" in a similarly metaphoric way, justified by the fact that the outcomes of the differential survival of business firms or of ventures within firms produced surviving dominant policies that could be so described, without imputing these subjective mental goals and processes to the individual decision makers involved. Properly elaborated, this might resolve the deep divisions in this conference volume. I have neither the space nor the competence to develop this argument but would begin with Aldrich (1979), Nelson and Winter (1982), and Kaufman (1985).

I.   Self-Interest Equals Inclusive Fitness

Rationality in economic theory is primarily a rationality of the means whereby individuals (whether biological persons or firms) maximize utilities. Especially where the behavior of persons is at issue, the content of the utilities is left open, unspecified by theory. While it is a maximization of "self-interest," the contents of self-interest are usually not specified by the theory. Merging such self-interest theory with evolutionary biology offers the promise of theoretical grounds for predicting such contents, that is, predicting what sorts of interests the products of biological evolution would be apt to have. The paper by Lucas (in this volume) makes the equation between adaptation and optimizing, which I am assuming.

The answer of sociobiology, based on Hamilton's (1964/1971) crucial papers and elaborated by Wilson (1975), Alexander (1979), and many others, is to derive all more specific interests from the ultimate goal of inclusive fitness, maximizing the frequency of one's genes in future generations. Through the related concept of kin selection, Hamilton and the others point out that this is furthered not only through one's own offspring but also, in diluted degree, by the progeny of relatives. Thus nepotism becomes an aspect of self-interest.

While economic theory may formally leave self-interest unspecified, in practice an individualistic self-centeredness is often assumed. This needs revising to include the interests of direct descendents and nephews and nieces. Thus "altruistically" hoarding wealth to pass on to children at the expense of one's own skin-surface hedonism becomes rational self-interest in the biological model. While my attention has been called (although I have lost the reference) to at least one economic study failing to support such a motive in wealth accumulation, I would counter with Baldus's (1973) massive assembly of evidence that the aged poor will endure personal deprivation to leave property to their heirs. I feel confident that the bulk of econometric analysis will support this revision.

II. The Rationality of Interests in a Modular Hierarchy of Goals and Subgoals

The larger critique of human rationality of which economic theory is inevitably a part must contain theory about the rationality of the goals, interests, or utilities for which we strive as well as about the rationality of decision making in the service of these interests.

From the standpoint of evolutionary biology, our innate pleasures, hungers, lusts, fears, and pains are subgoals, selected as mediating inclusive fitness. Learning takes place in the mediating of such goals. The message of cybernetics and purposive behaviorism (Tolman 1932; Miller, Galanter, and Pribram 1960) is that learning itself is a chaining not of muscle contractions but rather of "acts" organized around the achievement of subgoals. It was this recognition that weaned Karl Lashley (Lashley and McCarthy 1926) from Watson's behaviorism. A rat that learned a maze was still able to locomote it without entering any blind alleys after a cerebellar operation that paralyzed its rear legs: it still knew the route and achieved the subgoals, the choice points, by novel muscle movements. Similarly, much of the "instinctive" behavior even of insects is organized around subgoals, as McDougall and McDougall (1931) noted long ago in observing a mud wasp's repeated repair of an experimentally broken nest. Skinner's (1938) shift to operant behavior contains the same recognition: a rat that has acquired the subgoal of getting the lever depressed will continue to do so with its jaw if its front paws are tied (for elaboration, see Campbell [1963, pp. 135–48]).

The hierarchical nesting of subgoals organizes behavior into what Simon (1969, 1973) has called semidecomposable subunits in which the linking nodes are goals, or subgoals. The "informational" requirements of practical rationality, emphasized in his paper in this issue, depend in most instances on such subgoals being left unrevised, being instead treated as dependable units, the "rationality" of whose mediation is not continually being reexamined. This "neglect" is in the ser-

vice of an overall rational strategy for mastering complex environments in a cumulative way. (An important agenda for Simon is to
integrate explicitly these two lines of thought. Heuristics, too, involves
subgoals tentatively trusted.)

From this perspective on a pervasive hierarchy of "interests"—
innate, learned, and organized as subgoals that mediate more encom-
passing goals—it becomes clear that the issue of rationality of decision
making cannot be separated from that of the rationality of "interests."

III. Evolutionary Reasons for Irrational Interests

Evolutionary theory—biology or cultural—does not automatically
produce a "Panglossian" picture of perfect rationality or adaptedness.
Indeed its theoretical resources can be assembled to understand and
predict systematic dysfunction, and it may well be this potentiality that
might most modify economic theory were the merger to be carried
further.

Evolutionary processes posit slow adaptation to stable environments
where large populations of reproductive units are available. The "wisdom" of the products is wisdom about past worlds and loses any
"hypothetically normative" credibility if we have reason to believe the
organism (or organization) is now in an environment substantially different from the environment that shaped it (Campbell 1965).

Even within the constant environment of evolutionary shaping, the
adaptive mechanisms are built up from initially crude exploitation of
convenient approximations, complicated by subsequent approximative
corrective devices, but, starting from ignorance and without revelation, are never clairvoyant or fully informed. (In considerable part this
may correspond to the informational restraints stressed by Simon.)
The result is that irrationalities may persist for some tasks even within
the original environment of evolutionary shaping if the mechanism
(subgoals, etc.) is adaptive for the greater bulk of its uses.

Tversky and Kahneman's paper (in this volume) provides a possible
illustration of this last point. The Müller-Lyer illusion is probably best
explained as a by-product of generally adaptive visual inference habits,
innate and acquired, centered around gaining valid third-dimensional
information from two-dimensional line or edge displays (Segall, Campbell, and Herskovitz 1966; Deregowski 1980). While at least some animals and probably all humans are subject to the illusion to some degree
(enough to require the arrow-tipped line to be perhaps 4% longer than
the feathered one), those of us who live in "carpentered worlds"
abounding in rectangular solids have the "illusion" to a stronger degree (perhaps 20%) and at the same time are more adept at decoding
third-dimensional information from two-dimensional drawings: overall
the processes atypically sampled in the illusion drawing are adaptive.

Moving to the "irrational" response to equivalent wagers differently framed that are central to Tversky and Kahneman's (in this volume) work, one probably has to emphasize the shift-in-ecology argument: human brains formed in one ecology of problems are now being used in quite another. Without claiming competence in the large literature of alternative interpretations that their exciting work has generated (e.g., Cohen 1981, and critiques; Stich 1985), let me offer an illustrative possibility. In the formative ecology of perceptual and brain processes adaptation was achieved by modularly separate focal attention to desired objects on the one hand and to feared objects (aversive "goals") on the other, with cognitive neglect (and nonenumeration) of irrelevant objects. A brain thus shaped is ill adapted, in ways that Tversky and Kahneman specify, to two-valued logics or to an exhaustive-set, three-valued logic.

A special class of Simon's informational economy mechanism is the maladaptive hypertrophy of once usefully approximate proxy variables. Thus, in the biological theory of female choice in mate selection (to use an outmoded example), size of antlers may have once been a useful proxy variable for overall male capacity to contribute to the inclusive fitness of joint offspring. But once it becomes an innate female preference determiner, it may lead to maladaptive exaggeration. Similarly, in cultural evolution crude but useful proxies for leadership competence may be exaggerated into economically wasteful customs (see Boyd and Richerson 1985, chs. 6, 9).

Haldane (1932), in his greater unification of natural selection with Mendelian genetics, pointed out another biological evolutionary source of nonoptimality for social animals in which there is genetic competition for individual inclusive fitness among the cooperators. He founded the discussion of (self-sacrificial) "altruism" in evolutionary theory, an analysis that has its parallels in the economist's problems of free riders and collective goods (e.g., Olson 1968). This source of collective irrationality is the subject of my two final comments.

IV. Evolutionary Theory and Collective Goods

Human beings, like all fertile animals, are in direct competition with their kin (except their identical twins) and neighbors for the food and shelter available in their environment. This ubiquitous condition creates an obvious interest in controlling how other individuals behave and is best elaborated in David Wilson's (1980) interference theory. This produces a minimal form of the conflict of interests between the group as a whole and each individual as to how that individual should behave, thus getting into the problem of social control.

More significant is the fact that in a wide range of ecologies, such as in big-animal hunting and irrigated grain fields, cooperation increased food resources and shelter from predators. But individuals are once again in competition for the size of their shares of these increased resources. At this level, however, a novel form of collective interest emerges: individual competition for maximum share of the resources jeopardizes the benefits of cooperation and the cooperative organization itself. Greedy quarreling for maximum share reduces the pool of resources to be shared. In ecologies where cooperation can double or quadruple the per-capita resources available, there is a payoff for effective social control that protects the efficacy of cooperation from individual greed. That such mechanisms are rare and fragile is the conclusion of analyses coming from both the mathematical models of evolutionary biology (Haldane 1932; Williams 1966; Wilson 1975, ch. 5; Boorman and Levitt 1980; Wilson 1980) and economics (von Neumann and Morgenstern 1944; Hardin 1968; Olson 1968; Schelling 1971).

My own disagreement with the collective-goods economists is only one of emphasis. Their analyses, currently, seem to me to underestimate grossly the relative magnitude of collective goods to individual goods, particularly as projected into a future of exhausted natural resources. Their focus is thus predominantly one of liberating individual choice behavior from the restraints placed on ruthless individual optimizing by traditional morality and governmental edict, whereas I see effective restraint on intelligent individual covetousness as essential to the securing of collective goods of overwhelming importance. This is not a difference in theory but rather a difference in the estimates of parameters in a shared model.

It may help to minimize these differences if I present the covetousness-restraining moral norms as fundamentally motivated by a "selfish" (i.e., inclusive fitness) interest in how the other cooperators behave. The example of the social insects helps dramatize this (Campbell 1983). The predominant sterility of the cooperators is essential to this elaborate cooperative division of labor. It eliminates "genetic competition among the cooperators" and thus the motivation to be a free rider. But this sterility needs continual enforcement to be maintained. A female ant's first-choice strategy (facultative polymorphism) is to be the fertile queen. This failing, the sterile worker's second-choice strategy in implementing her inclusive fitness via nieces and nephews (following the argument for kin selection) is to keep her fellow workers (and soldiers, etc.) sterile. The cooperative nest system is so productive that this is in the net advantageous even if, in the process, her own sterility is also ensured. Thus the workers distribute to fellow workers, soldiers, and infants fertility-inhibiting pheromones produced by the queen, at the expense of their own fertility (Seeley 1985).

To abbreviate a much longer argument (Campbell 1982, 1983) for human complex social coordination that is achieved in spite of (rather than through eliminating) genetic competition among the cooperators, moral norms curbing ruthless intelligent individual optimization are rational selfish individual preferences as to how others behave. If the social organization is intact and if the collective goods are substantial, it is also rational to conform to such norms oneself if that is necessary for maintaining group membership. We probably have an innate ambivalence (facultative polymorphism) on this score: an available repertoire of cooperative group solidarity and another one of individual optimization at the expense of the group.

Trivers (1971) and Axelrod (1984) describe the requirements for the minimally social verion of such cooperative systems: pair-wise reciprocal altruism. (Trivers's article has never been fully reprinted, and I recommend it be read in the original.) The requirements include prolonged interaction with the same others, individual identifiability, good memory, and small populations of interactors. Accompanying the capacity for reciprocal altruism is the capacity for "moralistic aggression," inflicting vengeance on those who welch on their agreements. Somehow this reciprocal altruism gets expanded into clique selfishness, primary-group solidarity, fear of ostracism, and the like.

For larger social units the precarious establishment of cooperative social units has been accompanied by fantastic transcendental belief systems, with rewarding and punishing reincarnations and afterlives promising individuals a net hedonic gain optimized over a longer period than their own immediate lives. Consider the great gain in productivity of early irrigation civilizations, coming from a social order that builds and repairs irrigation canals and clearly worth maintaining from a collective rationality of collective inclusive-fitness optimizing. Contrast this rationality with the heroic waste (economically and biologically) accompanying the royal funerals in most (perhaps all) such early agricultural societies. Such waste is explicable only as a means to a still greater gain. My explanation (not fully convincing even to me; but see Campbell [1975]) is that this ritual testimony to the ruler's belief in an afterlife supported such beliefs among the citizens and was fundamental in protecting the production of collective goods against the erosion of individually optimizing free riding. Boyd and Richerson (1985, ch. 7) provide a model of cultural evolution that might make this possible. May I note in passing my belief that, where in the past either market mechanisms or legal restraints have worked well, it is because of the helpful residue of such awed indoctrination into moral restraint (Campbell 1982). If indeed the process Weber described as *die Entzauberung der Welt* (loss of the enchanted worldview) still proceeds apace, we must look to alternative means to protect collective goods.

While space limitations provide an excuse for not trying to fill the gaps right now, I would hope that eventually Kahneman et al.'s data on perceptions of fairness and on market responses of compliance to such perceptions could become a part of this perspective on collective rationality.

V. Nonoptimalities and Irrationalities due to Face-to-Face Group Solidarity

Economic and organization theory (e.g., March and Simon 1958) has noted dysfunctions from the point of view of the firm arising from managers' mixed agendas where optimizing their own interests conflicts with optimizing the firm's. In economics, "principal agent theory" (Jensen and Meckling 1976) is one articulation of this. The evolutionary perspective supports such emphases and adds to their understanding where nepotistic expressions of self-interest are involved.

Our biological heritage provides another equally powerful source of distortion for the optimization of the interests of the firm or of any other large organization. This is our capacity for face-to-face group solidarity. We are all responsive to signs of approval and disapproval coming from those whom we see face-to-face on a regular basis. We all have a dread of ostracism at some underlying level, if not consciously. The communications of approval and disapproval may be largely non-verbal and unconscious on the part of both sender and receiver. There results (in brief, see Campbell [1982, 1983] for some more extended argument) a tendency for every face-to-face aggregation in the organization to become an "in-group," with both those in other buildings at higher, equal-status, or lower echelons and those transient others, such as customers, becoming "out-groups." The clique interests of the primary groups lead to solidarity in furthering the comfort of in-group members, often at the expense of the interests of the larger group of which the face-to-face groups are a part (for an interesting example from Dengist China, see Walder [1985]).

Here is an area that, if developed, would provide, I believe, a great gain in our understanding of how individual and face-to-face group interests, rationally expressed, become a source of nonoptimality at the level of larger social units.

VI. Summary

As several economists have noted, there are numerous parallels favoring an integral relation between economic theory and evolutionary biology. Evolutionary theory also leads to predictions of the utilities that an organism is likely to maximize and, in the concepts of kin selection and inclusive fitness, expands self-interest to include nepotism. But for reasons of pragmatic economy evolutionary adaptations are never complete for the ecology adapted to and can be maladaptive in novel ecologies.

Evolutionary analyses of social insect and human complex division of labor systems point out the rationality of wanting to restrain the individual optimization of other cooperators where this threatens collective goods. If the collective goods are substantial and the social system intact, it becomes individually rational to conform to such inhibiting norms oneself. Face-to-face group solidarity can produce nonoptimalities for social organizations made up of several face-to-face groups.

References

Aldrich, H. E. 1979. *Organizations and Environments*. Englewood Cliffs, N.J.: Prentice-Hall.

Alexander, R. D. 1979. *Darwinism and Human Affairs*. Seattle: University of Washington Press.

Axelrod, R. 1984. *The Evolution of Cooperation*. New York: Basic.

Baldus, D. C. 1973. Welfare as a loan: An empirical study of the recovery of public assistance payments in the United States. *Stanford Law Review* 25, no. 2:123–250.

Becker, G. S. 1976. Altruism, egoism and genetic fitness. *Journal of Economic Literature* 14:817–26.

Boorman, S. A., and Levitt, P. R. 1980. *The Genetics of Altruism*. New York: Academic Press.

Boyd, R., and Richerson, P. 1985. *Culture and the Evolutionary Process*. Chicago: University of Chicago Press.

Campbell, D. T. 1963. Social attitudes and other acquired behavioral dispositions. In S. Koch (ed.), *Investigations of Man as a Socius*, vol. 6 of *Psychology: A Study of Science*. New York: McGraw-Hill.

Campbell, D. T. 1965. Variation and selective retention in socio-cultural evolution. In H. R. Barringer, G. I. Blanksten, and R. W. Mack (eds.), *Social Change in Developing Areas: A Reinterpretation of Evolutionary Theory*. Cambridge, Mass.: Schenkman.

Campbell, D. T. 1975. On the conflicts between biological and social evolution and between psychology and moral tradition. *American Psychologist* 30:1103–26.

Campbell, D. T. 1982. Legal and primary-group social controls. *Journal of Social and Biological Structures* 5:431–38.

Campbell, D. T. 1983. The two distinct routes beyond kin selection to ultrasociality: Implications for the humanities and social sciences. In D. L. Bridgeman (ed.), *The Nature of Prosocial Development: Interdisciplinary Theories and Strategies*. New York: Academic Press.

Cohen, L. J. 1981. Can human irrationality be experimentally demonstrated? [with 31 critiques and responses]. *Behavioral and Brain Sciences* 4:317–70.

Dawkins, R. 1976. *The Selfish Gene*. New York: Oxford University Press.

Deregowski, J. B. 1980. Perception. In H. C. Triandis and W. Lonner (eds.), *Handbook of Cross-cultural Psychology: Basic Processes*. Vol. 3. Boston: Allyn and Bacon.

Haldane, J. B. S. 1932. *The Causes of Evolution*. London: Longmans Green.

Hamilton, W. D. 1964. The genetical evolution of social behavior. *Journal of Theoretical Biology* 7:1–51. Reprinted in C. C. Williams (ed.), *Group Selection*. Chicago: Aldine-Atherton, 1971.

Hardin, G. 1968. The tragedy of the commons. *Science* 162:1243–48.

Hirshleifer, J. 1977. Economics from a biological viewpoint. *Journal of Law and Economics* 20:1–52.

Hirshleifer, J. 1978. Natural economy versus political economy. *Social Biological Structures* 1:319–37.

Jensen, M. C., and Meckling, W. H. 1976. Theory of the firm: Managerial behavior, agency costs and ownership structure. *Journal of Financial Economics* 3, no. 4:305–60.

Kahneman, D.; Knetsch, J.; and Thaler, R. In this volume. Fairness and the assumptions of economics.

Kaufman, H. 1985. *Time, Chance, and Organizations: Natural Selection in a Perilous Environment*. Chatham, N.J.: Chatham House.

Lashley, K. S., and McCarthy, D. A. 1926. The survival of the maze habit after cerebral injuries. *Journal of Comparative Psychology* 6:423–32.

Lucas, R. E., Jr. In this volume. Adaptive behavior and economic theory.

March, J. G., and Simon, H. 1958. *Organizations*. New York: Wiley.

McDougall, K. D., and McDougall, W. 1931. Insight and foresight in various animals— monkey, raccoon, rat, and wasp. *Journal of Comparative Psychology* 11:237–73.

Miller, G. A.; Galanter, E.; and Pribram, K. H. 1960. *Plans and the Structure of Behavior*. New York: Holt, Rinehart & Winston.

Nelson, R. R., and Winter, S. G. 1982. *An Evolutionary Theory of Economic Change*. Cambridge, Mass.: Belknap.

Olson, M. 1968. *The Logic of Collective Action*. New York: Schocken.

Samuelson, P. A. 1983. Complete genetic models for altruism, kin selection and like-gene selection. *Journal of Social and Biological Structures* 6:3–15.

Schelling, T. C. 1971. On the ecology of micromotives. *Public Interest* 25:61–98.

Seeley, T. D. 1985. *Honeybee Ecology*. Princeton, N.J.: Princeton University Press.

Segall, M. H.; Campbell, D. T.; and Herskovits, M. J. 1966. *The Influence of Culture on Visual Perception*. Indianapolis: Bobbs-Merrill.

Simon, H. A. 1969. *The Sciences of the Artificial*. Cambridge, Mass.: MIT Press.

Simon, H. A. 1973. The organization of complex systems. In H. H. Pattee (ed.), *Hierarchy Theory: The Challenge of Complex Systems*. New York: Braziller.

Simon, H. A. 1983. *Reason in Human Affairs*. Stanford, Calif.: Stanford University Press.

Simon, H. A. In this volume. Rationality in psychology and economics.

Skinner, B. F. 1938. *The Behavior of Organisms*. New York: Appleton-Century-Crofts.

Sober, E. 1984. *The Nature of Selection: Evolutionary Theory in Philosophical Focus*. Cambridge, Mass.: MIT Press.

Stich, S. P. 1985. Could man be an irrational animal? Some notes on the epistemology of rationality. In H. Kornblith (ed.), *Naturalizing Epistemology*. Cambridge, Mass.: Bradford.

Tolman, E. C. 1932. *Purposive Behavior in Animals and Men*. New York: Century.

Trivers, R. L. 1971. The evolution of reciprocal altruism. *Quarterly Review of Biology* 46:35–57.

Tversky, A., and Kahneman, D. In this volume. Rational choice and the framing of decisions.

von Neumann, J., and Morgenstern, O. 1944. *Theory of Games and Economic Behavior*. New York: Wiley.

Walder, A. G. 1985. Wage reform and the web of factory interest. Mimeographed. New York: Columbia University, East Asian Institute.

Williams, G. C. 1966. *Adaptation and Natural Selection*. Princeton, N.J.: Princeton University Press.

Wilson, D. S. 1980. *The Selection of Populations and Communities*. Menlo Park, Calif.: Benjamin/Cummings.

Wilson, E. O. 1975. *Sociobiology: The New Synthesis*. Cambridge, Mass.: Belknap.

James S. Coleman

University of Chicago

Psychological Structure
and Social Structure
in Economic Models

Economic theory can, for the purposes of what I shall say here, be seen as consisting of two parts. One part is the microfoundation of purposive action, using a model of action that is especially simple. The second part is the apparatus that derives system-level behavior from the actions of individuals whose goals have some relation. The paradigmatic way in which the interests or goals are related is that which exists in a private-goods market.

Economists are often concerned that their assumptions in the first part of economic theory are awry, or at least too simple. This conference is an expression of that concern. But there is also a second set of assumptions, namely, those embedded in the apparatus that carries individual action into systemic functioning. While the assumptions that go to make up the model of rational action can be called the psychological assumptions underlying economic theory, those embedded in the apparatus that carries individual action into system functioning can be called the sociological assumptions underlying economic theory.

This conference is of course about the first of these sets of assumptions. My comments will not be wholly diversionary; I will not attempt to refocus your attention on the sociological assumptions. What I do want to suggest, however, is that there are parallels between the ways the psychological assumptions deviate from reality and the ways the sociological ones deviate. These parallels have to do with the absence of structure: in the first case, structure within the individual; in the second case, structure among individuals.

I will attempt to show the parallel by use of the familiar red bus/blue bus problem. Let me state the problem by using an illustration that Gerard Debreu used in criticizing Duncan Luce's probabilistic theory of choice in an early review (for a discussion, see Tversky [1972]). Consider a person choosing between two records: a suite by Debussy and a Beethoven symphony. Assume that he is indifferent between the two. Then, putting this indifference to one side, suppose he is offered a choice between the original Beethoven symphony and another recording of equal quality of the same symphony. He is again indifferent between the two. Then what do we expect him to do if confronted with all three? Luce's theory of choice would predict that he would choose each with a probability of about one-third. Yet this seems quite unlikely. Instead it seems very likely that he would still have about a .5 probability of choosing the Debussy recording and about a .5 probability of choosing one of the two Beethoven recordings.

Amos Tversky's (1972) paper accounts for the way individuals make such a choice by introducing structure, that is, a multistage choice in which individuals first determine the most important "aspect" of the choice and then eliminate alternatives according to that aspect. Here the "aspect" is composer so that, according to Tversky's aspect theory, the individual would first choose between Debussy and Beethoven and then, if the choice was Beethoven, would choose between the two recordings. This three-stage, or "structured," choice would predict the results of the thought experiment that Debreu devised. The first stage is the selection of the dominant aspect that divides the alternatives. The second stage is selection between the two sets of alternatives grouped according to this aspect. In this case, the Debussy record is one set, and the two Beethovens make up the other. The third stage in this case is selection on the minor aspect, that is, between the two Beethovens if "Beethoven" was chosen in the second stage. If there are more alternatives in the set chosen, another aspect may be used to divide them before the final stage is reached. It should be noted that, in this case, if the second and third stages were reversed, choosing on the minor aspect first, the same prediction would hold. The crucial element of the theory is the introduction of structure through first determining the importance of aspects or qualities of the alternatives.

Now let me shift from processes within individuals to processes among individuals, that is, from psychology to sociology. Consider the following thought experiment about social choice. There are two nominees in an election, and polls show that each would receive about half the vote. Now another nominee is introduced who turns out to be very similar to the first. This third nominee turns out to be, in the polls, about equally attractive to the first and about equally attractive to the second in pair-wise choices. Suppose that it is an election in Lebanon for president. One nominee is Bashir Gemayal, from a prominent Christian family, and the second is a man from a prominent Moslem family. Suppose that the candidates are C and M for short. Then there comes a third nominee, Amin Gemayal, the brother of Bashir. So we now have C_1, C_2, and M.

Then the question arises, What will happen in an election? Simple rationality of individuals would predict, with reasonable individual preference orders, that Amin would get about a quarter of the votes, Bashir about a quarter, and the Moslem about half.[1] Is this what would occur? The answer is ordinarily no. This would occur only if the electorate were a set of disconnected individuals so that the outcome were a simple aggregation of individual preferences. The result would be collectively irrational (in that the dominance of the Moslem over the Christians does not reflect the balance in the population of voters), though the individuals are quite rational.

But what would almost certainly occur is something quite different. Structure would be introduced: within the Gemayal family, or among Christians as a whole, there would first of all be a choice between Amin and Bashir; and the general election would be between two candidates, one a Moslem and the other a Christian. Even if the two potential Christians, C_1 and C_2, were not from the same family, it appears very likely that the Christians would get together and choose between the two so that the resulting election would be between one Christian and one Moslem. In short, structure would be introduced in the social choice, with the choice occurring in stages.

When we consider political elections more generally, we recognize that this behavior of the social system is not limited to Christians and Moslems in Lebanon. Rather what we find in nearly every political system is a multistage choice process. The first stage, analogous in Debreu's example to the implicit decision that composer is the most important aspect or dimension, is formation of a political party. The subsequent stages follow: a choice process within the party (e.g., by a primary or a convention) and then a choice in which the parties' candidates are the only nominees.[2] Informally, there are certainly earlier stages in which there is a selection among possible candidates on the left, say, of a political party and among possible candidates on the right, with each subgroup within the party (and, before that, subgroups within subgroups) putting its best candidate forward to the party as a whole.

Altogether, what appears to be the case is that in social choice there has been a social evolution in which structure is introduced by subgroups who stand to lose if they do not introduce structure (such as the Christians in Lebanon in the example I introduced), resulting in multistage social choice processes.

Now let me return to the two components of economic theory—the

1. Preference orders that would give the particular combination are any in which about half the voters ranked the Moslem first, and, both among these voters and among those who ranked a Christian first, about half preferred Amin to Bashir, and half preferred Bashir to Amin.

2. Note that after the choice of dominant aspect the social choice proceeds in the opposite sequence to that proposed for individual choice by Tversky: elimination first within each party, and finally a choice between parties.

microfoundations and the apparatus for moving from individual action
to system behavior. The example I gave suggests that, both in the
microfoundations and in the apparatus for moving from individual to
system-level behavior, there is more structure than is assumed in neoclassical economic theory. For an example of social structure in markets there often seems to be a relatively stable structure that develops
among trading partners so that for any exchange each party in the
market considers only a small set of trading partners among those
potentially available—with a change in this set itself occurring only
infrequently.

But I want to go further than this. The implicit premise of this conference is, I believe, that revision of the rational action foundation of
economic theory, by constructing a more sophisticated model of action, is where the potential gains to the theory are greatest. For some
problems in economics this may be true. My argument, however, is
that, for most, it is incorrect; that the straightforward model of rational
action that satisfies normative theory will, despite all the evidence
about its descriptive deficiency, be adequate for most problems in
economic theory as a descriptive theory. It is deficiencies in the apparatus for moving from the level of the individual actor to the behavior of the system that hold the greatest promise of gain. The same
investment in modifications to this apparatus will bring considerably
greater benefit to the theory. The reasons, I believe, lie in part with
evolutionary processes in social and psychological organization: psychological organization has evolved more fully to bring individual action closer to efficient action than has social organization (where even
the definition of efficiency is more problematic than is true for a physical individual). The end result is that there is wider variability in social
organization through which individuals' actions combine to produce
system-level behavior. In the example I gave, social organization appears to be far more variable in the construction of multistage social
choices for a society than is psychological organization in constructing
multistage choices for the individual. Or, to move closer to economic
behavior, markets function differently and give different equilibrium
prices, depending on the institutions through which exchanges are organized—as Charles Plott's and Vernon Smith's experimentation with
market institutions have shown (see Plott 1982; Smith 1982). An English auction gives one set of outcomes; a central clearinghouse of bids
and offers gives another; sealed-bid auctions give another; a market
with prices established by sellers and modified to produce market
clearing gives another; and a wholly instructured market in which the
traders themselves must develop informal structure gives still another.
Information, of course, is part of the reason for the differences in
different kinds of markets, but not all. Social institutions and social
networks—which are not completely, but are largely, ignored in neo-

classical theory—can make differences in outcomes without any change at all in the model of rational action. It is elaboration in this direction that I believe will constitute the greater payoff for economic theory. The elaboration involves not only the introduction of structure into the theory when it is found in reality but also predicting the kind of structure that will, if individuals are rational, be introduced—as in the illustration I gave of the emergence of political parties in social choice.

References

Plott, Charles R. 1982. Industrial organization theory and experimental economics. *Journal of Economic Literature* 20 (December): 1485–1527.

Smith, Vernon L. 1982. Microeconomic systems as an experimental science. *American Economic Review* 72 (December): 923–55.

Tversky, Amos. 1972. Elimination by aspects: A theory of choice. *Psychological Review* 79, no. 4:281–99.

John P. Gould

University of Chicago

Is the Rational Expectations
Hypothesis Enough?

This note presents a model in which the rational expectations hypothesis does not restrict the number of equilibrium solutions in any meaningful way.[1] The techniques and assumptions used to obtain this result, though applied to a very simple duopoly model, are likely to generalize to a variety of rational expectations models. This result suggests that the rationality assumptions often used in economic models may not narrow the range of predicted economic behavior by very much. Such a result is troubling insofar as models that are able to narrow the range of predicted behavior significantly are often the most useful in empirical work.

There is a more positive way to state this result, for it suggests a potentially fruitful collaboration between economists and decision psychologists. From the viewpoint of economics, such collaboration may be a source of insight that can help to reduce the number of solutions that rational expectations models of the type presented here seem to generate. From the viewpoint of decision psychology, such collaborative research would provide a framework of equilibrium analysis (or even general equilibrium analysis) that might suggest new forms of experimentation and a broader context for the interpretation of experimental findings. It is worth mentioning in this respect that the feedback implied by the equilibrium framework of economics does not, in and of itself, depend on any rationality assumption but does recognize the effect of the interaction of an aggregation of numerous individual decisions on the individual decision makers themselves. So far as I can tell from my reading of the literature, such feedback from what might be described as the "macro" implications of the equilibrium process in economics seems to play little or no role in decision psychology.

A formal model is presented and discussed in the next section, and

---

1. A secondary objective is to discuss some methodological issues concerning the modeling of expectations in economics.

the concluding section considers the implications for both psychologists and economists in greater detail.

I. The Model

The model considered here is a simple duopoly involving linear conjectural variations and rational expectations. In these equations, q_1 and q_2 represent the outputs of firm 1 and firm 2, respectively, and p is the price. The variable q_1^e refers to firm 2's expectation of firm 1's output. Similarly, q_2^e is firm 1's expectation of firm 2's output. The terms a and b are demand function parameters, c is the constant average (and marginal) cost of output for each firm, and h_1, v_1, h_2, and v_2 are the parameters from the expectations equations. The terms r_1 and r_2 represent profit (the maximand) for firm 1 and firm 2, respectively.

The equations of the model are as follows:

demand:

$$p = a - b(q_1 + q_2); \tag{1}$$

profit for firm 1:

$$r_1 = pq_1 - cq_1; \tag{2}$$

profit for firm 2:

$$r_2 = pq_2 - cq_2; \tag{3}$$

expectations of firm 1:

$$q_2^e = h_1 + v_1q_1; \tag{4}$$

expectations of firm 2:

$$q_1^e = h_2 + v_2q_2; \tag{5}$$

rational expectations:

$$q_1 = q_1^e; \tag{6}$$

rational expectations:

$$q_2 = q_2^e. \tag{7}$$

The equilibrium for this model is given by the solution to the following set of equations:

first order for firm 1:

$$-2b(1 + v_1)q_1 = c - a + bh_1; \tag{8}$$

rational expectations for firm 1:

$$q_2 = q_2^e = h_1 + v_1q_1; \tag{9}$$

first order for firm 2:

$$-2b(1 + v_2)q_2 = c - a + bh_2; \qquad (10)$$

rational expectations for firm 2:

$$q_1 = q_1^e = h_2 + v_2q_2. \qquad (11)$$

The usual approach to (8)–(11) would be to solve the equations simultaneously for q_1 and q_2, treating all other values as given parameters. A well-known example of this approach is when $v_1 = v_2 = 0$. In this case the solution to these equations is the celebrated Cournot-Nash equilibrium:

$$q_1 = q_2 = \frac{a - c}{3b}.$$

In general, however, the solution will not exist because there are more equations (four) than there are unknowns (two). In other words, unless we are lucky, there will not be a rational expectations equilibrium for an arbitrary set of parameters. In this sense, rational expectations appears to narrow the set of admissible values for the parameters in this model and hence is useful empirically and theoretically.

There is another approach to solving (8)–(10), however, that maintains the rational expectations assumption while avoiding the problem of overdeterminacy in the set of equations. In this approach a quantity pair (q_1, q_2) is treated as given (or observed) as are the demand and cost parameters a, b, and c. These five values are then treated as parameters, and the four equations are solved simultaneously for h_1, h_2, v_1, and v_2. In other words, we are asking whether there exist expectations equations that are consistent with the observed quantities.

It is easy to characterize the solution to this second approach. Begin with the values of q_1 and q_2 and calculate p from the equation

$$p = a - b(q_1 + q_2).$$

It can be shown that the solution of (8)–(11) is then

$$v_1 = \frac{p - c}{bq_1} - 1, \qquad (12)$$

$$v_2 = \frac{p - c}{bq_2} - 1, \qquad (13)$$

and

$$h_1 = h_2 = q - \frac{p - c}{b},$$

where $q = q_1 + q_2$. The first- and second-order conditions are met if q_1 and q_2 are positive and $p > c$. Thus there is an infinite number of solutions that satisfy the rational expectations equilibrium. In particular any positive pair (q_1, q_2) that satisfies the inequality

$$q_1 + q_2 < \frac{a - c}{b}$$

will be a rational expectations solution.

This second approach to finding rational expectations equilibria is the methodological inverse of the usual approach. Instead of finding equilibrium values of q_1 and q_2 given the parameters of the conjectural variation equations, this second approach asks whether there are parameters of the conjectural variation equations that are consistent (in the rational expectations sense) with a given pair of quantities. The somewhat disturbing answer is that virtually any pair of quantities is consistent with rational expectations. In the next section this result is discussed in terms of some methodological issues in economics, and its relation to behavioral decision making is also considered.

II. Some Implications of the Model

It is a bit surprising that such a large number of rational expectations solutions can be generated using nothing more elaborate than linear conjectural variations. However, a little reflection shows why this is the case. To be specific, consider firm 1 for a moment. Given an output level for firm 2, firm 1's output decision will depend on how responsive firm 1 believes firm 2 to be to firm 1's output decision; that is, firm 1's output will depend on the parameter v_1. Similarly, firm 2's output decision will depend on how responsive firm 2 believes firm 1 will be to firm 2's output decision; thus firm 2's output depends on v_2. The explicit form of these dependencies can be seen in equations (12)–(13). This "responsiveness" belief plus the conjectured exogenous output level parameters, h_1 and h_2, provide enough degrees of freedom to generate the large number of rational expectations equilibria shown in the last section.

Many economists would object to this kind of equilibrium on the grounds that it might not be dynamically stable. In particular there is no mechanism to show how the system achieves such an equilibrium if it starts in a nonequilibrium state. While dynamic stability has an understandable intellectual and aesthetic appeal, its absence cannot be regarded as a serious methodological objection to this type of model. This model and others like it are essentially comparative static structures. Within the comparative static framework stability is assured at any of the indicated equilibria because neither firm has any incentive to deviate from its output decision given its beliefs. It is true that the firm may find that, if it does choose some other output, the other firm will not in fact respond as believed. However, since there is no reason in the model for either firm to choose a different level of output, the failure of each firm's conjecture is an off-equilibrium phenomenon and hence will not be observed. Thus, since all the observed evidence each firm has is consistent with its beliefs, any discrepancies between conjectured behavior and actual behavior are never observed, and hence the equilibrium is both rational and consistent in the comparative static setting. I note that this is also the sense in which the popular Cournot-Nash equilibrium is consistent. Indeed, the Cournot-Nash solution is one of the infinite number of solutions to this model.

A more sophisticated version of the dynamic stability objection is the effort to find equilibria in which the conjectural variation assumptions made by the firms are consistent with the model in the sense that output variations by either firm evoke the expected response by the other firm.[2] The fact that the equilibria described here are not always consistent conjectural equilibria is again not a serious methodological objection for reasons similar to those described above. The equilibria determined by consistent conjecture models are comparative static. Neither firm has the incentive actually to perform the conceptual experiment envisioned by the consistent conjectural equilibrium model since neither has the incentive to change its output. Similarly, neither firm can rationalize why the other firm would exogenously change its output as the model suggests because such behavior is not consistent with the view it has about the other firm. In short, all these models are similar in spirit to the one described in the last section in the sense that the equilibria they describe require that each firm hold beliefs about the other firm that are not true in off-equilibrium conditions. The inconsistencies are nonetheless irrelevant to the firms themselves because nothing in their behavior generates empirical evidence to contradict their beliefs.

It is possible that a fully dynamic model might be developed in which each firm's conjectures about the behavior of its rival would lead to dynamic paths that were consistent with these conjectures. I suspect, however, that it may well be possible to generalize the model of the last section to show that rational expectations would not be enough to establish a unique equilibrium path. Cyert and DeGroot (1974) have developed a Bayesian dynamic model that considers some of these issues. The dynamic path analyzed by Cyert and DeGroot deals with one out-of-equilibrium firm in an industry where the rest of the firms are assumed to be at equilibrium. In Cyert and DeGroot's model the equilibrium output is assumed to be known and is not determined endogenously, so the model does not directly address the uniqueness issue raised here.

---

2. This approach was taken by Tim Breshnahan (1981) in an interesting and widely read paper.

While it is understandable that in seeking to reduce the number of possible equilibrium solutions generated by a rational expectations model economists would look to the standard economic paradigm for help, it is not obvious why this is necessary or even desirable. For example, the particular beliefs a firm has about the potential off-equilibrium behavior of its rival could depend on sociobiological considerations. Such an equilibrium would be optimal in terms of the joint interests of the two firms for sociobiological reasons and also optimal in terms of the individual maximizing behavior of the firms for the usual economic reasons. This kind of dual optimality arises because the implied inconsistency never becomes an empirical reality for the firms themselves.

Similarly, the findings of psychologists working in the behavioral decision-making area may well help economists to make more precise statements about empirical phenomena by narrowing the range of predictions of rational equilibrium models. In other words, the large number of solutions that turn out to be consistent with rational expectations in models of the type considered here suggests that there may be opportunities for incorporating research findings from the area of behavioral decision making into economic research. For the reasons noted above, the apparent inconsistencies may not prove to be a serious barrier to progress along these lines.

Although I have focused my remarks on how the results from behavioral decision making might contribute to a deeper understanding of issues of interest to economists, I note that the reverse may be true as well. Psychologists working in the behavioral decision-making area are very careful about interpreting their findings in the context of the experimental environment from which they are derived. While this is scientifically prudent, one is inclined nonetheless to speculate about how some of these results might look in the general context of a market equilibrium. I suspect that some of the experimental results would have to be modified or reinterpreted in this broader context. For example, it would seem unlikely that findings concerning intransitivities at the level of individual decision makers would translate into persistent arbitrage opportunities at the level of market prices. This is not because no intransitive decision makers could survive in a market equilibrium, as some claim, but rather because the arbitrage opportunity in prices can be eliminated by the actions of only a few traders who are not subject to the intransitivity. More generally, the concept of market equilibrium has been a rich source of experimental results, as the research of Charles Plott, Vernon Smith, and others has shown, and additional research of this type is likely to prove interesting and valuable to both economists and psychologists.[3]

3. See, e.g., Smith (1962) and Plott and Smith (1978). A very interesting survey by Plott (1982) includes an extensive list of references.

By way of conclusion I cannot resist commenting on a certain irony that the papers at this conference have brought to mind. Economists have been using the rationality hypotheses that are being challenged by the psychologists largely for the development of a positive theory. To the extent that the psychologists' challenges to the positive theory turn out to be valid, the economists can take consolation from the fact that their positive theory will then have considerable normative merit.

References

Breshnahan, T. F. 1981. Duopoly models with consistent conjectures. *American Economic Review* 71 (March): 934–45.

Cyert, R. M., and DeGroot, M. H. 1974. Rational expectations and Bayesian analysis. *Journal of Political Economy* 82 (May/June): 521–36.

Plott, C. R. 1982. Industrial organization theory and experimental economics. *Journal of Economic Literature* 20 (December): 1485–1527.

Plott, C. R., and Smith, V. L. 1978. An experimental examination of two exchange institutions. *Review of Economic Studies* 45 (February): 133–53.

Smith, V. L. 1962. An experimental study of competitive market behavior. *Journal of Political Economy* 70 (April): 111–37.

Laurence E. Lynn, Jr.
University of Chicago

The Behavioral Foundations of Public Policy-making

Should we abandon the a priori postulates of neoclassical economics in favor of the empirically based postulates of cognitive psychology as Simon recommended in his presentation to the conference? The putative gain would be an increased supply of behavioral models characterized by greater descriptive accuracy and consistency. Or should we follow Becker's advice in his remarks to the conference and try to do better with models based on assumptions of rationality? The presumed gain would be models of greater power in making contingent predictions of aggregate behavior. Resolution of this issue would appear to be of vital importance to the study of policy-making, and these remarks are the reactions of a policy analyst to the proceedings thus far.

The study of policy-making is the study of behavior and its consequences: the behavior of individuals, groups, and organizations that produce or mediate the social conditions to which policymakers react. It is also the study of the behavior of policymakers themselves: legislators, elected and appointed executives, bureaucrats, and judges, whose decisions and other actions shape the role of the state in social and economic affairs. For purposes of providing intelligence for policy-making, an understanding of human and social behavior encompasses the ability both to explain it and to predict the behavioral consequences of changes in the values of explanatory variables and constraints, particularly changes in values that are created or influenced by government.

If policy analysis were concerned solely with description and explanation, its methods and its social role would not be much different from those of the social and behavioral sciences in general. Policy research would consist of constructing descriptively accurate models of individual and social behavior, logically deriving the implication of these models and assessing the significance of these implications for policy-making.

Policy analysis is also concerned, however, with the design of effective interventions in human affairs and thus with prediction of policy-relevant variables. It is concerned with social phenomena that actors in the policy-making process are inclined to regard as problems justifying official action and with the quality of these actors' responses to such problems. In its instrumental role—making conditional predictions that can be used as the basis for designing "social" actions, or, more particularly, governmental action—policy analysis cannot be confined to mere description. The value of analytic arguments must be judged not in terms of their descriptive accuracy or logical validity but "in relation to the special features of the problem, the quality of the data, the limitations of the available tools, and the needs of the clients" (Majone 1979, p. 9).

It is their commitment to prediction, to answering "what if" questions about possible governmental actions, that colors policy analysts' reactions to the issue raised by this conference. Analytic arguments are based on what are often termed craft judgments rather than on their conformity with mathematical or logical theorems, and choices of models are guided by practical considerations.

An example illustrates the point. Consider the following phenomenon, which has attracted the attention of policymakers. To an increasing extent, teenage girls are bearing children outside of marriage. These young mothers and their children are often poor and dependent on others—kin, neighbors, community agencies, and public bureaucracies—for sustenance. Both the mothers and their children are likely to find their future opportunities greatly restricted by the circumstances within which they must survive and grow, and long-term dependence on the state is a distinct possibility for many.

Public policy affects both the current levels of well-being of these mothers and children and, because public policies alter incentives, their future prospects as well. Depending on the effects of policies on incentives and on the behavioral responses of young mothers to these incentives, public policies may either increase or reduce the prospects for long-term dependence on public assistance, and they may affect future prospects in other ways.

If their task were "merely" to understand the problem, policy analysts would be justified in constructing descriptively rich, rather than descriptively parsimonious, explanations of individual behavior. Even in pursuit of this aspiration, these analysts would be venturing beyond the bounds of normal science and exercising craft judgments because they would necessarily need to assemble insights, empirical knowledge, and conjectures from numerous behavioral and social science disciplines and traditions, and there are few guidelines for how to do these syntheses. Thus no policy analyst committed to accurate description would want to be confined to the strong assumptions of rationality—of subjective expected utility maximization—because they would appear to be empirically inadequate. Nor, however, would they choose to confine themselves to cognitive/behavioral models, which neglect relations between cognition and behavior on the one hand and of social context on the other.

To understand why teenage girls become pregnant and bear children outside of marriage it would seem to be important to the study of policy-making cum social science to understand the complex behaviors underlying teenage pregnancy and illegitimacy. Why do these girls become sexually active? Why do they get pregnant? How do they make decisions about marriage and living arrangements? Why do they engage in particular forms of help seeking before, during, and after pregnancy? How do potential helpers view the situations of these girls, and why do they respond to them in the ways they do? Why do policy-makers make the choices they do concerning the structures and levels of support for programs affecting this population in the light of the alternatives they face? How do they form their understandings of the issues, and what kinds of evidence do they regard as informative? To form a sound basis for making policy choices, it can be argued, we need to understand the relevance to the behavior of teenage girls of cognitive structures, of ethical orientations, of patterns of association and dependence, of material incentives, of institutional structures, and of other potentially relevant variables.

If this "scientific" path to understanding the phenomenon of teenage pregnancy is taken, however, the policy analyst risks losing his or her audience long before any useful new knowledge emerges. The problem of deducing and testing hypotheses from complex, multidisciplinary models and of designing appropriate governmental action on the basis of the resulting empirical findings is likely to become intractable. Descriptively accurate models may be so complex that they are impractical. Programs of research based on their construction and testing may be exorbitantly expensive and offer little prospect of convergence or closure in a reasonable time. Another research strategy is called for.

As suggested, an appropriate strategy must be based on a clear idea of the policy problem to be addressed and of the predictions needed to design solutions. From the perspective of the policy-making process, teenage pregnancy constitutes a problem because of its aggregate manifestations. Increasing numbers of young girls, especially those who are black and living in inner-city ghettos, are bearing illegitimate children. The increasing numbers of black female-headed families become dependent for long periods of time on the range of services available from the welfare state, and their prospects for creating stable, independent lives on the basis of regular employment are dim. Indeed, many policymakers believe that the availability of services and support to pregnant teenagers is a cause of the problem. In these unpromising circumstances generations of children grow up with no prospects of their own for normal development and socialization. Thus fears of a growing urban "underclass" appear justified. Policy analysts cannot lose sight of the problem that justifies their efforts at achieving greater understanding of teenage pregnancy. The presumed goal of this understanding is useful ideas about how to prevent illegitimacy and dependency.

What kind of insight can the policy analyst cum craftsman hope to give to policymakers concerned with the problem of teenage pregnancy? The points of policy access may be numerous, at least in principle. Should we manipulate young women's perceptions of themselves and their social realities through information and public education? Should we attempt to alter their cognitive structures through direct interventions? Should we reorganize the institutions that touch their lives? Should we alter incentives by, for example, redesigning public assistance programs? Should we do nothing at all and let prevailing incentives, motivations, and demographic developments "solve" the problem?

Given the range of possibilities, deciding how to address the problem requires a high order of craftsmanship on the part of policy analysts. They must familiarize themselves with available data and with different analytic approaches to the problem. They must draw on insights into how policymakers learn and on the bases for their actions. Without giving in to preconceptions, they must rely on their feel for the advantages and disadvantages of different forms of policy intervention. Finally, they must create a conceptual framework that enables them to collect data in a timely manner and to use data relevant to addressing the concerns of this audience.

It may well be true that the policy studies community would be more effective in these pursuits if it invested more heavily in contemporary behavioral research. The kinds of policy insights that can result have been suggested by several of the presenters. However, the virtues of rational models for organizing thinking and data bearing on complex phenomena in a manner that permits testing and that, in addition, has action implications are considerable. I suspect that most of the contributions of social science to the content and results of public policy debate in recent years have depended on insights derived from the empirical application of rational models or from conjectures based on such models.

Maybe all this boils down to the proposition that you need a model to replace a model. Models of bounded rationality that addressed policy-significant behaviors in a more efficient way than did rational models would be welcome. As a policy analyst whose goal is to promote sensible policy-making, however, I would be reluctant to replace useful models with nothing because of their descriptive deficiencies. The choice of model for making predictions useful to policymakers depends on the question we are attempting to answer, the behavior we are attempting to predict. Policymakers are concerned with a wide variety of behaviors: teenage fertility, the securing of shelter, the consumption of medical care, participation in the paid labor force, saving for one's future income needs, and so on. As an empirical matter, models of rational choice doubtless will be more useful in explaining some of these behaviors than in explaining others. But the usefulness of the models is the issue.

The need to achieve understanding of aggregate behavior sufficient to inform action by actors in the policy-making process alters the incentives of policy analysts. The activity of achieving accurate description of individual behavior will now be viewed as costly, that is, as a competitor for scarce resources of time, attention, and research funds with the activity of developing more parsimonious models suitable for use with the kind of aggregate data common to policy-making discourse.

This choice of a focus for policy research does not imply an abandonment of principle, however. Regrettably, this question of analytic approach has been invested by many at this conference with great scientific and ethical significance, and abandoning neoclassical economics in favor of cognitive psychology is put forth as an ethically correct decision. From the perspective of policy-making, however, the question seems to be less one of ethics, or even of science, and more one of craftsmanship. It is a matter of how best to create useful knowledge about those social relationships and behaviors that attract the concern of policymakers. In this connection I would offer a number of additional observations of a sociological nature.

If we deemphasized rational models in favor of cognitive psychology, we might be merely trading in one style of casual empiricism, and one tradition of descriptive oversimplification, for another. Economists have no monopoly on tendencies toward confirming their conjectures with anecdotes or on offering heroic generalizations as truth. Psychologists have a distinguished history of a priori contributions to human understanding.

Similarly, we would be trading in one set of difficulties in constructing generally useful theories of real world aggregate behavior for another. The problems are bad enough in economics. The problems of constructing a well-behaved social welfare function from individual welfare functions are well-known. Theories that predict aggregate economic behavior are necessarily descriptively inaccurate at the level of the individual.

Constructing aggregate cognitive maps, or aggregate behavioral response functions, is no less problematic. In the limit, each individual's psyche and patterns of cognition are unique. Moreover, the benefits each individual derives from them are as incommensurable as are individual utilities. Psychologists who strive to reduce this complexity to more general laws, such as those of Freud or Skinner, raise the same questions as do neoclassical economists who do the same thing. Logically, how do you take aggregate measures on incommensurable individual attributes? As a practical matter, the question is, How many individuals must we understand—and to what extent must we understand anyone—before we can make tolerably accurate conditional predictions of behavior?

As a postscript, there may be a deeper significance to the questions raised by this conference. Once we introduce external and internal contexts into models of individual behavior, the focus on the individual decision may become hard to sustain. Making a decision is itself the product of a decision to do so. People decide to make decisions, they decide how to make decisions, and they decide what to do with themselves when they are not making decisions. The frequency and content of, and the approaches to, decisions are likely to be related to each other and to non–decision making in complex ways involving context and circumstances as well as personality.

Viewed in this way, my sense is that individuals are reasonably postulated as economizing on the use of scarce personal resources. They are trying to make some appropriately discounted stream of satisfactions as large as possible. Satisficing, or other methods of bounded rationality, may be viewed as ways of economizing on attention or search or emotional energy in connection with the pursuit of this larger goal.

Reference

Majone, Giandomenico. 1980. An anatomy of pitfalls. In Giandomenico Majone and Edward S. Quade (eds.), *Pitfalls of Analysis*. New York: Wiley.

Kenneth J. Arrow

Stanford University

Rationality of Self and Others in an Economic System*

I. Orientation

In this paper, I want to disentangle some of the senses in which the hypothesis of rationality is used in economic theory. In particular, I want to stress that rationality is not a property of the individual alone, although it is usually presented that way. Rather, it gathers not only its force but also its very meaning from the social context in which it is embedded. It is most plausible under very ideal conditions. When these conditions cease to hold, the rationality assumptions become strained and possibly even self-contradictory. They certainly imply an ability at information processing and calculation that is far beyond the feasible and that cannot well be justified as the result of learning and adaptation.

Let me dismiss a point of view that is perhaps not always articulated but seems implicit in many writings. It seems to be asserted that a theory of the economy must be based on rationality, as a matter of principle. Otherwise, there can be no theory. This position has even been maintained by some who accept that economic behavior is not completely rational. John Stuart Mill (1909, bk. 2, ch. 4) argued that custom, not competition, governs much of the economic world. But he adds that the only possible theory is that

Standard economic doctrine makes assumptions of rationality that have very strong implications for the complexity of individuals' decision processes. The most complete assumptions of competitive general equilibrium theory require that all future and contingent prices exist and be known. In fact, of course, not all these markets exist. The incompleteness of markets has several side consequences for rationality. For one thing, each decision maker has to have a model that predicts the future spot prices. This is an informational burden of an entirely different magnitude than simply optimizing at known prices. It involves all the complexity of rational analysis of data and contradicts the much-praised informational economy of the price system. It is also the case that equilibria become much less well defined. Similar problems occur with imperfect competition.

* This research was supported by the Office of Naval Research grant ONR-N00014-79-C-0685 at the Center for Research in Organizational Efficiency, Institute for Mathematical Studies in the Social Sciences, Stanford University, Stanford, California.

based on competition (which, in his theories, includes certain elements of rationality, particularly shifting capital and labor to activities that yield higher returns): "Only through the principle of competition has political economy any pretension to the character of a science" (1909, p. 242).

Certainly, there is no general principle that prevents the creation of an economic theory based on other hypotheses than that of rationality. There are indeed some conditions that must be laid down for an acceptable theoretical analysis of the economy. Most centrally, it must include a theory of market interactions, corresponding to market clearing in the neoclassical general equilibrium theory. But as far as individual behavior is concerned, any coherent theory of reactions to the stimuli appropriate in an economic context (prices in the simplest case) could in principle lead to a theory of the economy. In the case of consumer demand, the budget constraint must be satisfied, but many theories can easily be devised that are quite different from utility maximization. For example, habit formation can be made into a theory; for a given price-income change, choose the bundle that satisfies the budget constraint and that requires the least change (in some suitably defined sense) from the previous consumption bundle. Though there is an optimization in this theory, it is different from utility maximization; for example, if prices and income return to their initial levels after several alterations, the final bundle purchased will not be the same as the initial. This theory would strike many lay observers as plausible, yet it is not rational as economists have used that term. Without belaboring the point, I simply observe that this theory is not only a logically complete explanation of behavior but one that is more powerful than standard theory and at least as capable of being tested.

Not only is it possible to devise complete models of the economy on hypotheses other than rationality, but in fact virtually every practical theory of macroeconomics is partly so based. The price- and wage-rigidity elements of Keynesian theory are hard to fit into a rational framework, though some valiant efforts have been made. In the original form, the multiplier was derived from a consumption function depending only on current income. Theories more nearly based on rationality make consumption depend on lifetime or "permanent" income and reduce the magnitude of the multiplier and, with it, the explanatory power of the Keynesian model. But if the Keynesian model is a natural target of criticism by the upholders of universal rationality, it must be added that monetarism is no better. I know of no serious derivation of the demand for money from a rational optimization. The loose arguments that substitute for a true derivation, Friedman's economizing on shoe leather or Tobin's transaction demand based on costs of buying and selling bonds, introduce assumptions incompatible with the costless markets otherwise assumed. The use of rationality in these arguments is ritualistic, not essential. Further, the arguments used would not suggest a very stable relation but rather one that would change quickly with any of the considerable changes in the structure and technology of finance. Yet the stability of the demand function for money must be essential to any form of monetarism, not excluding those rational expectations models in which the quantity theory plays a major role.

I believe that similar observations can be made about a great many other areas of applied economics. Rationality hypotheses are partial and frequently, if not always, supplemented by assumptions of a different character.

So far, I have simply argued that rationality is not in principle essential to a theory of the economy, and, in fact, theories with direct application usually use assumptions of a different nature. This was simply to clear the ground so that we can discuss the role of rationality in economic theory. As remarked earlier, rationality in application is not merely a property of the individual. Its useful and powerful implications derive from the conjunction of individual rationality and the other basic concepts of neoclassical theory—equilibrium, competition, and completeness of markets. The importance of all these assumptions was first made explicit by Frank Knight (1921, pp. 76–79). In the terms of Knight's one-time student, Edward Chamberlin (1950, pp. 6–7), we need not merely pure but perfect competition before the rationality hypotheses have their full power.

It is this theme on which I will largely expand. When these assumptions fail, the very concept of rationality becomes threatened, because perceptions of others and, in particular, of their rationality become part of one's own rationality. Even if there is a consistent meaning, it will involve computational and informational demands totally at variance with the traditional economic theorist's view of the decentralized economy.

Let me add one parenthetic remark to this section. Even if we make all the structural assumptions needed for perfect competition (whatever is needed by way of knowledge, concavity in production, absence of sufficient size to create market power, etc.), a question remains. How can equilibrium be established? The attainment of equilibrium requires a disequilibrium process. What does rational behavior mean in the presence of disequilibrium? Do individuals speculate on the equilibrating process? If they do, can the disequilibrium be regarded as, in some sense, a higher-order equilibrium process? Since no one has market power, no one sets prices; yet they are set and changed. There are no good answers to these questions, and I do not pursue them. But they do illustrate the conceptual difficulties of rationality in a multiperson world.

II. Rationality as Maximization in the History of Economic Thought

Economic theory, since it has been systematic, has been based on some notion of rationality. Among the classical economists, such as Smith and Ricardo, rationality had the limited meaning of preferring more to less; capitalists choose to invest in the industry yielding the highest rate of return, landlords rent their property to the highest bidder, while no one pays for land more than it is worth in product. Scattered remarks about technological substitution, particularly in Ricardo, can be interpreted as taking for granted that, in a competitive environment, firms choose factor proportions, when they are variable, so as to minimize unit costs. To be generous about it, their rationality hypothesis was the maximization of profits by the firm, although this formulation was not explicitly achieved in full generality until the 1880s.

There is no hypothesis of rationality on the side of consumers among the classicists. Not until John Stuart Mill did any of the English classical economists even recognize the idea that demand might depend on price. Cournot had the concept a bit earlier, but neither Mill nor Cournot noticed—although it is obvious from the budget constraint alone—that the demand for any commodity must depend on the prices of all commodities. That insight remained for the great pioneers of the marginalist revolution, Jevons, Walras, and Menger (anticipated, to be sure, by the Gregor Mendel of economics, H. H. Gossen, whose major work, completely unnoticed at the time of publication [1854], has now been translated into English [1983]). Their rationality hypothesis for the consumer was the maximization of utility under a budget constraint. With this formulation, the definition of demand as a function of all prices was an immediate implication, and it became possible to formulate the general equilibrium of the economy.

The main points in the further development of the utility theory of the consumer are well-known. (1) Rational behavior is an ordinal property. (2) The assumption that an individual is behaving rationally has indeed some observable implications, the Slutsky relations, but without further assumptions, they are not very strong. (3) In the aggregate, the hypothesis of rational behavior has in general no implications; that is, for any set of aggregate excess demand functions, there is a choice of preference maps and of initial endowments, one for each individual in the economy, whose maximization implies the given aggregate excess demand functions (Sonnenschein 1973; Mantel 1974; Debreu 1974; for a survey, see Shafer and Sonnenschein [1982, sec. 4]).

The implications of the last two remarks are in contradiction to the very large bodies of empirical and theoretical research, which draw powerful implications from utility maximization for, respectively, the behavior of individuals, most especially in the field of labor supply, and the performance of the macroeconomy based on "new classical" or "rational expectations" models. In both domains, this power is obtained by adding strong supplementary assumptions to the general model of rationality. Most prevalent of all is the assumption that all individuals have the same utility function (or at least that they differ only in broad categories based on observable magnitudes, such as family size). But this postulate leads to curious and, to my mind, serious difficulties in the interpretation of evidence. Consider the simplest models of human capital formation. Cross-sectional evidence shows an increase of wages with education or experience, and this is interpreted as a return on investment in the form of forgone income and other costs. But if all individuals are alike, why do they not make the same choice? Why do we observe a dispersion? In the human capital model (a particular application of the rationality hypothesis), the only explanation must be that individuals are not alike, either in ability or in tastes. But in that case the cross-sectional evidence is telling us about an inextricable mixture of individual differences and productivity effects. Analogously, in macroeconomic models involving durable assets, especially securities, the assumption of homogeneous agents implies that there will never be any trading, though there will be changes in prices.

This dilemma is intrinsic. If agents are all alike, there is really no room for trade. The very basis of economic analysis, from Smith on, is the existence of differences in agents. But if agents are different in unspecifiable ways, then remark 3 above shows that very little, if any, inferences can be made. This problem, incidentally, already exists in Smith's discussion of wage differences. Smith did not believe in intrinsic differences in ability; a porter resembled a philosopher more than a greyhound did a mastiff. Wage differences then depended on the disutilities of different kinds of labor, including the differential riskiness of income. This is fair enough and insightful. But, if taken seriously, it implies that individuals are indifferent among occupations, with wages compensating for other differences. While there is no logical problem, the contradiction to the most obvious evidence is too blatant even for a rough approximation.

I have not carried out a scientific survey of the uses of the rationality hypothesis in particular applications. But I have read enough to be convinced that its apparent force only comes from the addition of supplementary hypotheses. Homogeneity across individual agents is not the only auxiliary assumption, though it is the deepest. Many assumptions of separability are frequently added. Indeed, it has become a working methodology to start with very strong assumptions of additivity and separability, together with a very short list of relevant variables, to add others only as the original hypotheses are shown to be inadequate, and to stop when some kind of satisfactory fit is obtained.

A failure of the model is attributed to a hitherto overlooked benefit or cost. From a statistical viewpoint, this stopping rule has obvious biases. I was taught as a graduate student that data mining was a major crime; morality has changed here as elsewhere in society, but I am not persuaded that all these changes are for the better.

The lesson is that the rationality hypothesis is by itself weak. To make it useful, the researcher is tempted into some strong assumptions. In particular, the homogeneity assumption seems to me to be especially dangerous. It denies the fundamental assumption of the economy, that it is built on gains from trading arising from individual differences. Further, it takes attention away from a very important aspect of the economy, namely, the effects of the distribution of income and of other individual characteristics on the workings of the economy. To take a major example, virtually all of the literature on savings behavior based on aggregate data assumes homogeneity. Yet there have been repeated studies that suggest that savings is not proportional to income, from which it would follow that distributional considerations matter. (In general, as data have improved, it has become increasingly difficult to find any simple rationally based model that will explain savings, wealth, and bequest data.)

The history of economic thought shows some other examples and difficulties with the application of the rationality hypothesis. Smith and the later classicists make repeated but unelaborated references to risk as a component in wage differences and in the rate of return on capital (e.g., Mill 1909, pp. 385, 406, 407, 409). The English marginalists were aware of Bernoulli's expected-utility theory of behavior under uncertainty (probably from Todhunter's *History of the Theory of Probability*) but used it only in a qualitative and gingerly way (Jevons 1965, pp. 159–60; Marshall 1948, pp. 842–43). It was really not until the last 30 years that it has been used systematically as an economic explanation, and indeed its use coincided with the first experimental evidence against it (see Allais 1979). The expected-utility hypothesis is an interesting transition to the theme of Section III. It is in fact a stronger hypothesis than mere maximization. As such it is more easily tested, and it leads to stronger and more interesting conclusions. So much, however, has already been written about this area that I will not pursue it further here.

III. Rationality, Knowledge, and Market Power

It is noteworthy that the everyday usage of the term "rationality" does not correspond to the economist's definition as transitivity and completeness, that is, maximization of something. The common understanding is instead the complete exploitation of information, sound reasoning, and so forth. This theme has been systematically explored in economic analysis, theoretical and empirical, only in the last 35 years or so. An important but neglected predecessor was Holbrook Working's random-walk theory of fluctuations in commodity futures and securities prices (1953). It was based on the hypothesis that individuals would make rational inferences from data and act on them; specifically, predictability of future asset prices would be uncovered and used as a basis for current demands, which would alter current prices until the opportunity for gain was wiped out.

Actually, the classical view had much to say about the role of knowledge, but in a very specific way. It emphasized how a complete price system would require individuals to know very little about the economy other than their own private domain of production and consumption. The profoundest observation of Smith was that the system works behind the backs of the participants; the directing "hand" is "invisible." Implicitly, the acquisition of knowledge was taken to be costly.

Even in a competitive world, the individual agent has to know all (or at least a great many) prices and then perform an optimization based on that knowledge. All knowledge is costly, even the knowledge of prices. Search theory, following Stigler (1961), recognized this problem. But search theory cannot easily be reconciled with equilibrium or even with individual rationality by price setters, for identically situated sellers should set identical prices, in which case there is nothing to search for.

The knowledge requirements of the decision maker change radically under monopoly or other forms of imperfect competition. Consider the simplest case, pure monopoly in a one-commodity partial equilibrium model, as originally studied by Cournot in 1838 (1927). The firm has to know not only prices but a demand curve. Whatever definition is given to complexity of knowledge, a demand curve is more complex than a price. It involves knowing about the behavior of others. Measuring a demand curve is usually thought of as a job for an econometrician. We have the curious situation that scientific analysis imputes scientific behavior to its subjects. This need not be a contradiction, but it does seem to lead to an infinite regress.

From a general equilibrium point of view, the difficulties are compounded. The demand curve relevant to the monopolist must be understood mutatis mutandis, not ceteris paribus. A change in the monopolist's price will in general cause a shift in the purchaser's demands for other goods and therefore in the prices of those commodities. These price changes will in turn by more than one channel affect the demand for the monopolist's produce and possibly also the factor prices that the monopolist pays. The monopolist, even in the simple case where there is just one in the entire economy, has to understand all these repercussions. In short, the monopolist has to have a full general equilibrium model of the economy.

The informational and computational demands become much stronger in the case of oligopoly or any other system of economic relations where at least some agents have power against each other. There is a qualitatively new aspect to the nature of knowledge, since each agent is assuming the *rationality* of other agents. Indeed, to construct a rationality-based theory of economic behavior, even more must be assumed, namely, that the rationality of all agents must be *common knowledge,* to use the term introduced by the philosopher David Lewis (1969). Each agent must not only know that the other agents (at least those with significant power) are rational but know that each other agent knows every other agent is rational, know that every other agent knows that every other agent is rational, and so forth (see also Aumann 1976). It is in this sense that rationality and the knowledge of rationality is a social and not only an individual phenomenon.

Oligopoly is merely the most conspicuous example. Logically, the same problem arises if there are two monopolies in different markets. From a practical viewpoint, the second case might not offer such difficulties if the links between the markets were sufficiently loose and the monopolies sufficiently small on the scale of the economy that interaction was negligible; but the interaction can never be zero and may be important. As usually presented, bargaining to reach the contract curve would, in the simplest case, require common knowledge of the bargainer's preferences and production functions. It should be obvious how vastly these knowledge requirements exceed those required for the price system. The classic economists were quite right in emphasizing the importance of limited knowledge. If every agent has a complete model of the economy, the hand running the economy is very visible indeed.

Indeed, under these knowledge conditions, the superiority of the market over centralized planning disappears. Each individual agent is in effect using as much information as would be required for a central planner. This argument shows the severe limitations in the argument that property rights suffice for social rationality even in the absence of a competitive system (Coase 1960).

One can, as many writers have, discuss bargaining when individuals have limited knowledge of each other's utilities (similarly, we can have oligopoly theory with limited knowledge of the cost functions of others [see, e.g., Arrow 1979]). Oddly enough, it is not clear that limited knowledge means a smaller quantity of information than complete knowledge, and optimization under limited knowledge is certainly computationally more difficult. If individuals have private information, the others form some kind of conjecture about it. These conjectures must be common knowledge for there to be a rationality-based hypothesis. This seems to have as much informational content and be as unlikely as knowing the private information. Further, the optimization problem for each individual based on conjectures (in a rational world, these are probability distributions) on the private information of others is clearly a more difficult and therefore computationally more demanding problem than optimization when there is no private information.

IV. Rational Knowledge and Incomplete Markets

It may be supposed from the foregoing that informational demands are much less in a competitive world. But now I want to exemplify the theme that perfect, not merely pure, competition is needed for that conclusion and that perfection is a stronger criterion than Chamberlin perhaps intended. A complete general equilibrium system, as in Debreu (1959), requires markets for all contingencies in all future periods. Such a system could not exist. First, the number of prices would be so great that search would become an insuperable obstacle; that is, the value of knowing prices of less consequence, those on events remote in time or of low probability, would be less than the cost so that these markets could not come into being. Second, markets conditional on privately observed events cannot exist by definition.

In any case, we certainly know that many—in fact, most—markets do not exist. When a market does not exist, there is a gap in the information relevant to an individual's decision, and it must be filled by some kind of conjecture, just as in the case of market power. Indeed, there turn out to be strong analogies between market power and incomplete markets, though they seem to be very different phenomena.

Let me illustrate with the rational expectations equilibrium. Because of intertemporal relations in consumption and production, decisions made today have consequences that are anticipated. Marshall (1948, bk. 5, chs. 3–5) was perhaps the first economist to take this issue seriously. He introduced for this purpose the vague and muddled concepts of the short and long runs, but at least he recognized the difficulties involved, namely, that some of the relevant terms of trade are not observable on the market. (Almost all other accounts implicitly or explicitly assumed a stationary state, in which case the relative prices in the future and between present and future are in effect current information. Walras [1954, lessons 23–25] claimed to treat a progressive state with net capital accumulation, but he wound up unwittingly in a contradiction, as John Eatwell has observed in an unpublished dissertation. Walras's arguments can only be rescued by assuming a stationary state.) Marshall in effect made current decisions, including investment and savings, depend on expectations of the future. But the expectations were not completely arbitrary; in the absence of disturbances, they would converge to correct values. Hicks (1946, chs. 9–10) made the dependence of current decisions on expectations more explicit, but he had less to say about their ultimate agreement with reality.

As has already been remarked, the full competitive model of general equilibrium includes markets for all future goods and, to take care of uncertainty, for all future contingencies. Not all of these markets exist. The new theoretical paradigm of rational expectations holds that each individual forms expectations of the future on the basis of a correct model of the economy, in fact, the same model that the econometrician is using. In a competitive market-clearing world, the individual agent needs expectations of prices only, not of quantities. For a convenient compendium of the basic literature on rational expectations, see Lucas and Sargent (1981). Since the world is uncertain, the expectations take the form of probability distributions, and each agent's expectations are conditional on the information available to him or her.

As can be seen, the knowledge situation is much the same as with market power. Each agent has to have a model of the entire economy to preserve rationality. The cost of knowledge, so emphasized by the defenders of the price system as against centralized planning, has disappeared; each agent is engaged in very extensive information gathering and data processing.

Rational expectations theory is a stochastic form of perfect foresight. Not only the feasibility but even the logical consistency of this hypothesis was attacked long ago by Morgenstern (1935). Similarly, the sociologist Robert K. Merton (1957) argued that forecasts could be self-denying or self-fulfilling; that is, the existence of the forecast would alter behavior so as to cause the forecast to be false (or possibly to make an otherwise false forecast true). The logical problems were addressed by Grunberg and Modigliani (1954) and by Simon (1957, ch. 5). They argued that, in Merton's terms, there always existed a self-fulfilling prophecy. If behavior varied continuously with forecasts and the future realization were a continuous function of behavior, there would exist a forecast that would cause itself to become true. From this argument, it would appear that the possibility of rational expectations cannot be denied. But they require not only extensive first-order knowledge but also common knowledge, since predictions of the future depend on other individuals' predictions of the future. In addition to the information requirements, it must be observed that the computation of fixed points is intrinsically more complex than optimizing.

Consider now the signaling equilibrium originally studied by Spence (1974). We have large numbers of employers and workers with free entry. There is no market power as usually understood. The ability of each worker is private information, known to the worker but not to the employer. Each worker can acquire education, which is publicly observable. However, the cost of acquiring the education is an increasing function of ability. It appears natural to study a competitive equilibrium. This takes the form of a wage for each educational level, taken as given by both employers and workers. The worker, seeing how wages vary with education, chooses the optimal level of education. The employers' optimization leads to an "informational equilibrium" condition, namely, that employers learn the average productivity of workers with a given educational level. What dynamic process would lead the market to learn these productivities is not clear, when employers are assumed unable to observe the productivity of individual workers. There is more than one qualitative possibility for the nature of the equilibrium. One possibility, indeed, is that there is no education, and each worker receives the average productivity of all workers (I am assuming for simplicity that competition among employers produces a zero-profit equilibrium). Another possibility, however, is a dispersion of workers across educational levels; it will be seen that in fact workers of a given ability all choose the same educational level, so the ability of the workers could be deduced from the educational level ex post.

Attractive as this model is for certain circumstances, there are difficulties with its implementation, and at several different levels. (1) It has already been noted that the condition that, for each educational level, wages equal average productivity of workers is informationally severe. (2) Not only is the equilibrium not unique, but there is a continuum of possible equilibria. Roughly speaking, all that matters for the motivation of workers to buy education are the relative wages at different educational levels; hence, different relations between wages and education are equally self-fulfilling. As will be seen below, this phenomenon is not peculiar to this model. On the contrary, the existence of a continuum of equilibria seems to be characteristic of many models with incomplete markets, as will be seen below. Extensive nonuniqueness in this sense means that the theory has relatively little power. (3) The competitive equilibrium is fragile with respect to individual actions. That is, even though the data of the problem do not indicate any market power, at equilibrium it will frequently be possible for any firm to profit by departing from the equilibrium.

Specifically, given an equilibrium relation between wages and education, it can pay a firm to offer a different schedule and thereby make a positive profit (Riley 1979). This is not true in a competitive equilibrium with complete markets, where it would never pay a firm to offer any price or system of prices other than the market's. So far, this instability of competitive equilibrium is a property peculiar to signaling models, but it may be more general.

As remarked above, the existence of a continuum of equilibria is now understood to be a fairly common property of models of rational market behavior with incomplete information. Thus, if there were only two commodities involved and therefore only one price ratio, a continuum of equilibria would take the form of a whole interval of price ratios. This multiplicity would be nontrivial, in that each different possible equilibrium price ratio would correspond to a different real allocation.

One very interesting case has been discussed recently. Suppose that we have some uncertainty about the future. There are no contingent markets for commodities; they can be purchased on spot markets after the uncertainty is resolved. However, there is a set of financial contingent securities, that is, insurance policies that pay off in money for each contingency. Purchasing power can therefore be reallocated across states of the world. If there are as many independent contingent securities as possible states of the world, the equilibrium is the same as the competitive equilibrium with complete markets, as already noted in Arrow (1953). Suppose there are fewer securities than states of the world. Then some recent and partly still unpublished literature (Duffie 1985; Werner 1985; Geanakoplos and Mas-Colell 1986) shows that the prices of the securities are arbitrary (the spot prices for commodities adjust accordingly). This is not just a numeraire problem; the corresponding set of equilibrium real allocations has a dimensionality equal to the number of states of nature.

A related model with a similar conclusion of a continuum of equilibria is the concept of "sunspot" equilibria (Cass and Shell 1983). Suppose there is some uncertainty about an event that has in fact no impact on any of the data of the economy. Suppose there is a market for a complete set of commodity contracts contingent on the possible outcomes of the event, and later there are spot markets. However, some of those who will participate in the spot markets cannot participate in the contingent commodity markets, perhaps because they have not yet been born. Then there is a continuum of equilibria. One is indeed the equilibrium based on "fundamentals," in which the contingencies are ignored. But there are other equilibria that do depend on the contingency that becomes relevant merely because everyone believes it is relevant. The sunspot equilibria illustrate that Merton's insight was at least partially valid; we can have situations where social truth is essentially a matter of convention, not of underlying realities.

V. The Economic Role of Informational Differences

Let me mention briefly still another and counterintuitive implication of thoroughgoing rationality. As I noted earlier, identical individuals do not trade. Models of the securities markets based on homogeneity of individuals would imply zero trade; all changes in information are reflected in price changes that just induce each trader to continue holding the same portfolio. It is a natural hypothesis that one cause of trading is difference of information. If I learn something that affects the price of a stock and others do not, it seems reasonable to postulate that I will have an opportunity to buy or sell it for profit.

A little thought reveals that, if the rationality of all parties is common knowledge, this cannot occur. A sale of existing securities is simply a complicated bet, that is, a zero-sum transaction (between individuals who are identical apart from information). If both are risk averters, they would certainly never bet or, more generally, buy or sell securities to each other if they had the same information. If they have different information, each one will consider that the other has some information that he or she does not possess. An offer to buy or sell itself conveys information. The offer itself says that the offerer is expecting an advantage to himself or herself and therefore a loss to the other party, at least as calculated on the offerer's information. If this analysis is somewhat refined, it is easy to see that no transaction will in fact take place, though there will be some transfer of information as a result of the offer and rejection. The price will adjust to reflect the information of all parties, though not necessarily all the information.

Candidly, this outcome seems most unlikely. It leaves as explanation for trade in securities and commodity futures only the heterogeneity of the participants in matters other than information. However, the respects in which individuals differ change relatively slowly, and the large volume of rapid turnover can hardly be explained on this basis. More generally, the role of speculators and the volume of resources expended on informational services seem to require a subjective belief, at least, that buying and selling are based on changes in information.

VI. Some Concluding Remarks

The main implication of this extensive examination of the use of the rationality concept in economic analysis is the extremely severe strain on information-gathering and computing abilities. Behavior of this kind is incompatible with the limits of the human being, even augmented with artificial aids (which, so far, seem to have had a trivial effect on productivity and the efficiency of decision making). Obviously, I am accepting the insight of Herbert Simon (1957, chs. 14, 15), on the importance of recognizing that rationality is bounded. I am simply trying to illustrate that many of the customary defenses that economists use to argue, in effect, that decision problems are relatively simple break down as soon as market power and the incompleteness of markets are recognized.

But a few more lessons turned up. For one thing, the combination of rationality, incomplete markets, and equilibrium in many cases leads to very weak conclusions, in the sense that there are whole continua of equilibria. This, incidentally, is a conclusion that is being found increasingly in the analysis of games with structures extended over time; games are just another example of social interaction, so the common element is not surprising. The implications of this result are not clear. On the one hand, it may be that recognizing the limits on rationality will reduce the number of equilibria. On the other hand, the problem may lie in the concept of equilibrium.

Rationality also seems capable of leading to conclusions flatly contrary to observation. I have cited the implication that there can be no securities transactions due to differences of information. Other similar propositions can be advanced, including the well-known proposition that there cannot be any money lying in the street, because someone else would have picked it up already.

The next step in analysis, I would conjecture, is a more consistent assumption of computability in the formulation of economic hypotheses. This is likely to have its own difficulties because, of course, not everything is computable, and there will be in this sense an inherently unpredictable element in rational behavior. Some will be glad of such a conclusion.

References

Allais, M. 1979. The so-called Allais paradox and rational decisions under uncertainty. In M. Allais and O. Hagen (eds.), *Expected Utility Hypothesis and the Allais Paradox*. Boston: Reidel.

Arrow, K. J. 1953. Le rôle des valeurs boursières dans la répartition la meilleure des risques. In *Econometrie*. Paris: Centre National de la Recherche Scientifique.

Arrow, K. J. 1979. The property rights doctrine and demand revelation under incomplete information. In M. J. Boskin (ed.), *Economics and Human Welfare*. New York: Academic Press.

Aumann, R. J. 1976. Agreeing to disagree. *Annals of Statistics* 4:1236–39.

Cass, D., and Shell, K. 1983. Do sunspots matter? *Journal of Political Economy* 91:193–227.

Chamberlin, E. 1950. *The Theory of Monopolistic Competition*. 6th ed. Cambridge, Mass.: Harvard University Press.

Coase, R. 1960. The problem of social cost. *Journal of Law and Economics* 3:1–44.

Cournot, A. A. 1927. *Researches into the Mathematical Principles of the Theory of Wealth*. Translated by N. T. Bacon. New York: Macmillan.

Debreu, G. 1959. *Theory of Value*. New York: Wiley.

Debreu, G. 1974. Excess demand functions. *Journal of Mathematical Economics* 1:15–23.

Duffie, J. D. 1985. Stochastic equilibria with incomplete financial markets. Research Paper no. 811. Stanford, Calif.: Stanford University, Graduate School of Business.

Geanakoplos, J., and Mas-Colell, A. 1986. Real indeterminacy with financial assets. Paper no. MSRI 717-86. Berkeley: Mathematical Science Research Institute.

Gossen, H. H. 1983. *The Laws of Human Relations*. Cambridge, Mass.: MIT Press.

Grunberg, E., and Modigliani, F. 1954. The predictability of social events. *Journal of Political Economy* 62:465–78.

Hicks, J. R. 1946. *Value and Capital*. 2d ed. Oxford: Clarendon.

Jevons, W. S. 1965. *The Theory of Political Economy*. 5th ed. Reprint. New York: Kelley.

Knight, F. 1921. *Risk, Uncertainty, and Profit*. Boston: Houghton Mifflin.

Lewis, D. 1969. *Convention*. Cambridge, Mass.: Harvard University Press.

Lucas, R., and Sargent, T. 1981. *Rational Expectations and Econometric Practice*. 2 vols. Minneapolis: University of Minnesota Press.

Mantel, R. 1974. On the characterization of excess demand. *Journal of Economic Theory* 6:345–54.

Marshall, A. 1948. *Principles of Economics*. 8th ed. New York: Macmillan.

Merton, R. K. 1957. The self-fulfilling prophecy. In *Social Theory and Social Structure*. Rev. and enlarged ed. Glencoe, Ill.: Free Press.

Mill, J. S. 1909. *Principles of Political Economy*. London: Longmans, Green.

Morgenstern, O. 1935. Vollkommene Voraussicht und wirtschaftliches Gleichgewicht. *Zeitschrift für Nationalökonomie* 6:337–57.

Riley, J. G. 1979. Informational equilibrium. *Econometica* 47:331–60.

Shafer, W., and Sonnenschein, H. 1982. Market demand and excess demand functions. In K. J. Arrow and M. Intriligator (eds.), *Handbook of Mathematical Economics*. Vol. 2. Amsterdam: North-Holland.

Simon, H. 1957. *Models of Man*. New York: Wiley.

Spence, A. M. 1974. *Market Signaling*. Cambridge, Mass.: Harvard University Press.

Sonnenschein, H. 1973. Do Walras's identity and continuity characterize the class of community excess demand functions? *Journal of Economic Theory* 6:345–54.

Stigler, G. J. 1961. The economics of information. *Journal of Political Economy* 69:213–25.

Walras, L. 1954. *Elements of Pure Economics*. Translated by W. Jaffé. London: Allen & Unwin.

Werner, J. 1985. Equilibrium in economies with incomplete financial markets. *Journal of Economic Theory* 36:110–19.

Working, H. 1953. Futures trading and hedging. *American Economic Review* 43:314–43.

Robert E. Lucas, Jr.

University of Chicago

Adaptive Behavior and Economic Theory*

I. Introduction

The relationship between psychological and economic views of behavior, once a subject of heavy dispute, is now understood in a very similar way by practitioners of both these disciplines and of our sister social sciences. In general terms, we view or model an individual as a collection of decision rules (rules that dictate the action to be taken in given situations) and a set of preferences used to evaluate the outcomes arising from particular situation-action combinations. These decision rules are continuously under review and revision; new decision rules are tried and tested against experience, and rules that produce desirable outcomes supplant those that do not. I use the term "adaptive" to refer to this trial-and-error process through which our modes of behavior are determined.

If one is interested in modeling particular decisions in any very explicit way, it is obviously necessary to think about rather narrow aspects of an individual's entire set of decision rules: his or her personality. Experimental psychology has traditionally focused on the adaptive process by which decision rules are replaced by others. In this tradition, the influence of the subject's (or, as an economist says, the agent's) preferences

This essay uses a series of examples to illustrate the use of rationality and adaptation in economic theory. It is argued that these hypotheses are complementary and that stability theories based on adaptive behavior may help to narrow the class of empirically interesting equilibria in certain economic models. An experiment is proposed to test this idea.

* Jacob Frenkel, Robin Hogarth, and Melvin Reder provided extensive and very helpful criticism of the version given at the conference.

are kept simple by choosing outcomes that are easily ordered (rewards vs. punishments), and the focus is on the way that behavior is adapted over time toward securing better outcomes.

Economics has tended to focus on situations in which the agent can be expected to "know" or to have learned the consequences of different actions so that his observed choices reveal stable features of his underlying preferences. We use economic theory to calculate how certain variations in the situation are predicted to affect behavior, but these calculations obviously do not reflect or usefully model the adaptive process by which subjects have themselves arrived at the decision rules they use. Technically, I think of economics as studying decision rules that are steady states of some adaptive process, decision rules that are found to work over a range of situations and hence are no longer revised appreciably as more experience accumulates.

From this point of view, the question whether people are in general "rational" or "adaptive" does not seem to me worth arguing over. Which of these answers is most useful will depend on the situations in which we are trying to predict behavior and on the experiences the people in question have had with such situations. It would be useful, though, if we could say something in a general way about the characteristics of social science prediction problems where models emphasizing adaptive aspects of behavior are likely to be successful versus those where the nonadaptive or equilibrium models of economic theory are more promising.

I do not know any general framework for addressing questions of this kind, so I will use the case method and discuss a series of examples. I will begin in Section II with an example of a social science question—the control of inflation—that has been successfully solved by economic methods. I hope that this example will work against a tendency that often appears in methodological discussions to disdain existing theories in favor of the yet-to-be-constructed models of the future. Economics works surprisingly well, under some conditions, and I think progress is more likely to follow from an understanding of the factors that have contributed to past successes and from trying to build on them than from attempts to reconstruct economics from the ground up in the image of some other science.

The rest of the paper consists mainly of more examples, each of which is drawn from recent work that is in some sense on the methodological boundary between economics and psychology. In each case, my focus will be on what methods I think of as "psychological" may contribute to the solution of economic problems of the sort described in Section II. Section III reviews a series of individual choice experiments with pigeons reported by Battalio et al. Section IV discusses some market experiments using undergraduate subjects conducted by Smith. Section V reviews a theoretical example by Bray on the stability of rational expectations equilibria. Section VI states a problem in monetary theory, and Section VII proposes an experimental resolution of it. In the course of discussing this research, I will also be advertising in passing a number of studies related to these. There is a good deal of current research on this interdisciplinary boundary, and I think that it has much promise for clarifying and advancing progress on some traditionally "economic" issues. I will expand on this belief, briefly, in Section VIII.

II. The Quantity Theory of Money

I will take an example of a solved economic problem from macroeconomics, partly because that is my own area of expertise but also because the aggregative character of macroeconomic problems serves to emphasize the distance between much of economics and the concerns of individual psychology. The particular theory I will discuss is called the quantity theory of money.

Consider the "equation of exchange,"

$$Mv = Py. \tag{1}$$

Here P denotes an economy's general level of prices at a point in time (as measured, say, by the consumer price index) and y denotes the rate of real production (real GNP, say). On the left, M is the quantity of money in circulation (say, M1, currency held by the public plus all checking deposits). Then v, velocity, is defined in terms of these other three magnitudes so that (1) always holds. One way of stating the quantity theory of money (there are many, not all consistent, as is true of most interesting theories) is to add to (1) the assumptions that velocity is constant and that movements in real output y are not affected by movements in M. Of course, neither of these assumptions is likely to be literally true (that velocity is not constant can be checked by plotting the observable series $P_t y_t / M_t$ against time for any economy), but this is to be expected in any theoretical model. If this theory were true, however, the rate of inflation, $(1/P)(dP/dt)$, would satisfy, from (1) and the assumption of constant velocity

$$\frac{1}{P}\frac{dP}{dt} = \frac{1}{M}\frac{dM}{dt} - \frac{1}{y}\frac{dy}{dt}.$$

Moreover, $(1/y)(dy/dt)$ would not vary systematically with $(1/M) \times (dM/dt)$. This way of stating the theory suggests that, if observations on $(1/P)(dP/dt)$ are plotted against corresponding observations on $(1/M)(dM/dt)$, the points so plotted should lie along a line with slope one: a 45-degree line shifted down by the rate of income growth. Figure 1 exhibits such a plot. (The graphics are from Lucas [1980], but the numbers were taken from Robert Vogel's [1974] study.)

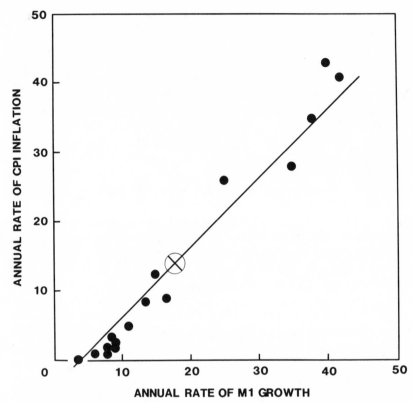

Fɪɢ. 1.—Sample averages from 16 Latin American countries, 1950–69

The X-coordinate for each point in figure 1 is the average rate of money growth for a single Latin American country over the period 1950–69, and the corresponding Y-coordinate is that country's average inflation rate for the same period. The line on the figure is drawn so as to pass through the average of all of these points, but its slope is 45 degrees, as predicted by the quantity theory. It is not fitted to the data. It is not easy to think of examples of nonvacuous social science theories that have recorded this kind of empirical success.

Not only does the quantity theory of money fit data, in the sense of figure 1, but it provides an operational answer to a problem of great social importance, the control of inflation. The rate of growth of money, in any country, can be controlled quite directly through government and central bank policy. That is, the location of a country on the X-axis of figure 1 is a matter of fairly simple policy choice. If, as figure 1 confirms, velocity and real income growth are largely independent of this choice, a society can thus indirectly dictate its long-run average inflation rate—its location on the Y-axis. This is what I meant in the introduction when I said that the problem of controlling inflation has been "successfully solved" in a scientific sense.[1]

So that we do not get carried away with this success, figure 2 (from my 1980 paper) also plots inflation rates against M1 growth rates, where in this case each observation is from a single quarter during the period 1955–75 for the United States. Where did the good fit go? To recover it, each observation in figure 2 can be replaced with a very long moving average of adjacent quarters' points, producing figure 3. Comparing figures 2 and 3 we can see that the use of averaged (over time) inflation and money growth rates was not incidental to the results displayed in figure 1. Without such averaging, the quantity theory (at least in the form that I have presented) does not provide a serviceable account of comovements in money and inflation.

What is the relationship between these three figures and economic theory? In particular, what role does the assumption that agents behave "rationally" play in equation (1) and in the assumptions I appended to this identity to obtain a nonvacuous model? This is not a simple question because each stage in the development of economic theory has produced its own collection of monetary theories, some consistent with the quantity theory and some not, so that it is possible to set out neither a set of agreed-on axioms on which monetary theory in general is "based" nor a set that is equivalent to the quantity theory in the form in which I have "tested" it. I think that this is a typical state of affairs in economics and not at all a deplorable one, but it does complicate the discussion.

It is certain that the quantity theory did not originate as an empirical generalization based on evidence such as that summarized in figure 1. When David Hume (1963) first enunciated the hypothesis, in 1742, the data needed to construct figure 1 were not collected for any economy. Nor did Hume deduce the theory from the axioms of utility theory, for the development of this useful equipment was more than a century in the future. Hume's argument was based on the idea that people hold money for the sole purpose of spending it on goods so that changes in money and prices in equal proportion "ought" to be pure units changes, affecting no one's decisions. The argument is tricky because a change in money does not automatically cause prices to move equiproportionally in any direct sense, so the proposition that individual behavior is invariant to units changes does not in itself give the result. One needs to argue, as Hume did, both that if prices move in proportion to the increase in money individuals will be willing to hold the increase and that, if prices do not move in proportion, money demand

1. Obviously, few societies have solved the problem of inflation in a political sense. I do not see this fact as qualifying my claim in the text, any more than I would view the current popularity of "creationism" as qualifying the scientific status of the theory of evolution.

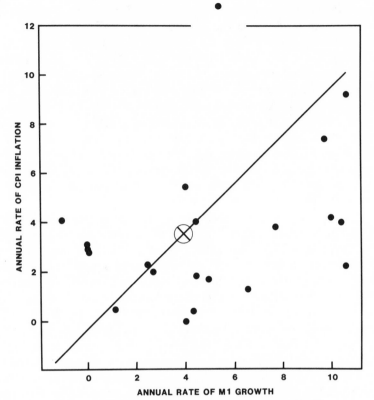

Fig. 2.—Original data for second quarters, 1955–75

cannot equal money supplied so that further price movements must follow. Nevertheless, there is a clear sense in which the theory rests on the hypothesis of individual rationality, at least in this limited sense that units that "ought" not to matter to "rational" people are assumed not to matter in fact.

In more recent times, a great variety of theories of monetary economies have been devised, in which the utility-maximizing behavior of agents and the environment in which they are assumed to interact have been made increasingly explicit. In the main, these theoretical developments have reinforced our understanding of and, I would say, belief in the quantity theory in roughly the form that I have stated it. But this theoretical work has also illuminated several distinct ways in which money can be "nonneutral," or ways in which changes in the rate of growth of money differ from pure units changes. Indeed, in Section VI, I will review one monetary model that has a continuum of equilibria, only one of which is quantity theoretic.

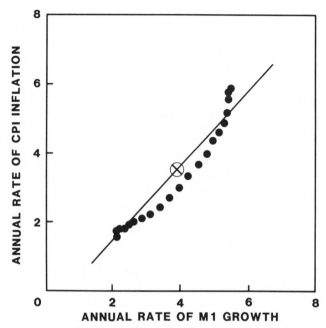

Fig. 3.—Smoothed data for second quarters, 1955–75

Given that Hume arrived at an empirically successful version of the quantity theory with relatively informal reasoning, what is the contribution of these more refined theoretical developments? I think there are several. First, by being explicit about agents' preferences, modern theory can illuminate the consequences of differing inflation rates on individual consumer welfare: equation (1) predicts that rapid money growth is inflationary but sheds no light on what is wrong with inflation. Second, theory that does not imply constant velocity under all circumstances suggests useful limits on the range of applicability of equation (1), as I have used it. Thus, the large movements in velocity observed during the onset of hyperinflations, predicted by more refined theory but not by (1), ought to reinforce our view that figure 1 is an important confirmation of the quantity theory: the theory works well when it "ought" to and fails when it "ought" to as well. The fact that we now view Newton's theory of gravity as a special case holding only in certain circumstances does not in any way compromise the usefulness of that theory. Third, and this is more an expression of hope than anything else, a main objective of more recent theorizing is to obtain models that are consistent with figures 1 and 3 and with figure 2. The simple form (1) of the quantity theory tells us nothing about the patterns (if there are any) shown in figure 2, nor does it suggest a line of attack on the problems of short-run monetary dynamics. I think the whole problem of the business cycle is hidden somewhere in this picture, but we do not yet have the monetary theory that can let us see if this conjecture is right or wrong.

Let me summarize. There are axiomatic developments of the quantity theory of money, but we do not believe that this theory is useful because it is built up from impeccable foundations. On the contrary, the more we understand the foundations, the more limits we see to the applicability of the theory. The empirical testing of the theory is critical precisely because we know that the axioms are abstractions, necessarily "false," so we need to know whether and under what range of circumstances these abstractions are adequate. Conversely, we learn very little about the axioms of utility theory from tests of its aggregative implications. Hume derived most of these implications before the theory of utility was discovered, and it seems likely to me (though we cannot know for sure in advance) that future evolution in utility theory will produce new statements of the quantity theory very similar to the ones we have now.

What is also clear is that adaptive elements of behavior have played no visible role in the theoretical development of the quantity theory or in its testing. If (as I have claimed) all behavior is adaptive, how can it be that important propositions about behavior can be obtained and applied without making any reference to this fact? Let us keep this question in mind.

III. An Individual Choice Experiment

The quantity theory of money provides a good illustration of the way that theoretical economic reasoning can lead to nonvacuous models that bear on questions of importance, but it is not a good context for isolating the contribution of rationality per se to economic modeling. Though all theoretical developments of the quantity theory assume some form of rational behavior, they require as well assumptions on the way agents interact and assumptions that certain theoretically possible feedback effects are small enough to be neglected. In this section and the next, I will draw on examples of research in which the separate effects of rationality and these other factors can be isolated and examined much more fruitfully.

There is an interesting and growing body of research, centered at Texas A&M University, involving experiments on individual choice with animals as subjects. The work is marked by its unusual mix of sophistication in the design and conduct of the experiments—methods drawn from psychological research—and in its use of the economic theory of choice. An excellent, recent example is provided by Battalio et al. (1981), who report results on commodity choice by pigeons. These experiments provided pigeons a choice between food and water in a controlled environment where "the price of each commodity was varied by altering the average time between deliveries of that commodity . . . while the income constraint was the total time available for the delivery of the two goods'' (p. 69). The pigeon exercised his choice with a single peck on a control key that determined whether his current income flow (out of a total stock of delivery time) was to go for food or for water. He could switch between these two goods at any time.

Battalio et al. are explicit about the background of the pigeons: "Four male White Carneaux pigeons with no previous experimental history served as subjects. . . . All [subjects] had extensive training with the procedures prior to the start of the experiment. Experimental conditions [i.e. prices] were changed when inspection of graphs of the data indicated an absence of any significant drift in consumption patterns'' (p. 71).

The main focus of the experiments is the degree to which the choice behavior of these pigeons satisfied the weak axiom of revealed preference. The statistic used to test this hypothesis used an average over the last 5 days of choices at "baseline" (original) prices and over the last 10 days at a new set of prices. Total days at each set of prices varied (over subjects and over price vectors) from 5 to 56 days.

The authors report on the conformity of the choice patterns to which each pigeon converges (roughly) with the axiom of revealed preference. For this particular set of experiments, it is high (though the indifference maps appear quite different across individual subjects). They also report on the adjustment paths or learning curves the subjects exhibited following switches from one price vector to another, finding interesting differences between responses to increases and decreases in relative food prices. For some subjects, repeating the baseline price vector later on induces roughly the original choices; for others, it does not.

To evaluate the results of this particular experiment would require a much more detailed description than I have provided, as well as familiarity with closely related work with pigeons and other subjects. But my present interest is rather in what is taken for granted about the relationship of economic theory to observed behavior in this work, both in the design of the experiments and in the interpretation of the results.

The main hypothesis tested is derived from the economic theory of choice. The theory was designed to refer to human decision making, not that of pigeons, and is on a different level from curve-fitting generalizations from earlier experimental work (such as psychological learning curves). The theory delivers nonobvious predictions about behavior in interesting circumstances, and these predictions are fairly well confirmed. These are striking and exciting findings.

It is assumed from the outset, however, that the economic theory of choice will fall well short of a complete model of the decision-making process of pigeons. First, the predictions are limited in scope to the behavior of average performance over several trials, with the averaged trials selected so as to exclude an initial period of changing behavior patterns. It is clear from the reported results that had these restrictions not been imposed, the theory would have fit the data very badly. Second, the theory, even interpreted as a model of these limited aspects of behavior, does not attempt to deal with choice at the more fundamental physiological level. That is, pigeons used food and water to stay alive (they had no access to either, outside the "price systems" imposed by the experiment), and, given that pigeons have survived as a species to this date, we can infer that they are equipped with internal mechanisms that detect deficiencies in existing "stocks" of both and trigger actions to deal with them. The economic theory is in no sense derived from a description of these underlying mechanisms, nor is it an attempt to provide such a description. The economic theory being tested, then, is limited both in scope and in depth.

This application of the theory of choice presupposes, then, the existence of a broader and deeper theory. Though this theory is not spelled out, certain features of it are taken for granted in the design of the experiment. It is assumed, in the first place, that the subject's behavior is adaptive. His initial behavior will be influenced by his genetic makeup and his previous experience (which is why aspects of both are given explicitly in describing the experiment). This behavior will involve some erratic or "experimental" actions on the pigeons' part, as well as a continuing evaluation of outcomes. Further, it involves some presumption (on the subjects' part) of stationarity in the environment, so actions that yield good outcomes are repeated and those that yield bad ones are not, or are at least used less frequently.

The economic theory of choice is thus interpreted as a description of a kind of stationary "point" of this dynamic, adaptive process. The pigeons' demand functions are decision rules arrived at after a process of deliberate experimentation and assessment of outcomes. The behavior implied by these decision rules is "rational" in the sense that economists use that term. But not only is it consistent with adaptive, trial-and-error behavior; the experiment designed to discover this rationality assumes that, if it exists, it is the outcome of some (unspecified) adaptive process.

Would it be possible to reinterpret this entire process as "rational" in this sense, as the solution to some more complex maximum problem? I assume so. Every "point" must be at the top of some hill, in some "space."[2] But what would be the empirical reward from doing

---

2. The subjects, e.g., could be modeled as having a prior distribution over possible experimental setups and choose pecks on the control key so as to maximize the expected value (with respect to this distribution) of an objective that assigns value both to the immediate food-water reward and to the new information gained at each stage.

so? It is clear that the time path of a subject's behavior will depend on his "initial conditions"—on what he makes of the experimental scene when he is first introduced to it—and we have no way of knowing what these are. Battalio et al. sidestepped this problem by hoping that, whatever these initial conditions look like, their influence will disappear over time (that the underlying process is stable). By giving up on an empty theory of the entire process, they obtained in return a theory with real content about certain very important aspects of it.

On the second limitation of the theory of choice—its physiological shallowness—it seems to me that much more could be done. Battalio et al. have some interesting speculations about mechanisms that might underlie the observed asymmetry in subjects' responses to upward and downward movements in the relative food price. I think that these could be modeled and that such models would have additional testable implications and would also illuminate the economic theory—the indifference maps of pigeons over food-water combinations. Battalio et al. do not pursue this (perhaps this is on the agenda for future work), but, even if they had, I think it is likely that they would have been led to progressively more pigeon-specific models, models with less transferability to behavior of other subjects or to pigeons in other situations. Economists apply essentially the same model of choice to pigeon choices over food-water pairs as to, say, a corporation's choice over capital goods of differing durability. Insofar as much decisions can successfully be viewed in a unified way, it is not likely to be at the physiological level.

In summary, it is clear that the research on economic rationality in animal subjects rests on a maintained idea that behavior is determined by an adaptive process, with the economic theory of choice interpreted as applying to some kind of stationary point of this process. This is the way in which Battalio et al. interpret their results with pigeons, and it seems to me the only interpretation that is tenable. Moreover, it is inconceivable to me that this same general idea cannot be carried over, in some form, to interpreting the application of economic theory to human behavior in actual market situations. But this is getting slightly ahead of my story.

IV.   Market Experiments with Human Subjects

Applications of economic theory to market or group behavior require assumptions about the mode of interaction among agents as well as about individual behavior. For example, a competitive equilibrium (the concept typically—though not necessarily—underlying quantity-theoretic models) assumes that each agent takes prices as given and that no trading occurs at non-market-clearing prices. Just as the assumption of individual rationality abstracts from the adaptive aspects we know are present in actual individual behavior, so does the assumption of competitive (or Nash) equilibrium abstract from adaptive aspects of group behavior. The consequences of this quite different abstraction can also be isolated and studied experimentally.

A large body of experimental results bearing on this aspect of the applicability of economic theory has been obtained by using human subjects in market systems. In this research, subjects are simply given a preference function by the experimenter, who pays them in dollars according to how well they succeed in maximizing their induced "utility." Hence no information about subjects' actual preferences over goods is obtained. On the other hand, subjects are left quite free as to how they choose to interact—to trade—with one another. The objective is to see under what conditions the predictions of competitive market equilibrium theory (given the artificially induced preferences of subjects) conform to the actual quantities exchanged and the prices at which these exchanges actually take place.

Vernon Smith's (1962) paper was the pioneering effort along this line.[3] Smith divided subjects into two groups, buyers and sellers, assigning to each buyer a "reservation price" giving the maximum amount he or she could pay for 1 unit of a good (no buyer could purchase more) and to each seller a minimum price at which he or she could sell the 1 unit of the good with which he was endowed. Each subject was rewarded in proportion to the difference between his maximum (minimum for sellers) price and the price at which he actually transacted. Subjects interacted during trading rounds lasting from 5 to 10 minutes, during which they were free to make public, verbal offers of any kind. On acceptance of an offer, the buyer-seller pair so matched withdrew from the market. On completion of a round, a new round, identical in structure and with identical preferences, opened. The process continued for two to six rounds.

"The most striking general characteristic of tests 1–3, 5–7, 9 and 10 is the remarkably strong tendency for exchange prices to approach the predicted equilibrium for each of these markets. As the exchange process is repeated through successive trading periods with the same conditions of supply and demand prevailing initially in each period, the variation in exchange prices tends to decline, and to cluster more closely around the equilibrium" (Smith 1962, p. 116). (In the exceptions, tests 4 and 8, the results exhibited a kind of bargaining power not

---

3. Since experimental methods have undergone considerable evolution since 1962, a more recent example might have been a more suitable basis for this discussion. But in comparing Smith (1982) to the main conclusions of Smith (1962), I am struck with the extent to which the main early findings of this research have stood up over time and over many replications.

predicted by competitive theory.) Smith obtained these results with about 10 subjects on each side of the market.

In 1874, Leon Walras (1954) had provided the first explicit theoretical description of a set of market "rules" under which it could usefully be asked whether and/or how a collection of economic agents could arrive at an equilibrium price—a price at which the quantity demanded by buyers of a good would equal the amount sellers wished to supply. Walras's scenario is centered on an auctioneer who initiates the process by announcing an arbitrary trial price. Agents then indicate how much they would be willing to buy or sell if this price should prevail. They have an incentive to answer this hypothetical question truthfully; if the announced price does in fact prevail, they are required to deliver or purchase whatever they said they would be willing to do. If the trial price equates demand and supply, it does prevail and trade is consummated. If it does not "clear the market," all bets are off and the auctioneer selects a new trial price. Under some quite reasonable conditions, this adaptive process (though it is only the auctioneer who does any adapting) converges to the market clearing price.

In Smith's experiment, as in subsequent experimental work, the market mechanics are not at all Walrasian: subjects set prices as they please, with no auctioneer to guide them. In Walras's auction, either price converges to the competitive equilibrium, or no trade occurs at all. In Smith's, trade can occur at any price that any buyer-seller pair can mutually agree on. Equilibrium prices in Smith's setting turned out to be stable (even when they differed from the competitive prediction), but patterns of convergence were not well described by Walras's adjustment hypothesis.

Walras's point of departure was the idea that an economic equilibrium is not an empirically interesting object unless one can imagine some way that a group of economic agents, with ordinary human mental equipment, might actually hit on it. The mechanism he proposed has the virtues of being concrete, of relying only on simple adaptive capacities, and of being, under a wide range of circumstances, stable. Smith's experimental setting retained these important features, but shifted the task of adaptation from the auctioneer to the same agents whose preferences determine the equilibrium, and permitted trades to be consummated whenever mutually agreeable, just as they are in actual free markets. In doing this, he reformulated the problem of stability of equilibria as a question (or set of questions) about the behavior of actual people—as a psychological question—as opposed to a question about an abstract and impersonal "market." His and subsequent experimental work has done much to illuminate this question, but in so doing it has left the standard theory of stability far behind.

V. Stability Theory: An Example

Recent work in stability theory has begun to examine situations in which convergence to equilibrium rests on adaptive behavior of individual agents (as opposed to the Walras auctioneer). An example given by Margaret Bray (1983) will serve to illustrate the main ideas.[4]

Bray's example concerns a sequence of spot markets where the market clearing price at date t, p_t, depends on the price that agents expect will prevail next period, date $t + 1$. (It is easy to think of models that would have this character. One example will be provided in the next section.) Call this expected price p_{t+1}^e (an expectation formed in t about an event in $t + 1$) and assume

$$p_t = a + bp_{t+1}^e + \epsilon_t. \tag{2}$$

Here $\{\epsilon_t\}$ is a sequence of independently and identically distributed normal "shocks" with mean zero. Following Muth (1961), call the price expectation

$$p^e = \frac{a}{1 - b} \tag{3}$$

rational because, if (for some reason) people always expect next period's price to be given by (3), the actual prices $\{p_t\}$ will be a sequence of independently and identically distributed normal random variables with mean $a/(1 - b)$ and the expectation that (3) will be confirmed, on average, by experience.

In (2), the current price p_t is market clearing, set presumably by some stable process such as Walras's or Smith's. Any adapting that takes place must be on individuals' common forecast p_{t+1}^e of next period's price. In particular, what if people begin with some price expectations that are not rational in the sense of (3), as they would if the situation were new to them, as in Smith's experiments? They will need to form some belief about p_1 in order to engage in trade at date $t = 0$. Thereafter, they will need to decide how to use their accumulating experience with actual prices $p_0, p_1, \ldots, p_t$ in forming an expectation about the next term in the sequence, p_{t+1}. But what actually happens

4. Bray (1982, 1983), Blume and Easley (1982), and others have studied convergence to rational expectations equilibria under various adaptive hypotheses. Townsend (1978) and others have examined the same general question from the point of view of Bayesian decision theory (see n. 2 above). In the latter approach, the entire path of approach to the rational expectations equilibrium is itself an equilibrium of a suitably specified game. In the former, it is not. The two approaches are complementary and both have their uses, but if the question is how or whether adaptive behavior on the part of "irrational" agents will lead to "rational" behavior over time, only the first is germane. I found the brief discussion in Blume, Bray, and Easley (1982) helpful in clarifying the relationship between these two ideas of stability. Another adaptive approach to this stability question is sketched in Lucas (1978). In that paper, agents' preferences over market goods are formed adaptively, as agents learn about the utility actually yielded by purchased goods.

will depend, in turn, on what people expect to happen: actual and expected prices are simultaneously determined.

Bray assumed that people simply use an average of past actual prices as a forecast of the next price,

$$p_{t+1}^e = \frac{1}{t} \sum_{i=0}^{t-1} p_i. \tag{4}$$

Under this hypothesis, both actual and expected prices are well-defined stochastic processes (given an initial price expectation p_1^e), and it is shown that, provided $|b| < 1$, $\{p_t^e\}$ converges over time, with probability one (over realizations of the shocks $\{\epsilon_t\}$) to the rational expectation (3), for all initial values of p_1^e. In this specific sense, then, the rational expectations equilibrium is stable, given adaptive behavior of the form (4).

What is the empirical content of this model (or of more realistic and complicated models that involve the same basic elements as this example)? Does one take the rational expectations equilibrium, (2) and (3), as the model's prediction about the behavior of actual prices, or the adaptive path, (2) and (4)? Except in the limit, the two are not the same. It does not seem to me that this question is usefully posed in the abstract.

In applications such as that described in Section II, one would clearly take only the rational expectations equilibrium itself as a serious (though possibly empirically unsuccessful) hypothesis. The initial dates of 1950 or 1955 are not $t = 0$ in any behavioral sense; they are just the points at which Vogel's or my data sets happened to start. Moreover, we have no way of knowing what agents' beliefs about future prices were in various countries in 1950 and no reason at all to imagine that these beliefs were the same across countries or across individual agents within a country. In any case, using any adaptive scheme amounts to the conjecture that we econometricians, using only aggregate data on variables like M1 and the consumer price index, can discover rents that were available to, say, Argentinians during 1950–69 but were invisible to Argentinians themselves, who we know were processing thousands of data points in addition to those in our data sets. In aggregative applications of this character, then, one would take the rational expectations equilibrium—the appropriate analogue to (2)-(3)—as the model to be tested and view the adaptive hypothesis (4) as being, at most, an adjunct to the theory that serves to lend it plausibility.

In applications such as those described in the last section, in contrast, in which a group of subjects is observed from the first date at which they are introduced to a particular economic situation and begin to operate within it, it seems clear that subjects could hit on the behavior (2)-(3) from the outset only by coincidence so unlikely as not to be an empirically serious possibility. One would test (2)-(3) only as a prediction about behavior after many trials, exactly as in Bray's theory, or as in the experiments described in Sections III and IV. For predicting actual behavior from $t = 0$ on, an adaptive hypothesis like (4) would be a serious candidate for describing actual behavior. Even if it should work poorly (as I think it would, based on Smith's and others' experimental results), the general idea of averaging past experience on which it is based is a flexible one, and it seems likely that some scheme of this type could provide a good description of the adaptive behavior we do observe.

VI.   A Problem in Monetary Theory

For many problems in applied economics, then, the fact that people behave adaptively is of little or no operational consequence: one assumes that people have long ago hit on decision rules suited to their situations—"rational" rules—and utilizes theories about these rules to predict behavior. But this is certainly not true of all problems of interest. Even so well-established a theory as the quantity theory of money, reviewed in Section II, is subject to difficulties that I do not believe can be resolved on purely "economic" grounds. These difficulties involve the multiplicity of perfect foresight or rational expectations equilibrium paths in a Samuelson-type overlapping-generations model of a monetary economy. I will use an example to state the theoretical issue in this section. In the next, I will describe an experiment that I think is capable of fully resolving it.

The issue can be stated briefly, using a specific version of Paul Samuelson's (1958) model. The economy runs in discrete time, forever. Each period, N agents are born, each living for 2 periods, each endowed with 1 unit of a nonstorable consumption good in the first period of life and none in the second. An agent born in t has preferences $U(c_t^y, c_{t+1}^o)$ over consumption at t, c_t^y, and consumption at $t + 1$, c_{t+1}^o. Feasible allocations are nonnegative and satisfy $c_t^y + c_t^o = 1$, all t.

At $t = 0$, old agents each hold 1 unit of fiat money. Trade involves the young exchanging goods for the money held by the old. Letting q_t be the inverse of the price level (goods per unit of money), the decision problem of a young trader born in t is then

$$\max_{m} U(1 - q_t m, q_{t+1} m),$$

where m is the money balances he chooses to acquire in trade. In equilibrium, the first-order condition for this maximum problem must be satisfied (I assume increasing, concave U) at $m = 1$. Thus, one equilibrium condition is

$$U_1(1 - q_t, q_{t+1})q_t = U_2(1 - q_t, q_{t+1})q_{t+1}. \qquad (5)$$

Nonnegativity adds another,

$$0 \leq q_t \leq 1. \qquad (6)$$

Any solution to the implicit first-order difference equation (5) that satisfies (6) is a "perfect foresight" or "rational expectations" equilibrium.

Note that stationary solutions to (5) (sequences $\{q_t\}$ with q_t constant) correspond to the quantity theory of money. If the money supply is constant, so is the inverse q of the price level. If the money supply is initially doubled, the stationary equilibrium value of q is halved. Other solutions to (5) will not have these properties. Note also that (5) provides an example (though a nonlinear one) of an equilibrium condition of the form (2) postulated by Bray.

Until U is specified, this theory has a lot of possibilities. Since it is not my purpose here to explore all of these, let me specialize to the particular preferences

$$U(c_t^y, c_{t+1}^o) = (c_t^y)^{1/2} + 2(c_{t+1}^o), \qquad (7)$$

so the equilibrium condition (5) becomes

$$q_{t+1} = \frac{1}{4} (1 - q_t)^{-1/2} q_t. \qquad (8)$$

Figure 4 plots the right-hand side of (8) against the 45-degree line.

The stationary points of (8) are $q = 0$ and $q = 15/16$. The solution 15/16 is the quantity-theoretic equilibrium. The solution $q = 0$ describes a situation in which no agent has the faith that other traders will accept money at later dates, in which case money is valueless. Any solution to (8) with $q_0 > 15/16$ will violate (6) for some t. All solutions with $0 \leq q_0 \leq 15/16$ satisfy (6) for all t. All these solutions are perfectly legitimate equilibria. It is abundantly clear from much theoretical work that this multiplicity of equilibria does not in general disappear as this intergenerational model is complicated in various ways, provided all agents are assumed to be finitely lived. The simplicity of the example reveals the existence of a continuum of equilibria but it does not create them.

Indeed, if one thinks of trade in this economy as taking place in a sequence of spot markets, as seems necessary given its demographic structure, there are still many more sequences $\{q_t\}$ that may be interpreted as equilibrium prices. Suppose, for example, that at $t = 0$ a price $q_0 \in (0, 15/16)$ is established by young agents who believe, unanimously, that q_1 is given by (8). As established above, this is equilibrium behavior, no matter what q_0 value in this interval is hit on. Next period,

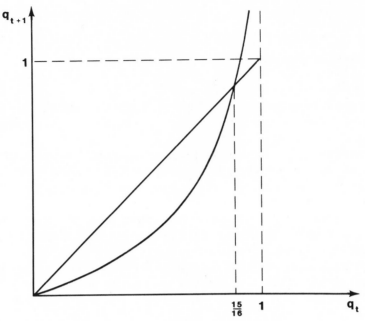

FIG. 4.—Price-level dynamics of eq. (8)

a new generation arrives, facing a situation that is exactly the same, in all respects, as that faced by the preceding generation. (Calendar time is clearly immaterial, as is history in the definition of a perfect foresight equilibrium.) Hence, for this new generation as well, any $q_1 \in (0, 15/16)$ is an equilibrium price. Continuing in this way, any sequence $\{q_t\}$, $0 \leq q_t \leq 15/16$, represents equilibrium behavior.

It is instructive to compare this theoretically confused situation with an otherwise identical economy with a finite life T and a given terminal price q_T of money. With such a given boundary condition, (8) has a unique solution $\{q_t\}$ for any $q_T \in [0, 1]$. If $q_T = 0$, this solution is $q_t = 0$, all t. If $q_T \in (0, 1]$, it is clear from figure 4 that an equilibrium $\{q_t\}$ must remain close to 15/16 most of the time, moving toward q_T appreciably only close to the terminal time. (With $q_T = .01$, e.g., and rounding prices to two places, $q_t = .94$ [$\cong 15/16$] until $T - 5$, following the sequence .92, .79, .45, .14, .04, .01, home from this point on.)

In this finitely lived economy, then, the multiplicity of equilibria in the sense of solutions to (8) is entirely absent. So too, then, is the additional multiplicity arising from the irrelevance of calendar time. Calendar time does matter in the finite system since each generation is 1 period closer to the end than its predecessor and hence faces an objectively different solution.

The simplicity of the finite model contrasted to the apparently hopeless complexity of the infinite one has seemed to many to hold the promise that there is some purely mathematical way by which the paradoxes raised by the infinite-horizon case might be resolved. Cannot one simply let T go to infinity in the finite case and conclude that the limiting equilibrium behavior ($q = 15/16$, in our example) is the "right" equilibrium for the infinite case? Viewed as a purely economic question, the answer is no. The infinite horizon case offers genuine equilibrium possibilities that are not approximated by the limits of sequences of finite-horizon equilibria.[5]

The stability theory proposed by Bray does offer a resolution to the multiplicity problem arising in the infinitely lived economy. Thus write (8) as

$$q_{t+1}^e = \frac{1}{4} (1 - q_t)^{-1/2} q_t, \quad t = 0, 1, 2, \ldots, \qquad (9)$$

where q_{t+1}^e is a point expectation formed at time t about the price in $t + 1$. This plays the role of (2). Then, as in (4), suppose q_t^e is formed adaptively; as a simple average of past, actual prices and the initial expectation q_t^e,

$$q_{t+1}^e = \frac{t}{t+1} q_t^e + \frac{1}{t+1} q_{t-1}, \quad t = 1, 2, \ldots. \qquad (10)$$

Given an initial expectation q_1^e, the actual price q_0 is obtained from (9). Then the new forecast q_2^e is given by (10), q_1 by (9), and so forth. It is easy to show diagrammatically (fig. 5) that the sequences $\{q_t\}$ and $\{q_t^e\}$ so generated satisfy

$$\lim_{t \to \infty} q_t = \lim_{t \to \infty} q_t^e = \frac{15}{16} \qquad (11)$$

for all $q_1^e \in (0, 1)$. (If $q_1^e = 0$, which would imply that no one initially believes the money will be valued in the future, the solution is $q_t^e = q_t = 0$, all t.) That is, the system converges to the stationary rational expectations equilibrium.[6]

Figure 5 illustrates the proof of (11) for the case $0 < q_1^e < 15/16$. Given q_{t+1}^e on the vertical axis, the actual price q_t on the horizontal axis can be read off the curve $1/4(1 - q)^{-1/2} q$. Since the curve is below the 45-degree line, $q_t > q_{t+1}^e$. Then the new forecast q_{t+2}^e, being an average of the old one and something larger, exceeds q_{t+1}^e, which implies that $q_{t+1} > q_t$, and so on. Bray's stability hypothesis comes close to running

5. McCallum (1983) has proposed as a "methodological principle" that equilibria with a "minimal set of state variables" be preferred. This principle, in the present context, would select the stationary equilibrium, but it is unclear what the behavioral rationale for this principle is. I think that the experiment proposed in Sec. VII is, however, very much in the spirit of McCallum's argument.

6. Proposition 2 in Wallace (1980, p. 56) is almost identical to the proposition illustrated in fig. 5.

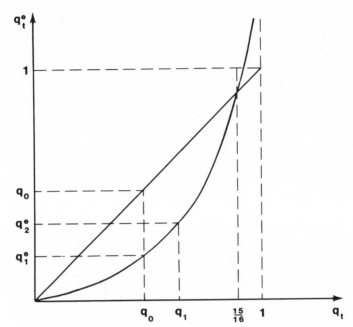

FIG. 5.—Price-level dynamics of eqq. (9) and (10)

the unstable difference equation (8) backward, converting it into a stable one.

The kind of adaptive behavior captured in this simple model seems to me to be a plausible conjecture as to how people might actually behave. Since it singles out the stationary equilibrium 15/16 as the one that would be converged to it seems to give this equilibrium a special substantive interest not shared by the infinity of other equilibria. But as a purely theoretical argument, this stability example does not seem to me to settle anything. The adaptive behavior it assumes is not based on any economic principle: (8) exhausts the implications of competition and "rationality," and it does not single out any one equilibrium path. Figure 5 is roughly consistent with what we know psychologically about the way people tend to behave in new situations, but so would be innumerable other adaptive schemes, different from the above, that one could have as easily worked through. In any case, the fact that one can produce an adaptive scheme that singles out a particular equilibrium does not rule out the possibility of producing other adaptive schemes that single out other equilibria or even suggest that this would be difficult to do.

The most that can be offered by the kind of stability argument just given seems to me to be the suggestion of the kind of experiment that might genuinely single out a particular equilibrium as being of more substantive interest than the others. The issue involves a question concerning how collections of people behave in a specific situation. Economic theory does not resolve the question. One can imagine other principles that would, but this cannot rule out the possibility that still other principles might resolve it quite differently. It is hard to see what can advance the discussion short of assembling a collection of people, putting them in the situation of interest, and observing what they do.

VII. A Proposed Experiment

The problem involved in convincing a collection of experimental subjects that they are in an infinite-horizon environment seems to me insurmountable. (Even to spell out what this means is not easy.) The central issues—whether people initially behave adaptively and, if so, what form this adaptive behavior takes—are as easily stated in the finite horizon case as in the infinite one. This observation (by Nancy Stokey) leads to the following proposed design.

Take N to be a number large enough to assure roughly competitive behavior in static experimental situations (say, 8 or 10), and let the number of subjects be $3N$, divided into three groups of N each. At $t = 0$, one group will be "old," each endowed with 100 white chips, each representing 0.01 units of fiat money (one "cent"). A second group will be endowed with 100 blue chips each, each representing 0.01 units of goods. The third group is in waiting; they will play the role of the young at $t = 1$. These groups are to rotate through ages 0, 1, and "nonexistent" for the duration of the experiment and are so informed.[7]

All subjects are informed that, at the end of each period as a young agent, each is to turn in all blue chips retained, and each is scored in proportion to the square root of this amount. At the end of each period as an old agent, each is to turn in all blue and white chips, and scores are given in proportion to twice the number of blue chips. The total pay each subject is to receive over the life of the experiment is simply the sum of the rewards so acquired in all of his successive "lives." Any white chips returned by subjects at "death" are redistributed as equally as possible to the newly "old" generation (acquired at price of zero) as of the beginning of the next period.

Subjects are convincingly informed that the experiment will last exactly T periods and that, at the conclusion of period T, the group playing the role of the "young" at that time will receive a fixed number q_T of blue chips for each white chip held at the end of that period. No other information as to the intrinsic value of white chips is given any subject at any time.

Subjects will be left free, in each period, to exchange white chips for

---

7. Sunder (1985) is currently conducting experiments of this general structure.

blue (or not to do so) on any terms they choose, on an entirely individual basis, exactly as in the Smith experiment described in Section IV. A period ends when no pair of subjects wishes to engage in further exchange. Thus blue chips and white will be traded, in general, in a variety of quantities and prices. Each period, the ratio $\hat{q}_t$ of total blue chips surrendered to total white chips surrended in exchange is recorded, and the history $(\hat{q}_0, \hat{q}_1, \ldots, \hat{q}_{t-1})$ is clearly displayed to all traders in period t. The sequence $(\hat{q}_0, \hat{q}_1, \ldots, \hat{q}_{T-1})$ is regarded as the outcome of experiment (T, q_T). The series of experiments here proposed involves varying T over various values (e.g., $T = 10, 50, 100$) and varying q_T over the interval $[0, 1]$ at discrete values most definitely including the end points.

An immediate benefit from the discipline imposed by the attempt to set out an operational experimental counterpart to the theoretical economy of Section VI is that one is led to take that theory seriously as an aid in thinking about how actual people might really behave in the given situation. One is led to ask, In what respects is equation (8) a serious model of human behavior, and in what respects is it not?

Surely it is unlikely that any sizable group of subjects would unanimously realize that their collective behavior "should" be described by (8), whatever this means. Even if they did, it is less likely still that all would solve (8) backward from the given terminal condition (T, q_T) to the "correct" value of q_0. Yet if this turn of events is wildly implausible, how much less plausible is it that similar subjects, situated in an infinite stage version of this same economy, should unanimously hit on the identical, wholly arbitrary value of q_0 that sets them and (somehow) their successors off on one of this economy's unstable equilibrium paths? Insofar as "perfect foresight" or "rational expectations" equilibria are useful social-scientific constructs, it must be in some other sense than this.

The sense in which these constructs are useful is, I think, something like this. The subjects in the experiment just described will have to take some kind of guess as to what white chips acquired today in trade will be worth tomorrow. Without knowing a good deal more about these people than that they are "rational," it seems obviously impossible to predict in any reliable way what these guesses will be. Even rational people assess new situations in the light of their own experience and without knowing much about these experiences; how can one predict their assessments? Yet unless all subjects are convinced that white chips are forever valueless (and I do not believe this can be brought about even by *telling* them that $q_T = 0$ if T is as large as 10 or 15), trade will occur and some positive value for money will be established.[8] If

---

8. This conjecture is not entirely without foundation, since the experiments proposed above are similar in many respects to experiments with repeated Prisoner's Dilemma

so, and if q_t is much off the value 15/16, subjects will see that available rewards have been passed over in the past and will adapt their behavior in the direction of claiming these rents in the future.

These conjectures are very much in the spirit of Bray's stability model, and, indeed, it would be interesting to see if the simple average forecasting rule that she assumed performs well as a description of price formation in early rounds of trading. My guess is that it would not—subjects in Smith's and subsequent experiments seem to behave more erratically, perhaps because they are themselves experimenting a little, than would be consistent with averaging alone—but I would also guess that whatever price formation patterns are observed would have stability properties identical to those derived by Bray.

VIII. Conclusions

This paper has been an inquiry into the role, actual and potential, of adaptive elements in empirically oriented economic theory. Rather than attempt a general characterization of this role, I have proceeded by the method of cases, using examples of specific social science research that seemed to be capable of shedding light on this general issue. I will conclude by sketching some generalities that these cases suggest.

I began with an example of empirical success in economics: the quantity theory of money. The example is not typical, for it involves the use of theoretical reasoning to arrive at testable propositions that subsequently, and in ways the originators of the theory could not have foreseen, enjoyed striking empirical confirmation. The nature of the theoretical reasoning involved is quite varied. Some element of "rationality" is involved in all versions, in the sense that units that "ought" not to matter to people are assumed in fact not to matter. More recent models involve formal utility theory in a much more explicit way than did the original versions, as well as explicit notions of market equilibrium. It is interesting that more refined theory has not been found to vindicate or provide a "foundation" for the testable versions of the theory. On the contrary, it has suggested a number of qualifications or possible deviations between theory and observation. We do not "believe in" the theory because it is built up from impeccable axioms about more fundamental aspects of behavior. It is also interesting to note that the theory succeeds empirically only on data

---

games, as reported, e.g., by Axelrod (1981). In these games, there is a unique Nash equilibrium that can be calculated by "backward induction" from a simple terminal condition, yet subjects often pursue nonequilibrium cooperative strategies (the analogue to exchanging goods for ultimately valueless money in the model of Sec. VI).

that are heavily time averaged. The theory has virtually no ability to account for month-to-month comovements in prices and money.

The experimental work with pigeons and other animal subjects permits an examination of the role of "rationality" at a level that obviously cannot be carried out with aggregative data on entire economies. In this work, the relationship between adaptive and rational behavior is clear: the presumption that behavior is adaptive is built into the experimental design and the interpretation of the results. Working out the implications of utility theory involves calculations (by the experimenters) that we do not believe have counterparts in the mental processes of pigeons.

Experimental work with human subjects in market situations involves adaptive behavior as well, but of an entirely different character. Here subjects are using experience not to trace out their own preferences but to determine how other "players" are likely to react to their own moves. Again, it is possible for the experimenter to calculate certain features of the outcome of this adaptive process theoretically, but these calculations are not a description or a model of the adaptive process itself.

This experimental work bears on the question of the stability of economic equilibria, but the results suggest (as Smith observed in his original paper) processes very different from those treated in received stability theory. More recently, theorists such as Margaret Bray have begun to develop a stability theory that seems to correspond much more closely to the adaptive behavior documented by Smith and other experimentalists.

The models studied by Smith and Bray have unique equilibria. Their results, experimental and theoretical, have the effect of making us feel more comfortable with the predictions of certain theoretical models but do not lead to modifications or improvements in the predictions of these models (though I think they have the potential for doing so). In Section VI, I introduced a well-known example from monetary theory in which there is a continuum of equilibria so that the theory is virtually vacuous. Bray's stability theory selects exactly one of these as stable. In Section VII, I proposed an experiment that would, I believe, select out this same equilibrium as the stable one (although the process might well differ from that proposed by Bray).

Recent theoretical work is making it increasingly clear that the multiplicity of equilibria illustrated in Section VI can arise in a wide variety of situations involving sequential trading, in competitive as well as finite-agent games. All but a few of these equilibria are, I believe, behaviorally uninteresting: They do not describe behavior that collections of adaptively behaving people would ever hit on. I think an appropriate stability theory can be useful in weeding out these uninteresting equilibria, an important application of the Correspondence Principle that Samuelson (1947) proposed long ago. But to be useful, stability theory must be more than simply a fancy way of saying that one does not want to think about certain equilibria. I prefer to view it as an experimentally testable hypothesis, as a special instance of the adaptive laws that we believe govern all human behavior.

Each "point" in figure 1 represents the behavior over a period of 20 years of all the individual households and business firms in a single Latin American country. To a sociologist or an anthropologist, these 16 countries exhibit an enormous variety of quite different cultures. To a political scientist, they cover a range from liberal democracy through military dictatorship. To a psychologist, they consist of millions of individual personalities, with most of those alive at the end of the period not yet born at its beginning. To an economist, they are 16 points lying (more or less) on a theoretically predicted 45-degree line.

To observe that economics is based on a superficial view of individual and social behavior does not, in these circumstances, seem to me to be much of an insight. I think it is exactly this superficiality that gives economics much of the power that it has: its ability to predict human behavior without knowing very much about the makeup and the lives of the people whose behavior we are trying to understand.[9] Yet an ability such as this necessarily has its limits, and I have spent most of this essay on cases that seem to me to lie close to these limits, for this is where they can best be seen and, perhaps, transcended.

References

Axelrod, R. 1981. The emergence of cooperation among egoists. *American Political Science Review* 75:306–18.

Battalio, R. C.; Kagel, J. H.; Rachlin, H.; and Green, L. 1981. Commodity choice behavior with pigeons as subjects. *Journal of Political Economy* 89:67–91.

Blume, L. E.; Bray, M. M.; and Easley, D. 1982. Introduction to the stability of rational expectations equilibrium. *Journal of Economic Theory* 26:313–17.

Blume, L. E., and Easley, D. 1982. Learning to be rational. *Journal of Economic Theory* 26:340–51.

Bray, M. 1982. Learning, estimation and the stability of rational expectations. *Journal of Economic Theory* 26:318–39.

Bray, M. 1983. Convergence to rational expectations equilibrium. In Roman Frydman and Edmund S. Phelps (eds.), *Individual Forecasting and Aggregate Outcomes.* Cambridge: Cambridge University Press.

Hume, D. 1963. *Essays Moral, Political and Literary.* London: Oxford University Press.

Lucas, R. E., Jr. 1978. Asset prices in an exchange economy. *Econometrica* 46:1429–46.

Lucas, R. E., Jr. 1980. Two illustrations of the quantity theory of money. *American Economic Review* 70:1005–14.

Muth, J. F. 1961. Rational expectations and the theory of price movements. *Econometrica* 29:315–35.

McCallum, B. T. 1983. On non-uniqueness in rational expectations models: An attempt at perspective. *Journal of Monetary Economica* 11:139–68.

9. What I am here calling "superficiality" in economic theory is described more fully and more neutrally in Simon (1969).

Samuelson, P. A. 1947. *Foundations of Economic Analysis*. Cambridge, Mass.: Harvard University Press.

Samuelson, P. A. 1958. An exact consumption-loan model of interest with or without the social contrivance of money. *Journal of Political Economy* 66:467–82.

Simon, H. A. 1969. *The Science of the Artifical*. Cambridge, Mass.: MIT Press.

Smith, V. L. 1962. An experimental study of competitive market behavior. *Journal of Political Economy* 70:111–37.

Smith, V. L. 1982. Microeconomic systems as an experimental science. *American Economic Review* 72:923–55.

Sunder, S. 1985. Unpublished notes. University of Minnesota.

Townsend, R. M. 1978. Market anticipations, rational expectations, and Bayesian analysis. *International Economics Review* 19:481–94.

Vogel, R. C. 1974. The dynamics of inflation in Latin America, 1950–1969. *American Economics Review* 64:102–14.

Wallace, N. 1980. The overlapping generations model of fiat money. In J. H. Karaken and N. Wallace (eds.), *Models of Monetary Economies*. Minneapolis: Federal Reserve Bank of Minneapolis.

Walras, L. 1954. *Elements of Pure Economics*. Translated by William Jaffe. Homewood, Ill.: Irwin.

Sidney G. Winter

Yale University

Comments on Arrow and on Lucas*

Such a number of interesting and provocative things are put forward in Lucas and in Arrow (in this volume) that I would like to be able to dissect them in detail. For example, Lucas states that "the problem of controlling inflation has been 'successfully solved' in a scientific sense" (p. 221). I am tempted to explore the limits of the set of problems that might be said to be scientifically "solved" in the Lucas sense, but I fear that this would take up a good deal of space. Arrow deplores the use of homogeneity assumptions as a device for adding content to otherwise inconclusive economic theories, but presumably he does not believe that the Sonnenschien-Mantel-Debreu theorem is the ultimate conclusion regarding the useful content of the propositions of general equilibrium theory. Some restrictions of intermediate strength are presumably called for, and I would like to make the case that strong empirical generalizations about the nature of human actors—such as those describing the biological requirements for survival—are available and relevant in this connection. This too would take some space to develop in detail, though not as much as the first subject.

Given the constraints, I must choose a focus. I will focus on what I take to be the main message that Lucas has put forward regarding the relationship between "adaptive behavior" and the rationality assumptions employed in standard economic theory. This message is recognizable as the intellectual descendant of similar discussions by Friedman and Machlup in the 1940s and 1950s, and the ideas involved remain extremely influential in the discipline today. I will present and comment on my own statement of this position, which I (following Blaug [1980]) will call the "Classic Defense" of the rationality-as-

* Helpful comments on an earlier draft were received from R. Antle, J. Demski, and O. Williamson. Errors that I have persisted in, willfully or otherwise, are definitely not their responsibility. Research support from the Sloan Foundation is also gratefully acknowledged.

optimization paradigm in economic theory. This discussion will provide a framework for occasional more detailed comments on both Lucas and Arrow.

Although there are significant distinctions to be made among the various views put forward by Friedman, Machlup, Lucas, and others, there is a major common theme that is the characteristic feature of the Classic Defense. This is the willingness to concede that the rationality assumptions of economic theory are not descriptive of the process by which decisions are reached and, further, that most decisions actually emerge from response repertoires developed over a period of time by what may broadly be termed "adaptive" or learning processes.

Lucas is unusually explicit in his acknowledgment of these points; in my view, this explicitness represents progress in the statement of the Classic Defense: "We use economic theory to calculate how certain variations in the situation are predicted to affect behavior, but these calculations obviously do not reflect or usefully model the adaptive process by which subjects have themselves arrived at the decision rules they use. Technically, I think of economics as studying decision rules that are steady states of some adaptive process, decision rules that are found to work over a range of situations and hence are no longer revised appreciably as more experience accumulates" (Lucas, in this volume, p. 218). This statement may be compared with Friedman's use (1953, p. 22) of the analogy between the behavior of a businessman and that of a skilled billiards player, and Machlup's discussion of the routine decisions of a driver overtaking a truck (1946, pp. 534–35).

I have argued elsewhere (Winter, 1975 pp. 89–95) that the willingness not only to limit the scope of theoretical propositions by the "as-if" principle but also to concede in general terms the character of the underlying reality is an important and underemphasized aspect of the long-standing "realism of assumptions" controversy (see also Nelson and Winter 1982, pp. 91–95). It leaves the door open (at least a crack) for those of us who advocate more explicit reliance on empirically grounded behavioral generalizations at the foundations of economic theory. Lucas's statements in his paper here open the door wider and might even be read as proposing the terms of a possible modus vivendi between standard theory and a more empirically based behavioralism. But they leave me even more puzzled than ever as to how the proponents of as-if optimization manage to derive their familiar bottom-line endorsement of "business as usual" in economic theorizing from the premises of their argument. As I read Lucas's firm repudiation of (unidentified) "attempts to reconstruct economics from the ground up in the image of some other science" (p. 218), I am led once again to suspect that the premise from which this methodological conservatism derives is conservatism itself, otherwise known as behavioral inertia (cf. Winter 1975, pp. 111–13).

Both the strengths and the limitations of the Classic Defense seem to me to have been left somewhat obscure by the long discussion of economic methodology.[1] That discussion has tended to focus on matters of high principle that transcend disciplinary boundaries, rather than on the more specific issues surrounding the concept of rational economic behavior. What follows is an attempt to restate the Classic Defense in what is intended to be a sympathetic fashion—but since my reserves of sympathy are limited, I cannot fairly attribute this viewpoint to Lucas or other proponents of the position I seek to characterize. It is a view that I am at least tempted to agree with—but it may not be what they believe.

The argument is in seven steps. (1) The economic world as a whole, or some identifiable sector thereof, is reasonably viewed as being in proximate equilibrium. (2) Individual economic actors repeatedly face the same choice situation or a sequence of highly similar choice situations. (3) Actors have stable preferences and thus evaluate the outcomes of individual choices made according to stable criteria. (4) Given repeated exposure, any individual actor could identify and would seize any available opportunity for improving outcomes (and, in the case of business firms, would do so on pain of being eliminated by the competition of others who would identify and seize such opportunities). (5) Hence, no equilibrium can arise in which individual actors fail to maximize their preferences—any superficially stationary position involving nonmaximization would be altered according to the logic of the previous point. (6) Since the world is, as noted, in proximate equilibrium, it must exhibit, at least approximately, the patterns implied by the assumption that actors are maximizing. (7) The details of the adaptive processes referred to in point 4 are complex and probably actor and situation specific; by contrast, the regularities associated with optimization and equilibrium are comparatively simple. Considerations of parsimony therefore indicate that the way to progress in economic understanding is to explore these regularities theoretically and to compare the results with observation.

Although I concede some force to this argument, I have reservations about every step. Some of these are beyond the limited scope of the present discussion; others are at least briefly noted below. The first point of the argument deserves special attention, however, for it marks a psychological divide that is fundamental to one's outlook on economics. To be willing to limit the aspirations of economic science to the study of the steady states of adaptive processes is presumably to view vast realms of apparent rapid change as either unimportant or illusory; it is to join with the writer of Ecclesiastes in maintaining that "there is no new thing under the sun." I, on the other hand, side with Hera-

1. For an excellent overview of the discussion as it relates to the theory of the firm, see Blaug (1980, ch. 7).

cleitus in arguing that "you could not step twice into the same river, for new waters are ever flowing on to you." It is the appearance of stability that is illusory; just look a little closer or wait a little longer.[2] We Heraclitean types find it difficult to understand what the Ecclesiastes types are talking about, what with the universe expanding, the continents drifting, the arms race racing, and the kids growing up. The observed predictive performance of economic models also seems to us to be considerably more consonant with the Heraclitean view than with the alternative. Still, it is ultimately a question of philosophical outlook, and *de gustibus non disputandum* (except among philosophers, of course).

The Classic Defense provides, nevertheless, an important perspective on where economic science stands today. To the extent that our science does have empirical successes to its credit that are theoretically explained by the rationality-as-optimization paradigm, I believe it is largely because the various conditions set forth in the Classic Defense are approximately satisfied in some particular segment of economic reality over an extended period of time: approximate equilibrium prevails, similar choices are faced repetitively, a stable set of preferences roughly separable from other domains of preference is applied, and so forth. To cite an important example, I believe that the efficient markets hypothesis must be scored as an empirical success for the standard approach and that the Classic Defense provides the meta-explanation for this feat of successful (but partial) explanation of the functioning of financial markets. Any effort to "reconstruct economics from the ground up" should be one that preserves the discipline's major empirical successes, and the Classic Defense provides useful guidance as to where these successes are to be found and how they might be explained in a theory with quite different foundations.

My objections to the Classic Defense pale into insignificance compared with my objections to an alternative image of economic rationality that seems to have ever-increasing influence among theorists. This is the image of the economic actor as superoptimizer.[3] When the question is raised, as it often is, whether a particular choice problem is not just a subproblem of some higher-level optimization problem, the answer for the superoptimizer is always yes—and he or she has that one correctly solved too. Thus, the superoptimizer never makes an ordi-

2. For thoughtful essays from the Heraclitean viewpoint, see Day (1984) and Solow (1985).

3. I first encountered this useful term in Mirrlees and Stern (1972). Various authors have discussed the possibility that paradox or contradiction may arise when the attempt is made to apply the notion of full "superoptimizing" rationality in a world in which all information processing is costly (though the term itself is not used in most of these discussions). (See Winter 1964, 1975; Savage 1967; Radner 1968; Day 1971; Nozick 1981.)

nary human mistake, whether in making the first transaction in one of Plott's (in this volume) experimental games or in choosing the consumption level in the first instant of a program calculated to maximize an integral of discounted utility over a lifetime. Superoptimizer never departs from the rules of Bayesian inference, applied within the framework of the prior distribution with which he or she is somehow endowed at "birth." Subtle inferences from observations to underlying conditions are always correctly made, as in models of fully revealing rational expectations equilibrium or in recent models of reputation effects (Kreps et al. 1982).

Above all, the superoptimizer has unlimited access to free information-processing capacity. Were it not so deeply ingrained in the intellectual routines of the discipline, this characterization of human capability would be recognized as being totally inappropriate in a science concerned with the social implications of resource scarcity. Even to minds inured by disciplinary tradition to the violence that this assumption suffers from common sense and everyday observation, Tversky and Kahneman's results (in this volume) on "framing effects" should be profoundly disturbing. These results refute, as squarely as an empirical result ever can, the assumption that human beings have effectively unlimited information-processing capacity. Superoptimizers cannot display framing effects because, to them, no logical problem is "opaque."

Lucas makes passing, and possibly whimsical, reference to superoptimization in footnote 2 of his paper. He suggests that the pigeons in the experiments of Batallio et al. (1981) might be modeled as superoptimizers who are making fully rational choices from the very first peck of a control key. To his credit, he appears to deprecate the usefulness of this sort of approach and returns to his endorsement of the Classic Defense. Arrow appears to be concerned that recent theorizing under the rubric of "common knowledge"—the latest example of the trend toward ever more subtle conceptions of economic rationality—may be pressing beyond the limits of what is sensible. Of course, if the evidence on framing effects is taken seriously—and it seems that Arrow (1982) does take it seriously—then it should be apparent that those limits were breached some time ago.

But if economic man is not a superoptimizer, what sort of optimizer can he be? There is no logically defensible stopping point in the hierarchy of N-meta rationalities since the behavior characterized at any particular level is always subject to rational critique and elaboration at the next higher level. This is the conundrum that has driven theory down the path it has taken; the disciplinary rituals that are believed to mandate this theoretical odyssey have been performed by the discussants and referees of thousands of papers. They are right; there is no logical reason to limit the process, and the race to be the first to explore the next level drives the climbers on.

There are, however, empirical reasons for limiting the process and closely related reasons involving the requirements for a fruitful relationship between theory and empiricism in economics. The great virtue of the Classic Defense is that it does not represent human beings as superoptimizers, and it offers, albeit implicitly, an empirical basis for deciding when the impulse to impute more rationality should be checked. The suggestion is that the experience of the actor with the situation envisaged has a lot to do with the level of rationality the actor should be expected to display in that situation—provided that by "rationality" one means nothing more than the sorts of consistency properties that are the core of the economist's notion of rationality.

As a forceful and elegant elaboration of this same idea, let me submit my favorite quotation from the writings of Joseph Schumpeter, originally published in 1911.

> The assumption that conduct is prompt and rational is in all cases a fiction. But it proves to be sufficiently near to reality, if things have had time to hammer logic into men. Where this has happened, *and within the limits in which it has happened,* one may rest content with this fiction and build theories upon it. . . . Outside of these limits our fiction loses its closeness to reality. To cling to it there also, as the traditional theory does, is to hide an essential thing and to ignore a fact which, in contrast with other deviations of our assumptions from reality, is theoretically important and the source of phenomena which would not exist without it. [1934, p. 80; emphasis added]

The problem with the notion of the economic actor as superoptimizer is it denies that any such limits exist. The problem with the Classic Defense is that its proponents, while they acknowledge the reality of the limits, do little to help define them and nothing to explore the important phenomena that lie beyond them.

From Schumpeter's basic question whether things have had time to hammer logic into men, some more specific observations about the scope of the Classic Defense may be derived. (1) It is the actions actually taken in a steady-state situation that are subject to repeated testing, not the decision rules that underlie those actions. For this reason, the support that the Classic Defense provides for standard comparative statics results is much weaker than is commonly supposed (Winter 1964; Nelson and Winter 1982, ch. 7). (2) Since the defense by itself provides no indication as to how long it takes for adaptive processes to reach something like steady-state conditions, it provides no guidance regarding the quality of the predictions that standard economic models may be expected to provide in particular cases. (3) Since sophisticated learning requires sophisticated arrangements for the collection, storage, and analysis of information, it may be expected in general to be more characteristic of firms than of consumers—a distinction the defense does not make explicit. (4) The Classic Defense offers no support when the decision under consideration is unique (such as the choice of a lifetime policy) or irreversible.[4] (5) Finally, if taken seriously, the Classic Defense would condemn economists to silence on major policy questions in a world undergoing path-dependent historical change, since change is continually presenting economic actors with truly novel choice situations (or so it appears to a Heraclitean type).

From my own historically unique vantage point and subject to the qualifications inherent in my own bounded rationality, the following conclusions seem to emerge. Although the Classic Defense applies to a domain of inquiry that is significant, that domain is far too small to be acceptable as a definition of the limits and ambitions of the discipline. There is an important role for inquiry into the learning and adaptive processes of boundedly rational economic actors who are forced to act in a changing world that they do not understand. What economics needs is to hold on to the empirical successes it has achieved within the scope of the Classic Defense, recognize that that scope is drastically narrower than the allocation of theoretical effort would imply, and get on with the important business of building a successful empirical science that extends beyond the scope of the Classic Defense.

References

Arrow, K. J. 1982. Risk perception in psychology and economics. *Economic Inquiry* 20 (January): 1–9.

Arrow, K. J. In this volume. Rationality of self and others in an economic system.

Battalio, R. C.; Kagel, J. H.; Rachlin, H.; and Green, L. 1981. Commodity choice behavior with pigeons as subjects. *Journal of Political Economy* 89 (February): 67–91.

Blaug, M. 1980. *The Methodology of Economics.* Cambridge: Cambridge University Press.

Day, R. H. 1971. Rational choice and economic behavior. *Theory and Decision* 1:229–51.

Day, R. H. 1984. Disequilibrium economic dynamics: A post-Schumpeterian contribution. *Journal of Economic Behavior and Organization* 5 (March): 57–76.

Friedman, M. 1953. The methodology of positive economics. In *Essays in Positive Economics.* Chicago: Chicago University Press.

Kreps, D. M., et al. 1982. Rational cooperation in finitely repeated Prisoner's Dilemma. *Journal of Economic Theory* 27 (August): 245–52.

Lucas, R. E., Jr. In this volume. Adaptive behavior and economic theory.

---

4. Consider, e.g., the sort of rational expectations model with overlapping generations studied in Lucas's paper. He suggests that results from experimental economics might be used to sharpen the predictions of such models by offering an empirically based choice among the many theoretically possible equilibria. His proposal, however, involves the giant step of substituting a repetitive choice situation where learning is possible for a choice situation that is unique for the actors in the underlying model. Since real actors "only go around once in life," it is not clear that the experimental results would warrant any confidence in the corresponding predictions about reality—even assuming the results to be supportive in the fashion Lucas expects.

Machlup, F. 1946. Marginal analysis and empirical research. *American Economic Review* 36 (September): 519–54.

Mirrlees, J. A., and Stern, N. H. 1972. Fairly good plans. *Journal of Economic Theory* 4 (April): 268–88.

Nelson, R. R., and Winter, S. G. 1982. *An Evolutionary Theory of Economic Change.* Cambridge, Mass.: Harvard University Press.

Nozick, R. 1981. *Philosophical Explanations.* Cambridge, Mass.: Harvard University Press.

Plott, C. R. In this volume. Rational choice in experimental markets.

Radner, R. 1968. Competitive equilibrium under uncertainty. *Econometrica* 36 (January): 31–58.

Savage, L. J. 1967. Difficulties in the theory of personal probability. *Philosophy of Science* 43 (December): 305–10.

Schumpeter, J. A. 1934. *The Theory of Economic Development.* Cambridge, Mass.: Harvard University Press.

Solow, R. M. 1985. Economic history and economics. *American Economic Review* 75 (May): 328–31.

Tversky, A., and Kahneman, D. In this volume. Rational choice and the framing of decisions.

Winter, S. G. 1964. Economic "natural selection" and the theory of the firm. *Yale Economic Essays* 4 (Spring): 225–72.

Winter, S. G. 1975. Optimization and evolution in the theory of the firm. In R. H. Day and T. Groves (eds.), *Adaptive Economic Models.* New York: Academic Press.

Richard Zeckhauser
Harvard University

Comments: Behavioral versus Rational Economics: What You See Is What You Conquer*

Among geologists a battle now rages whether the earth contains a substantial, buried pool of methane gas that was formed with the planet rather than from the decay of plant and animal bodies. Each side, though respecting the other's natural brilliance, looks askance at its science on this subject and its empirical support. One is reminded of the spirited battle between the rationalists and behavioralists in economics—but the geologists' conflict is subject to empirical test, a monumentally expensive bore. (It may be substantially resolved by a 3-mile-deep drill for gas now being undertaken by Sweden in an area where an ancient collision with a meteorite may have created a reservoir to trap such gas.) The behavioralist-rationalist debate, in contrast, is unlikely to be resolved any time soon because the two schools look for evidence in very different arenas. In some ways, it is more a debate between religions than between scientific theories.

Thomas Kuhn's (1970) notion of the struggle among paradigms offers another metaphor for thinking about battles among theories. Celestial bodies provide useful examples once again, whether it be replacing the heliocentric theory of the universe or supplanting the pulsating universe theory with the big bang. In most of the cases Kuhn describes, the struggle is titanic, in part, but only in part, because the evidence is hard to mount. The battle is usually won only after some time, often when disciplines of the new theory have come of age.

I. The Behavioral versus Rational Battle

This volume contains elegant, often persuasive documents in the battle between behavioral and rational economics. The specific papers I have

* Malcolm Brachman, Harvey Brooks, and Nancy Jackson provided helpful comments. This research was supported by the Business and Government Center, Harvard University.

been asked to comment on, by Arrow and by Lucas (in this volume), are deep and thoughtful presentations by as forceful combatants as either side could hope to muster. Supporters of the behavioral and rational schools will rally round their respective champions. But I believe that this battle will differ significantly from the intellectual struggles over theories regarding primordial gas or the origins of the universe. There are many common elements—deep passions, academic careers at risk, and the emergence of theories long before conclusive evidence could be marshaled. Ultimately, the other conflicts are (or will be) resolved. But prospects for a settlement of the rational-versus-behavioral battle seem dim.

Too Many Battlefields

I do not think that the conflict between rationalists and behavioralists will be resolved in an intellectual generation, or even 3 such generations. There are simply too many battlefields. Each side can select the ones most favorable to its own cause. From time to time there will be mutually agreed-on skirmishes. Major recent ones have centered on macroeconomics, where the evidence remains exceedingly controversial and inconclusive, and finance, where the markets work exceedingly well but not perfectly—an outcome sufficiently ambiguous to enable both sides to claim victory. In the future, I suspect, the behavioralists will continue mounting experiments or micro evidence of nonrational choices, for there are an infinite number to be found. The rationalists will take succor from the overwhelming power of their model, which had a lot to do with its success in the first place, and the absence of any equivalently powerful competitor.[1] Should behavior in certain salient areas be found to violate rationality, it will be treated as beyond economics. Decisions on religion and, conceivably, on family choices or personal habits thus may command the rationalists' attention, if they behave well; otherwise, they may be classified in the same category as the source of preferences or values, something about which we have little to add as economists.

This is not a Kuhnian struggle among paradigms, but a turf battle.[2] Each side has some secure territory. Figure 1 is perhaps suggestive,

---

1. Arrow demurs on this point. See the discussion of his contribution below.
2. Philosophers of science are hardly agreed on Kuhn's formulation. Harvey Brooks suggested to me that competing theories in physics tend to coexist for periods of time because each explains most of the facts. Moreover, "a new conceptual framework does *not* sweep away all that has gone before. Relativity *reduced* to Newtonian mechanics in the domains of parameters for which Newton's mechanics had been established. Newton's mechanics is entirely adequate for space vehicles and planatary probes, for example." Though the gap is not as large, the rational-versus-behavioral economics debate does not fit this pattern either, to judge by the assessments of most participants. There is too much disagreement on basic assumptions. Behavioral theories of economics do not readily reduce to rationality in limited domains.

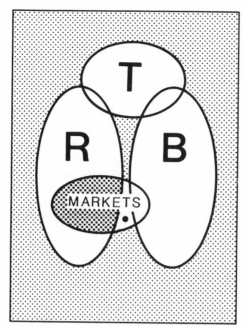

Fig. 1.—Domains of decision

revealing areas where each theory is likely to have its greatest strengths. An impartial draftsman has allotted equal space to the rational and behavioral explanations, denoted by the ovals R and B, but viewers can stretch the diagram where they wish along any dimension. Much territory is not covered by either model. Frequently, third categories of explanation—theology, oval T, is the example in the diagram—hold sway, though these may have a rational or behavioral accompaniment.

The shaded area, rational participants in markets, is the one most studied by the rational camp. That camp's most insistent claim, and one for which there is a great deal of evidence, is that no hypothesis other than rationality could describe the observed behavior with equivalent elegance and power. Most other explanations are introduced ad hoc, on an area-by-area basis, and hence consist of no explanation at all. Some braver souls (Gary Becker is the most celebrated) make forays into rational explanations of nonmarket behavior. And there are some market areas, perhaps the dot representing the market for poetry, that the rationalists gladly leave as booty for others.

The behavioralists, well schooled in understanding our pursuits of, say, food, take delight in showing nonrational market behavior. Occasionally the evidence consists of poorly behaving markets. Financial markets are too volatile (Shiller 1979); price variations from seller to

seller in competitive markets are too great (Pratt, Wise, and Zeckhauser 1979); people gamble. They also employ laboratory experiments and survey evidence to show that behaviors needed for effective
performance in the market, the most salient being the accurate processing of information and adherence to consistent preferences for
decisions under uncertainty, are beyond the inclinations or capabilities
of most human decision makers (see the essays in Kahneman, Slovic,
and Tversky [1982]).

But surely this formulation is too simple. To capture the confusion of
the struggle between rationalists and behavioralists, perhaps we should
imagine that the combatants have wandered into four-dimensional
space. Each side resides in its own three dimensions, only two of
which overlap the other's space. The three-dimensional boulders
thrown by one side are thus highly unlikely to hit the other, though
they will show up as direct hits on the launching side's radar screen.

II. The Moderate Assessment

If the four-dimensional battle analogy is apt, the moderate in this debate, seeing deep intellectual structure on both sides, is due for frustration. The debate is not being joined and will not be joined in the future,
for each side is triumphant in the areas it surveys. When progress can
no longer be made in an area, it is not uncommon to introduce some
axioms, statements that are either so obvious or so untestable that they
can enter the debate in no other fashion.

Axioms and Corollaries

AXIOM 1. For any tenet of rational choice, the behavioralists (e.g.,
Amos Tversky) can produce a laboratory counterexample.

AXIOM 2. For any "violation" of rational behavior discovered in a
real world market (e.g., the fact that hardware stores do not raise snow
shovel prices shortly after a storm), the rationalists (e.g., Gary Becker)
will be sufficiently creative to reconstruct a rational explanation.

AXIOM 3. Elegant abstract formulations will be developed by both
sides, frequently addressing the same points, but because there are
sufficient degrees of freedom when creating a model, they will come to
quite different conclusions.

If these axioms are accepted, we cannot expect much progress in
convincing the diehard believers in either camp that the other is correct. Future disciples must be expected on both sides. The task of
sorting out thus falls to the moderates. Empirical support should be our
criterion. Moreover, we moderates should be happy if we can merely
label the world, knowing where rational models effectively hold sway
and where behavioral explanations are likely to be more successful.
Each of the axioms has a corollary for the moderate's agenda.

COROLLARY 1. The behavioralists should focus their laboratory experiments on choice patterns with important real world implications or, better yet, directly on important real world phenomena.

COROLLARY 2. The rationalists should define the domains of economics where they can demonstrate that the preponderance of evidence supports their view.

COROLLARY 3. The choice among elegant abstract formulations that conflict with one another should not be based on their elegance, though that would surely tempt us behavioralists, or the opportunities they offer for additional work, a lure to us rationalists, but rather on the consistency of their predictions with real world observations. (This is not the place to rehash the hoary debate whether we must worry about the accuracy of the rationalist's assumptions.)

Responses of the Combatants

The behavioralists have produced work that is both dazzling and disturbing, particularly to those of us who worship at the Bayes-Savage shrine for decision making under uncertainty. But they have only begun to demonstrate the importance of their formulation. (Kahneman, Knetsch, and Thaler's article [in this volume] is a good example of a search for importance.)

The rationalists have been more interested in conquering new territory—the battle of the theory of rational expectations for the heart of macroeconomics is a salient example—than in identifying which areas within their identified spheres of influence are not critical to their well-being. Robert Lucas's article (in this volume) is a significant, welcome exception. In a highly conscientious fashion, it clearly identifies priority areas for explanation by rational models and other areas where the rational flag need not wave. He draws evidence from animal experiments and history and demonstrates that certain abstract "refutations" of rational explanations may not be refutations at all.

Arrow (in this volume) works in the spirit of my third corollary, examining abstract economic formulations to identify where the rationality assumption is critical. He concludes that it imposes an "extremely severe strain on information-gathering and computing abilities . . . incompatible with the limits of the human being" (p. 213). We moderates knew that and felt that the appropriate inquiry was then the following: given the distribution of economic decisions that citizens confront and their limitations as information processors, will they come reasonably close to a first-best performance? I know of no hard evidence on this question. But research through anecdote collection suggests that people do much better on recurring, everyday choices than on major decisions, such as the selection of a spouse, occupation, or retirement plan.

Arrow also raises two other classes of troubling observations. First,

theory suggests that, when markets are incomplete or information im-
pounded, rational behavior is not sufficient to define a single equilibrium; rather, there is a continuum. Second, the exchange of assets due
to differences in information, such as is found on stock markets, is
inconsistent with a view that individuals rationally gather and process
all information. I shall return to the arguments of Arrow and Lucas.

What the Two Sides See

In the debate between rationalists and behavioralists, each side is
triumphant in the landscape it views. Let me now describe where I
think each side holds sway.

Nonrational behavior in economics is a bit like an optical illusion.
Just as you cannot always trust your eyes, you cannot always trust
your behavior to be rational. But are optical illusions predominantly a
laboratory curiosity or an important issue in problems ranging from the
design of buildings to the training of athletes? I am inclined toward the
former view, though I recognize that in special situations (e.g., warning
a desert soldier where he will not find water), optical illusions may be a
life-and-death matter. Although an understanding of the phenomenon
may help explain how our brains work, it is probably irrelevant to our
ability to perceive situations accurately in the overwhelming majority
of real world situations.

If we believe that nonrational behavior in economics is as unimportant to real world resource allocation as optical illusions are to real
world perception, the subject should be left to those few psychologists
who wish to use economics as the area in which they explore thought
processes. Importance here is a product of frequency of occurrence
times impact—the magnitude of the deviation from what rational behavior would produce. Economics, unfortunately, seldom attempts to
measure magnitudes of deviations. Thus, in welfare economics, for
example, we have too often been satisfied to say, "Aha, the external-
ity," without worrying about its size. To repeat: measuring the real
world consequence is the major challenge to the behavioralists.

An Underlying Agenda

Many, though not all, of the participants in these struggles see a deeper
underlying agenda: once it is perceived that the individual participants
are not rational, the important theorems on the allocational accom-
plishments of the market no longer hold. We can no longer make the
efficiency claim that normally counterbalances arguments for greater
central intervention in the economy. Intervention is thus more
justifiable. This is an argument to convince not economists but rather
those on the sidelines whom they have sometimes mesmerized.

Consider the following thought experiment. There are two equally
important sectors of the economy, food and shelter. When making

transactions in one sector, food, the participants are highly rational. But their decisions in housing reveal numerous psychological traps.[3] By law, we must impose a substantial government presence in precisely one of these two sectors. Which one should it be? I know of no theory or empirical study that provides an answer to this question; hence, there seems to be no logic to the nonrational-hence-intervene argument. Therefore, it is disturbing—though hardly surprising—to observe the correlation between political values and participation in the rational-versus-behavioral battle.

III. Assessing the Arguments

The central question in this debate is who controls which territory. That question is too controversial to settle here, but it should be possible to generate some agreement on comparative advantage. As is true in the world of international trade, as the resources of a productive entity—be it a nation or a scholarly school—expand, it will begin to produce an ever-increasing menu of products. Alas, the rational-versus-behavioral debate takes place in a many-factor world. Here is one man's speculation on how advantage might break down on various dimensions (see table 1). Most of these categories are clear. I shall elaborate on a few.

Identifying States and Alternatives

Since the time of Frank Knight, economists have paid attention to the distinction between risk (where probabilities are known) and uncertainty (where they are unknown). This distinction motivates a number of the early behavioralist "refutations" of the rational choice model, such as the Allais and Ellsberg paradoxes. But real world violations of the rational decision prescription, particularly under conditions of uncertainty, often relate to a third class of problems, namely, failure to define or consider alternatives. Even when alternatives are well defined, states of the world may be unknown.

Ignorance might be an appropriate term to describe situations in which states of the world or alternatives are simply unknown. Howard Raiffa tells an informative story about himself. In a lecture on fault trees at the National Academy of Sciences, he illustrated with the concept of a probabilistic diagnosis of a car failing to start. After finishing the lecture, he walked to his nearby rental car, got in, inserted the key, and found that he could not start it. He was embarrassed to discover not only that he had gotten into the wrong car but that getting into the wrong car was not an identified state on his fault tree.

---

3. For example, people may fail to change their consumption bundle when relative prices change, and the value of their house rises fantastically.

TABLE 1   Comparative Advantage

Rational		Behavioral
Steady state	vs.	Adaptive
Recurring situation	vs.	Unique
Continuous allocation	vs.	Discrete
States of the world identified	vs.	States of the world need to be identified
Alternatives clear	vs.	Alternatives need to be identified
Price taking	vs.	Negotiation or strategic
Goods	vs.	Time, health, faith, love
Subject to arbitrage	vs.	No poaching

In many cases, even if one thinks for a very long time, one can only identify states of the world that capture, say, 90% of the possible outcomes. The less familiar the situation, the greater the density of the complementary catchall category. (For example, try to think of the possible ways the world may end.) When surprises arise, new models may be appropriate. Daniel Ellsberg used to discuss a hypothetical decision situation in which one flips a coin to determine whether it is fair or has two heads. Five trials produce two heads and three landings on edge. Merely stating that the odds are four to one for the two-headed coin does not seem to capture the situation.

In a strict sense, ignorance of alternatives is just a special case of ignorance of states of the world. But it causes problems so frequently that it merits separate investigation. In the typical economics text, the available alternatives are clearly delineated; in early chapters, for example, they are likely to lie along a budget line. But in the real world, even simple choice situations, such as which college to attend, often involve an anterior decision as to which goods should even be considered. In many instances, the space of alternatives may be hard to define. A likely, often significant, error is to fail to consider some attractive alternative, including the alternative of looking further.

Perhaps some of the laboratory irrational behavior that we observe, where the alternatives are usually well specified, is really due to people's attempts to protect themselves against unspecified states in a *hostile world*. In the Ellsberg and Allais contexts, for example, subjects may be concerned that the experimenter is working against them. After all, that is what usually happens in the real world, where most economic uncertainties relate to the behavior and interests of other parties, not nature's choices. If an unfamiliar mechanic disparages our car—"I don't like that right front ball joint; I wouldn't go over 40 mph. But it will probably last for a month or so"—we all suspect that he may not be giving us a fair portrayal of his assessment of the odds. If our customary decision making under uncertainty allowed for manipulation of the probabilities, usually against us, that would at worst be an instance of invoking reasonable rules of thumb, a form of bounded rationality. In laboratory experiments, however, we cannot determine what other situations are being blended in the decision maker's mind.[4] In this instance, the failure to consider alternatives is that of the experimenter, who is not alert to all that may be happening. The failure to identify alternatives may also be related to the misallocation of time.

Misallocation of Time

Among important economic commodities, time is perhaps the one that individuals allocate least well. Research by introspection will convince most readers that they consistently misallocate time and that their biases are predictable. For example, most of us spread time too evenly. Given a $100 decision and a $10,000 decision, we are likely to spend relatively too much time on the former. We have bias toward spasm response, at the expense of long-term planning. Many professors at Harvard, I have discovered, have not spent 1 hour selecting among alternative retirement plans and have not even considered some highly favorable, tax-advantaged programs.[5] Though virtually every reader of this article is convinced of the importance of portfolio diversification, probably only a small percentage have any personal holdings in foreign stocks, which would substantially increase expected returns for any level of risk. Most people have never taken the 5 minutes needed to determine that the problem was worth considering and the 10 minutes to find out how to purchase.

IV. From Observations to Deductions about Behavior

I have attempted to define some areas where individuals will be able to make decisions that come closer to the rational ideal and others where greater explanatory power may be provided by behavioral models, which unfortunately do not carry over nearly so easily from situation to situation. But as the debate continues, we should also consider how to extrapolate from what we observe to what we believe about individual's behavior. For example, if we mistakenly assume an individual is deciding under nature's uncertainties, when in fact he believes himself to be in a hostile world, we will interpret his behavior incorrectly. Even

4. I earned my spending money through college by participating in psychological experiments. My principal conclusion was that, when the experimenter said something like, "You are each an undergraduate trying to estimate which design is better," the chances were nine in 10 that one of the subjects was a confederate, that the experiment had little to do with judging designs, or both.

5. Perhaps too equal spreading of time helps explain the Pratt et al. (1979) results. Price variations among standardized, high-priced goods were vastly too great to justify on a search theory basis, given estimates of the value of time, including estimates derived from price variability among low-priced goods.

if the experimenter is not hostile or the car mechanic is honest, is the suspicious decision maker necessarily irrational to think otherwise?[6]

Arbitrage versus No Poaching

The natural selection paradigm provides powerful comfort to supporters of the rational behavior assumption. Even if there are many nonrational participants, they will in effect starve. When economic activity is judged on a value-weighted basis, we will find that rational behavior predominates. A small variety store may misprice, but not a major chain. This formulation applies as long as there is free poaching, that is, that rational actors can move in on arenas where irrational decisions now prevail. This requires that entry be feasible and that rational capabilities spread readily. Financial markets offer poaching opportunities. It is as easy to buy 1,000,000 as 100 shares of stock, and K-Mart may be able to expand so as to drive even local variety stores out of business. But it is hard to see how one could make a profit capitalizing on the irrationality of the Harvard professors who failed to consider their retirement plans adequately.

The implication is that, if we look in areas where poaching is easy, prices and quantities will be arbitraged into relationships predicted by rational formulations. The stock market will look pretty good on this basis. But the aggregate outcome of a cluster of personal nonpoachable decisions—such as insuring appropriately, planning for retirement, or having babies in or out of wedlock—will be more heavily influenced by a behavioral component.

Decisions versus Games

Las Vegas is an affront to the rational decision model unless one gives weight to the pleasure of playing games. The vast volumes that are often traded on commodities and futures exchanges are no less an affront, not only because, as Kenneth Arrow points out, information-based trades strictly between speculators cannot make sense for both parties but also because these markets cost so much to operate, particularly in terms of the gains of the floor traders and certain big players. If we ever do come to understand gambling behavior, I suspect we will find that it offers powerful psychological benefits such as hope, ego gratification, and reward for outsmarting the other player or the system. Each person keeps his or her own score; perhaps a single big win offsets many losses that are larger in total. Gambling, of course, is an area where there are effective poachers, the effective professionals and

---

6. Some decision situations are rigged in your favor. Television game shows such as "Let's Make a Deal" are designed to let the contestants come off as winners. Smart children learn that their parent competitors make purposeful mistakes or even cheat to help their offspring.

those who run the house. Presumably they design their games to max-imize the dollars extracted per unit of benefit offered. The possibility of injecting a little pseudoscience seems to help in creating additional rewards for the suckers. In the commodities markets, you can chart, guess the weather, be a fundamentalist, or undertake correlational analyses. Without such opportunities, perhaps fewer people would want to play the negative-sum game (see Niederhoffer and Zeckhauser 1983).

Individual Choice versus Working for Others

When we use small classroom gambles in discussing the elements of utility theory, we find that some married students are peculiarly risk averse. Though they invest far larger sums in the stock market, they cannot bear to tell their spouse that they lost money on a gamble. A good time to join many poker games is near the end of the evening, when some men bet against odds to get positive and "go home to the wife" as a winner. Corporate executives keep the profits increasing at a steady rate, often sacrificing substantial expected profits for their diversified shareholders. When others are kibitzing our decisions, we may suppress information on the performance of alternatives, even if we might make a subsequent switch.

If such actions were taken by an isolated individual, they might appear irrational. But once others are involved, even the most thor-oughly rational individual will take actions that appear to violate Sav-age's prescriptions. With prediction the goal, whether we adhere to the rational or behavioral paradigm, we would undoubtedly prefer a world in which agency problems vanished along with other problems, for example, so that everyone would be always a price taker and never a negotiator.[7]

But that is not the real world. Hence, we must calibrate the infer-ences we draw from observed behavior to the circumstances in which it occurred. If we are willing to admit to a limited amount of bounded rationality and assume that individuals adopt good overall decision procedures that are not necessarily perfect in each instance, we must also recognize that they learn to operate in a world where nature is rarely the generator of uncertainties, hostile people manipulate percep-tions, and one must worry about monitoring and being monitored. Think of the unreliability of predictions made in a group decision situa-tion, such as a faculty appointment or a Washington tax bill delibera-

7. The rationalists, for reasons that may relate to the underlying agenda, tend to accord less importance to agency problems, non-price-taking behavior, and so on. Greater recognition of such difficulties would provide a more secure defense of rational behavior. For example, a corporate executive who seeks a satisfactory level of profits, rather than trying to maximize their expected value, may be behaving in a fully rational behavior given directors' and shareholders' monitoring limitations.

tion, where preferences strongly influence alleged judgments of outcomes.

V. The Arrow and Lucas Contributions

The papers by Arrow and by Lucas (in this volume) push forward the debate substantially. As primary protagonists, they took the unusual course of focusing more on clarifying arguments than on scoring points.

Arrow identifies the vacuous nature of the assumption of rational behavior by itself, showing that virtually all observed microeconomic and macroeconomic phenomena can be derived from other foundations. Moreover, to derive interesting predictions from the rational behavior model, additional assumptions of a quite different nature are required, such as the assumption that differences in individuals' utility functions depend on observable magnitudes, for example, family size. Arrow's logic is penetrating. But his beliefs, as revealed in his writings more generally, show a deeper appreciation for the contributions of the rationality assumption, a perspective shaped by Arrow's observations of real world behavior. He appears to be a closet moderate.

I suspect that Arrow would agree that no alternative theory would predict nearly as well as rationality over a wide range of economic circumstances. With bounded rationality (see Simon, in this volume), a theory of behavior favored by Arrow, most predictions are much less precise, unless we add additional information. Perhaps rationality explains 50% of the variance, and boundedness explains an important additional 5%.

Arrow provides a valuable service with his crisp historical overview of the use of the rationality assumption in economics. He reminds us that, with incomplete or imperfect markets, the predictions of rationality are weak. Often there are continua of equilibria, for example. Arrow suggests that limiting rationality may offer a way out, reducing the number of equilibria. But my guess is that a theorist as brilliant as Arrow could easily conjure up seemingly reasonable situations where limitations on rationality multiply rather than reduce the number of feasible outcomes.

The deep conundrum about real world outcomes is that they look so sensible relative to the ranges of possibilities that our models permit. Dramatic disequilibria rarely arise. Prices, for the most part, move reasonably. Signaling equilibria fall within familiar bounds. Undoubtedly there are other determining factors selecting equilibria, and with experience we have learned what to expect. (A mother is much better at predicting the behavior of her child than would be any psychologist armed with theoretical models.) Perhaps there are some forces of natural selection that drive out unreasonable equilibria. In the microeconomic domain, it appears, the world is vastly more tractable than our models would predict. Nowadays, even self-confident macro modelers employ fudge factors to adjust their predictions with judgment.

Lucas took seriously the challenge of the behavioral approach to economics, deriving primarily from psychologists views of human behavior. He concedes that economic theory does not "usefully model the adaptive process by which subjects have themselves arrived at the decision rules they use." He thinks of economics, which includes the assumption of rational behavior, as "studying decision rules that are steady states of some adaptive process, decision rules that are found to work over a range of situations and hence are no longer revised appreciably as more experience accumulates" (p. 218).

His explicit choice of battlefield is in the spirit of my comparative advantage discussion and indeed helped inspire it. I judge him the victor on this turf and suspect that most behavioralists would do so as well. Accepting Lucas's formulation, there remains the question of defining alikeness classes, situations in which the same forms of behavior should be employed. At my university, the dean normally sets faculty salaries—or so I assume. If a faculty member acts as a price taker when he or she is really in a negotiating situation, is he irrational, boundedly rational, maximizing given his psychological propensities, or merely buying relief from a minute of embarrassment by sacrificing an expected thousand dollars or two?

Lucas takes to the battle, having achieved many successes from such behavior in the past. He identifies a great range of areas where rational, steady-state behavior provides a sound explanation for important phenomena. His discussion of the quantity theory of money and the implied relationship between inflation and M1 growth under certain circumstances (see his fig. 1) is convincing, though it seems fair to point out that, if agents were merely boundedly rational with the same motivations, the pattern might be the same.[8]

Lucas observes that the quantity theory may fail during hyperinflations and concludes that this should "reinforce our view that figure 1 is an important confirmation of the quantity theory: the theory works well when it 'ought' to and fails when it 'ought' to as well" (p. 223). He invokes an analogy to Newton's theory of gravitation as a special case of great usefulness. But wouldn't Lucas have been even more pleased if the quantity theory worked even in extreme circumstances? And would we not think Newton's mechanics more robust if they applied even when velocities were comparable to the speed of light?

Lucas ranges widely in marshaling evidence. He reports on experi-

8. Lucas, appropriately, is not troubled that any of a variety of adaptive menus might have led to this pattern as well, for the steady state reflects "rational" behavior. In this spirit, pigeons who consume according to demand theory reinforce the rational model.

ments with pigeons whose behavior converged to adhere to the weak
axiom of consumer preference. We all know that nature optimizes, at
least over the long run. Leaves turn to the light effectively; bumblebee
economics is well established. The question is whether human beings
can do as well in the much richer and more rapidly changing environment they confront. Experiments reveal that pigeons' brains can respond to information on the prices of nourishment. But if we found that
pigeons gave insufficient pecks to "invest" to get a new, more generous control key to operate, would we therefore begin to worry about
the adequacy of capital theory? And would we be concerned if in a
choice of lotteries mice violated stochastic dominance?[9]

Lucas attacks the multiple-equilibrium problem head on and refutes
a too common mode of attack on rational models, that is, the use of an
adaptive model that singles out a particular equilibrium. Other adaptive
schemes may lead to other equilibria, as Lucas observes; he then
makes the important point that we need models that "genuinely single
out a particular equilibrium as being of more substantive interest than
the others" (pp. 236–237). Lucas concludes with an elegant, intriguing proposed experiment to determine how price expectations are
formed in an overlapping-generation, finite-horizon model with two
kinds of money, white chips for trading and blue chips for trading or
eating. This experiment might provide the basis for a reputational bet
between Arrow and Lucas, both concerned with models with multiple
equilibria.[10] But I suspect Arrow would not ante up since this is a
battlefield constructed by Lucas. When the experiment is conducted,
the results will probably support his side.

VI. Conclusion

The battle between rational and behavioral economics is likely to remain predominantly an effort to stake turf.[11] Little blood need be shed
if, as I have suggested, the two schools operate in substantially different dimensions. But substantial progress will require spilled blood or at

9. There is the possibility that human beings have been too harsh on animals. See
Griffin (1984) for an interesting speculative account.
10. See Hofstee (1984). With most proposed reputational bets, one side can intuit what
will happen. The other, understanding the Arrow article better than most investors,
knows enough not to bet. Three criteria for a reputational bet are (1) neither side knows
the answer, (2) the matter is important, and (3) both sides will accept. Given the multiple-
battlefields problem, it would be pleasing, though surprising, if the two sides could agree
on reputational bets.
11. We should not lose track of the sibling rivalry nature of this struggle. When
someone outside the economics family ventures in—say, to propose the use of price
controls in an oil shortage—we are likely to close ranks. Whether we are rational,
boundedly rational, or adaptive, we still believe in elasticity of demand. Maybe we can
even learn to divorce the rationality debate from our views on how well the market
performs.

least bumped noses. Success will mean that we can systematically employ our understanding of psychology to make nonobvious predictions about behavior in a range of problems of economic import.

References

Arrow, Kenneth. In this volume. Rationality of self and others in an economic system.

Brooks, Harvey. 1986. Personal communication.

Griffin, Donald R. 1984. *Animal Thinking*. Cambridge, Mass.: Harvard University Press.

Hofstee, Willem K. B. 1984. Methodological decision rules as research policies: A betting reconstruction of empirical research. *Acta Psychologica* 56:93–109.

Kahneman, Daniel; Slovic, Paul; and Tversky, Amos, eds. 1982. *Judgment under Uncertainty: Heuristics and Biases*. New York: Cambridge University Press.

Kahneman, Daniel; Knetsch, Jack L.; and Thaler, Richard H. In this volume. Fairness and the assumptions of economics.

Kuhn, Thomas S. 1970. *The Structure of Scientific Revolutions*. 2d ed. Chicago: University of Chicago.

Lucas, Robert, Jr. In this volume. Adaptive behavior and economic theory.

Niederhoffer, Victor, and Zeckhauser, Richard. 1983. Futures markets as ecological systems: Survival? Efficiency? Rational participants? Paper presented at the meeting of the American Economics Association, December.

Pratt, John; Wise, David; and Zeckhauser, Richard. 1979. Price differences in almost competitive markets. *Quarterly Journal of Economics* 94 (May): 189–211.

Shiller, Robert J. 1979. The volatility of long-term interest rates and expectations models of the term structure. *Journal of Political Economy* 87:1190–1219.

Simon, Herbert. In this volume. Rationality in psychology and economics.

Merton H. Miller

University of Chicago

Behavioral Rationality in Finance: The Case of Dividends*

I. Introduction

As the title suggests, this paper attempts to get to the specifics of the behavioral rationality theme of this conference by focusing on an area in the main core of finance, namely, the demand and supply of dividends, where, by common consent, the essentially "rationalist" paradigm of the field seems to be limping most noticeably. Important and pervasive behavior patterns on both the paying and the receiving ends have despairingly been written off as "puzzles" even by theorists as redoubtable as Fischer Black (see esp. his much-cited 1976 article). Behaviorists have homed in on precisely these same dividend-related soft spots in the current body of theory (see esp. Shefrin and Statman 1984). We seem to have, in sum, an ideal place to look for signs of an imminent "paradigm shift" in the behavioral direction of precisely the kind envisioned by some of the other contributors to this conference.

The dividend-related difficulties and supposed anomalies at issue here are more than just the parochial concern of finance specialists. The

Dividends seem a natural area in finance where the introduction of behavioral/cognitive elements might help resolve long-standing anomalies, particularly the seeming failure of supply to adjust to tax-induced price penalties. A closer look at the empirical record, however—particularly at evidence of responsiveness to major structural changes—shows behavior of the aggregates to be less anomalous than conventional handwringing might suggest. Behavioral/cognitive elements, whatever they might contribute to the description of particular microdecisions, do not appear to be essential adjuncts to the basic finance model in the major, comparative static applications for which it was intended.

* Helpful comments on an earlier version of this paper have been received from Nai-fu Chen, Jean-Marie Gagnon, Gur Huberman, Kose John, James Poterba, and especially Melvin Reder.

finance model of the firm, after all, *is* the standard economists' model of the firm, but with some of the components grouped differently. The finance version, focusing on the interaction between the firm and the capital markets, subsumes the details of optimizing output, product pricing, and factor-input combinations into a single intertemporal "transformation function" of current resource inflows to future resource outflows. The firm in finance becomes, as it were, simply an abstract engine that "uses money today to make money tomorrow," as Alfred P. Sloan, that most quintessential of finance-oriented business executives once (almost) described his General Motors Corporation. The firm's objective function, reflecting the specifically intertemporal statement of the firm's problem, must go beyond the familiar rubric of maximizing "profits" to maximizing the net present value of future cash flows. But that is the merest of details.[1] The two models of the firm, the finance model and the price theory model, are variations on a single theme; moreover, the anomalies burdening any one class of users must be of some concern to the other classes as well.

How much concern should they show at this point about our dividend anomalies? Less, I will argue here, after a fresh look at the evidence, than I and others in finance may once have thought (see, e.g., the introduction to Miller and Scholes [1978]). This is not to say that we do not have our share and more of still-unsolved problems. Finance, after all, is one of the newer specialty areas in economics. But I do not see us in such disarray, even on the much-mooted dividend issues, that we must think of abandoning or even drastically modifying the basic economics/finance paradigm on which the field has been built.

The first task of the paper will be to sketch out briefly what the supposed dividend anomalies are all about. Their perception as anomalies will then be shown to a considerable extent to be traceable to a misinterpretation of the basic model, to a misreading of the empirical record, and perhaps also to exaggerated expectations of what our models can hope to accomplish.

II. The Dividend Anomalies

The dividend anomalies at issue here are mainly tax related. They are instances in which a substantial body of corporate managers, presumably acting on behalf of their shareholders, appears to have been responding or, more precisely, failing to respond over long periods to large and persistent incentives in the tax system.

Recall the essential tax facts. Under U.S. law, the net income of the large, publicly held corporations that are our main concern is first

---

1. The relation of the two models is discussed at length in Fama and Miller (1972), esp. ch. 3.

subject to tax at progressive rates that quickly reach 46%. Marginal rates at these levels (and higher) were first reached during World War II and have been maintained with only minor changes over the entire period since then. Any dividends paid by the corporation out of its current or accumulated past after-tax earnings are subject to tax (with the inevitable minor exceptions) at the regular progressive rates under the personal income tax.[2] These rates currently peak at 50%, their low point for the postwar era; but the maximum has reached as high as 92% in the years during and immediately following World War II. The dividends received would also be taxable under state income taxes as well.

By contrast, the portion of the after-corporate-tax profits not paid out in dividends, but retained in the firm, is not directly subject to personal income tax.[3] The earnings retained by the corporation may still be reached by the tax system, but by a somewhat more indirect route. The retained earnings increase the value of the shares—or at least that is the presumption in the model whose anomalies are being probed. Should the share subsequently be sold at a price greater than its original cost, the price appreciation will constitute a taxable capital gain. The rates applied to such gains are hard to describe briefly, but, for individual holders, the rates on realized capital gains are never higher than those on ordinary income and are typically lower. For securities owned for more than a minimum holding period—which has varied from 6 months to 1 year in the post–World War II era—the statutory rate on gains has rarely been more than half the regular rates and then only for taxpayers who have triggered one of the minimum-tax provisions that Congress tends to enact in its periods of loophole-closing frenzy. The maximum rate on capital gains was capped for much of the postwar era at 25%, so the maximum gap between the top rate on ordinary income and on capital gains could have been as much as 67 percentage points! Remember, that is for *realized* gains only. Shares not sold during one's lifetime but held for one's estate escape the capital gains tax altogether.

Our tax law, in sum, thus places a substantial penalty on dividends as opposed to retained earnings/capital gains. Why, then, in the face of these penalties, do firms continue to pay them? Before the modern finance model was developed, economists and public finance specialists may have presumed that firms had no better alternative. Invest-

2. For tax years after 1981, the first $100 of dividends ($200 on a joint return) could be excluded from income. Special provisions, which expired at the end of 1985, were also made for the dividend reinvestment plans of utilities. Prior to 1936, dividends were exempt from the low, flat-rate normal tax but fully subject to the progressive surtaxes.
3. Small, closely held corporations, but only such, may elect to be taxed as partnerships under subchap. S of the Internal Revenue Code, in which case, no corporate income tax is levied and the entire net profit of the corporation, whether distributed or not, is taxed as ordinary personal income to the shareholders.

ment in projects at declining rates of profitability could proceed until the marginal return on internally financed investments had been driven to equality with the stockholders' after-tax dividend return. But thereafter, paying out the funds and taking the dividend tax hit would dominate further pouring of funds into low-return rat holes. In the finance model, however, there are better alternatives to dividend payouts than wasteful real investments. The technological concavity in the opportunity set imposed by the law of diminishing returns on real investment can be bypassed, as it were, for any one firm by adjoining the essentially linear technology of transactions in securities in well-functioning capital markets. The production function in the finance model of the firm is only weakly concave, not strictly concave.[4]

In such a setting, the firm is pictured as taking any internally generated funds remaining after profitable real investment opportunities have been exhausted and using them not for paying tax-disadvantaged dividends but for the purchase of securities, either its own or those of other firms (or governments). On these financial investments the firm will presumably earn not a rat-hole return but the same market, risk-adjusted return that serves as its own capital budgeting cutoff. The firm's shareholders, moreover, whatever their tax status, would, if they are behaving rationally, also seem to be unanimous in favoring such a strategy.[5] Some of the shareholders, like pension funds and university endowments, are themselves tax exempt and hence have no incentive to shun dividends. But, by the same token, they would seem to have no tax incentive to oppose the efforts of their taxable brethren to improve their lot by transforming the firm's return from fully taxable dividends to untaxed or at least lower-taxed capital gains. It may be a weak-inequality form of unanimity, but it is still unanimity.[6]

---

4. The critical role of external securities in the dividend supply function was first noted explicitly by Miller and Modigliani (1961). That was indeed a major thrust of their paper, though somewhat obscured perhaps by the more controversial and provocative material on the valuation of shares. Their point, however, is also a fairly direct implication of the standard Fisherian model of the finance firm, as can clearly be seen from the discussion in ch. 2 of Fama and Miller (1972).

5. Not quite. Nothing in our tax law ever seems that clear-cut. Corporations holding shares in other corporations are permitted to exclude 85% of intercorporate dividends received. The effective maximum tax on intercorporate dividends is thus about 7%, which is substantially below the corporate capital gains tax rate. Corporate holdings of shares for investment purposes, however, are predominantly in the form of preferred stocks. Corporate shareholding is worth a mention but is not a major part of the story to be developed here.

6. Another qualification should be entered for the record. Where a firm has adopted a dividend reinvestment plan (DRIP) with a significant price discount (frequently as high as 5%) on the shares acquired, its institutional investors would no longer be neutral between dividends and capital gains but would strongly prefer dividends. By reinvesting the dividends and then immediately selling off the shares so acquired, they pick up a substantial quasi-arbitrage profit. Relative to the issues of concern here, however, DRIP are of too recent an origin and too limited a scope to play any major explanatory role.

Such, then, is the anomaly plaguing the current finance model of the dividend-paying firm. It rests essentially on the belief that firms are systematically failing to benefit their shareholders by converting high-taxed dividends to low-taxed capital gains. Most nonspecialists will suspect that the most likely route for resolving the anomaly is on the cost-of-conversion side. Surely, they will presume, there can be no free lunches in conversions. They will certainly be correct with respect to one of the main financial strategies for conversion suggested by the underlying model, namely, buying the securities of other firms (and governments). It may be instructive, therefore, to get at least that class of distractions out of the way before turning to the more serious issues raised by the other conversion strategy of buying back the firm's own securities.[7]

III. The Costs of Avoiding Cash Payouts by Buying Outside Securities

A first look at the finance model can all too easily lead one to the belief that even investing in government bonds normally would be better (and never worse) for the shareholders than paying out cash dividends. Not so, however. In fact, holding significant amounts of government bonds or other purely financial instruments is not even a feasible alternative for corporations under U.S. tax laws.

The infeasibility is more than just a matter of Internal Revenue Code section 532, which imposes a penalty tax for "improper accumulation of surplus." That provision has indeed been part of the code almost from its inception, and its purpose has been precisely to keep shareholders from avoiding the personal income tax on dividends by piling up cash in the corporation. But few firms have ever been caught in its meshes.[8]

The moral to be drawn from this lack of bite, however, is precisely the opposite of that usually drawn, which is that the section is a tooth-

---

7. Although the emphasis in this paper will be on the conversion opportunities available to firms, individuals too have methods for converting dividends to capital gains. In principle, as shown in Miller and Scholes (1978), these tactics could make the corporate conversion possibilities redundant; but, in practice, these techniques are likely to be availed of only by the small (but possibly important) minority of stockholders who regularly buy stocks on margin.

8. The penalty will not be invoked if the firm can show that its accumulations have a "valid business purpose," and proving that presents little challenge to even a moderately competent tax lawyer. In the last few years, the Internal Revenue Service has begun to put some additional muscle behind its enforcement efforts and to reach firms substantially larger than had earlier been the case. But the firms affected have all been closely held or at least clearly controlled by a dominant shareholder. No publicly traded firm with widely dispersed ownership (of the kind that the finance model is concerned with) has ever been hit by sec. 532. The similarly motivated personal holding company penalties are also confined to closely held corporations.

less tiger, not even worth mentioning as a deterrent to cutting back on dividends. Clearly, from the section's existence and history we know that both Congress and the Internal Revenue Service are aware of the potential for dividend tax avoidance via corporate hoarding as well as of the steps that would have to be taken to close off that route. That they have not troubled to do so suggests that the route is not being sufficiently traveled to make an effort via section 532 worthwhile.

Section 532 has been rendered largely superfluous for publicly held corporations by another and much more fundamental tax provision, the corporation income tax itself. Under that tax, the interest earned on any government bonds in the corporate hoards would be taxable in principle at the full marginal corporate rate of 46%.[9] Hence any pension fund or other institutional holder offered a choice between receiving an immediate cash dividend or having the corporation invest the cash in government bonds would not be indifferent, or anywhere close to it, even though the institution itself was tax exempt and subject to no tax on either dividends or capital gains. Nor are institutional investors the only body of shareholders disadvantaged when a taxable corporation uses otherwise available funds to purchase securities that those investors could acquire directly. Taxable shareholders can also be hurt if the numbers are such that the front-end bite of the dividend tax on the dollars paid out turns out to be less than the present value of the stream of additional corporate tax payments incurred on the funds invested. Precisely where that boundary lies need not be spelled out in detail. The present concern is simply whether observed corporate dividend behavior can be regarded as anomalous relative to the standard finance model because investment in securities by the firm would be a uniformly or even weakly superior alternative to paying dividends. Merely establishing that a cutoff exists means that the answer is no.[10]

9. The inevitable qualification: the IRS will tolerate a limited amount of stashing away of tax-free investments by "overfunding" the firm's pension fund.

10. The argument in this section about the purely tax disadvantages of financial investment relative to dividends was first made in the finance literature, as far as I am aware, by David Emanuel (1983). Essentially the same point could have been made, though in a less transparent way, in terms of standard finance "capital structure" models. In a so-called before-tax equilibrium world, as in Modigliani and Miller (1963), e.g., any investment in taxable, interest-bearing securities would be "negative leverage" and hence would, ceteris paribus, lower the value of the shares. In an "after-tax equilibrium" world, as in Miller (1977), holding of taxable securities by the firm would deprive the tax-exempt and low-bracket shareholders of the "bondholders' surplus" that they could earn with the funds on their own. Investments by corporations in preferred stock of other taxable corporations are less tax disadvantageous to institutional and low-bracket holders than investments in interest-bearing securities, thanks to the 85% exclusion on intercorporate dividends received. Hence the great popularity in recent years of new instruments such as ARPs (adjustable rate preferreds) or MARs (multiple adjustable rate preferreds) as temporary abodes for cash. To the extent, however, that yields adjust and issuers recapture some of the tax benefits, as appears to be the case, the corporate buyers are paying what Scholes, Mazur, and Wolfson (1984) have dubbed an "implicit

To dispose of a dividend-related anomaly by invoking a tax argument is never entirely satisfactory even when, as here, the anomaly itself is tax induced. The dividend policies of firms and individuals today are similar, at least in broad outline, to those found before the present tax system and in countries with tax regimes very different from our own. It is worth emphasizing, therefore, that the tax case against corporate hoarding is offered here in the sense of sufficiency, not necessity. No shortage exists of other costs and drawbacks to a policy of holding securities at the corporate level beyond the liquidity needs of the business. Too much of the benefits would accrue to the firm's creditors, and, more to the point, the treasures might attract raiders, as the story of the Rhine Maidens and their ring reminds us. Indeed, much of the presumed motivation of the acquirers, and certainly much of their rhetoric, in recent highly publicized takeover struggles has focused precisely on getting underproductive assets out of corporate solution and into the hands of the shareholders.[11] Hoarding, in sum, is not a feasible alternative to dividends. With that established, we can turn now to some dividend-conversion strategies available to the firm that make the tax anomaly less easy to shrug off.

IV. Share Repurchase and the Supply of and Demand for Dividends

Rather than buy government securities or the securities of other firms, a firm, in this country at least, always has the option of purchasing its own securities.[12] This route can get excess funds out of corporate

---

tax" over and above the nominal 7% (i.e., .46 × .85). For holdings of common stock by corporations, the implicit tax on the dividends is smaller. Some would argue, as we shall see, that it is substantially negative because dividends sell at such a substantial discount. Even if true, however, it would clearly be a self-referencing paradox to imagine every cash-rich dividend-paying corporation to be avoiding payment of dividends by investing in the dividend-paying shares of other cash-rich corporations. Of course, the cash-rich firms could purchase the shares of the cash-poor corporations. Indeed, some, but only some, of the seeming merger wave of recent years has been so motivated. But merger activity that eliminates one firm's securities from the capital markets is perhaps more appropriately treated as real investment than as financial investment. (I have benefited from discussions of these issues with my colleague Gur Huberman but absolve him from responsibility for any errors.)

11. Interestingly enough, the raiders have been zeroing in on hoards of passive investment funds even when held in tax-exempt form in overfunded pension plans; see, e.g., Asinof (1985). For a discussion of some moral hazard problems in overfunding pension plans, see also Ippolito (1985). Recent spin-offs of developed oil field properties into limited partnerships (not subject to corporate income tax) offer additional examples of efforts to get what amounts to passive "investment income" out of corporate form and attendant tax burdens.

12. The qualification is made because the frequently heard, conventional wisdom is that corporate law in Great Britain and in most European countries rules out share repurchase. Perhaps so, if taken literally; but one suspects that there must be other, equivalent tactics that permit a business to reduce in size. In Belgium, the explicit restrictions appear to apply only to self-tenders, not to open-market purchases. In

solution, thus avoiding the class of difficulties just seen but without creating dividends, which are taxable as ordinary income under the personal income tax.

At first sight, the policy of share repurchase may seem to benefit only those shareholders who choose to take the other side of the firm's offer to buy. But that is not so. The policy of share repurchase, like the quality of mercy, is twice blessed. It blesses not only those who sell but also those who do not. In fact, the nonsellers are thrice blessed because their benefit takes the form, not of realized, but of unrealized capital gains.[13] Note also that, when allowance is made for the taxes, stayers under the buy-back plan might be better off than under a dividend plan, even if the firm had to pay the sellers a premium over the market price, as is often the case when the firm tenders for the shares. The gain from nontaxability more than offsets the loss from dilution.[14]

Share repurchase is thus clearly superior to corporate hoarding as a method of transforming current dividends into current capital gains. But it is not a costless alternative to paying dividends. Brokerage fees must be incurred, and, in the case of tenders, often underwriting expenses must be paid as well. Still, transaction costs of this kind seem small when compared with the statutory tax differentials between divi-

---

Canada, Jean-Marie Gagnon of Laval University in Quebec, commenting on an earlier version of this paper, notes that share repurchase very definitely is permitted under Canadian law, subject, however, to the standard restrictions on actions damaging to the firm or its creditors. He suspects that a misinterpretation of those restrictions may be the source of the folk belief that share repurchase is somehow illegal.

13. For nonspecialists, perhaps the following numerical example may help sort things out. Suppose, to keep things simple, there were no taxes to complicate calculations, and suppose a firm with 1 million shares outstanding had set aside $4 million for return to the shareholders. Suppose further that, after it announced the setting aside of $4.00 per share, the *cum-dividend* price of each share at this time were to be $44. After the dividend was paid, each shareholder would have $4.00 in cash plus an *ex-dividend* share worth $40, ceteris paribus. Imagine now that, instead of paying the dividend, the firm had used the same $4 million to buy 90,909 shares at the predistribution price of $44. The nonselling shareholders receive no cash, of course, but each of their shares now represents a larger fraction of the firm. In fact, each will be worth $44 ($40,000,000 ÷ 909,091). Thus every stockholder winds up with the same net worth of $44 per share no matter which policy the firm follows in disposing of the cash. The only difference is in how the net worth is divided between cash and shares (a uniform $4.00 in cash and $40 in shares for every holder under the dividend route vs. $44 in cash for the sellers and $44 in stock for the stayers under the buy-back route).

14. But the premium cannot be set too high or the procedure becomes self-defeating. If everyone tenders and is prorated, the cash distribution is "proportional" and will be treated as a dividend for tax purposes. Under present rules, a reduction in fractional interest in the corporation of 20% or more is required to assure any stockholder that payments received in a share self-tender offer are not deemed to be merely disguised dividends. These restrictions do not apply to open-market repurchases and are moot, of course, even under self-tenders for nontaxable institutional shareholders. But that does not mean that such investors will be indifferent between dividends and self-tenders. A tender offer at a premium above market (but not so far above to get even the taxable holders to tender) may well be better for them than a dividend after all costs have been taken into account.

dends and capital gains. So much so, in fact, that it might be daunting to a behavioral theorist of the firm to venture even a boundedly rational explanation of why dividends continue to be paid (at least by firms other than public utilities).

Remember, however, that in the finance model of the supply of dividends, whose possibly anomalous status is our concern, the tax differentials under the personal income tax do not enter the firm's objective function directly. The managers of large, widely held corporations are not pictured there as solving dividend decision problems by performing "thought experiments," as we here have been doing, about what might or might not be in the best interests of this or that group of the shareholders—though they may well tend to couch their explanations in those terms. Rather, as with constructing any other supply function in the theory of the firm, the managers are assumed to be responding to the signals conveyed to them by market prices. The process is a bit harder to visualize for dividends, perhaps, because the price of dividends relative to capital gains is not quoted directly, as such, in the columns of the *Wall Street Journal*. But that price can be *inferred,* at least within tolerable limits, from the stock prices and dividend yields reported there and from the analyses, formal and informal, performed on that and other relevant data by financial analysts within and outside the firm.

For the finance model of dividend supply to be held anomalous, therefore, or at least as requiring important structural modifications (including, quite possibly, the grafting on of major elements from the behavioral theory of the firm), it would be sufficient (and, in my view, also necessary) to show that the observed market price of dividend return can confidently be placed too far below the observed market price of capital gain return to be plausibly attributed to the likely cost of converting current dividends to current capital gains. The feeling that empirical research has established that dividends have, in fact, long been selling at a substantial discount appears to be the major contributor to the sense of unease within the profession about the status of the model. It is important, therefore, to be clear about what has and what has not been shown about the market price of dividends relative to capital gains.

V. The Empirical Record

The conventional impression that academic empirical research has shown a large and long-standing price penalty on dividends is perhaps nowhere so neatly capsulized as in a "box score" table added to the last edition of Brealey and Myers's (1984) excellent textbook on corporate finance. Ten separate statistical studies of the average cross-sectional relation between risk-adjusted stock returns and dividend yields are summarized in the table (p. 348). In eight of the 10 studies, the regression coefficient representing the return premium for dividends—or, equivalently, the price discount for dividends—was substantial both in absolute size (equivalent, say, to an effective "tax differential" on dividends over capital gains of from 25% to as high as 56%) and relative to its reported standard error. There were only two exceptions to the modal result.[15] One was the classic study by Black and Scholes (1974). If the results of the Black-Scholes study had to be expressed as a single point estimate, then it too would have been a dividend discount on the order of 20%. But the essential message of the paper, stressed repeatedly by the authors themselves, was that, with the data and techniques then available, the differential in the weight on dividends relative to capital gains could not be pinned down in size or even in sign.

The other study departing from the general trend was one by Miller and Scholes (1982). In that study, however, our concern was not to provide the best estimate of the dividend coefficient but to show that the dividend coefficient reported in another and very influential study (Litzenberger and Ramaswamy 1979) was sensitive to seemingly small adjustments in the definition of dividend yield used. In addition, and more to the present point, we showed that what Scholes and I called the "short-run measure" of dividend yield used by Litzenberger and Ramaswamy was, for a variety of reasons, inappropriate for measuring the market price obtainable for dividends supplied. On that score, at least, something approaching a consensus has emerged, and virtually all recent cross-sectional empirical work on the dividend issue has relied on so-called long-run measures of dividend yield, in the same spirit as the original Black-Scholes study, though with some improvements in detail.[16]

15. There is even one very small piece of evidence often cited in support of the position that the relative price of dividends may actually be *higher* rather than lower than that of capital gains. This is the case of Citizens' Utility as reported by Long (1978). The company was allowed by the Treasury to issue two classes of shares, one paying cash dividends and the other dividends in stock, with the stock dividend shares convertible to the cash dividend shares. The ratio of the stock dividend to the cash dividend was subject to change (and hence to some uncertainty at the time of purchase). But after making reasonable adjustments, Long concludes that the cash dividend shares were selling at a premium relative to the stock dividend shares. It is difficult, however, to know how much weight to place on observations on a stock so thinly traded. For an updated look at Citizens' Utility that comes to somewhat different conclusions, see Poterba (1985).

16. The use of short-run measures of dividend yield makes a test essentially one of the size of the momentary cum-dividend/ex-dividend (cum-ex) differential. The substantial body of literature attempting to use the direct, cum-ex route to establish the discount for dividends has established that the differential is certainly affected by taxes but that transactions costs, dividend "arbitrage" games, and the distortion of the normal patterns of transactions around ex days make it impossible to draw any reliable inferences about the price of dividends over the longer intervals that are relevant for the supply curve of dividends. For an account of the current state of the cum-ex experiments, see Grundy (1985).

One of the most provocative of these post-Black-Scholes studies is that of Marshall Blume (1980). Blume showed that, looking solely at firms that were actually paying dividends, there did indeed appear to be a substantial average cross-sectional dividend yield premium—an excess return so large, in fact (as Blume noted), as to be beyond plausibility as a compensation for tax differentials. But the cross-sectional scatters showed that the relation between risk-adjusted returns and dividend yields—which, when properly scaled, is the sought-for measure of the market price of dividends—was U-shaped. The market appeared to demand a return premium both from those firms paying the most in dividends and from those paying the least (i.e., zero).

Attempting to account for puzzling extreme observations can sometimes turn up important neglected aspects of the problem under study, and such indeed proved to be the case with Blume's U. Donald Keim (1982) noticed that the firms at the two ends of the U—the zero-dividend firms and the highest-dividend-yield firms—were primarily small companies. What made that observation so interesting was the rapidly building mountain of research on the so-called small-firm effect.

The small-firm effect is the finding, by now amply documented both here and abroad, that small firms, even after adjustment for the standard CAPM-based measures of risk, appear to earn significantly higher rates of return than do large firms (for a recent survey, see Schwert [1983]). These higher returns, moreover, appeared to have a marked seasonal pattern: they occurred mostly in January (Keim 1983). The same was true of the dividend-yield return premiums on each arm of Blume's U. What, therefore, were all the dividend studies measuring? Dividend effects? Small-firm effects? January effects? All the above? None of the above?

Since Keim's work, the focus of empirical research has shifted to seeking more powerful econometric methods for isolating the separate contributions of these effects. The search, however, has yet to produce much in the way of results. This should not be entirely surprising in view of the high degree of collinearity between each of the intertwined effects and between each of them and the CAPM-based risk measure. There is the further complication that the true functional form of the relation between returns and the variables may not be the linear one to which we are effectively restricted. If, then, we happen to turn up a significant coefficient for one or more of our variables, how can we be confident that we are seeing genuine economic contributions and not mere correlations of the variable with residuals induced by the misrepresentation of the functional form?

Until recently, at least, we could hope that these difficulties would someday be overcome and that eventually we would get a sharp enough fix on the market price of dividends to determine whether the aggregate corporate supply of dividends has really been in long-standing disequilibrium relative to the predictions of the standard, value-maximizing model of the firm. My colleagues Nai-Fu Chen, Bruce Grundy, and Robert Stambaugh (1985), however, have been devoting their not inconsiderable econometric prowess to this task and have reluctantly concluded that the estimating equations are too sensitive even to small variations in the risk measure to establish confidently whether dividends sell at a discount relative to capital gains. We are back to Black and Scholes!

This inconclusiveness is certainly not the best that one could have hoped for; but it is also not the worst. At least, it puts to rest the charge that the corporate sector has systematically failed to respond to the price signals being sent by the market. No clear and steady signal to management to reduce dividends is coming through the noise.[17]

But we can actually do somewhat better than this. We may not be able to say as much as we would like about the long-run equilibrium *price* of dividends, but, as will be shown in Section VI, evidence is accumulating that the *quantity* of dividends brought to market does vary appropriately in response to significant exogenous shocks to demand or supply.[18] After all, comparative statics—explaining and predicting the economy's adjustment to change—is why we build maximizing models in the first place.

VI.   The Response to Shocks

The most promising place to look for experiments testing the dividend supply and demand model is along the fault line between corporate and personal income taxes. While a method of integrating the two taxes that is not open to serious attack on economic or political grounds has

17. If the tax penalty on dividends does not show up in the price of dividends, where can it have gone? The answer to be offered in Sec. VI (and proposed earlier by Black and Scholes, though in somewhat different terms) is that the quantity of dividends supplied has adjusted. The current equilibrium price of dividends, at the intersection of demand and supply, is now not easily distinguished from the price of capital gains, suggesting that the fabled "marginal shareholder" is a tax-exempt institution, or at least someone with a low cost of switching between dividends and capital gains.

18. Soon we may also have at least some indirect evidence as to whether the market for dividends is so far out of equilibrium as to generate substantial arbitraging side flows between "clienteles," i.e., between those who might have high relative demand prices for dividends and those who might have low demand prices. Recent Treasury rulings have permitted one firm, the Americus Trust, to purchase shares of ordinary corporations and reissue them in two pieces, one giving rights (essentially) to the dividends and the other (essentially) to the capital appreciation. The two pieces can be recombined at any time and turned in to the trust for a single underlying share. At present, only two stocks are involved, AT & T and Exxon, but more are promised. A separation of dividends and capital gains has long been available, though less efficiently, via so-called dual funds. The aggregate holdings of all such funds, however, represent only a tiny fraction of corporate shares outstanding.

yet to be found (and, indeed, may not exist), the possibility of switching to a different, more fashionable method of integration is always on the tax policy agenda. When such switches in tax regime are implemented, drastic, order-of-magnitude changes can occur in the relative demand price of dividends, supply price of dividends, or both.

In the United States, such changes in regime have unfortunately (or perhaps fortunately) been rare. A deduction at the corporate level for part of dividends paid was a feature of the recent Treasury tax reform proposals and the subsequent House of Representatives tax reform bill, but it remains unlikely that academic researchers will ever have the benefit of observing that particular comet. Aside from these periodically proposed and usually aborted integration schemes (which would not leave even a trace for an event study) and some trivial relief under the personal income tax such as the flat $100 dividend exclusion (which, of course, effects no decisions at the margin), I am aware of only one major, detectable change of regime in the United States since the income tax took its modern form during World War I. I refer to the Undistributed Profits Tax of 1936. This now-all-but-forgotten piece of New Deal legislation levied a tax on corporate profits remaining after corporate income taxes (then at a rate of 11% in the top bracket), interest on U.S. government securities, and payment of taxable cash dividends. The rates of the undistributed profits tax were progressive, starting at 7% of undistributed profits and reaching a maximum rate of 27% when 100% of after-tax income was retained.

The tax was in full force for only 2 years, 1936 and 1937. It was still technically on the books in 1938, but by then it had been virtually emasculated (see Rolbein 1939, esp. pp. 221–22, n. 3). During the 2 years of 1936 and 1937, when the cost of not paying dividends was increased so sharply, the flow of cash dividends paid surged dramatically. A study undertaken shortly after the incident, while memories were still fresh, puts the extra flow of dividends (beyond what might normally have been expected at that stage of the business cycle) at about 33⅓% (see Lent 1948). A collapse of equivalent magnitude occurred in 1938, when the tax was, mercifully, put to death.

Although the episode of the Undistributed Profits Tax exhausts the list of major regime changes in the United States, the set of instructive experiments can be expanded substantially by drawing on experience from abroad. In 1973, for example, Canada abandoned its long-standing policy, common to tax systems adapted from the old British model, of exempting from tax all capital gains and losses (except for brokers and others in the business of dealing in securities). The same Canadian statute also reduced effective tax rates on dividends so that the combined effect (though not uniform across all income levels) amounted on balance to a substantial tipping of the scales in favor of dividend income.

For the period immediately after the shift, Khoury and Smith (1977) report a significant increase in the rate of growth of dividends on the part of a representative sample of Canadian firms. They also find significant differences in the predicted direction between the dividend payout policies before and after the tax change of their Canadian sample, relative to a matched sample of comparable U.S. firms.

In Great Britain, as many as five distinct changes in tax regime can be discerned in the post–World War II era as Labour and Conservative governments alternated their tenure in office (for a detailed description, see Poterba and Summers [1985]). The direction of change in the relative burdens on dividends and capital gains was not always uniform across all income levels; also, dividend responses by firms were inhibited over part of the period by direct controls on dividends.[19] Still, Poterba and Summers are able to document reasonably clear signals of the appropriate kind being sent to management by changes in stock prices in the period following the changes and of an appropriate adaptation of dividend flow to those signals when firms had the freedom to do so.

Although changes in tax regime provide the most dramatic and hence informative experiments, changes in the rate structure, if sudden enough and drastic enough, can be almost as effective. In the United States, for example, the transition of the income tax from a minor nuisance to a major engine of income redistribution was a matter of only a few years. Surtax rates on ordinary income, which would include dividends, surged upward in the mid-1930s and were ratcheted up again during the rearmament period of the late 1930s and the war years of the early 1940s. The adjustments of corporate payout policies (and of individual portfolio strategies) to the new environment was masked for a while by concern with other, even more massive tax effects on corporate profits (notably, those coming from the excess-profits tax and the carryback of postwar losses and unused credits against wartime taxes). But by the early 1950s, the increased reliance on retained earnings by U.S. corporations, compared with their payout practices in the 1920s and early 1930s, was widely noted among economists. In fact, it is worth remembering that the classic dividend study of John Lintner (1956) was undertaken precisely in response to the then-controversial issue of whether there had indeed been a fundamental shift in the corporate propensity to save. Lintner concluded that there had not been a shift. But a subsequent, much more detailed study

19. The United States too has been known to institute dividend controls. Under the Nixon price controls of 1973–74, dividend growth was to be "voluntarily" restricted by firms to 5%. A noticeable bulge in share repurchases occurred during this period. In fact, some cynics regarded the spectacle of leading corporate officials standing at the side of Arthur Burns and calling for voluntary dividend restrictions as a classic example of the Brer Rabbit tactic of pleading not to be thrown into the briar patch.

by John Brittain (1966) showed quite convincingly that a downward shift in corporate dividend payout policies had occurred and that it could not be attributed to any of the proposed explanatory factors other than the change in the tax environment.[20]

Although major tax changes of the kind discussed above are likely to provide the most direct demonstrations of the comparative statics of the finance/dividend model, they are certainly not the only detectable shocks to which the underlying demand curves and supply curves are subject. We seem, in fact, to be undergoing just such a major shock at the moment in the form of a dramatic reduction in the cost of going back and forth between cash and securities.

These costs of getting in and out of cash are important to the model if only because they are presumed to be a major part of what justifies our speaking of a demand curve for dividends. The direct and indirect costs of converting shares to cash, if high enough, create a demand for cash dividends, even on the part of taxable investors, that would support a nonzero equilibrium supply of dividends by the corporate sector. With the coming of discount brokers, however, and with new financial instruments such as Cash Management Accounts that can make a portfolio of stocks the virtual equivalent of a checking account, the liquidity benefits of dividend-paying shares are fast eroding. The demand curve for cash dividends would thus appear to be shifting to the left.[21] Furthermore, casual observation of corporate share repurchase activity (especially, but not only, in connection with well-publicized takeovers and recapitalizations) suggests that supply too is adjusting—but slowly. In the last analysis, it may well be this slowness to adjust, as well as the seemingly endless persistence on both sides of the market of long-outmoded habits of thought about dividends, that is at least partly responsible for the concern within the profession about the predictive power of the underlying model.

Some of what appears to be sluggishness in corporate dividend policies relative to model predictions can be traced to the failure, in the short run, of the model's strong information assumptions. The equilibrium conditions in the model are worked out under essentially "double dummy" rules in which all the players are presumed to know each other's cards. Over the long pull, disclosure policies, both mandatory and voluntary, may make this a reasonable enough approximation. But

20. Poterba and Summers (1985, p. 270) report that the shift in supply first noted by Brittain appears to have been a permanent one. They find no signs in the period after Brittain's study of any return to prewar payout patterns.

21. It was thus somewhat ironic that dividend relief was included among the administration's and the Ways and Means Committee's tax reform proposals. The technological improvements and regulatory changes that have lowered the cost of security transactions by individuals have also done so for corporations. Reductions at that level have reduced the cost of both increasing dividends (by outside finance) and decreasing dividends (by share repurchase) so that the net effect remains unclear.

in the shorter run—and certainly at the time that any single particular dividend in the temporal sequence is under active consideration—management can be presumed to know more than outside investors about the current and immediate prospects of the firm. Under these conditions of asymmetric information, dividend decisions can take on an additional strategic dimension that, on balance, tends to inhibit changes in policy. That inhibition is likely to be particularly strong where, as at present, the objective conditions seem to be suggesting a fall in the demand for dividends. Passing or cutting the dividend has often been taken by the market as a bad-news signal despite the most elaborate educational preparation by the management and its public relations support teams. Many, indeed, are the corporate treasurers who have wished to be the *second* major firm in their industry to slash dividends.

Taking these strategic and information-related elements more formally into the basic model is clearly desirable and is, in fact, currently the focus of much research (for a survey of some recent efforts, see Miller [in press]). But developments of the underlying apparatus in these directions should not be taken as implying any systematic drawing away from the rationality postulate. If anything, signaling models and other models in information economics tend, in some ways, to place even greater demands on the rationality assumption than the valuation models from which they take off.[22]

VII. Conclusion: What Role for Behavioral Models of Dividends?

The purpose of this paper has been to show that the rationality-based market equilibrium models in finance in general and of dividends in particular are alive and well—or at least in no worse shape than other comparable models in economics at their level of aggregation. The framework is not so weighed down with anomalies that a complete reconstruction (on behavioral/cognitive or other lines) is either needed or likely to occur in the near future.

Having tried to establish that, let me conclude on a more conciliatory note by freely conceding again (see, e.g., Miller 1977, esp. pp. 272–73) that, at the most micro decision level, behavioral/cognitive elements are very much a part of the picture. If the concern is primarily with the fine details of specific cases—as it may well often tend to be in many business school finance classes—they cannot be ignored. It was not a lack of command over standard theoretical tools that led John Lintner (1956) to encapsulize his months of observation of actual dividend

---

22. The same strong thread of rationality also runs through another and even larger current stream of research in finance, i.e., the literature on agency theory and optimal contracting.

decisions in the neat little behavioral model we have all come to call the Lintner model. (I assume it to be a behavioral model, not only from its form, but because no one has yet been able to derive it as the solution to a maximization problem, despite 30 years of trying!) Nor should we be surprised to find evidence of "satisficing," "organizational slack," "rules of thumb," or "bounded rationality" in the making of individual dividend decisions. Corporate treasurers have many other, and often vastly more important, problems to contend with on a day-to-day basis, particularly in the highly volatile and takeover-jittery capital markets of recent years. The amounts of money involved in a quarterly dividend are typically not large in relation to corporate cash and financing flows (though crises do occasionally arise), and many corporate finance officers find it convenient under normal conditions to defer (or, at least, to pretend to defer) to the judgment of the firm's directors, who have the technical responsibility for declaring the dividend. Policy reviews and changes do occur, but only fitfully and at a pace that all recently hired M.B.A.'s are bound to regard as maddeningly slow.

The behavioral/cognitive elements in decisions involving dividends (including, perhaps, even some of the cognitive, cash-preference illusions imagined by Shefrin and Statman [1984]) are also likely to loom larger for individual investors who hold modest amounts of stock directly and who, unlike institutional and other large investors, do not rely heavily on professional portfolio advisers. For these investors, stocks are usually more than just the abstract "bundles of returns" of our economic models. Behind each holding may be a story of family business, family quarrels, legacies received, divorce settlements, and a host of other considerations almost totally irrelevant to our theories of portfolio selection. That we abstract from all these stories in building our models is not because the stories are uninteresting but because they may be too interesting and thereby distract us from the pervasive market forces that should be our principal concern.

References

Asinof, L. 1985. Excess pension assets lure corporate raiders. *Wall Street Journal* (September 22).

Black, F. 1976. The dividend puzzle. *Journal of Portfolio Management* 2 (Winter): 72–77.

Black, F., and Scholes, M. 1974. The effects of dividend yield and dividend policy on common stock prices and returns. *Journal of Financial Economics* 1, no. 1 (May): 1–22.

Blume, M. 1980. Stock returns and dividend yields: Some more evidence. *Review of Economics and Statistics* 62 (November): 567–77.

Brealey, R., and Myers, S. 1984. *Principles of Corporate Finance*. 2d ed. New York: McGraw-Hill.

Brittain, J. 1966. *Corporate Dividend Policy*. Washington, D.C.: Brookings.

Chen, N.-F.; Grundy, B.; and Stambaugh, R. F. 1985. Changing risk, changing expectations and the relation between expected return and dividend yield. Mimeographed. Chicago: University of Chicago, Graduate School of Business.

Emanuel, D. 1983. Debt and taxes, dividends and taxes, and taxes. Mimeographed. Dallas: University of Texas.

Fama, E., and Miller, M. H. 1972. *The Theory of Finance*. New York: Holt, Rinehart & Winston.

Grundy, B. 1985. Trading volume and stock returns around ex dividend days. Mimeographed. Chicago: University of Chicago, Graduate School of Business.

Ippolito, R. A. 1985. The economic function of underfunded pension plans. *Journal of Law and Economics* 28, no. 3 (October): 611–51.

Keim, D. B. 1982. Further evidence on size effects and yield effects: The implications of stock return seasonality. Mimeographed. Chicago: University of Chicago, Graduate School of Business.

Keim, D. B. 1983. Size-related anomalies and stock return seasonality: Further empirical evidence. *Journal of Financial Economics* 12, no. 1 (June): 13–32.

Khoury, N. T., and Smith, K. V. 1977. Dividend policy and the capital gains tax in Canada. *Journal of Business Administration* 8, no. 2 (Spring): 19–37.

Lent, G. E. 1948. *The Impact of the Undistributed Profits Tax, 1936–37*. New York: Columbia University Press.

Lintner, J. 1956. The distribution of incomes of corporations among dividends, retained earnings and taxes. *American Economic Review* 46 (May): 97–113.

Litzenberger, R., and Ramaswamy, K. 1979. The effect of personal taxes and dividends on capital asset prices. *Journal of Financial Economics* 7, no. 2 (June): 163–95.

Long, J. B., Jr. 1978. The market valuation of cash dividends: A case to consider. *Journal of Financial Economics* 6, no. 3 (June/September): 235–64.

Miller, M. H. 1977. Debt and taxes. *Journal of Finance* 32, no. 2 (May): 261–75.

Miller, M. H. In press. The informational content of dividends. In J. Bossons, R. Dornbusch, and S. Fischer (eds.), *Macroeconomics: Essays in Honor of Franco Modigliani*. Cambridge, Mass.: MIT Press.

Miller, M. H., and Modigliani, F. 1961. Dividend policy, growth, and the valuation of shares. *Journal of Business* 34, no. 4 (October): 411–33.

Miller, M. H., and Scholes, M. S. 1978. Dividends and taxes. *Journal of Financial Economics* 6, no. 2 (December): 333–64.

Miller, M. H., and Scholes, M. S. 1982. Dividends and taxes: Some empirical evidence. *Journal of Political Economy* 90, no. 6 (December): 1118–41.

Modigliani, F., and Miller, M. H. 1963. Corporate income taxes and the cost of capital: A correction. *American Economic Review* 53, no. 3 (June): 433–43.

Poterba, J. 1985. The citizens utility case: A further dividend puzzle. Working Paper no. 339. Cambridge: Massachusetts Institute of Technology.

Poterba, J. M., and Summers, L. H. 1985. The economic effects of dividend taxation. In E. Altman and M. Subrahmanyam (eds.), *Recent Advances in Corporate Finance*. Homewood, Ill.: Irwin.

Rolbein, D. L. 1939. Noncash dividends and stock rights as methods for avoidance of the undistributed profits tax. *Journal of Business* 12, no. 3 (July): 221–64.

Scholes, M.; Wolfson, M.; and Mazur, M. 1984. A model of implicit taxes and their effect on empirical estimates of income tax progressivity. Mimeographed. Stanford, Calif.: Stanford University.

Schwert, G. W. 1983. Size and stock returns and other empirical regularities. *Journal of Financial Economics* 12, no. 1 (June): 3–12.

Shefrin, H., and Statman, M. 1984. Explaining investor preference for cash dividends. *Journal of Financial Economics* 13, no. 2 (June): 253–82.

Allan W. Kleidon
Stanford University

Anomalies in Financial Economics: Blueprint for Change?*

I. Introduction

Beginning with Herbert Simon's (in this volume) opening paper and his call for data and testing of theories, it is clear that participants at this conference, whether their primary orientation is as "psychologists" or as "economists," emphasize rigorous standards of research and evidence. Indeed, calls have been made by Richard Thaler and Richard Zeckhauser for carefully framed experiments on which individuals may place "reputational bets": if the outcomes are not as predicted, there will be no further chance to explain/rationalize the outcome. Such proposals are close to the notion of crucial experiments in, say, Popper's view of the philosophy of science.[1] The presumption is that the failure of such a crucial experiment is sufficient to overturn the theory and signals that change is required.

However, Kuhn (1970) claims that examination of the history of science shows that such a model of the process of scientific activity is

This paper examines the case for major changes in the behavioral assumptions underlying economic models, based on apparent anomalies in financial economics. Arguments for such changes based on claims of "excess volatility" in stock prices appear flawed for two main reasons: there are serious questions whether the phenomenon exists in the first place and, even if it did exist, whether radical change in behavioral assumptions is the best avenue for current research. The paper also examines other apparent anomalies and suggests conditions under which such behavioral changes are more or less likely to be adopted.

* This paper was prepared for the Conference on Behavioral Foundations of Economic Theory at the University of Chicago, October 1985. Helpful comments have been received from the participants at that conference and the finance seminar at Stanford University, especially Michael Gibbons, Paul Pfleiderer, Mel Reder, and Myron Scholes. Partial financial support was provided by the Program in Finance, Stanford University.

1. Popper (1972, p. 266), e.g., suggests: "And look upon your experiments always as tests of a theory—as attempts to find faults in it, and to overthrow it."

more a caricature than a characterization of typical actual behavior. He argues (p. 81):

> How, then, to return to the initial question, do scientists respond to the awareness of an anomaly in the fit between theory and nature? What has just been said indicates that even a discrepancy unaccountably larger than that experienced in other applications of the theory need not draw any very profound response. There are always some discrepancies. Even the most stubborn ones usually respond at last to normal practice. Very often scientists are willing to wait, particularly if there are many problems available in other parts of the field. We have already noted, for example, that during the sixty years after Newton's original computation, the predicted motion of the moon's perigee remained only half of that observed. As Europe's best mathematical physicists continued to wrestle unsuccessfully with the well-known discrepancy, there were occasional proposals for a modification of Newton's inverse square law. But no one took these proposals very seriously, and in practice this patience with a major anomaly proved justified. Clairaut in 1750 was able to show that only the mathematics of the application had been wrong and that Newtonian theory could stand as before.

Although there are obvious differences between the two fields, it seems odd to require adherence by the social sciences to idealistic standards of behavior that often are not observed in the natural sciences. Moreover, there are important reasons why the proposed critical experiments are seldom performed, irrespective of how noble the ideal may be. Not least of all, it is costly to expend the amount of resources required to formulate an unambiguous, ultimate experiment, which so carefully handles every possibility, however unlikely, that researchers agree in advance to accept the results of the experiment without further question. For the nature of the questions dealt with at this conference, the costs may well prove prohibitive.

For this and other reasons, it is likely that we will always be contending with anomalies recently generated by empirical research. Many of these will be dispelled by more refined observation, but, as in the past, some will persist and cause revisions of relevant theory. At any given time, researchers are forced to decide whether a seeming anomaly is of the former—transitory—kind or presents an opportunity for viable reconstruction of theory.

In financial economics, such a seeming anomaly has been generated by some recent research that challenges an underlying model, namely, that stock prices can be regarded as the present value of rationally forecasted future cash flows. Initially, work by LeRoy and Porter (1981) and Shiller (1981a, 1981b, 1981c) examined one restrictive form of this model, which assumed constant discount rates, and argued that stock price movements greatly exceed those consistent with the (restrictive) model. Attempts to explain the results in terms of changes in discount rates have had little success, leading Shiller (1984a, p. 459) to conclude "that mass psychology may well be the dominant cause of movements in the price of the aggregate stock market."

In some ways, the initial tests assuming constant discount rates appear to have some of the characteristics of a critical experiment, at least for the constant rate model. The theory underlying the tests seems straightforward (see Sec. II), and the violations of the predictions appear very strong. Indeed, recent literature appears to take for granted that these tests provide clear evidence against the model; for example, Tirole (1985, p. 1085) states that the model can be seen to be violated "simply by looking at Figures 1 and 2 in Shiller [1981b]."

However, despite the apparent simplicity of the predictions and the apparent grossness of the violations, it turns out that this work demonstrates the pitfalls inherent in the concept of crucial experiments. Section II examines the evidence that is primarily relied on for the claim that stock prices show gross excess volatility relative to what would be expected if they constituted rational expectations of the present value of future cash flows.[2] This section demonstrates that much of what has been presented as evidence against the "rational valuation" model is really a misinterpretation of the data and that key results in this ("variance bounds") literature depend critically on questionable assumptions about the properties of the relevant data. Contrary to claims made in this literature, excess volatility of stock prices has not been adequately demonstrated.

Granted the validity of the argument in Section II, debate over possible responses to the alleged anomaly loses much of its immediate purpose. Nevertheless, Section III addresses the issue of how the economics discipline would respond to the alleged anomaly if—contrary to the argument of Section II—the empirical results proved sustainable. In particular, it considers what evidence would justify considering stock prices as being largely the irrational outcome of mass psychology, as advocated by Shiller. It is suggested that better alternatives are available than abandonment of the rationality assumption. The point of this (counterfactual) exercise is that the finance literature contains a number of other anomalies, based on much firmer evidence than that advanced in support of the so-called excess volatility of stock prices. Section IIIC discusses two examples of such anomalies and suggests that, if changes in behavioral assumptions are to occur (and there is little current support for such changes in the finance literature), they are more likely to be made in areas where it is relatively easier to model (at least implicitly) the aggregation theorems that are necessary

---

2. This section draws heavily on material from Kleidon (in press).

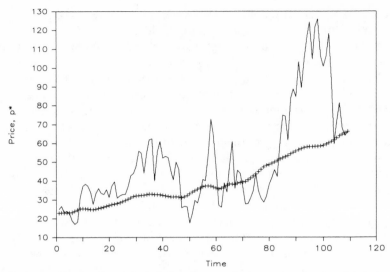

FIG. 1.—Standard and Poor's (real) annual composite stock price index, 1926–79, augmented with Cowles Commission common stock index, 1871–1925 (solid line), and corresponding "perfect foresight" series, including terminal condition ($p_t^* = p_T$).

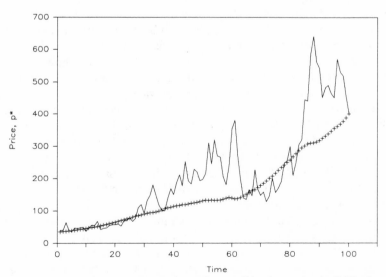

FIG. 2.—Nonstationary (geometric random walk) price series (solid line) and corresponding "perfect foresight" series, including terminal condition ($p_t^* = p_T$).

to predict the effect of individual behavior on the variables under study. Concluding remarks are offered in Section IV.

II. Evaluation of Evidence from Variance Bounds Literature

A. *Introduction*

The empirical nature of anomalies presupposes the existence of data with sufficient integrity to allow some disciplinary consensus as to whether the predictions of theory are satisfactorily achieved in the data. The better the data—and, of course, the better developed the theory and empirical technique—the more likely that inadequacies in theory or application will result in anomalies that are recognized as such by the relevant community. It is not altogether surprising then that recent results that challenge theoretical foundations of economics should come from research using stock price data. Whatever interpretation is given to stock prices, they represent a preeminent data source for economics, with few rivals in terms of quality or quantity of recorded prices. The existence of these data has led to relative sophistication in the questions asked of stock price research. Are results of tests affected by bid-ask spreads or by whether trades occur more or less frequently than for a typical stock? Is the discreteness of price (to within eights) a source of error that affects experiments?

Of course, these questions could not be asked if broader, more fundamental questions about the nature of prices, stock prices in particular, had not apparently been already answered with sufficient precision. Although stock prices have sometimes been regarded as unworthy of the attention of economists—for example, Roberts (1959, p. 3) expressed the hope that "perhaps the traditional academic suspicion about the stock market as an object of scholarly research will be overcome"—relatively recent work has seen the apparent success of a broad range of empirical investigations of stock prices using models based firmly within the disciplinary framework of economics. Starting with the work of Merton Miller and Franco Modigliani (Modigliani and Miller 1958, 1959; Miller and Modigliani 1961) and extending through the early work of the sixties using the CRSP data base from Chicago, this work has changed suspicion of stock prices to reliance on them. A generation of graduate students grew up to believe that stock prices are, at least prima facie, explainable within the context of models based on rational behavior by stock market participants (or their representative agents).

One important expression of this belief is the proposition that stock prices are set rationally as the present value of expected future cash flows. But, as mentioned above, a recent literature has challenged this proposition.[3] The work of Grossman and Shiller (1981), LeRoy and Porter (1981), and Shiller (1981a, 1981b, 1981c, 1984a, 1984b), among others, has used what have become known as variance bounds or volatility tests to examine the validity of this model. The primary claim of this literature is that the model is grossly violated in empirical tests—so grossly violated, in fact, that "for the aggregate stock market, there is no evidence at all that stock price movements have been followed by corresponding dividend movements" (Shiller 1984a, p. 476). The literature claims that stock prices show excess volatility and that "the variability of stock prices cannot be accounted for by information regarding future dividends" (Grossman and Shiller 1981, p. 222). Although early tests assumed constant discount rates, subsequent attempts to explain price changes in terms of changes in the discount rate have had little success. For example, Shiller (1981a) argues that the discount rates estimated by Grossman and Shiller (1981) in an attempt to reconcile stock prices with rational valuation models are not consistent with those implied using the same techniques on other assets such as real estate.

Building on the alleged failures of theories based on an assumption of rationality to explain the behavior of stock prices, Shiller asserts "that mass psychology may well be the dominant cause of movements in the price of the aggregate stock market" (1984a, p. 459) and argues, "If . . . the reader goes back to a rational expectations model in which information about potential dividend movements, rather than discount rate movements, causes stock prices to move, then since actual aggregate dividend movements of such magnitude have never been observed, what is the source of information about such potential movements? Can we be satisfied with a model which attributes stock price movements and their business cycle correlation to public rational expectations about movements in a variable which has, in effect, never yet been observed to move?"

These provocative questions are answered by showing that the apparent evidence against the possibility of price changes reflecting information about potential dividend movements is ill founded.

B. Ostensible Evidence

The model most often used in the excess volatility or variance bound literature is the dividend valuation model,

---

3. As shown by Miller and Modigliani (1961), there are alternate (equivalent) ways of stating the model under attack, including the present value of net cash flows into the firm (the earnings-investment approach) or from the firm to shareholders (the dividend approach). Note also that there is no necessary assumption of constant discount rates in these statements, although clearly some restrictions on the expected returns used for discounting (as provided, e.g., by the capital asset pricing model) are necessary to avoid a tautology.

$$p_t = \sum_{\tau=1}^{\infty} \frac{E(d_{t+\tau}|\Phi_t)}{(1+r)^\tau}, \tag{1}$$

where r is an assumed constant discount rate and $(X|\Phi)$ denotes the conditional distribution of the random variable X given the information Φ. A new variable, p_t^*,[4] is defined as

$$p_t^* \equiv \sum_{\tau=1}^{\infty} \frac{d_{t+\tau}}{(1+r)^\tau}. \tag{2}$$

A comparison of (1) and (2) shows

$$p_t = E(p_t^*|\Phi_t), \tag{3}$$

which implies the variance bound,

$$\text{var}(p_t) \leq \text{var}(p_t^*). \tag{4}$$

The basis for this inequality is that, since the price rationally forecasts p_t^* by (3), the variance of the forecast (the price) should be less than that of the variable being forecast.

Figure 1 plots Standard and Poor's (1980) annual composite stock price index 1926–79 augmented with the Cowles Commission (1938) common stock index 1871–1925 (the solid line) and p_t^* calculated from the following recursion implied by definition (2),

$$p_t^* = \frac{p_{t+1}^* + d_{t+1}}{(1+r)}, \tag{5}$$

subject to a condition that equates the terminal p_T^* to the terminal price p_T. It seems obvious from figure 1 that the bound in (4) is grossly violated, with the consequent implication that prices cannot be set by the model (1). Since (1) implies that changes in price are driven by changes in expectations of future cash flows, it seems reasonable to infer that something else might be causing the large variation in prices; Shiller's conclusion is that the "something else" is mass psychology or fads.

The data shown in figure 1 were used in Shiller (1981b), but similar behavior is observed in other data as well. Consider figure 2, which also plot prices p_t (the solid lines) and the corresponding p_t^* series. The relevant characteristics are very similar to those in figure 1. It would once again seem obvious that the bound (4) has been violated and that consequently the valuation model (1) is empirically untenable.

However, in the case of figure 2, such a conclusion would be abso-

---

4. This variable is called the "perfect foresight" price in much of the variance bound literature (e.g., see Shiller 1981c, p. 292), although it is not necessarily the price that would prevail under perfect foresight since the discount rate r is not necessarily appropriate under those conditions. For more discussion on this point, see Kleidon (in press).

lutely unfounded. Figure 2 is based not on real data but on simulated data that by construction are generated by the rational valuation model (1). The variance bound (4) is not violated, and absolutely nothing can be inferred from the data plots about the validity of the model (1).

This seems startling at first glance. Much of the effect of the variance bounds literature has come from the apparently clear violation of the inequality (4) by plots such as figure 1. Indeed, it has been claimed that an inspection of these plots provides such obvious evidence against the inequality (4) and the valuation model (1) that formal empirical tests of (4) need not be relied on (see Shiller 1981a, pp. 4, 7; 1984b; Tirole 1985). This interpretation is clearly false if plots virtually identical to figure 1 can be readily created when (1) holds by construction.

It is to be emphasized that the price process used in figure 2 is not an unusual or artificial construct; rather it is the (geometric) random walk traditionally regarded in finance as an excellent empirical description of the price process in actual data.[5] Kleidon (in press) examines Standard and Poor's series in some detail and demonstrates empirically that the traditional process used to construct figure 2 is consistent with Standard and Poor's price series in figure 1.

The explanation for the compatibility of plots such as figures 1 and 2 with the variance bound (4) is given in detail in Kleidon (in press). I now highlight the primary results of that paper, both for the interpretation of time series plots such as figure 1 and concerning the use of sample variances of price and p_t^* to test the inequality (4). First, key results concerning conditional variances are outlined (Sec. IIC). Section IID discusses the interpretation of time series plots of price and p_t^*, including the work of Grossman and Shiller (1981) based on nonconstant discount rates. Finally, Section IIE discusses the use of sample variances to test the bound (4).

C. Conditional Variances of Price and p_t^*

The characteristic of the time series plots of price p_t and p_t^* that seems most at odds with the claim that $\text{var}(p_t^*) \geq \text{var}(p_t)$ is the striking "smoothness" of p_t^* compared with the price series. The most common interpretation is that this provides evidence against the inequality (see, e.g., Shiller 1981b, p. 421; Grossman and Shiller 1981, p. 224). However, this interpretation is incorrect, and in fact the variance bound does not address the issue of how smooth one time series is compared with the other. The literature has incorrectly identified the variances used in the inequality (4) with smoothness or "short-term variation" in time series plots of price and p_t^*.

---

5. For construction details, see Kleidon (in press, sec. 2.1). Note also that the primary characteristics of time series plots such as figs. 1 and 2 do not depend on the nonstationarity assumption and are present even in stationary AR(1) processes for prices. See Kleidon (1986) for more detail on the stationary case.

Although the variance inequality found in the literature is almost always given in terms of unconditional variances as in (4), Kleidon (in press) shows that similar inequalities hold for conditional variances, that is,

$$\text{var}(p_t^*|\Phi_{t-k}) \geq \text{var}(p_t|\Phi_{t-k}), \quad k = 0, \ldots, \infty, \qquad (6)$$

where Φ_{t-k} is information at $t - k$ that is always included in information at t (i.e., traders do not forget) and where the limits as $k \to \infty$ of the conditional variances in (6) are equal to the unconditional variances in (4). The "smoothness" of time series plots of price and p_t^* is also determined by conditional variances, although they differ from those in (6) and do not satisfy an inequality such as (6). Instead, the conditional variance that determines the smoothness of the p_t^* series implies less short-term variation in p_t^* than is implied for the price series by the corresponding conditional variance of p_t.

The smoothness or amount of short-term variation in price and p_t^* is determined by the variance conditional on past values of the series, that is, $\text{var}(p_t|p_{t-k})$ and $\text{var}(p_t^*|p_{t-k}^*)$.[6] Note that $\text{var}(p_t|p_{t-k})$ is equivalent to the conditional variance of price in (6) if information comprises current and past prices. However, the conditional variance $\text{var}(p_t^*|p_{t-k}^*)$ that determines the smoothness of the time series of p_t^* is not equivalent to $\text{var}(p_t^*|\Phi_{t-k})$ since, by the definition of p_t^* in (2), past values of p_t^* depend on future outcomes of dividends that are not known at or prior to time t. Consequently, there is no necessity for the conditional variances $\text{var}(p_t|p_{t-k})$ and $\text{var}(p_t^*|p_{t-k}^*)$ to satisfy an inequality such as (6), and indeed they do not.

To illustrate these distinctions, consider the following dividend process (which ignores irrelevant means for current purposes):

$$d_t = \rho d_{t-1} + \eta_t, \qquad (7)$$

where η_t is independently and identically distributed $(0, \sigma_\eta^2)$.

This process includes both stationary dividends $(|\rho| < 1.0)$ and non-stationary random walk dividends $(\rho = 1.0)$. If prices are set by (1) and information comprises current and past dividends given by (7), then Kleidon (in press) shows that

$$\begin{aligned} p_t &= ad_t \\ &= \rho p_{t-1} + a\eta_t, \end{aligned} \qquad (8)$$

where

$$a \equiv \frac{\rho}{(1 + r - \rho)}.$$

6. An early version of Kleidon (in press) drew the distinction between the unconditional variances in (4) and conditional variances similar to these, and this distinction was adopted in LeRoy (1984) in terms of these conditional variances.

Kleidon (in press) gives the variances of the conditional distributions $(p_t|\Phi_{t-k})$ and $(p_t^*|\Phi_{t-k})$, where Φ_{t-k} is limited to current and past dividends or equivalently from (8) to p_{t-k}. The limit as $k \to \infty$ gives the unconditional distributions. The variances of the appropriate conditional distributions verify (6), but for the random walk case when $\rho = 1.0$, the conditional variances are well defined but the unconditional variances are not. We have

$$\text{var}(p_t|\Phi_{t-k}) = \text{var}(p_t|p_{t-k})$$

$$= \sigma_\eta^2 a^2 \left(\frac{1 - \rho^{2k}}{1 - \rho^2} \right), \tag{9}$$

$$\text{var}(p_t^*|\Phi_{t-k}) = \text{var}(p_t^*|p_{t-k})$$

$$= \sigma_\eta^2 a^2 \left[\left(\frac{1 - \rho^{2k}}{1 - \rho^2} \right) + \frac{(1 + r)^2}{\rho^2(2r + r^2)} \right] \tag{10}$$

$$= \text{var}(p_t|p_{t-k}) + \frac{\sigma_\eta^2 a^2 (1 + r)^2}{\rho^2(2r + r^2)}.$$

It can be verified that the limits (as $k \to \infty$) of the conditional variances in (9) and (10) equal the corresponding unconditional variances:

$$\text{var}(p_t) = \frac{\sigma_\eta^2 a^2}{(1 - \rho^2)}, \tag{11}$$

$$\text{var}(p_t^*) = \frac{\sigma_\eta^2(1 + r + \rho)}{(1 + r - \rho)(1 - \rho^2)(2r + r^2)}. \tag{12}$$

Further, for the random walk case ($\rho = 1.0$), we have

$$\lim_{\rho \to 1} \text{var}(p_t|p_{t-k}) = \frac{\sigma_\eta^2 k}{r^2}, \tag{13}$$

$$\lim_{\rho \to 1} \text{var}(p_t^*|p_{t-k}) = \frac{\sigma_\eta^2}{r^2} \left[k + \frac{(1 + r)^2}{2r + r^2} \right]. \tag{14}$$

This shows that the unconditional variances of p_t and p_t^* are not defined for the random walk so that, strictly speaking, the bound (4) involves undefined terms. However, the corresponding conditional variances satisfy inequality (6).

The variances (9)–(14) are defined in the cross-sectional sense of (unobserved) variances at t across different possible economies. To illustrate this notion, figure 3 shows the values for p_1 and p_1^* for 20 replications of the simulated economy that is used to generate figure 2, where the model used is the (geometric) random walk for prices tradi-

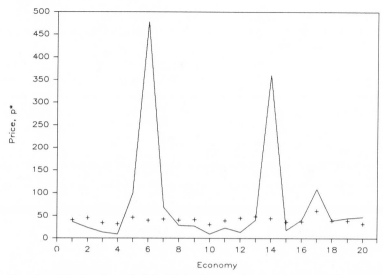

FIG. 3.—Distribution of p^* (solid line) and prices at time 1 across 20 economies that are identical at time 0.

tionally used in finance.[7] In each economy the starting price is set at p_0 = 40.0, and the same dividend process is used in each replication (although obviously different dividend outcomes occur).

From (6), we know that the variance of p_1, given p_0, should be less than the variance of p_1^* given p_0, and figure 3 shows precisely this result. Values of p_1 across the 20 economies vary between a low of 30.48 (economy 10) and a high of 61.35 (economy 17). Much greater variability across economies is seen in p_1^*, as the theory predicts, and values range from 8.99 (economy 4) to 477.83 (economy 6).

To complete the picture, figure 4 shows time series plots of 100 observations of p_t and p_t^* for three of the 20 economies shown in figure 3. The three economies are 2, 4, and 6; the latter two are chosen because they give the lowest and highest values of p_1^*, respectively. It is obvious from figure 4 that the wide variation in p_1^* is simply the result of different ex post draws of dividends over time for the different economies. Each is possible at time zero since the same stochastic process and same initial price p_0 prevail in each economy. Ex post quite different worlds could be encountered, and each would imply its own value of p_1^*. The variance bounds hold across these different economies.

It is obvious, however, that the striking smoothness of the plots of p_t^* shown in figures 1 and 2 also appears in each of the time series plots of

---

7. For simulation details, see Kleidon (in press, sec. 2).

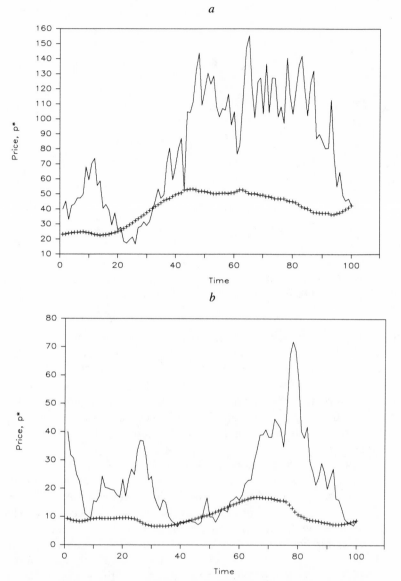

Fig. 4.—Plots of time series of nonstationary price series (solid line) and corresponding p_t^* series, for economies 2, 4, and 6 from 20 replications shown in fig. 3.

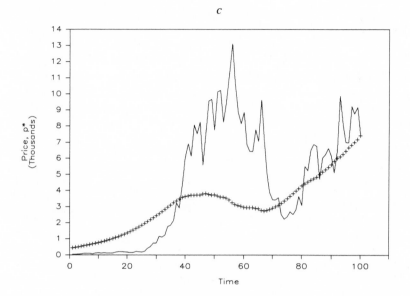

p_t^* in figure 4. Smoothness of p_t^* is defined here to mean that, for small k,

$$\text{var}(p_t^*|p_{t-k}^*) < \text{var}(p_t|p_{t-k}).$$

It is clear that as $k \to \infty$ the conditional distribution $(p_t^*|p_{t-k}^*)$ approaches the unconditional distribution of p_t^*, so that the bound (4) will indeed hold for sufficiently large k (assuming that the variances of the unconditional distributions exist). What is not obvious is the behavior of $(p_t^*|p_{t-k}^*)$ for small k. Kleidon (in press, proposition 5) derives (subject to realistic parameter restrictions on r):

$$\text{var}(p_t^*|p_{t-k}^*) = \text{var}(p_t^*)(1 - \rho_k^2), \tag{15}$$

where

$$\rho_k \equiv \text{cov}(p_t^*, p_{t-k}^*)\text{var}(p_t^*)$$

$$= \frac{\rho^{k+1}(2r + r^2) - (1 - \rho^2)(1 + r)^{1-k}}{(1 + r + \rho)(\rho + r\rho - 1)}.$$

It can be verified that the limit (as $k \to \infty$) of $\text{var}\{p_t^*|p_{t-k}^*\}$ in (15) is $\text{var}(p_t^*)$ and that for the random walk case ($\rho = 1.0$)

$$\lim_{\rho \to 1} \text{var}(p_t^*|p_{t-k}^*)$$

$$= \frac{\sigma_\eta^2[(k + 1)(2r + r^2) - (1 + r)(3 + r) + 2(1 + r)^{1-k} + 1]}{r^2(2r + r^2)}.$$

Again in this case, the conditional variances $\text{var}(p_t^*|p_{t-k}^*)$ are well defined for $k < \infty$.

The limits as $k \to \infty$ of the conditional variances $\text{var}(p_t^*|p_{t-k}^*)$ and $\text{var}(p_t|p_{t-k})$ give the unconditional variances in (11) and (12), respectively. Hence for k large enough, $\text{var}(p_t^*|p_{t-k}^*)$ must exceed $\text{var}(p_t|p_{t-k})$ since the bound (4) holds for unconditional variances (assuming that they exist). However, the key insight is that short-term variances show the opposite result. For small k,

$$\text{var}(p_t^*|p_{t-k}^*) < \text{var}(p_t|p_{t-k}),$$

and this can hold for quite large k depending on the parameter ρ in the dividend process.

This result is discussed in detail in Kleidon (in press), but the fundamental intuition for the greater smoothness of p_t^* relative to prices is that the former series gives the present value of the ex post dividend outcomes by the definition (2), while actual prices give the present value of *expected* dividends. A change in current dividends from past levels rationally implies a change in all future expected dividends if dividends are given by the process (7). Consequently, the price should change by the present value of those changes in expected future dividends, which will typically be much larger than the current dividend change itself. However, since p_t^* by definition already uses full knowledge of the ex post dividend stream, there are no revisions in expectations as a result of changes in current dividends. In fact, (2) implies that consecutive changes in p_t^* are limited to the capital gain that, together with current dividends, will give exactly the return r, and this change in p_t^* will typically be smaller than the change in prices.

D. Interpretation of Plots of Price and p_t^*

Given the results from Section IIC above for reasonable values of r and ρ, it is clear that time series plots of p_t^* *should* be smoother than prices if prices are rationally set by the valuation model (1). Consequently, figures 1 and 2 cannot be interpreted as evidence aginst (1) simply because of the clearly different time series properties of price and p_t^*. However, much of the evidence cited against (1) rests precisely on this difference between the series.

One of the most influential papers using this argument is Grossman and Shiller (1981). They assume a constant relative risk-aversion utility of consumption function,

$$U(c) = \frac{1}{1 - A}c^{1-A}, \quad 0 < A < \infty, \tag{16}$$

and calculate (p. 223) the "perfect foresight price" p_t^* with constant and nonconstant discount rates.[8] Under the assumption that investors

8. Some papers use the notation P_t^* and P_t, as in Grossman and Shiller (1981), while others use the lowercase notation p_t^* and p_t, which is used throughout this paper.

know the whole future path of consumption (p. 223), they calculate implied discount rates from (16) for different values of the risk-aversion parameter and attempt to infer the parameter value that makes the observed stock price series consistent with market efficiency (p. 224). The risk-neutrality case ($A = 0$) gives constant discount rates (assuming constant time preference), and p_t^* appears much closer to the actual price series for $A = 4$ (nonconstant rates), at least for the period up to about 1950. Their results are reproduced here as figure 5.

Grossman and Shiller select the risk-aversion parameter $A = 4$ in figure 5 (1981, p. 224) because of the smoothness of p_t^* when discount rates are assumed constant:

> Notice that with a constant discount factor, P_t^* just grows with the trend in dividends; it shows virtually none of the *short-term variation* of actual stock prices. The larger A is, the bigger the variations of P_t^* and $A = 4$ was shown here because for this A, P, and P_t^* have movements of very similar magnitude. . . . The rough correspondence between P^* [$A = 4$] and P (except for the recent data) shows that if we accept a coefficient of relative risk aversion of 4, we can to some extent reconcile the behavior of P with economic theory *even under the assumption that future prices are known with certainty.* [Emphasis added]

The statement concerning a certainty assumption is crucial, and I return to it shortly. More recently, Shiller (1984*b*) relies exclusively on plots such as figure 5 as a "particularly striking way of presenting the evidence" that stock price changes cannot be explained in terms of "some new information about future earnings" (p. 30). He uses virtually the same plot as figure 5 (extended to 1981) and claims (1984*b*, p. 31):

> [Figure 5] shows that actual dividend movements of the magnitude "forecast" by price movements never appeared in nearly a century of data. We *might* have observed big movements in [p_t^*, $A = 0$] that correspond to big movements in [p_t] and that would mean that movements in [p_t] really did appropriately forecast movements in future dividends. On the other hand, this just did not happen. Look, for example, at the stock market decline of the Great Depression, from 1929 to 1932. [p_t^*, $A = 0$] did not go down then, but only very slightly, far less than the decline in [p_t]. The reason is that real dividends declined substantially only for the few worst years of the Depression. These few lean years have little impact on [p_t^*, $A = 0$], which depends in effect on the longer-run outlook for stocks.

Shiller's (1984*b*) claim that the stock price should not have declined as much as it did between 1929 and 1932, because dividends declined substantially only in the few worst years of the depression, is at best incomplete since the argument assumes that stockholders knew that the lower dividends they were seeing would not last far into the future.

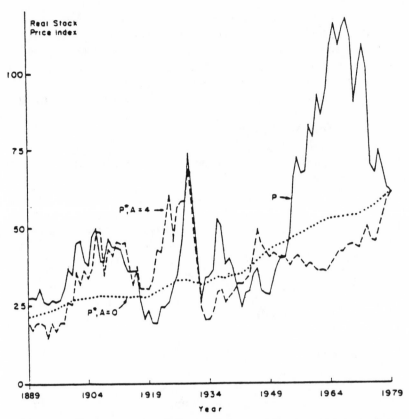

FIG. 5.—"Grossman and Shiller's (1981) series of actual and perfect foresight stock prices, 1889–1979. "Note: The solid line P_t is the real Standard and Poor Composite Stock Price Average. The other lines are: P_t^* (as defined by expression (6) and (7) [Grossman and Shiller]), the present value of actual subsequent real dividends using the actual stock price in 1979 as a terminal value. With $A = 0$ (dotted line) the discount rates are constant, while with $A = 4$ (dashed line) they vary with consumption" (Grossman and Shiller (1981, fig. 1, p. 225). (Reprinted by permission of the American Economic Association from Grossman and Shiller [1981, fig. 1, p. 225].)

Grossman and Shiller (1981) are more explicit and add an assumption of certainty about future prices. However, it is clear that this assumption is not part of the model ostensibly being tested. The original model, given as (1) above, writes price in terms of expected future dividends, in contrast to p_t^*, which uses the ex post outcomes. Although we would expect p_t^* to correspond to the actual price series in a world of certainty—if discount rates were estimated correctly and the price series were rational, they should be identical—the actual stock prices shown in figure 5 were of course not set in a world of omniscience. Consequently, we should expect deviation between the ex ante expectations reflected in prices and the ex post outcomes given by p_t^*.

The issue is addressed by Shiller (1984*b*, p. 35), but he does not present sufficient evidence to allow inference about the degree of divergence to be expected: "Of course, people do not have perfect foresight, and so actual stock prices [p_t] need not equal [p_t^*]. We [i.e., Grossman and Shiller 1981] argue that even under imperfect information we might expect [p_t] to resemble [p_t^*], though if information is very bad the resemblance could be very weak." This illustrates precisely the difficulty in examining plots such as figures 1 and 5. Until we know how imperfect the information is, we cannot interpret how weak the resemblance should be. A fundamental misinterpretation of such figures has been to make inferences about the validity of the valuation model (1) without specifying the yardstick necessary to allow such inferences.

To see whether the degree of correspondence between p_t^* and price in figure 1 is consistent with the valuation equation (1), we need a model that specifies the information available to the market about future cash flows. One possibility—favored by Grossman and Shiller—is to assume that shareholders have a large amount of information about future dividends. Then the only way that prices could be rational is if discount rates vary greatly because of changes in aggregate consumption, which is their solution. However, not only does this explanation fail to explain stock price behavior in figure 5 after about 1950, but, as noted in Shiller (1981*a*), it also fails when applied to other data.

An alternative explanation for the lack of correspondence between the p_t and the p_t series is much more consistent with the data, namely, that there is considerable uncertainty about future dividends when prices are set. Using the (geometric) random walk for prices traditionally used in finance and assuming that the only information available at time t is the past history of dividends, figures 2 and 4 show that there is sufficient uncertainty about future cash flows to imply the large divergence between prices and p_t^* seen in Standard and Poor's data in figures 1 and 5. Note that the procedures used to construct figures 2 and 4 are conservative since discount rates are strictly constant by construction and no dividend smoothing is assumed.

Despite the potential for confusion in plots such as figure 5, they have been heavily relied on in the literature and have even been treated as stronger evidence against (1) than formal tests of the bound (4). Shiller (1981*a*, pp. 4, 7; 1984*b*) and Tirole (1985, p. 1085) claim that figure 5 alone is sufficient to show that stock prices are inconsistent with the valuation model (1). This is simply incorrect. However, as Shiller (1981*a*) acknowledges, more formal tests of (4) based on time series data for a single economy also have problems, which are now addressed.

E. Time Series Tests of Variance Bounds

The assumption typically made to test the bound (4) using time series data is that the relevant variables (namely, dividends and prices for the dividend discount model being discussed here) follow stationary and ergodic processes. If this is true, then the sample moments are consistent estimators for the moments of the unobservable distributions used in the inequality, assuming a sufficiently long time series of realizations from those distributions.[9]

However, there are at least two important reasons to question whether the extra assumptions underlying these tests are valid empirically. First, Kleidon (in press, sec. 3.3) shows that the data used in many of the variance bounds tests are consistent with the assumption that prices follow a nonstationary random walk. If so, the unconditional variances in (4) do not exist, and the use of sample variances of p_t and p_t^* as estimators of population unconditional variances is invalid.

Assuming prices are nonstationary, Kleidon (in press, sec. 3.1) shows that the apparent gross violations of the variance bound (4) reported in the current literature using sample variances of p_t and p_t^* are not surprising. Shiller (1981b) uses a (real) discount rate of 0.048 per annum for detrended data, or 0.063 per annum for nondetrended data, and finds that the ratio of the sample standard deviation of price to that of p_t^* is 5.59. Kleidon (in press, fig. 2) applies Shiller's procedures to Monte Carlo simulations of nonstationary processes with parameter values equal to those for Standard and Poor's price series. The simulations show that when the discount rate is assumed to be 0.05, the ratio of sample standard deviation of price to that of p_t^* exceeds five in about 40% of the replications (with the largest ratio in 1,000 replications being 14.65). For an assumed discount rate of 0.065 (0.075), almost 15% (5%) show these apparent gross violations of the bound. Further, although the use of these sample variances of price and p_t^* as estimators of population unconditional variances is invalid when prices are nonstationary, it is valid to estimate conditional variances. Kleidon (in press, sec. 3.2) shows that Standard and Poor's data do not violate the conditional variance inequalities in (6).

The second problem, that of dividend smoothing, has important implications for all research that attempts to infer the properties of an infinite stream of future dividends from some finite ex post set of dividends that are under some control of management. Empirical evidence suggests that management takes pains to create a smooth short-run dividend series that may not reflect one-for-one the fortunes of the firm

9. See Fuller (1976, p. 230). Just how long is "sufficient" in this context, even assuming stationarity and ergodicity, is investigated in detail in Kleidon (1983, ch. 5; 1986). See also Flavin (1983).

as determined primarily by its earnings and investment opportunities.[10] Ceteris paribus, the less variable the dividend stream, the more variable will be the price series that comprises the present value of future dividends. For example, a firm seeking to finance expansion internally may withhold all dividends over some finite period, with an implicit promise of some future (perhaps liquidating) dividend.

If dividends are smoothed, the time series may be covariance nonstationary and violate the assumption of ergodicity necessary to allow estimation of valid cross-sectional variance bounds with time series data. The issue of dividend smoothing can have striking implications for some more recent tests that attempt to overcome criticisms of early variance bounds tests. For example, West (1984) derives and tests the inequality that the variance of changes through time in the present value of expected dividends will be greater when the information set comprises only current and past dividends than when it comprises a larger set. However, as discussed in Kleidon (in press), dividend smoothing may violate the necessary assumption that dividends follow an auto-regressive integrated moving average (ARIMA) process and potentially invalidates his bound.

Although the issue of dividend smoothing is potentially very important in interpreting the results from any particular test, Kleidon (in press, sec. 3) shows that, even ignoring smoothing, the current apparent gross violations of the bound (4) are not surprising if prices follow a nonstationary (geometric) random walk with parameters corresponding to Standard and Poor's price data[11] and that Standard and Poor's series do not violate the conditional bounds given by (6).

F. Conclusions

This section shows that the key claims of the variance bound literature (used as evidence that stock price variability cannot be explained in terms of rational changes in expectations of future cash flows) are subject to severe reservations. Many who examine time series plots of price and p_t^* misinterpret the greater smoothness of the p_t^* series as evidence that price changes are not caused by changes in expectations of future cash flows. However, for relevant dividend processes, if prices are set by the valuation model (1), greater smoothness follows by construction. Moreover, more formal tests based on sample variances of price and p_t^* are inappropriate when prices follow a nonsta-

10. See, e.g., Lintner (1956) and Fama and Babiak (1968). This does not deny that dividends may contain some information, as in the signaling hypotheses of Ross (1977) and Bhattacharya (1980).

11. Marsh and Merton (1986) show that if the terminal value p_t^* is set equal to the average sample price, the bound (4) is always violated if prices follow this process, although they do not indicate whether "gross" violations are to be expected. See Kleidon (in press, n. 23) for further discussion.

tionary random walk, which cannot be ruled out in the data used to test
the variance bounds. It is shown that application to nonstationary data
of the procedures used in current variance bounds tests frequently
yields precisely the results reported in the literature.

Two further issues remain. First, the observations made here concerning ostensible evidence of excess volatility of stock prices do not
address the question whether discount rates are constant as in (1).
Although plots such as figure 1 are not sufficient to constitute evidence
against (1), including the constant discount rate assumption, the validity of that assumption is important theoretically as well as empirically
and is not ruled out by these results.[12]

Second, it is not claimed that the material presented here constitutes
positive evidence in support of the notion that prices are set rationally
as the present value of expected future cash flows (with appropriate
discount rates). However, it can be shown that a large part of observed
price changes is associated with changes in expectations of future cash
flows, using simple models and a few information variables. For example, Shiller (1984b, p. 31) contends that the failure of p_t^* to decline
(over the period 1929–32) to the same extent as price constitutes evidence against the hypothesis that price changes reflect changes in expectations of future cash flows. As we have seen, this logic is invalid
since it confuses expectations with ex post outcomes. Moreover, Standard and Poor's (accounting) earnings index fell during 1929 by about
the same percentage as did the price index, and this was followed in the
next year by a similar percentage decline in dividends. The simple
random walk model used to construct figures 2 and 4 predicts that
equal percentage changes should be seen in prices and dividends.[13]

I now turn to the question of how the economics profession should
react to ostensible anomalies, including the results from the variance
bounds literature.

III.   A Change in Behavioral Foundations?

If it is true that the profession will always be faced with some anomalous differences between theory and data, when does an anomaly cease
being regarded as a challenging puzzle to be solved within the current
framework, to become regarded as evidence that some fundamental
change in worldview is desirable? The issue revolves around the
benchmark that is used to measure successful reconciliation of data

12. See Kleidon (in press, sec. 4) for more discussion.
13. For more formal evidence linking price changes to changes in expectations of
future cash flows in the context of simple valuation models, see Kleidon (1983, ch. 6).
Note also that, although roughly similar percentage changes are seen in Standard and
Poor's prices, earnings, and dividends series prior to about 1950, since that time dividends appear considerably more highly smoothed than either earnings or prices.

with theory since what is anomalous from one viewpoint may be self-evident from another. This section examines these questions and suggests, first, that some kinds of anomalies are more likely to lead to serious changes in the behavioral foundations of economics than others and, second, that not all subfields or models in economics are equally susceptible to changes of this nature.

The major current proposal for radical change in the behavioral assumptions underlying economic models of stock prices comes from Shiller, particularly as articulated in (1984a). Section IIIA suggests some general principles to be considered when making major changes in the foundations of a discipline such as financial economics. Section IIIB applies these principles to the variance bounds literature, particularly to the arguments of Shiller (1984a), and examines some published reaction by economists to those arguments.

The conclusion reached here is that it is unlikely that the profession will adopt Shiller's (1984a) framework, in which virtually all price movements are assumed to be driven by fads and mass psychology rather than by rational expectations of future dividends or prices, with or without constant discount rates.[14] Such adoption is unlikely for two reasons. First, as shown above, the results that are relied on as evidence of excess volatility within the simple present value models are in serious dispute. Second, even if this were not so, other models may explain "excess volatility" without rejecting the assumption of rational expectations. As discussed below, Fischer (1984) argues that this would be more attractive to many economists.

Section IIIC briefly examines some anomalies in financial economics and their potential for changing the behavioral foundations of the discipline. The conclusion reached is that changes are more likely to be made in areas where it is easier to model (at least implicitly) the aggregation theorems that are necessary to predict the effect of individual behavior on the variables under study. Not all questions arise within the same institutional framework, and not all models assume the same degree of market competition and aggregation of data. Consequently, when potentially richer individual environments require more complicated mechanisms to produce the aggregate data under study, the trade-offs involved are likely to differ across subfields or models.

Two examples of different institutional environments are examined, and the behavioral assumptions that ultimately prove necessary to explain observed data may differ between them. The first concerns models of risk and expected return, in the context of highly competitive and largely anonymous environments such as the stock market. The second concerns mergers and acquisitions, in which the behavior of particular individual participants may be more easily traced to ultimate

14. See, e.g., Shiller (1984a, fig. 2).

merger bids. The major current models of risk and expected return do not differ greatly in the standard behavioral assumptions they make; however, as discussed below, Roll (1986) has proposed a significant change in behavioral assumptions underlying models of mergers.

A. What Justifies Major Theoretical Changes?

Kuhn (1970, p. 84) suggests that, historically, there have been three responses to significant anomalies (which in his terminology produce a crisis for the affected discipline). First, what initially appeared to be anomalous may be subsequently explained within the original disciplinary framework. Second, the problem may be regarded as insoluble with the current state of knowledge and left for future generations. Third, and most relevant here, the disciplinary foundations may change so that, within the new framework, the anomaly is explained.

The issues faced by disciplines when considering major foundational changes provide insight about when and why economists may countenance major changes in the behavioral assumptions of their field. If anomalous results suggest an alteration in accepted theory, typically one requirement of the new theory will be that it explain the original anomaly. Second, a highly desirable characteristic of a new theory is that it not destroy "too much" of what was originally explained, that is, what was known under the previous framework. The trade-off is clear. Resources may be devoted to further attempts to explain the anomaly within the old framework, or the field may cut bait and start (at least partially) afresh with a new theory. This choice is never easy, and individual scientists have always differed in their judgments. But without putting too fine an economic explanation on the group behavior, it seems clear that the greater the loss of current knowledge occasioned by acceptance of a new theory, the less likely is a field to accept it. Similarly, key determinants of the probability of change are the perceived importance to a field of providing an explanation for the phenomenon under dispute and the amount of resources anticipated as necessary to explain the anomaly within the current framework (which is potentially infinite if the field sees no hope of reconciliation).

A third requirement of an alternate theory is that it provide promise for the future. Such promise is afforded by precise explanations of phenomena well handled within the original framework, by the suggestion of explanations of what had previously been regarded as inexplicable, and by the breaking of paths for research previously unimagined. Finally, the standards that caused an anomaly to be deemed sufficiently important as to justify a major theoretical change presumably must also be met in research done under the new framework. These general notions are now applied to the variance bound literature.

B. *Variance Bounds and Changes in Behavioral Foundations*

The first question concerns whether the variance bounds literature has produced the type of anomaly that will cause the economics profession to alter its theoretical foundations radically. As discussed in Section II, much of what has been regarded as evidence of a major anomaly in stock prices is at best controversial, or it is explainable within the current framework of economic theory. Although the issues are still alive in the literature, it is significant that one of the original proponents of the variance bounds approach (LeRoy 1984, p. 186) concludes "that the burden of proof is now on those who contend that asset prices are too volatile, rather than on those who view the observed behavior of asset prices as consistent with market efficiency."[15] Fisher (1984, p. 504) also believes that "the balance of the argument for excess variability is now weaker than it was a few years ago" and suggests what may be "a new round in the econometric battle." In any event, one reaction of the profession has been precisely to attempt to explain the apparent anomaly within the existing framework—an example of how "economists revel in showing how apparently anomalous behavior is in fact consistent with the maintained hypothesis" (Hogarth and Reder 1985, p. 5).

Nevertheless, since at first there appeared to be strong evidence of excess volatility and since some economists still view the ostensible evidence as convincing, we have an opportunity to investigate the reaction of the profession to a perceived major anomaly. For purposes of the following discussion, I will assume, contrary to the evidence presented in Section II, that stock prices show excess volatility relative to a rational valuation model. I first examine Shiller's proposal for rejection of market rationality in favor of mass psychology and fads, in terms of the criteria suggested above for a new theory, and then examine the profession's reaction to his proposal.

Is Shiller's proposed explanation for stock price movements able to explain the observed volatility of the stock market? The answer is yes if only because Shiller does not propose a specific model of what causes particular price changes but suggests rather that it is possible that fads or social movements *may* have caused any particular change. He argues (1984a, p. 470), "The evidence is not intended to provide a tight theory of the movements of stock prices but to show that large

---

15. Note that LeRoy does not equate market efficiency with constant discount rates, as Shiller (1984a) does in much of his paper. Commenting on Shiller (1984a), Fischer (1984, p. 501) emphasizes the distinction between an assumption of constant discount rates and stock market rationality, as does, e.g., Fama (1976, p. 211). Note also that Summers's characterization of Shiller's work as simply showing that discount rates are not constant (1985, p. 635) appears to ignore the conclusions and inferences drawn by Shiller himself about fads and market irrationality, as in Shiller (1984a).

social movements appear to have occurred *that may plausibly* have had a great impact on stock prices. In fact, there is a superabundance of plausible reasons for the movements of the market" (emphasis added). Examples of what Shiller has in mind are given by the following (1984*a*, p. 473):

> There is in the postwar period evidence of substantial changes in behavior big enough to have a major impact on the market. For example, the percentage of people who said that religion is "very important" in their lives fell from 75 percent in 1952 to 52 percent in 1978 ["Religion in America" 1984]. The birth rate hovered around 2.5 percent throughout the 1950s and then began a gradual decline to around 1.5 percent in the 1970s. These changes may reflect changing attitudes toward the importance of family, of heirs or of individual responsibility for others.
>
> Of all such changes, the one with perhaps the most striking importance for demand for shares in the postwar period is the pervasive decline in confidence in society's institutions after the bull market period.

Assuming then that the approach advocated by Shiller is sufficiently open-ended to explain observed price movements, I turn to the second issue, that of how much of existing knowledge is likely to be lost by his suggested approach. Clearly, the answer is very much since virtually all extant results based on stock price data rely strongly on the informational content in prices to allow the required inference. For example, consider event studies, in which stock prices are used in relatively standard procedures to infer the effect of some particular event. Although much of the early work was sufficiently novel to constitute doctoral dissertations, these studies are now commonplace and even accepted as evidence by the courts. Today, arguments are appearing in courts to the effect that the variance bound literature has demonstrated that evidence based on stock prices should be disregarded.[16]

The potential effect of the variance bound literature was brought home sharply to me shortly after my arrival at Standford. A graduate student in the economics department came to see me, with a well-defined research project that required the use of stock prices to test the particular model with which he was working. However, his adviser had suggested that he drop the project, on the grounds that the work of Bob Shiller had shown that stock prices are irrational.

Given that the proposed changes in behavioral assumptions have the potential to destroy much of 2 decades of knowledge of stock prices, I turn to the third issue, namely, the potential for future research. What would research in economics look like if prices were assumed to be

---

16. Clearly, the incentive to invoke this argument is not independent of the outcome of the now-traditional analysis of stock prices around the event in dispute.

primarily determined by irrational fads and social waves? Suppose, for example, that an investigator wished to determine the effect on prices of a change in the tax structure. Shiller's approach of suggesting that some past social changes may in some sense have been related to stock price changes is, by itself, of no assistance for future predictions because no explicit model is presented to allow such predictions.

Indeed, the model suggested by Shiller to explain stock price movements explicitly does not model the behavior of the "blockheads" (Stanley Fischer's term [1984, p. 500] for what Shiller calls "ordinary investors"), "who include everyone who does not respond to expected returns optimally forecasted" (1984*a*, p. 477). Instead, Shiller argues, "let us suppose that they overreact to news or are vulnerable to fads. We will not make assumptions about their behavior at all, but merely define Y_t as the total value of stock demanded per share by these investors." The approach followed is to model explicitly the behavior of the "smart money" (and the model used in Shiller's [1984*a*] fig. 2 explains very little of the observed stock price movement) and to attribute the large unexplained remainder as constituting the blockhead's demand Y_t.

Unless there is a different approach to the explanation of stock price changes within the fads framework advocated by Shiller, many economists may well remain unconvinced that Shiller's approach is the most desirable. Given current knowledge, I suspect, it will prove difficult to take vague observations about such things as changes in attitude toward religion and model in a predictive sense stock price changes that significantly improve on the simple rational economic models from Section II. Of course, this would not be cause for complaint with Shiller's approach if current models were also unable to explain any price changes; but, as noted above (n. 13), this is not the case.

It is instructive to examine some of the published reactions of economists to Shiller's proposals.[17] While reaction has not been uniform, much criticism has focused on the following issues: whether the presumed anomaly is in fact well established, the vagueness of the alternative suggested by Shiller, and Shiller's apparent rejection of an alternate explanation more closely linked to traditional economic assumptions. The discussion of the last of these concerns is instructive on how economists react to attacks on their behavioral assumptions. Thus, Fischer argues (1984, p. 500), "Surprisingly, Shiller dismisses the speculative bubble literature, which is one explanation for excess volatility of the market and which has produced increasingly sophisticated empirical work. Apparently he objects to both the rational expectations assumptions in the speculative bubble approach and to the

17. See "Comments and Discussion" (1984).

implication that there are no excess returns expected even when the bubble is full blown.''

Fischer's concluding statements reflect the importance placed on explicit predictive content of economic theories (1984, p. 504):

And despite Shiller's appeal for the use of qualitative evidence when statistical tests are weak, the outcome will turn on statistical tests. The reason is that there is no way of knowing how important are the fashions and fads described in the first section [of Shiller 1984a] without quantitative evidence on the extent of departures from market efficiency. With the evidence of the last few years on varying real interest rates, the new tests will have to allow for changing discount rates on stocks. They will also in all likelihood be more closely related to the speculative bubble literature than to the fads literature—if indeed those approaches are ultimately different.

What lessons have been learned from the variance bound literature concerning the adoption of alternate behavioral assumptions in economic models? While making no claims of completeness, I would suggest the following.

First, the existence of the original apparent anomaly is still unsettled, and continuing research aims at explaining the results in a satisfactory fashion within the current disciplinary framework. This illustrates the observation that the current framework, with its attendant set of solved puzzles and consequent "knowledge," is likely to imply inertia for the discipline.

Second, the profession has come to expect certain standards of compatibility with assumptions found successful in other applications (such as rational expectations), specificity of modeling and prediction, and past and future empirical success. Although these standards may be overturned if the situation is deemed drastic enough, the resulting losses will likely be perceived as large, and the efforts to maintain the standards correspondingly strong. Consequently, the introduction of new behavioral assumptions, including fads or the effects of social psychology, will most likely be attractive to economists if these current standards are maintained.

Links between economics and the behavioral sciences are potentially very fruitful, but the example of the variance bounds literature suggests that there are stringent requirements for a succesful melding of the assumptions of these different disciplines. A likely scenario for such success will include the existence of an important anomaly, which is generally perceived as such in the relevant community; a low likelihood of solving the problem using traditional assumptions; a well-structured alternate hypothesis, preferably with proven success in other applications, that explains the anomaly in terms of different behavioral assumptions; and promise of future success in other applications.

Although these ingredients appear to be missing from the attempt to substitute "fads" for traditional economic analysis of stock market volatility, there are other anomalies in financial economics in which some of them may be present.

C. Other Anomalies in Financial Economics

Several anomalies in financial economics are more firmly established than excess volatility in stock prices and, not surprisingly, have had more direct effect on the discipline. While the following comments are by no means complete, and the (possible) anomalies may not be mutually exclusive, they provide some insight into the current reaction to various anomalies, especially with respect to possible changes in behavioral assumptions.

Perhaps the major anomalies at present concern unexplained seasonalities in stock returns, particularly the well-documented "January effect" of Keim (1983) and the related "small-firm effect" (see Banz 1981; and Reinganum 1981). Other seasonalities have been documented for some time, including apparent negative returns over weekends (see French 1980; and Gibbons and Hess 1981), but these have received relatively little attention as compared with the size and January effects.

It is not certain that such seasonalities cannot be accommodated by existing theories, but certainly they were not expected by the discipline. Potential explanations include data errors, more sophisticated equilibrium models that explicitly allow for such seasonalities, and modification of models to allow for transactions costs or taxes. Many of these were not explicitly ruled out by the prevailing equilibrium theories, in particular the Sharpe-Lintner capital asset pricing model (CAPM) or its multiperiod extensions such as Merton (1973) and Breeden (1979).[18] Nevertheless, realization that the initial versions of these models had not led to an expectation of the observed seasonalities changed the way in which the models were viewed. At present, a different approach to deriving models of asset pricing, based on the arbitrage pricing theory (APT) of Ross (1976), is attempting to reconcile some of these empirical findings in a model possessing the desirable characteristics of an alternate theory outlined above.[19] The issue of the relative merits of these two different approaches (i.e., CAPM and APT) is not settled, but much of the current debate in the financial literature concerns the questions whether (how well) the APT can account for these empirical results, how readily the model can be implemented in this and other applications such as mutual fund evalua-

---

18. However, negative weekend returns are particularly troublesome.

19. See, e.g., Chen (1983); Chen, Roll, and Ross (1984); Connor and Korajczyk (1985); Lehmann and Modest (1985).

tion, and how well the model allows testing of its predictions relative to other approaches.

Note, however, that the APT has not attempted to change the fundamental behavioral assumptions underlying the earlier equilibrium models, along the lines suggested by Shiller. The APT relies primarily on lack of arbitrage rather than expected utility maximization by individuals (although more recent arbitrage models such as Connor [1984] incorporate utility maximization). Nevertheless, the approach requires assumptions of individual maximizing behavior in the construction of arbitrage portfolios to exploit any mispricing, which, of course, results in the APT's prediction of no arbitrage opportunities remaining in prices. Those unhappy with such assumptions will find little comfort in the differences between the models. At this level, and at least for the moment, the discipline appears to place a high value on precise, testable models that can be used to confront the data currently available.

Obviously, individual behavior does not conform to these assumptions, and most economists and behavioral scientists have some knowledge of at least the broad issues and standard responses of the respective disciplines. Aggregation theorems that encompass both empirically observed individual behavior and empirically observed aggregate behavior are neither trivial nor commonplace. One frequent defense for the behavioral assumptions in economics, as articulated, for example, by Alchian (1950), relies on competition to produce the observed (or at least predicted) aggregate behavior of the model, even if individuals do not behave as the model assumes. If such a defense is plausible, it is most likely to apply to markets where competition is strongest, and the stock market is a prime candidate.[20] Consequently, the reliance on standard economic assumptions in asset pricing models such as the CAPM or the APT is not surprising.

An interesting contrast in terms of the degree of competition in markets is provided by the case of mergers. Although general industry conditions may be competitive, the classic model of prices determined by the atomistic behavior of numerous individuals seems far from the process involved in a typical merger, especially the well-publicized takeover battles. Is there a role for changes in behavioral assumptions about participants in these activities?

At least one researcher in finance believes the answer is a firm maybe. Roll (1986) proposes a "hubris hypothesis" for corporate takeovers, by which "hubris on the part of individual decision makers in bidding firms can explain why bids are made, even when a valuation above the current market price represents a positive valuation error"

20. Even here, however, current evidence on intraday price behavior may lead to a questioning whether the activities of large (say, institutional) traders do not leave traces in the data.

(1986, abstract). While conceding that "this interpretation may not turn out to be valid," Roll suggests that "it has enough plausibility to be at least considered in further investigations" (p. 198).

The approach taken by Roll to establish his case is, perhaps, indicative of the challenge faced by those wishing to change explicitly the behavioral underpinnings of economic models. Not only does he consider a litany of possible objections as early as the introduction, he also sifts through current empirical evidence on mergers and takeovers point by point. With some irony, he argues (p. 212) that "the hubris hypothesis can serve as the null hypothesis of corporate takeovers because it asserts that all markets are strong-form efficient." If this were so, in Roll's view, only the hubris hypothesis remains to explain any above-market premium.

Despite the care given to justifying the argument, this hypothesis does not appear to be regarded as firmly established in the discipline, at least at present. On the other hand, it is an example of the kind of link between individual behavioral assumptions and empirical financial research that may emerge in the future, especially as continued detailed investigation of the available data and continued refinement of theory and technique reveal areas where agreement between current theory and data leaves something to be desired.

IV. Conclusions

The analysis in this paper suggests that the case for radical change of behavioral assumptions underlying economic models based on the results of variance bounds tests may be easily overstated. There are serious questions concerning whether the phenomenon of excess volatility exists in the first place and, if it did, whether abandonment of assumptions of rational expectations in favor of assumptions of mass psychology and fads as primary determinants of price changes is the best avenue for current research.

Nevertheless, the links between individual behavior and aggregate outcomes are both intriguing and little understood. It seems inconceivable that at some time in the (perhaps distant) future, there will not be much more explicit recognition of the interaction that occurs between individual and aggregate phenomena.

The economics literature shows first steps toward such links, in at least two directions. The first is the experimental evidence discussed by others at this conference. These methods, together with much sounder knowledge of the behavior of prices (e.g., through better intraday data bases), offer the potential for considerable improvement in our understanding of both individual and aggregate behavior. Separate but potentially related work based on information theory also offers insights into the mechanisms at work in transforming individual activity into aggregate prices. Although still at an early stage, these models may explain, for example, why price changes show greater variance over periods when markets are open than closed (see French and Roll [1984] 1985).

It is still too early to tell which, if any, of these puzzles will prove incorrigible within the current framework of financial economics and consequently call the disciplinary foundations into serious question. What is clear at this stage, however, is that none of them is sufficiently well formulated to allow it to take the role of a critical experiment discussed earlier. In short, whether or not their existence eventually leads to a significantly different disciplinary framework, they do not provide a "blueprint" for such change.

References

Alchian, A. A. 1950. Uncertainty, evolution, and economic theory. *Journal of Political Economy* 58:211–21.

Banz, R. 1981. The relationship between return and market value of common stocks. *Journal of Financial Economics* 9:3–18.

Bhattacharya, S. 1980. Nondissipative signaling structures and dividend policy. *Quarterly Journal of Economics* 95:1–24.

Breeden, D. T. 1979. An intertemporal asset price model with stochastic consumption and investment opportunities. *Journal of Financial Economics* 7:265–96.

Chen, N. 1983. Some empirical tests of the theory of arbitrage pricing. *Journal of Finance* 38:1393–1414.

Chen, N.; Roll, R. W.; and Ross, S. A. 1984. Economic forces and the stock market. Unpublished manuscript. Los Angeles: University of California, Los Angeles, Graduate School of Management.

Comments and discussion. 1984. *Brookings Papers on Economic Activity*, no. 2, pp. 499–510.

Connor, G. 1984. A unified beta pricing theory. *Journal of Economic Theory* 34:13–31.

Connor, G., and Korajczyk, R. A. In press. Performance measurement with the arbitrage pricing theory: A new framework for analysis. *Journal of Financial Economics*.

Fama, E. F. 1976. *Foundations of Finance*. New York: Basic.

Fama, E. F., and Babiak, H. 1968. Dividend policy: An empirical analysis. *Journal of the American Statistical Association* 63:1132–61.

Fischer, S. 1984. Stock prices and social dynamics: Comments and discussion. *Brookings Papers on Economic Activity*, no. 2, pp. 499–504.

Flavin, M. A. 1983. Excess volatility in the financial markets: A reassessment of the empirical evidence. *Journal of Political Economy* 91:929–56.

French, K. R. 1980. Stock returns and the weekend effect. *Journal of Financial Economics* 8:55–70.

French, K. R., and Roll, R. 1985. Stock return variances: The arrival of information and the reaction of traders. Working Paper no. 121. Chicago: University of Chicago, Graduate School of Business, July. Revised version of Is trading self-generating? Unpublished manuscript. Chicago: Univeristy of Chicago, Graduate School of Business, 1984.

Fuller, W. A. 1976. *Introduction to Statistical Time Series*. New York: Wiley.

Gibbons, M. R., and Hess, P. J. 1981. Day of the week effects and asset returns. *Journal of Business* 54:579–96.

Grossman, S. J., and Shiller, R. J. 1981. The determinants of the variability of stock market prices. *American Economic Review* 71:222–27.

Hogarth, R. M., and Reder, M. W. 1985. Conference on behavioral foundations of economic theory: Some preliminary comments. Unpublished manuscript. Chicago: University of Chicago, Graduate School of Business.

Keim, D. B. 1983. Size-related anomalies and stock market seasonality: Further empirical evidence. *Journal of Financial Economics* 12:13–32.

Kleidon, A. W. 1983. Stock prices as rational forecasters of future cash flows. Ph.D. thesis, Stanford University, Graduate School of Business.

Kleidon, A. W. 1986. Bias in small sample tests of stock price rationality. *Journal of Business* 59:237–61.

Kleidon, A. W. In press. Variance bounds tests and stock price valuation models. *Journal of Political Economy*.

Kuhn, T. S. 1970. *The Structure of Scientific Revolutions.* 2d ed. Chicago: University of Chicago Press.

Lehmann, B. N., and Modest, D. M. 1985. The empirical foundations of the arbitrage pricing theory. I. The empirical tests. Working Paper no. 821. Stanford, Calif.: Stanford University, Graduate School of Business.

LeRoy, S. F. 1984. Efficiency and the variability of asset prices. *American Economic Review* 74:183–87.

LeRoy, S. F., and Porter, R. D. 1981. The present-value relation: Tests based on implied variance bounds. *Econometrica* 49:555–74.

Lintner, J. 1956. Distribution of incomes of corporations among dividends, retained earnings and taxes. *American Economic Review* 46:97–113.

Marsh, T. A., and Merton, R. C. 1986. Dividend variability and variance bounds tests for the rationality of stock market prices. *American Economic Review* 76:483–98.

Merton, R. C. 1973. An intertemporal capital asset pricing model. *Econometrica* 41:867–

Miller, M. H., and Modigliani, F. 1961. Dividend policy, growth, and the valuation of shares. *Journal of Business* 34:411–33.

Modigliani, F., and Miller, M. 1958. The cost of capital, corporation finance, and the theory of investment. *American Economic Review* 48:261–97.

Modigliani, F., and Miller, M. 1959. The cost of capital, corporation finance and the theory of investment: Reply. *American Economic Review* 49:655–69.

Popper, K. R. 1972. *Objective Knowledge: An Evolutionary Approach.* Oxford: Clarendon.

Reinganum, M. R. 1981. Misspecification of capital asset pricing: Empirical anomalies based on earnings yields and market values. *Journal of Financial Economics* 9:19–46.

Religion in America. 1984. *Gallup Report,* no. 222 (March).

Roberts, H. V. 1959. Stock market "patterns" and financial analysis: Methodological suggestions. *Journal of Finance* 14:1–10.

Roll, R. 1986. The hubris hypothesis of corporate takeovers. *Journal of Business* 59:197–216.

Ross, S. A. 1976. The arbitrage theory of capital asset pricing. *Journal of Economic Theory* 13:341–60.

Ross, S. A. 1977. The determination of financial structure: The incentive-signalling approach. *Bell Journal of Economics* 7:23–40.

Shiller, R. J. 1981a. Consumption, asset markets and macroeconomic fluctuations. Paper presented at the Money and Banking Workshop, University of Chicago.

Shiller, R. J. 1981b. Do stock prices move too much to be justified by subsequent changes in dividends? *American Economic Review* 7:421–36.

Shiller, R. J. 1981c. The use of volatility measures in assessing market efficiency. *Journal of Finance* 36:291–304.

Shiller, R. J. 1984a. Stock prices and social dynamics. *Brookings Papers on Economic Activity,* no. 2, pp. 457–98.

Shiller, R. J. 1984b. Theories of aggregate stock price movements. *Journal of Portfolio Management* (Winter), pp. 28–37.

Simon, H. A. In this volume. Rationality in psychology and economics.

Standard & Poor's. 1980. *Security Price Index Record.* New York: Standard & Poor's.

Summers, L. H. 1985. On economics and finance. *Journal of Finance* 40:633–35.

Thaler, R. In this volume. Comments on Simon, on Einhorn and Hogarth, and on Tversky and Kahneman.

Tirole, J. 1985. Asset bubbles and overlapping generations. *Econometric* 53:1071–1100.

West, K. D. 1984. Speculative bubbles and stock price volatility. Unpublished manuscript. Princeton, N.J.: Princeton University, Department of Economics.

Zeckhauser, R. In this volume. Comments: Behavioral versus rational economics: What you see is what you conquer.

Robert J. Shiller

Yale University

Comments on Miller and on Kleidon

Both Allan W. Kleidon's and Merton H. Miller's papers (in this volume) are organized around the list of "anomalies" or "puzzles" that seem to be challenging the efficient markets "paradigm." They both are referring to the Kuhn model of scientific revolutions. Maybe something as dramatic as a scientific revolution is in store for us. That does not mean, however, that the revolution would lead to (as Kleidon attributes to critics of market efficiency like me) "the abandonment of assumptions of rational expectations in favor of mass psychology" (p. 313). Obviously the efficient markets theory does capture an element of truth. For example, when important concrete information about the future earnings potential of a corporation becomes public, of course the price of the stock in that company tends to jump immediately. Thus, a prediction of the efficient markets theory is borne out. This is so even if there is also another component to movements in the price of the stock of that company, a component not explainable by any fundamental information. It might even be that, in stocks in which important concrete information does not become available, price movements may be dominated primarily by changes in fashions or attitudes of investors. Even in this case, there are still senses in which the conventional efficient markets models may be regarded as quite useful. The models will be durable concepts in finance from now on.

I tend to view the study of behavioral extensions of these efficient markets models as leading in a sense to the enhancement of the efficient markets models. I could teach the efficient markets models to my students with much more relish if I could describe them as extreme special cases to consider before moving to the more realistic models. These models would look so much more appealing as first approximations to more complicated and more accurate theories, rather than as the only models that the profession has to offer.

Perhaps what we need is not something so dramatic as a "scientific revolution" so much as a little softening of the dogmatic adherence to the efficient markets viewpoint among people in academe. If you look in finance journals, you will find a nearly total absence of any mention of the possibility that fashions or fads may be at work. Those who bring up such a possibility are viewed as if they were bringing up astrology or extrasensory perception. I find that, as a consequence, many people in academic finance show little indication of having thought much about how fashions or fads might affect financial markets.

The bottom line on Merton Miller's appraisal of the importance of behavioral models in finance is that behavioral models are important for the "fine details of specific cases" but that "we abstract from all these stories in building our models . . . not because the stories are uninteresting but because they may be too interesting and thereby distract us from the pervasive market forces that should be our principal concern" (p. 283). This could be interpreted in a couple of ways. One is that nonoptimizing behavior might explain only unimportant phenomena. The other is that theories of nonoptimizing behavior, if such behavior is important, will never get far. I do not see that either conclusion follows from his paper.

Miller's conclusion that equilibrium models are "alive and well" seems a little overstated, given his evidence on dividends. He never offered a reason why it would not be rational for stockholders to expect firms to buy back shares rather than pay dividends. They do issue dividends, so somebody is not behaving rationally. The econometric evidence on the market price of dividends versus capital gains shows only that firms are not necessarily behaving irrationally, given market behavior. Given this evidence on stockholder behavior, psychological models of investor preference for dividends, like the "self-control" model of Shefrin and Statman (1984), are what seems called for.

Miller looks at studies relating risk-corrected returns on stocks to dividend yield as having only one purpose: "To determine whether the aggregate corporate supply of dividends has really been in long-standing disequilibrium relative to the predictions of the standard, value-maximizing model of the firm" (pp. 277–278). But one would think that the direction of the effect is also relevant to the fads theory. If fads are independent of dividends, one would suppose that times of high dividend-price ratio would be times when high returns are to be expected. Unfortunately, this effect cannot be disentangled from the tax effect. Moreover, with his conclusion that you just cannot pin down the size of the coefficient, it is going to be very hard to judge one way or the other from these data whether a fads model is a good one. So perhaps he is right in not looking to these results to refute or confirm a fads model for prices.

Still, I think that other evidence can be brought to bear on the importance of fads in financial markets. I think the truth may well be that financial prices can be successfully modeled as reflecting proper anticipations of those future movements in dividends that can be predicted plus a term reflecting the anticipation of fashions or fads among investors. I say the "anticipation of" because it is likely that market prices move as soon as a fad becomes imminent. Such a model follows from the assumption that there is smart money as well as ordinary faddish investors but that the smart money is not abundant enough to dominate the market fully (see my paper [1984]).

There is, it is important to remember, no theoretical reason to expect that, in the presence of departures from market efficiency, smart money should "take over the market" by accumulating wealth through profitable trading. The accumulation of wealth is limited by other forces: smart money wealth is also depleted by consumption of wealth and by the limits imposed by the life cycle. If smart money were able to accumulate very quickly and efficiently, we might expect them nonetheless to take over the market. But it is hard to see why relatively slow moving fashions or fads (of the kind we associate, say, with the "bull market" of the 1920s or of the 1950s) should create such profit opportunities. One does not know when the fad will end, and one does not observe the end of the fad very often.

Allan Kleidon has presented a criticism of my discussion (1979, 1981) and that of LeRoy and Porter (1981) on the apparent excess volatility of prices of speculative assets. Let me say that there is some merit in his argument as it applies to the original papers that he discusses here. I myself argued before that, if the dividend is a random walk, the simple variance inequalities that I derived would not be valid. I did not know then that, as Marsh and Merton (1986) first pointed out, if the dividend process is a random walk and there is no information about future changes in dividends, then p^* will have a lower variance in the sample than p, as Kleidon illustrates in his figures. In my (1981) paper, I had given a simpler example of an efficient markets model in which the sample variance of p^* tends to be below that of p: the example was one involving a low-probability big event of an enormous change in dividends, an event that chanced not to occur in the sample period. His example may seem a little more appealing, but in fact we can reject the random-walk pattern for the aggregate log dividend series using a Dickey-Fuller test (Shiller 1981).[1]

It is interesting to note that Kleidon's (in press) own work and that of Marjorie Flavin (1983) offer some reason for hope for the rejection of efficient markets by the volatility tests even when the log-dividend process is a random walk. Kleidon (in press) found that the probability

1. A regression of the log of the dividend on its lagged value and time for 1872–1978 produced a coefficient of lagged dividend of .807, far below one. Using a test based on that coefficient in table 8.5.1 in Fuller (1976), the null hypothesis of a random walk was rejected at the 5% level. Kleidon (in press) did a similar test and did not reject, but he used only half as much data for his test.

that $\sigma(p)/\sigma(p^*) > 5$ in a sample of 100 with a discount rate of .075 is .046.[2] Those are roughly the relevant parameters; in my sample, $\sigma(p)/\sigma(p^*)$ was 5.6. Thus, his results show a sense in which the high volatility that I observed was unlikely even in the random-walk case.

Two papers have recently come up with alternative ways of handling the nonstationarity of dividends (West 1986; Mankiw, Romer, and Shapiro 1985). The same reasoning that led to var(p^*) > var(p) also leads to var($p^* - p^0$) > var($p - p^0$) and var($p^* - p^0$) > var($p^* - p$), where p^0 is anything in the public information set. Mankiw et al. take p^0 equal to d/r, while West in effect takes p^0 as a univariate ARIMA forecast based on lagged dividends. Both reject the simple efficient markets model.

Mankiw et al. (1985) have also shown analytically that the random walk case is, among the class of AR(1) processes, essentially the worst possible case for the volatility tests, in the sense that the ratio of the expected value of var(p) to the expected value of var(p^*) is near its maximum when the autoregressive coefficient is one. The variance bounds would be much less likely to be violated under the efficient markets hypothesis if the autoregressive coefficient were substantially less than one or greater than one.

Kleidon makes much in his paper of the fact that the p series need not under the efficient markets hypothesis be smoother in appearance than the p^* series. He is right, of course, and I said much the same thing in my (1979) work on the volatility tests, though in the context of the term structure of interest rates.[3] The model I considered in that paper was formally identical to the efficient markets model used here, so the conclusions there carry over to the present discussion. I showed that there is still a sense in which the price series ought to be somewhat smooth, and this sense can be expressed formally in terms of an upper bound to a weighted integral of the spectral density of the price, where high weight is given to the higher frequencies. That weighted integral is just the variance of a filtered price series, and some of the variance inequalities found to be violated in my papers on stock prices were formally identical to such weighted integrals. But Kleidon makes no mention of these inequalities in this paper.

In essence, though, the picture of p^* and p (Kleidon's fig. 1) is evidence of a different sort, regardless of the validity of the volatility tests as tests of the efficient markets model (1). It is evidence suggesting that a model that attributes all the variability of aggregate stock prices to changing fashions or fads is certainly at least as consistent with the data as is the efficient markets model. Intuitively, it is hard to see how a model that makes p^* roughly a trend with p bounced around

2. See his table 2, row 6, col. 2 (Kleidon, in press).
3. See the mathematical app. to my paper (Shiller 1979).

this trend by fashions or fads could ever be rejected by these data in favor of a model that says that price movements anticipate dividends. Many people appear to suppose that the mass of evidence in the efficient markets literature can be taken as somehow implying that stock price movements really do forecast dividends in a manner appropriate to the efficient markets model (1). This might conceivably have been proven to be so by figure 1 if p^* moved around a lot and were substantially correlated with p. This would be expected to happen given the model (1) if people have a lot of information about future dividends movements. If figure 1 did happen to come out that way, we could say that it presents impressive evidence for the efficient markets theory. It did not. We should not be hesitant to mention fads or fashions as the true source of the bulk of the price movements that characterize the aggregate stock market.

References

Flavin, M. 1983. Excess volatility in the financial markets: A reassessment of the empirical evidence. *Journal of Political Economy* 91 (October): 929–56.

Fuller, W. A. 1976. *Introduction to Statistical Time Series*. New York: Wiley.

Kleidon, A. W. In this volume. Anomalies in financial economics: Blueprint for change?

Kleidon, A. W. In press. Variance bounds tests and stock price valuation models. *Journal of Political Economy*.

LeRoy, S. F., and Porter, R. D. 1981. The present value relation: Tests based on implied variance bounds. *Econometrica* 49 (May): 555–74.

Mankiw, N. G.; Romer, D.; and Shapiro, M. D. 1985. An unbiased reexamination of stock market volatility. *Journal of Finance* 40 (May): 677–87.

Marsh, T. A., and Merton, R. C. 1986. Earnings variability and variance bounds tests for the rationality of stock market prices. *American Economic Review* 76 (June): 483–98.

Miller, M. H. In this volume. Behavioral rationality in finance: The case of dividends.

Shefrin, H. M., and Statman, M. 1984. Explaining investor preference for cash dividends. *Journal of Financial Economics* 13 (June): 293–82.

Shiller, R. J. 1979. The volatility of long-term interest rates and expectations models of the term structure. *Journal of Political Economy* 87 (December): 1190–1219.

Shiller, R. J. 1981. The use of volatility measures in assessing market efficiency. *Journal of Finance* 36 (May): 291–304.

Shiller, R. J. 1984. Stock prices and social dynamics. *Brookings Papers on Economic Activity*, no. 2, pp. 457–98.

West, K. 1986. Speculative bubbles and stock price volatility. National Bureau of Economic Research Working Paper 1833. February.

Index